The Color of Equality

THE COLOR OF EQUALITY

Race and Common Humanity
in Enlightenment Thought

Devin J. Vartija

PENN

UNIVERSITY OF PENNSYLVANIA PRESS

PHILADELPHIA

Published by
University of Pennsylvania Press
Philadelphia, Pennsylvania 19104-4112
www.upenn.edu/pennpress

Printed in the United States of America on acid-free paper
10 9 8 7 6 5 4 3 2 1

A Cataloging-in-Publication record is available from the Library
of Congress
ISBN 978-0-8122-5319-1

To my parents

CONTENTS

INTRODUCTION

Enlightenment thinkers present us with a predicament: they politicized the concept of equality while simultaneously making the naturalization of inequalities between Europeans and non-Europeans thinkable. What are we to make of this tension in Enlightenment thought? Scholars have often viewed this situation as a dichotomy: either the Enlightenment was an emancipatory intellectual movement foundational to the modern, liberal democratic defense of human rights, or it is the primary culprit in the dark side of modernity, from scientific racism and sexism to colonialism and even genocide. Sensible intellectuals have interjected that this dichotomy between "acceptance" or "rejection" of the Enlightenment is in fact misguided. As Barbara Taylor explains, the "Enlightenment project" that postmodernists chastise and liberals defend "cannot survive even a cursory glance at the noisily argumentative world of Enlightenment, with its multiple renditions of reason and truth purveyed by lively minds of diverse sorts, from Encyclopedists and philosophical theologians to bluestockings and Grub Street hacks of both sexes."[1] Over the past three to four decades, our appreciation for just how noisy that argumentative world of Enlightenment was has been deepened thanks to the pluralization of the Enlightenment. What was once seen as a relatively monolithic intellectual movement centered around the ideas held by a handful of men in mid-eighteenth-century Paris has now become a vast collage of women and men active in various seventeenth- and eighteenth-century European and colonial cities, belonging to a variety of institutions, and holding a diverse array of ideas.

In these debates, equality and race are recurrent themes, as it is generally accepted that Enlightenment thinkers fundamentally altered the way we think about human sameness and difference. Whereas people were once viewed as equal only in terms of souls in an otherworldly realm, Enlightenment thinkers postulated the basic equality of human beings in this world, based on shared rational and emotive capacities. Yet just as worldly hierarchies were being called into question, the philosophes also sought naturalistic explanations of human differences and thus laid the groundwork for postulating that natural inequalities might permanently separate human groups from one another. As our understanding of the Enlightenment has become more capacious, it makes it difficult to disentangle the messy history of Enlightenment, equality, and racial classification. This study aims to make sense of this complicated history by searching for the ways in which equality and race, human sameness and difference, may have been linked in Enlightenment thought.[2] How was the tension between these ideas dealt with and possibly resolved? And what do transformations in thinking about equality and race tell us about the Enlightenment as an intellectual movement?

To address these questions, I have chosen three influential Enlightenment encyclopedias as my main corpus of primary sources: Ephraim Chambers's *Cyclopaedia* (London, 1728), Denis Diderot and Jean le Rond d'Alembert's *Encyclopédie* (Paris, 1751–1765), and Fortunato Bartolomeo De Felice's *Encyclopédie d'Yverdon* (Yverdon, 1770–1775).[3] These encyclopedias form a genealogy in that each work explicitly drew on the material of its predecessor. Chambers's *Cyclopaedia* may be considered the first "modern" encyclopedia, because it was alphabetically ordered, was grounded in Lockean epistemology, and popularized Newtonian science.[4] Diderot and d'Alembert's *Encyclopédie* began as a translation of Chambers's work but, principally thanks to Diderot's leadership, was expanded immensely and is widely considered the most important work of the European Enlightenment.[5] With the *Encyclopédie d'Yverdon*, De Felice aimed to update and correct its Parisian predecessor, as well as to excise the more libertarian and atheistic ideas and install liberal Protestant theology in their place. While much remains the same between these two encyclopedias, scholars stress that many of the important, lengthy articles—those that extend beyond a simple definition of a few sentences—were reworked by De Felice and his collaborators.[6] These encyclopedias capture three moments in the intellectual history of the Enlightenment: early eighteenth-century England, mid-eighteenth-century France, and mid- to late eighteenth-century Switzerland. This set of sources thus brings forth not only the distinctiveness of particular national or regional political, philosophical, and religious debates but also the pan-European nature of the Enlightenment.

Because my focus is primarily on Enlightenment ideas of equality and race, my use of encyclopedias in general, as well as these encyclopedias in particular, as a main corpus of primary sources requires explanation. Encyclopedias were immensely important texts in early modern Europe, as they responded to the surge of printed material following the invention of moveable type print and aimed to distill essential information from the ever-expanding mass of printed texts into an easily accessible reference work.[7] In the prospectus to the *Encyclopédie*, Diderot attributed the spread of "enlightenment" since the Renaissance to, in large measure, the availability and use of reference works: "One cannot dispute that since the rebirth of letters among us, we partially owe to dictionaries the general enlightenment that has spread throughout society and this germ of science which imperceptibly disposes minds to a more profound knowledge."[8] Charles-Joseph Panckoucke, the most important publisher in late eighteenth-century France, echoed this sentiment, stating that "the *Encyclopédie* will always be the first book of any library or cabinet."[9]

These specific encyclopedias will allow me to bring to the fore some of the key issues in the development of Enlightenment thought. John Locke and Isaac Newton have long been associated with the early Enlightenment, and Chambers's work fits well into the consolidation of what we might call an "early Enlightenment culture."[10] From its inception in the 1740s, contemporaries recognized the *Encyclopédie* as crystallizing and embodying an intellectual movement, one that pushed forward the struggles surrounding Newtonianism and philosophical liberty, as well as the attack on both orthodox religious dogma and absolute political authority.[11] Including the *Encyclopédie d'Yverdon* allows me to interrogate how thinkers of a different confessional standpoint within the Enlightenment used ideas of equality and race. Given that the issue of a "radical" versus a "moderate" Enlightenment, in addition to various confessional Enlightenments, is a pressing topic in the current historiography, the *Encyclopédie d'Yverdon* provides an interesting case study to assess the interplay between religion, philosophy, and politics in the Enlightenment.

Besides offering a window onto the cultural and social milieu from which they emerged, encyclopedias can be seen as expressions of and contributors to key trends in Enlightenment culture: namely, making knowledge accessible to as broad a public as possible to facilitate debate and conversation across national and social divides.[12] Diderot's *Encyclopédie* in particular occupies a central place in Enlightenment scholarship because the work was founded on a spirit of equality and reciprocity and committed to gathering knowledge together for the service of humanity.[13] The work reflects one of the central tenets of Enlightenment thought: the individual's power to rationally understand the world.[14]

Interestingly, scholars opposed to a sanguine view of the advance of *philosophie* in the century of light have seized upon these same encyclopedias, Diderot's *Encyclopédie* in particular, to highlight the sinister workings of the power/knowledge dynamic. Michel Foucault famously referred to the eighteenth century as "the age of the catalogue" and argued that the eighteenth century was a turning point in which new classifications and modes of thinking worked in menacing ways to produce social control.[15] Charles Withers follows Foucault's lead in his investigation of the connections between geography, encyclopedism, and natural history, referring to an "Enlightenment project" characterized by "an imperializing masculinist gaze" that aimed to understand and subdue all of nature.[16] Likewise, Gunnar Broberg remarks that "the same ambition to keep possession of what had been discovered, indeed conquered, characterized both the *Systema Naturae* and the great French *Encyclopédie*."[17] In our current postcolonial moment, more attention has been paid to the ways in which dictionaries and encyclopedias reinforce stereotypes and biases.[18] Race has been found to be a biologically incoherent concept, but it continues to be a powerful organizing principle in politics and society, and even in science, in a modified form. Given that many experts single out the eighteenth century as the beginning of both "race thinking" and racism, it is particularly illuminating to discover whether Enlightenment encyclopedias reflect the state of the "givenness" of race that some researchers argue took hold in eighteenth-century Europe.

For many scholars, there is thus an umbilical connection between classification, Enlightenment, and domination, and in this regard, it is entirely fitting to investigate how eighteenth-century encyclopedists included racial classifications in their reference works. While these scholars have brought the ethical issues involved in creating classificatory systems to the fore, classification is a necessary precursor to the employment of our faculty of understanding and, as such, is inescapable. Issues of power and social control will become abundantly clear when we analyze how these Enlightenment thinkers engaged with racial classifications, but to reduce their reflections on human diversity to apologies for European hegemony alone would be misguided. As we will see, equality became politicized to a degree unseen in reference works before the eighteenth century. The postcolonial reading of Enlightenment reference works, while important, is not the only reading that one should put forward, as Aude Doody has demonstrated in her study of Pliny's *Natural History* and its reception. Doody shows that both the present-day postcolonial criticism of Pliny's imperial Roman politics and Diderot's appropriation of Pliny as a subversive philosophe are valid, representative as they are of the concerns of different ages.[19] Encyclopedias, which are necessarily expressive of an era's attitudes and biases, are particularly apropos to studying the tension between an emerging egalitarian perspective and nascent racial science.[20]

Enlightenment encyclopedias sat on a thin line between confident syntheses of knowledge and interventions in polemical debates, and, as such, using these sources offers a unique perspective into the co-construction of difference and equality in eighteenth-century thought. Louis de Jaucourt's article "Natural Equality" was the first entry in a major European encyclopedia to treat equality as a political concept rather than as a logical or mathematical concept, and his entry "Slave Trade" put equality to novel usage in what was the most fervent abolitionist text published in French thought up to that volume's publication, in 1765.[21] At the same time, however, the French colonial administrator Jean-Baptiste-Pierre Le Romain contributed an article that offered a summary of the principal characteristics of various African ethnicities in order that slave owners may better manage their human chattel.[22] These encyclopedias thus put into particularly sharp relief the tensions raised by European colonialism and slavery and addressed by Enlightenment thinkers, a tension between the desire to "change the common mode of thinking" in the direction of a more humane society and to serve a useful governmental and administrative function.

I have used the methodology of the so-called Cambridge School of intellectual history to understand how these encyclopedists used and transformed the concepts of equality and race. In the chapters that follow, I analyze these encyclopedias in chronological order, placing each in its particular political and social context. To study an idea in context means that we can understand the meaning of any given idea only if we study the unique sphere of meanings to which it once belonged by looking at its procedures, aims, and vocabularies.[23] This robust method serves to guard against anachronism and to, as far as possible, discover an author's intentions in writing a given text.[24] Quentin Skinner has demonstrated the importance of considering the conventions of a given genre when studying the history of thought, because only then, and not by reading the same text "over and over," can we better understand a past thinker's innovations and aims.[25] As we will see, Diderot and some of his collaborators deliberately played with the conventions of the reference work, and this impacts how we should make sense of its content. We should, however, be careful not to grant Cambridge-style contextualism a global and exhaustive theory of meaning.[26] Cultural history and intellectual history can supplement one another, since cultural historians might be more attuned to the logic of culture as a set of practices, while intellectual historians guard against totalizing ideas of culture.[27]

As J. G. A. Pocock has remarked, "Languages plainly denote, both consciously and unconsciously, elements of experience, feeling, and conditioning outside the structure of intellectuality" and that, as a historian, one strives to make the implicit explicit to discover meanings in a context of which the author was not perhaps aware.[28] In this regard, I have sought to recover the emotions inherent in new ideas.[29] With regard to equality, its vindication entailed crucial affective elements, because the idea of natural equality had to be internalized in some way before it could have any political consequence.[30] The potential political consequences that equality might have depend at least to a certain extent upon empathy and compassion.[31] Eighteenth-century thinkers themselves, of course, reflected extensively on "the passions" and "sentiment" and their role in our moral and political lives.[32] While I consider these writings, I also attempt to recover the ways in which affect, empathy in particular, can help us to better understand how equality came to resonate with more and more eighteenth-century Europeans.

I analyze how the encyclopedists reflected upon political and social equality within their own societies as well as the ways in which concepts of common humanity and cross-cultural equality operate in these texts. I have narrowed my focus to the encyclopedic entries concerning peoples of the Americas, Africa, and China—with the peoples of Europe as the often implicit point of reference—sufficiently limiting my scope to allow for a more in-depth analysis of how these encyclopedists situated themselves among populations that they considered distinct in crucial ways.[33] In the conjectural historical scheme that acquired greater theoretical complexity in the Enlightenment, Native Americans were broadly considered to be "closer to nature" than Europeans, whether in a noble or ignoble state. The blackness of sub-Saharan Africans was taken to be the major axis of difference in the racial discourse of the eighteenth century, and the institution of slavery was the most important context in which Europeans interacted with Africans; thus, consideration of writings on Africans and slavery/abolitionist debates are particularly pertinent for understanding both racial and egalitarian

thinking. Europeans considered China to be the most autonomous intellectual entity outside of Europe—a sophisticated, ancient civilization whose inhabitants were ethnically distinct from Europeans. Rather than investigating
how these various eighteenth-century peoples and places "actually" were, my
main focus is on how eighteenth-century European encyclopedists perceived
them to be. Taken together, these three cases allow a thorough investigation
into how eighteenth-century European thinkers positioned themselves
within the panoply of human diversity and consideration of the influence of
ideas of civilizational progress on their racial and egalitarian thinking.

Because all eighteenth-century encyclopedists relied heavily on previous
dictionaries and encyclopedias or copied large sections from other published material, I have tried to identify the sources that the encyclopedists
used.[34] This is an important aspect of the contextual analysis of the encyclopedias, enabling an assessment of which debates the encyclopedists entered
into and the often-interesting ways in which they subtly altered the texts
they relied upon. As Marie Leca-Tsiomis has stated, "Borrowing is . . . a law
of lexicographical work and what is interesting to study is not the similarities, which are obvious, but the differences."[35] Leca-Tsiomis has made an
important contribution to the comparison of Diderot's *Encyclopédie* and
Chambers's *Cyclopaedia*, but she and others remark that more work remains
to be done.[36] Although my focus is on the ideas of equality and race in Enlightenment thought and not on the publishing history or impact of the encyclopedias I am using, I hope that my study will also contribute to the body
of scholarship on the nature and importance of eighteenth-century reference works.

While issues of authorship are certainly important, and Frank and Serena Kafker's work has been indispensable in this regard, I approach these
reference works from the general reader's perspective.[37] I am not interested
in encyclopedia readers' accounts or a general pattern of readership but rather
in the reader imaginatively addressed by the texts.[38] In my analysis, I bring
together cross-cultural equality and racial classification, themes that were
not necessarily brought together by eighteenth-century thinkers themselves
but that were nonetheless linked in interesting ways. Most significantly, the
philosophes often grounded their defenses of equality in the authority of
nature. Simultaneously, however, physical differences and a myriad of inequalities that many imagined to accompany these differences were also ascribed to nature. Thus, Montesquieu's aversion to torture results from, as he
stated, "the voice of nature crying out against me," while Thomas Jefferson

wrote that although the cause of dark skin is not well understood by natural philosophers, "the difference [between Black and White] is fixed in nature."[39] Then, as now, the understanding of nature was capacious enough to accommodate such tensions, even contradictions.[40] How have historians made sense of these contradictions? We now turn to a brief overview of some of the most important attempts at making sense of the ambiguities of Enlightenment thinkers' transformations of race and equality.

The Contours of the Debate on Race and Equality in the Enlightenment

It is tempting to search for a "good Enlightenment" of thinkers committed to equality and human rights and for a "bad Enlightenment" of thinkers who laid the foundations of racial science. Indeed, such an approach has been pursued. In Jonathan Israel's monumental multivolume study of the Enlightenment, materialist-monist thinkers from Baruch de Spinoza onward take the starring role as defenders of a sweeping list of a "package of ideas" that includes, but is not limited to, equality: "The Enlightenment— European and global—not only attacked and severed the roots of traditional European culture in the sacred, magic, kingship, and hierarchy, secularizing all institutions and ideas, but (intellectually and to a degree in practice) effectively demolished all legitimation of monarchy, aristocracy, woman's subordination to man, ecclesiastical authority, and slavery, replacing these with the principles of universality, equality, and democracy."[41] Such an approach is misguided for at least three reasons. First, it anachronistically sets up camps of thinkers who upheld a list of values that supposedly logically hang together but that, upon closer inspection, fall apart. As Darrin McMahon puts it, "Even Israel's most intrepid radicals never completed the package, were never doctrinally pure."[42] Second, Antoine Lilti argues that Israel's conception of what it meant to be radical may be misguided, as what was really novel about free-thinking in the Enlightenment was its public usage.[43] Last, it ignores the modern discourses of inequality that the Enlightenment produced, racial classification among them, as Siep Stuurman has demonstrated in his magisterial history of equality in world history.[44]

In addition to wholesale defense, some quarters on the political left have also pleaded for wholesale rejection of the Enlightenment because of its sexism and racism. For example, it has been stated that "the Enlightenment scientists rationalized that 'subhumans' were genetically inferior, and behaviorally irrational (of course, according to the criteria they devised). They created intelligence/power in their own image. How convenient."[45] Or, take Catherine Belsey on the Enlightenment's role in the history of misogyny: "The Enlightenment commitment to truth and reason, we can now recognize, has meant historically a single truth and a single rationality, which have conspired in practice to legitimate the subordination of . . . women."[46] And reading some postcolonial scholarship would make one believe that slavery, colonialism, and inhumane treatment did not exist before the Enlightenment, but instead were uniquely the progeny of the intellectual movement.[47] While many scholars do not adhere to either of these two poles, such a sketch helps us to understand the contours of the discussion and why the debate on the Enlightenment and its legacy continues at a fairly high temperature.[48]

The argument presented here extends a line of inquiry that has long been part of Enlightenment studies and is positioned somewhere in between the extremes outlined above: one that remains committed to the promise of individual and collective emancipation through Enlightenment while simultaneously recognizing Enlightenment thinkers' exclusions and blind spots. The Enlightenment's most important legacy lies in its self-reflexivity, not in a set of rationalist or moral premises that must be defended.[49] In an older historiography, equality was taken to be an integral part of the Enlightenment. In the preface to his classic *The Crisis of the European Mind*, Paul Hazard wrote that, for eighteenth-century thinkers, "the one absorbing dream was Equality."[50] While the advance of freedom took center stage in postwar Anglophone Enlightenment historiography, equality was nonetheless an important concept in classic works like those of Peter Gay, Robert Darnton, Roy Porter, and Jonathan Israel, in what Annelien de Dijn has called "the modernization thesis."[51] In French-language Enlightenment historiography, equality has played as important a role, as demonstrated by Paul Hazard in the 1930s and continued by Alphonse Dupront in the 1960s and Daniel Roche in the 1990s.[52]

With the postmodern challenge and the impact of such key texts as Edward Said's *Orientalism*, the Enlightenment's complicity in, even fundamental contribution to, "othering" became one of the most important and fruitful new avenues of research from the 1970s onward.[53] In addition to Said's seminal work, which did not really touch on the Enlightenment at any length, Michèle Duchet and a number of other scholars drew explicit attention to the Eurocentric, neocolonial, and sometimes even racist aspects of Enlightenment thought.[54] One of Duchet's principal aims was to expose the anti-colonialism of the Enlightenment as a myth.[55] She demonstrated that although many philosophes critiqued colonialism and slavery, this was launched from a perspective that she calls neocolonial, in that they aimed to reform the system not because of their humanitarian ideals, but because changes had to be made in order to keep European colonial rule intact.[56] Using such examples as the encyclopedist Jean-Baptiste-Pierre Le Romain, she argues that Le Romain and other "philosophes-administrators" demonstrate the tight connection between the Enlightenment and European imperialism.[57] The power of Duchet's work was to give agency to non-Europeans in the eighteenth-century fight against colonialism and slavery, as she showed that the philosophes' humanism evolved in response to slave revolts and other insurrections against European domination.[58]

In a similar vein as Duchet's work, William B. Cohen's *The French Encounter with Africans* went against the then-reigning consensus that France was and had always been a fundamentally anti-racist country.[59] In the chapter "The Philosophes and Africa," he identifies the Enlightenment as a key moment in the transformation of French attitudes of superiority over Black Africans: while the perspective of a heathen, "savage" other had dominated French discourse from the sixteenth century, the eighteenth century saw the displacement of this religious framework with a "biological" one that continued to emphasize African inferiority in another key.[60] Although most of the philosophes believed that Africans were Europeans' potential equals and a thoroughgoing and systematic racism is absent from their thought, Cohen nonetheless placed the emphasis on their views of Africans as degenerated from an implicitly white, "superior" standard. Duchet and Cohen's research—and that of many others—was immensely important because it demonstrated the centrality of the European colonial project to Enlightenment reflections on humanity's natural history and brought the issue of European and non-European agency to the forefront of the discussion. Duchet and Cohen wrote in the thick of the rise of postmodernism and can thus be placed in the context of a more critical distancing from the Enlightenment because of its Eurocentrism and racialism.[61]

Writing after the peak of postmodernist debates on the Enlightenment and highlighting a very different strand of Enlightenment thought than Duchet and Cohen's focus on colonialism, Sankar Muthu developed an incisive and influential argument concerning the robustness of Enlightenment anti-colonialism in which equality comes forcefully to the center of Enlightenment debates. In *Enlightenment Against Empire*, he argues that in the thought of three influential Enlightenment thinkers—Diderot, Immanuel Kant, and Johann Gottfried Herder—there developed the most robust criticism of colonialism since the beginning of the Columbian exchange. While there had been critics of European colonialism since the early sixteenth century, Muthu shows that these critics focused on the *manner* in which Christianity and European lifestyles were spread, not on the fundamental injustice of colonial domination itself. An anomalous and short-lived line of thought developed in the mid- to late eighteenth century that postulated that humans are constitutively cultural beings, a view that Muthu calls "humanity as cultural agency."[62] While Muthu's argument is convincing on the whole, it sometimes elides the importance of the development of a natural historical and racialist perspective on humanity in the very thinkers who are central to his analysis, particularly Diderot and Kant. As such, my study extends his argument by confronting the tensions between the inequality that so often accompanied racialist views of humanity and the cross-cultural equality that Muthu demonstrated lies at the basis of Enlightenment anti-colonialism.

One of the most important recent contributions to the history of race and anthropology in the French Enlightenment is Andrew Curran's fine study *The Anatomy of Blackness*.[63] He presents a very detailed analysis of how and why blackness went from being a "variety" to a "race" in the period from intensified European interactions with sub-Saharan Africa in the fifteenth century to the end of the eighteenth century, comparing eighteenth-century anatomy with other fields or modes of inquiry into human diversity. He is acutely aware of the Eurocentric and prejudiced views that underlay much of Enlightenment "scientific" interest in blackness, which conflicted with the nascent and growing secular antislavery movement, and argues that one of the best explanations of this seeming paradox can be found in the different genres that Enlightenment writers engaged with to write about blackness and slavery. Writing about Black people from the perspective of natural history entailed different assumptions and modes of argument than writing in defense of Black peoples' equal rights: "In both of these cases, Diderot's so-called convictions regarding the black African were perhaps less real beliefs than they were the reflection of specific intent, conventions of genre, and competing Enlightenment-era epistemologies."[64] I draw on numerous insights from Curran's rich book throughout this study but, overall, my book complements his important intervention because the full breadth of cross-cultural equality in Enlightenment thought doesn't receive sustained analysis in *The Anatomy of Blackness*. Curran seems to take it for granted that an egalitarian leaning underpinned Enlightenment thinkers' view of humanity. Such a perspective, I would argue, cannot be taken for granted, and I investigate how and why Enlightenment thinkers put equality to new uses and, thereby, politicized it, a topic to which I now turn.

Equality as a Foundational and an Essentially Contested Concept

The contributors to these three encyclopedias certainly did not agree upon what consequences follow from the natural equality of humankind, but they put the concept to use in novel ways in their discussions of religious toleration, antislavery, and the justice of the society of orders.[65] I argue that in so doing the philosophes transformed equality into both a foundational and an essentially contested concept.[66] Present-day philosophers distinguish between many different kinds of equality: legal, political, social, economic, and moral.[67] I am primarily interested in what Siep Stuurman has called "modern equality," an idea that had to gain traction before the myriad contemporary theories of equality could even become thinkable. In his intellectual biography of the Cartesian thinker François Poulain de la Barre, Stuurman develops the concept of "modern equality" to refer to the simple yet revolutionary move that Poulain made in the second half of the seventeenth century to make equality the basis of his social philosophy. Poulain drew together the languages of equality available to early modern Europeans: natural law, the Christian conception of spiritual equality, the cultural relativism of some travelogues, and the Cartesian vindication of the equality of reason.[68] In bringing these languages together, Poulain also abstracted from all of them, transforming equality into a universalist concept. Equality rather than inequality was given the benefit of the doubt. In this study, I focus on the politicization of basic or moral equality, an idea with ancient roots but one that, when combined with a deepening commitment to the equal right of each adult individual to moral autonomy, would have revolutionary consequences in the eighteenth century.[69]

Chambers's defense of religious toleration and the open, cosmopolitan ethos that undergirds his reflections on cultural diversity demonstrate that equality constitutes a significant subtext in his *Cyclopaedia*. In Chapter 2, I demonstrate that a vindication of equality of rights underpinned early Enlightenment defenses of religious toleration, elements of which we find throughout Chambers's *Cyclopaedia*. Diderot, De Felice, and their collaborators transformed the concept of equality in fascinating ways at mid-century, as equality went from a subtext in Chambers's work to a concept of explicit reflection and fundamental contestation in both Francophone encyclopedias. We will see that the eighteenth-century encyclopedists I analyze begin from a premise of common humanity and basic equality and then go on to argue how and why inequality within society is either necessary or beneficial. Rather than assuming the naturalness of hierarchy and inequality, such disparities must now be justified. Poulain's egalitarian thought reverberated across the late seventeenth and eighteenth century not only in the work of such major thinkers as John Locke, Montesquieu, and Jean-Jacques Rousseau but also in the Francophone encyclopedias I analyze.[70] Stuurman has demonstrated that Louis de Jaucourt, the author of more than a quarter of the *Encyclopédie* entries, was probably Poulain's student at the *collège* in Geneva, and Jaucourt's article "Wife" indicates that his teacher's defense of the equality of the sexes certainly influenced his thinking.[71] Regardless of the mixture of arguments for or against women's equality that are to be found in these encyclopedias, one notices that this mixture testifies to the destabilization of gender in the Enlightenment.[72]

Beyond the impact that Poulain's egalitarian social philosophy had on eighteenth-century thinkers, I argue that the transformation of equality into a foundational concept can be understood in the context of the invention of "society" as the ontological frame of our collective existence in the Enlightenment, an invention that the *Encyclopédie* both reflected and reinforced.[73] Keith Michael Baker and Brian Singer, among others, have demonstrated that rather than being a self-evident truth, the modern concept of society, understood as the fundamental domain of human interdependence, was abstracted from the religious imaginary in the Enlightenment.[74] Rather than having legitimacy through a transcendental principle from without, society became the ground of meaning. And in rejecting the notion of a cosmic moral order that purportedly lay outside of society and gave it its legitimacy, the individual was imbued with an unprecedented level of dignity and respect.[75] As Louis Dumont has shown, accepting the ontological primacy of the individual has important political and philosophical consequences because society is reduced to the interaction between free and equal individuals.[76] Although individualism does not always or even often lead to an egalitarian political philosophy,[77] individualism had unmistakable egalitarian consequences in Enlightenment thought because the philosophes found dependence to be particularly odious.[78] As such, they were primarily concerned with advancing and expanding individual autonomy and viewed the equality and liberty of individuals as interdependent, a standpoint expressed most succinctly by Jaucourt in the *Encyclopédie*: "Equality is the principle and foundation of liberty."[79] Elements of this new conceptualization of society can be found in Chambers's *Cyclopaedia*, where the sacral and civil community are separated. But this deeper social and cultural change becomes an element of more conscious reflection in the Francophone encyclopedias.

In the existing historiography on the Enlightenment concept of equality, much is made of the limitations that the philosophes imposed on the concept, as judged by a normative, usually postrevolutionary, egalitarian standard. For example, in an important article on the subject, Harvey Chisick writes of the "conservative intention and use of one of the most potentially radical Enlightenment social values."[80] And Jean-Marie Goulemot argues that the demand for equality remained rare throughout the Enlightenment and appeared "archaic" to most philosophes.[81] I do not propose to go to the opposite extreme and make revolutionaries out of the philosophes, as this would be equally misguided. But I would like to argue that this emphasis on the conservative nature of equality in the Enlightenment overlooks the significance of how Enlightenment thinkers used and transformed the concept.[82] The philosophes politicized equality by putting it to new uses, as they called into question the legitimacy of the society of orders and slavery, to name two of the institutionalized inequalities that many philosophes found particularly troublesome. While we should be aware of the limitations that eighteenth-century thinkers placed on the concept, Lynn Hunt reminds us that perhaps the more pressing and interesting question to ask is: "How did these men, living in societies built on slavery, subordination, and seemingly natural subservience, ever come to imagine men not at all like them and, in some cases, women too, as equals?"[83] Rather than prosecuting eighteenth-century thinkers before a twenty-first century tribunal, I emphasize that analyzing their ideas in context demonstrates the novelty and importance of their discussion of equality and rights.

Where did the force that equality acquired during the Enlightenment originate? Many developments converged in the Enlightenment to produce a politically consequential notion of equality. In addition to the elements

Siep Stuurman has brought together in his analysis of modern equality and to Louis Dumont and Keith Michael Baker's sketches of the advent of individualism within a novel understanding of society, I focus on the affective elements of egalitarian thinking.[84] I argue that focusing on the emotional elements of egalitarian thought can help us to make sense of the complex relationship between philosophy, politics, and religion in the Enlightenment. Support for equality did not spring from any single religious or philosophical tradition but evolved in the context of changes in religion and belief.[85] As David Bell has argued, "It was only when the French ceased to see themselves as part of a great hierarchy uniting heaven and earth, the two linked by an apostolic church and a divinely ordained king, that they could start to see themselves as *equal* members of a distinct, uniform, and sovereign nation."[86] The essentially human order of society, composed of improvable individuals, made equality a real possibility, not just an outmoded feature of an atavistic "golden age."

The language of fellow feeling underpins some of the most important defenses of equality one finds in eighteenth-century texts, including the encyclopedias I analyze. For example, in his abolitionist article "Slave Trade," Jaucourt grounds his argument in an empathic appeal to common humanity: "It is thus an obvious inhumanity on the part of the judges in the free countries where he [the slave] is transported not to immediately emancipate him by declaring him free, *because he is their fellow human, having a soul like them*."[87] De Felice and his circle intensified the attack on slavery, drawing particularly from the most radical passages of Guillaume Thomas Raynal's *Histoire des deux Indes* (*History of the Two Indies*).[88] I thus pay particular attention to the matrix of empathy, equality, and antislavery sentiments in these encyclopedias.[89] In short, the political force that equality acquired in the eighteenth century did not spring from any particular religious or philosophical viewpoint—Christian, materialist, or otherwise. Rather, the force it gained stemmed at least partially from a deeper empathic commitment to a new understanding of humanity as composed of sentient and autonomous moral agents.

Racial Classification and the Natural History of Humanity

Running counter to the expanding purview of equality in Enlightenment thought was the invention of a powerful discourse of inequality: modern

racial classification. Scholars continue to debate when and where racial classification and its corollary racism began, variously contending that we must
look to antiquity,[90] the Middle Ages,[91] the early modern period,[92] or only the
modern era.[93] From the outset, it is important to distinguish between race
and racism.[94] "Race" has obscure origins but appeared in many European
vernaculars by at least the fifteenth century, originally referring to the lineage of prized animals such as dogs and birds of prey and later to noble
families.[95] It maintained its connection to the idea of noble blood well into
the Enlightenment. By the eighteenth century, the word had come to incorporate both heredity, or lines of descent, and phenotypic similarity, though
eighteenth-century thinkers often did not consistently distinguish it from
related concepts like species, variety, nation, or people.[96] Racism, on the
other hand, was a nineteenth-century neologism and has influentially been
defined as hostility that combines difference and power and that "regards
'them' as different from 'us' in ways that are permanent and unbridgeable."[97]
I thus reject Thierry Hoquet's contention that "a history of race [is] also, inextricably, a history of racism."[98] This is of course not to assert that racism
really began only when the word was coined, which would be absurd, but
simply that it is possible and important to analytically separate race from
racism in order to think historically and to recognize that one may believe
both that races exist and be committed to a nonracist politics.[99] It should be
clear that one can assert that a given peoples has a distinct ancestry from
another given peoples without positing fundamental inequalities or unbridgeable differences between them.

Although there is no consensus concerning when racial classification
was invented, the eighteenth century occupies a prominent place in much of
the scholarship on the subject. Sue Peabody has asserted that "it is a truism
that the modern or scientific racism that emerged in the late eighteenth
century and flourished throughout Europe, the United States, and much of
Latin America in the nineteenth and twentieth centuries was new and different from the collection of prejudices, myths and attitudes that circulated
during the early modern and even earlier periods."[100] In a sense, racial classification fits into the systematizing spirit of the Enlightenment, since using
physical features to group humanity into a finite number of categories was a
way of reducing the complexity of human diversity. But there is nothing
"natural" about using physical features to classify humanity and, given that
the so-called races of humanity are not natural kinds, issues of power and
social control are intimately bound up with how we conceptualize human

difference. Historians generally agree that the salience that physical features gained in seventeenth- and eighteenth-century classificatory systems owes much to slavery. Eric Williams, in his seminal work *Capitalism and Slavery*, wrote that "slavery was not born of racism: rather, racism was the consequence of slavery."[101]

While Seymour Drescher and others have disproved Williams's thesis of the unprofitability of slavery at the time of its abolition, Williams's contention that race, racism, and slavery are connected has largely withstood the test of time.[102] Susan Amussen's investigation of how the English established slavery in seventeenth-century Barbados and Jamaica demonstrates that (White) servitude and (Black) slavery developed in distinct ways in these colonies which contributed to the establishment of racial categories. She has assiduously studied legal changes in these colonies from the 1660s onward, demonstrating that colonial officials began to identify slavery as inherent in bodies and thus collapsed social status into skin color.[103] Cristina Malcolmson has shown that the scientific gaze was bound up with the colonial project from the very origins of the Royal Society and this partially explains the preoccupation of its members with "racial" difference.[104]

Similarly, for the French case, Sue Peabody and others have demonstrated that it was in the second half of the eighteenth century that racial ideology took root and suggests that this was because race served as a justification for the enslavement of Black Africans.[105] These historians have established that the economic and political exigencies of the enslavement of sub-Saharan Africans gave skin color and other physical features an unprecedented importance and that these concerns flowed back to Europe from the West Indies. Crucially, the origin of racial theory was intimately tied to economic exploitation and racist social practices.[106] We will see that the social and economic context of slavery in the European colonies is indeed indispensable for understanding the evolution of the concept of race across these encyclopedias.

Yet this is not the only story to be told regarding the development of the race concept in the early modern world, particularly in the Enlightenment. As Silvia Sebastiani has written, "Ideas might have a distinct trajectory from socioeconomic relations."[107] In his polemical essay from the early 1970s, "The Philosophical Basis of Eighteenth-Century Racism," Richard Popkin argues that when one looks more closely at some of the Enlightenment's most important thinkers, one is confronted with a "paradox": from the heart of the venerable Enlightenment humanist tradition sprang abhorrent theories

of the inferiority of non-Europeans.[108] Following my investigation of the
strands of both equality and race in Enlightenment thought, I aim to shed
light on Popkin's paradox by suggesting that the physical diversity of humanity was a real intellectual problem to which the Enlightenment philosophes responded and that racial classification as part of a novel natural
history of the human species was one of their answers.[109] Because race is a
social construction, scholars of the humanities and the social sciences
have sought an explanation of the phenomenon in the workings of power
alone. I point to the ways in which the matter was more complicated than
the creation and maintenance of an allegedly superior white race, even if
that is one of the most important stories to be told of the creation of concepts of race.

Moving beyond the intractable issue of when race or racism began, what
is undoubtedly the case is that the early modern migration, both forced and
voluntary, of an unprecedented number of peoples to new climes called climatic theory in its ancient guise into doubt and this, combined with the
overall disintegration of the classical and biblical worldview, placed questions of human origins and diversity on a new intellectual plane.[110] I argue
that while we cannot lose sight of the context of European colonialism and
exploitation when studying the origins of modern racial classification, we
can theoretically separate issues of hierarchy, genealogy, and classification,
even if they were intertwined in practice.

The use of such a major Enlightenment philosophe as Montesquieu by
administrators whose aim was to reform colonial laws in order to maintain
the slave system demonstrates the complexity of the issues at hand and the
legitimacy of what has been called a "colonial Enlightenment."[111] Nonetheless, it is important to note the rifts that grew within Enlightenment thought,
particularly in the post-1750 period, as the language of human rights gained
currency in what David Brion Davis has called a "remarkable shift in moral
consciousness."[112] In his study of human diversity in the French Enlightenment, David Allen Harvey remarks, "Certainly, the defenders of the Caribbean plantation complex had no illusions as to which side the 'philosophers
of Paris' were on, and their complaints regarding the naïve humanitarianism and utopian egalitarianism of Enlightenment thinkers abound in the
French colonial archives."[113] Additionally, the origins of racial prejudice
among the French colonial elite toward Amerindians resulted primarily
from the failure of *francisation* in the experience of colonization itself, and
such racialist policies predated the publication of the major philosophes'

anthropological and natural historical reflections.[114] In his sweeping survey of early modern European attitudes toward non-Europeans, Joan-Pau Rubiés emphasizes the differences between imperial metropolitan attitudes towards racialized others and the attitudes of colonial elites, as the latter were much more concerned with the creation and maintenance of a racial hierarchy.[115] While color prejudice often accompanied racial classificatory schemes, the former does not logically or inevitably follow from the latter.[116]

By analyzing the reflections on human diversity in Chambers's *Cyclopaedia* and its Francophone successors, I argue that within Enlightenment philosophy, racial classification was not thinkable outside of the framework of natural history. We should understand Enlightenment race thinking as the view that human physical diversity results from natural processes that combine environmental influences and mechanisms of inheritance in a worldview that superseded appeals to divine intervention to explain human physical diversity.[117] Most of the Enlightenment thinkers I analyze understood the "races" or "varieties" of humankind as dynamic entities, making these concepts distinct from the more static and fixed status of many nineteenth-century conceptualizations of race. The so-called races of humanity are not natural kinds, but the eighteenth-century thinkers analyzed here sought to explain humanity's physical diversity through naturalist causes, just as their twenty-first-century heirs continue to do.

Beginning with Chambers's *Cyclopaedia*, we see that the civilized/savage divide frames his discussion of human diversity more than a racialist perspective.[118] In his dedication to the king of Great Britain, Chambers explains: "'Tis by These [the Arts and Sciences], the Parsimony of Nature is supplied, and Life render'd easy and agreeable under its numerous Infirmities. By these the Mind is reclaim'd from its native Wildness; and enrich'd with Sentiments which lead to Virtue and Glory. 'Tis these, in fine, that make the Difference between your Majesty's Subjects, and the Savages of *Canada*, or the *Cape of Good Hope*."[119] Chambers consolidated an idea that was already widespread in seventeenth-century Europe: that societies pass from savagery to civilization over time and that Europe, Great Britain in particular, stands proudly at the apex of this development. As we will see in Chapter 2, Chambers's *Cyclopaedia* and the *Supplement* (1753) are particularly interesting because they register the subtle shifts taking place in conceptualizing human sameness and difference at mid-century: older notions of European civilizational superiority are accompanied by the emergent anatomical and natural historical interest in human physical diversity.

When we come to the Francophone encyclopedias, we see a marked difference in the treatment of human physical diversity compared with Chambers's reference work. Namely, humanity is explicitly included in natural history as one species among many that must be described and classified as a life form within the ambit of nature. Diderot and De Felice's encyclopedias appeared in the wake of Carl Linnaeus and Georges-Louis Leclerc, Comte de Buffon's monumental natural histories, the latter in particular looming large in both reference works. In Chapters 3 and 4, I investigate the importance of Buffon for the transformation of the concept of race in the Enlightenment. While we find both discourses of equality and inequality in Buffon's anthropology and in Diderot's appropriation of it,[120] I argue that we can better understand Enlightenment perspectives on human physical diversity as an inchoate combination of various ideas that were not understood as definitive answers but instead constituted the new approaches the philosophes adopted to answer old questions.[121] Many philosophes held that motion inheres in particles of matter, that these particles of matter form a coherent whole—nature—and that our understanding of life, including human life, must be placed within this evolutionary materialist worldview.[122] Race moved from the realm of theology to the realm of biology across the early modern period, and rather than projecting the later history of fixed and hierarchical racial categories back into the eighteenth century, it is more fruitful to view the philosophes' contributions to racial classification as a new method of looking at human diversity.[123]

In Chapters 3 and 4, as well as in the conclusion, I will demonstrate that questions relating to heredity, humanity's deep past, and our place in the natural world were central to the philosophes' understanding of race. My aim is not to exculpate the philosophes from the charge of prejudice (of which we will find much to discuss) but rather to better explain what would otherwise be a confounding historical phenomenon: the fact that some of the most radical Enlightenment critics of European colonialism and naturalized inequalities, such as Diderot, also contributed to racial discourse. Race in Enlightenment thought touched upon broader questions of human origins and relatedness that had been newly raised by advances in the new philosophy and the new science. This is not to vindicate the naturalness of the races of the eighteenth century (or any century, for that matter) but instead to emphasize that understanding humanity as an animal species within the fold of nature rather than as God's special creation between angels and brutes was a significant Enlightenment intellectual revolution and this is one eighteenth-century context into which we can place race.

The discovery of time and its relationship to race in the Enlightenment has been tackled in an important recent study. Silvia Sebastiani has demonstrated that the concept of race in the Scottish Enlightenment was engendered by novel eighteenth-century conjectural histories that described human progress in stages, most often from a monogenist perspective.[124] The idea of the progress of humanity as described in stadial histories made the perceived "stagnation" of some peoples a problem, and she argues that the concept of race served to explain the divergent developmental paths of various peoples by attributing them to physical and moral causes that, depending on the thinker, could be either a "hard" or "soft" conceptualization of racial differences. She demonstrates that stadial history was a form of natural history, and her elegant study stresses the unresolved tensions between universality and hierarchy in the Scottish Enlightenment. My argument differs from Sebastiani's in that she focuses on conjectural history and theories of progress while I concentrate on the introduction of time into debates within Enlightenment life science, particularly theories of inheritance and the effect of climate on species' form. The philosophes' conception of race—the idea that the environment and inheritance act together to produce distinct varieties within the human species—served to firmly place humanity in nature's purview, as a species with a deep history extending across unimaginably vast stretches of time, beyond the confines dictated by Genesis, and susceptible to the effects of climate.[125]

It is nonetheless important to acknowledge that while a hardened racism remains largely absent from the philosophes' writings, paternalistic attitudes toward non-Europeans, as well as to the lower classes within Europe, generally permeate their thought.[126] This paternalism was often couched in the language of philosophical history, in which non-Europeans were viewed as "primitive" and only potentially equal to Europeans because they lay further back on the arrow of time.[127] There is in fact an inequality built into the very concept of Enlightenment, as the philosophes positioned themselves as the enlightened few in contrast to unenlightened others, whether European or non-European. Nonetheless, we see the development of the concept of the human being as a constitutively cultural agent in the Enlightenment, which opened up the space both for new theories of history and culture, as well as for robust anti-colonial arguments—themes to which we will return.[128]

The Enlightenment continues to absorb our attention for a variety of reasons. This attention can sometimes appear excessive, but I hope to demonstrate that given our continued commitment to the value of equality and the persistence of structural inequalities, particularly with regard to race and sex, the Enlightenment has much to teach us. The value of studying race and equality in Enlightenment thought does not lie in looking back to see "how far we've come" in terms of our commitment to equality and our rejection of racism. Although equality and the passions associated with it have been at the center of various crises throughout history, there are no perennial questions in intellectual history; Enlightenment thinkers raised a new set of questions when they put equality to new uses. By looking at this moment in intellectual history, perhaps we can better understand a concept that increasingly holds our attention.

There are also crucial respects in which we must still position ourselves within the legacy of the Enlightenment even regarding race, despite its being "man's most dangerous myth."[129] By this I mean that rather than seeing race as an *object* "out there" in nature, which it definitively is not, race can also be construed as a *method* of looking at and understanding human diversity.[130] Our task, as Toni Morrison has memorably stated, is "to convert a racist house into a race-specific yet nonracist home."[131] The Enlightenment has been called a "double-edged sword," because the intellectual movement made nineteenth-century scientific racism thinkable at the same time that it called into question Jewish ghettoization and Black slavery.[132] We would stay truer to the quintessential *esprit de critique* of the Enlightenment if we work to sharpen the sword's edge that cuts deepest into the enduring inequalities and injustices that continue to plague our world.

The book is structured as follows. In Chapter 1, I provide an overview of the transformation of early modern European thinking on equality and human diversity in order to better situate the debates into which the encyclopedists entered. Chapter 2 is an analysis of equality and race in Ephraim Chambers's *Cyclopaedia*, demonstrating that equality formed a significant subtext in the reference work, which was primarily linked to defenses of religious toleration, while the civilized/savage divide is the primary frame through which Chambers discusses human diversity. The *Supplement* to his *Cyclopaedia*, published in 1753, reveals that the natural history of humanity and the concept of race gained greater importance in the course of the eighteenth century. In Chapter 3, I delve into the world of Diderot and d'Alembert's *Encyclopédie*, not only highlighting the ambiguities in thinking about human equality and diversity, but also stressing the numerous ways in which the reference work represents a break from what came before. In short, the most radical encyclopedists, such as Diderot, sought naturalist explanations for human diversity and, simultaneously, entrenched the view that inequality is non-natural. In Chapter 4, I analyze the *Encyclopédie d'Yverdon* and how its contributors' position within what might be called a Protestant Christian Enlightenment impacted their transformation of race and equality. In the conclusion, I offer a framework for making sense of equality and race, human sameness and difference, in Enlightenment thought and reflect on the enduring importance of this framework for understanding many facets of our own world.

CHAPTER 1

Early Modern Debates on Human Sameness and Difference

No two human beings are exactly alike and thus they are unequal in a very basic sense. Looking at the empirical world, a positivist would conclude that inequality is palpable, natural, and perhaps inevitable, and this is what makes equality so significant, because it must be invented and imagined.[1] An in-group notion of equality as fairness has arguably always been a part of human communities, but so too has some measure of hierarchy, not to mention hostility toward foreigners.[2] With the first Western theorizations of equality, in the context of the Greek polis, Aristotle's reflections stand out for their enduring impact. He famously asserted that justice is a "kind of equality," yet in his *Politics*, he also posited the existence of natural slaves.[3] This potentially contradictory position is circumvented because justice means treating like alike, and, because nature has created an inferior class of human beings, one need not, in fact *must* not (according to Aristotle's argument), treat natural slaves as the equals of free citizens.[4] While nearly all of the major early modern philosophers rejected Aristotle's idea of natural slavery, they seem to have performed a similar argumentative maneuver in restricting the applicability of such universalist statements as "all men are created equal." Although assertions of the natural equality of human beings were a common feature of early Greek and Roman philosophy and Christian theology which endured through the medieval period, prominent thinkers seem not to have been troubled in defending strict social hierarchies or even slavery, often justifying such inequalities as a consequence of humankind's fallen state.[5]

These past "shortcomings" in egalitarian thinking are sketched not to praise present-day moral and ethical consistency or achievement, but rather to demonstrate that professing human equality as a fact or ideal is not sufficient for its thoroughgoing defense in a given political or social system. We have to place reflections on equality and inequality—the interplay between reflections on what we share and what sets us apart and why they matter—in a specific context in order to understand what a given thinker was trying to achieve in writing about natural equality or inequality. This chapter lays out the early modern context of European debates concerning human origins and history, physical diversity, and equality in order to better understand the significance of the Enlightenment encyclopedists' interventions. Because the modern racial classificatory system developed within the discipline of natural history, I pay particular attention to this field of inquiry. With regard to equality, natural law and arguments for women's equality were particularly important in the evolution of Enlightenment thinking on the subject, and so I concentrate on these genres and perspectives to illuminate how eighteenth-century thinkers transformed egalitarian thought. I conclude with remarks on how these ideas overlapped and what the present research contributes to the existing historiography.

All but a handful of early modern European theories of human diversity took for granted the monogenetic creation story of Genesis and the descent of humankind from Noah's three sons following the biblical flood.[6] The traditional Christian account held that Europeans could trace their origins to Japhet; Africans, to the cursed Ham; and Semites, to Shem. Disdain for non-Christians and dark pigmentation is evident in this myth, because blackness was considered a curse.[7] More generally, blackness was often associated with sin, evil, and heresy in Christian mythology, though not uniformly given the use of black clothing by some Christian religious orders.[8] Skin color and other physical features, while remarked upon by early modern travelers, were not used as the basis of a classificatory system until the late seventeenth century. In her classic study of sixteenth- and seventeenth-century anthropological and ethnological thought, Margaret Hodgen remarks that while skin color may have been a divisive factor in cultural interactions, it would be anachronistic to speak of race in the modern sense for this period.[9] Instead, Europeans tended to classify peoples based on shared language and religion. Christianity played an important role here, bequeathing to early modern Europeans a powerful monogenetic legacy and an emphasis on humanity's linguistic and religious diversity, as opposed to physical diversity. However, scholars have also noted that this did not prevent deeply racialist interpretations of Scripture throughout the centuries of European expansion.[10]

The Expansion of Natural History and
the Transformations of a Racial Worldview

As Michel de Montaigne wrote, "Human eyes cannot perceive things but in the shape they know them by."[11] We can apply this general insight to make sense of the ways in which early modern Europeans incorporated Native Americans into their worldviews, underpinned as they were by a canon of texts from a circumscribed number of classical and Christian thinkers, in addition to the Bible.[12] Following the incorporation of Aristotelian anthropological categories into Christian thought by Albertus Magnus and Thomas Aquinas in the thirteenth century, "barbarian" referred to both non-Christians and to peoples who behaved in "uncivil" ways.[13] Throughout the sixteenth century, Europeans made one-to-one comparisons of New World peoples with Ethiopians and with Aristotle's favorite barbarians, the Thracians. In the initial debates concerning the status and nature of Native Americans among theologians of the Castilian crown in the late fifteenth and early sixteenth century, Aristotle's argument for the existence of natural slavery was used to justify the enslavement of the Antillean population, which was "uncivilized" in the rudimentary sense that they did not live in cities.

The debate changed, however, upon the discovery of the Aztec and Incan Empires in the early sixteenth century. Francisco de Vitoria, one of the most influential theologians in the so-called School of Salamanca, rejected that the New World peoples were Aristotelian natural slaves, since they fulfilled the basic requirements of "civil life." Nonetheless, the European colonists maintained that New World peoples were cannibals and that some performed human sacrifice, characteristics that denigrated the status of Native Americans. Sixteenth-century Europeans thought that cannibalism went against the law of nature (*ius naturale*), and Vitoria argued that the Native Americans had thus failed to interpret the natural world correctly but, as civil beings, they possessed reason *in potentia*.[14] In this way, Anthony Pagden argues that Vitoria brought Native Americans "into" the European worldview at the lowest possible social and human levels.[15] Even when Vitoria and some of his contemporaries criticized the cruelty of Spanish colonialism, they still argued that Native Americans had to be converted to

Christianity, revealing what Siep Stuurman has called the "limits of Christian equality."[16]

Other important sixteenth-century Spanish theorists who would have an enduring impact on early modern ethnology were Bartolomé de Las Casas and José de Acosta. In his *Apologética historia summaria de las gentes destas Indias* (*Apologetic History of the Indies*, 1536), Las Casas aimed to show that precontact Native American societies were civil in an Aristotelian sense and that their "barbarism" was not primary and absolute but relative. To explain why their societies were so radically and shockingly different from European society, Las Casas drew on Hippocratic climatic theory and Aquinas's idea of adherence to perverse customs.[17] He argued that the difference of Native American society was not one of kind but of degree, as all peoples had performed human sacrifice in the distant past and that these peoples were simply at an earlier stage of a developmental process.[18] José de Acosta, a Jesuit missionary who lived in South America for seventeen years, would elaborate on this developmental view of history in his *Historia natural y moral de las Indias* (*Natural and Moral History of the Indies*, 1590), which was quickly translated into every major European language. It was a remarkable work for the time, as a "moral history," or a history of customs, was highly unusual, and it would remain the most popular work on Spanish America throughout Europe until the publication of William Robertson's *History of America*, in 1777, and Francisco Javier Clavijero's *Historia Antigua de Mexico*, in 1781. Acosta's masterpiece can be read in two keys—religious and secular. On the one hand, he interprets the religious practices of Native Americans as the work of the devil, rejects Copernican heliocentrism, and attempts to reconcile all of the empirical observations of the New World with Christian and classical scholarship. On the other hand, significant parts of his work can be read as a more secular ethnographic study: he postulates that the Americas were populated by an as-yet undiscovered land bridge between the Eurasian continent and the Americas, and he draws constant comparisons between the Native Americans' customs and religion and those of the Ancient Egyptians, Greeks, and Romans.

The two registers of the work are demonstrated by Acosta's assessment: "First, although the darknesse of infidelitie holdeth these nations in blindnesse, yet in many things the light of truth and reason works somewhat in them."[19] In numerous passages, he even calls European prejudice against Native Americans into question, as when he states that his aim is "to confute that false opinion many doe commonly holde of them [Native Americans],

that they are a grose and brutish people, or that they have so little understanding."[20] He reprimands his fellow Spaniards who burned an Aztec book
of natural history because it was thought to be superstitious, writing of these
Spaniards' "foolish and ignorant zeal."[21] Acosta clearly believes that the Native Americans possess reason and are capable of being taught to live virtuous Christian lives. In the more secular mode of analysis, he posits that the
first inhabitants of America were nomadic hunters, peoples who had degenerated to the point where they were "without King, Law, God, or Reason," a
state in which, he says, one could still find various Native American populations.[22] That view fits with the wider perception among late medieval and
Renaissance thinkers that the lateral transmission of culture was associated
with corruption and degeneration, because it was linked to the rupture of
the original monolithic Edenic culture.[23]

Acosta argues that American societies developed beyond this initial
degenerated state in varying degrees across the continent, such that upon
European contact one could find three stages of development. There were
those who still lived in the utterly "degenerated" nomadic state, those who
established some kind of "barbarous" political order, and those who had established great empires. Other sixteenth-century European authors also argued
that Native Americans lived like all peoples had once lived at an early stage
in historical development, as Louis Le Roy wrote in his *De la vicissitude ou
variété des choses en l'univers* (*Of the Interchangeable Course, or Variety of
Things in the Whole World*, 1575): "They which have navigated thither, have
found many people living yet as the *first men*, without letters, without Lawes,
without Kings, etc."[24] In this secular key, Le Roy and Acosta perceived the
historical evolution of human societies, a theme that would be taken up and
further developed by numerous seventeenth- and eighteenth-century thinkers. Thus, as Anthony Pagden points out, Vitoria, Las Casas, and Acosta all
buried "the first crude image of the American Indian as an unreasoning
creature of passion, non-cultural 'natural man,' and thus made some kind of
comparative ethnology, and ultimately some measure of historical relativism, inescapable."[25]

With the global expansion of the sixteenth and seventeenth centuries,
Europeans were confronted with a veritable explosion in newly discovered
plants, animals, and peoples. The sharp increase in the amount of travel literature available to European readers in the early modern period illustrates
this. In the case of France, 805 books on the geography of extra-European
lands were published in the seventeenth century, as opposed to 263 in the

sixteenth century.[26] One of the overriding intellectual concerns from the beginnings of early modern European expansion was to integrate the newly discovered peoples, plants, and animals into a classical and Christian worldview, an increasingly difficult task by the seventeenth century. By way of example, when the botanical garden of Leiden University first opened in 1594, it contained 1,060 plants, whereas just 600 plants were known from ancient sources.[27] Unsurprisingly, classification became a central concern for many thinkers during the Scientific Revolution.[28] This preoccupation would have ramifications for how Europeans viewed the human species, as exemplified in Francis Bacon's *Novum Organum* (1620).[29] Bacon calls on the learned men of his day to undertake the observational study of nature, including human beings, writing that one must investigate the "History of Man," including the "History of the Figure and external Members of Man, his Size, Frame, Face and Features; and of their variations by People and Climate, or other minor differences."[30] In this regard as in many others, Bacon had an immense influence on Enlightenment thinkers, with d'Alembert referring to him as "the greatest, the most universal, and the most eloquent of the philosophers."[31]

Indeed, a novel classificatory scheme of the human species originated in the work of a devout follower of Francis Bacon's "new philosophy," the English political economist and statistician Sir William Petty. Petty has been described as the first thinker to fragment the unity of the human species into distinct races,[32] but this is an anachronistic reading of his *Of the Scale of Creatures* (1676–77). The historian Rhodri Lewis has shown that Petty in fact defended the scriptural account of creation against the heterodox views of Isaac La Peyrère, who had caused a storm with the publication of his polygenetic account of creation in his *Prae-Adamitae* (1655).[33] Petty did not consider the human form to be an adequate criterion on which to base the Great Chain of Being, since he placed the elephant above the great apes in this divine ordering, privileging the elephant's superior memory and intelligence above the more obvious anthropomorphic anatomy of the great apes. Petty also subscribed to the geohumoral theory of human difference. It would thus be misleading to consider William Petty as the first racial taxonomist. Nonetheless, his attention to the physical variation of the human species was indicative of the Baconian turn of mind. Bacon's call to study the "Book of Nature" as opposed to the large tomes of ancient thinkers also fits with the rise of the modern discipline of natural history.[34]

More generally accepted as one of the first racial classifiers is the French physician and traveler François Bernier. Unlike Petty, Bernier was not a prisoner of sacred history, because he formulated his theory of the races of humankind with no reference to the lost tribes of Israel or the sons of Noah in his essay "New Division of the Earth" (1684).[35] The principal significance of Bernier's text lies in its nature as an intellectual experiment in which he moves beyond the parameters of religion and language imposed by scriptural history and uses physical features alone to classify humanity into a finite number of groups.[36] Contrary to Siep Stuurman's interpretation of Bernier's intellectual innovations, Claude-Olivier Doron argues that Bernier was in fact continuing an older tradition in using "race" and "species" interchangeably in a logical, not a taxonomical, manner, rather than in the innovative genealogical way that Buffon would later use it.[37] Doron is not convincing that Bernier's use of the concept does not serve taxonomical purposes or that Bernier's text was not innovative. First, it is not clear why Doron insists that Bernier's use serves purely logical and not taxonomical purposes, given that his entire article is an attempt at a new classificatory system which is, by definition, a taxonomy. Second, Doron's point that Bernier is not concerned with genealogy is not entirely compelling, since Bernier's main criterion for distinguishing his "first" (European) race from his "second," black African, one is the fact that the dark pigmentation of sub-Saharan Africans he takes to be "essential," resulting from their sperm and blood. He states that their sperm and blood look the exact same as the rest of humanity's, but that their dark pigmentation is different from that of Indians and Egyptians, for example, whose darkness is "accidental," resulting from the sun, whereas that of sub-Saharan Africans is heritable.[38]

Bernier, as a follower of Pierre Gassendi, had a more empirical turn of mind than the Cartesians and wrote of human beings as possessing a dual nature—spiritual/rational and sensitive/irrational. In "New Division of the Earth," he categorizes the human species into four races. His "first" race comprises the inhabitants of Europe, North Africa, the Middle East, India, Southeast Asia, and America. The second race comprises sub-Saharan Africans, the third encompasses East and Northeast Asians, and the fourth includes only the Sami, or "Lapps." The first race is the standard by which he measures the other races. Bernier also considers the beauty of women from various regions, which is rejected by some as fanciful French writing but in fact fits with the sexualized male gaze that was so instrumental in the invention of the modern racial classificatory system. Eighteenth-century racial taxonomists can be described as successors of Bernier's secular, empirical, and systematic attempt at a "New Division of the Earth." Bernier points to a rupture in the assumptions made concerning human origins: biblical and classical exegesis dominated the first two centuries of debates on the origins of the Native Americans and, inseparably, all of human history, whereas Bernier was able to move beyond such a perspective.[39]

Bernier's work reveals the role of gender in the development of racial classificatory schemes in the early modern period. Londa Schiebinger has demonstrated the centrality of the beard in the science of race, as Bernier and many other racial taxonomists commented on the presence or absence of beards among the males of the various races they studied.[40] Schiebinger writes, "Eighteenth-century male anatomists in Europe were obsessed with black men (the dominant sex of an inferior race) and white women (the inferior sex of the dominant race). It was these two groups, and not primarily women of African descent, who challenged European male elites in their calls for equal rights and political participation."[41] Buffon, for example, wrote of the beauty of women among the various races he described in his chapter "Varieties in the Human Species," and also of the power of a mother's ability to alter the shape of newborn infants' skulls.[42]

The final element that went into making human diversity a prominent and controversial topic by the early Enlightenment was the debate surrounding epigenesis and preformationism. The invention and improvement of the microscope in the seventeenth century had given impetus to fierce debates concerning the mechanism of inheritance, as male gametes were viewed for the first time. William Harvey, famed for his discovery of the circulation of blood, also investigated the material aspects of reproduction in the mid-1600s.[43] He postulated the existence of eggs in all female animals, including humans, as a necessary part of reproduction, essentially inaugurating the modern controversy between epigenesis and preformationism. Preformationism is the theory that the embryo develops from a completely preformed version of the organism, which resides either in the egg or sperm cell, and epigenesis is the now-accepted theory that the embryo develops from an undifferentiated egg cell after fertilization. Added to the preformationist theory was the "preexistence of germs" theory at the end of the seventeenth century, which held that preformed organisms existed "in germ" and that these germs were created directly by God at the time of creation.[44] Preexistence was the dominant theory of generation in the late seventeenth and early eighteenth century and was defended by some of the leading microscopists of the day, such as Jan Swammerdam and Antonie van Leeuwenhoek.[45] But if one follows the preexistence theory to its logical conclusion, one must be committed to polygenism, because it would mean that God created separate races of humankind that existed in the ovary of Eve and that He caused to be born at a given point in time.[46] Despite some of the awkward aspects raised by this theory, it fit neatly into these thinkers' providential worldview.[47] We will see that, in the *Encyclopédie*, the controversy between preexistence and epigenesis bears on the philosophes' transformation of the race concept.

In analyzing the development of modern racial classification, we should also be careful not to overemphasize the role of male European thinkers. Nancy Shoemaker has persuasively argued for the agency of Native Americans in the creation of categories of "red," "white," and "black" in New World British and French colonies, because "red" was first used by Native Americans *themselves* and only belatedly adopted by Europeans. She posits two hypotheses for the emergence of a red identity: "red" was a response to strange new peoples who called themselves "white" to distinguish themselves from their "black" slaves; or "red" was an identity marker circulating among Native Americans prior to the arrival of Europeans.[48] These possibilities are not mutually exclusive, and Shoemaker argues that it was probably a combination of the two. In the southeast of the present-day United States, the evidence supports the hypothesis of a red identity in response to "white" and "black." Many of the English colonizers in the Carolinas migrated from Barbados, where a "white," as opposed to "Christian," identity likely developed as a result of the growth of the enslaved African population in the Caribbean.[49] Native American leaders adopted a red identity by drawing from indigenous mythical symbols connected to geographical elements, such as the red granite native to certain parts of eastern North America. Modern racial theory thus had complex roots in both European and non-European cultures and interacted with other forms of linguistic, religious, and cultural identity.

In addition to, or perhaps even because of, increased intergroup interaction in the colonial world, the Enlightenment has been accurately described as the age of classification, within which the inchoate science of race fits well. Charles Withers argues that Enlightenment philosophes named, described, and possessed natural objects and peoples in the quest to understand the world and put that newly acquired knowledge to a useful social enterprise.[50] Anthony Pagden expresses a similar sentiment when he writes that understanding the world and shaping it to meet Europeans' ends were related projects.[51] Connected with this drive to classify and understand, the Enlightenment witnessed an increase in anatomical investigations of human beings, as well as other animals, making the issue of the animal-human divide one of central concern in Enlightenment human science.[52] The Dutch physician Nicolaes Tulp performed and published one of the first anatomical observations of a great ape in Europe in his *Observationes Medicae*, in 1641. Tulp called it "homo sylvestris," or "orang-outang," but it was probably a chimpanzee from Angola.[53] In 1699, Edward Tyson added even more detail with his anatomical investigation of a chimpanzee (what he and many others also called an orangutan; the nomenclature did not become precise until the nineteenth century), published as *Orang-Outang, sive Homo Sylvestris: Or, the Anatomy of a Pygmie*, in which he clearly demarcated the great apes from human beings but also stressed the anatomical similarities. Tyson's essay inaugurated a period of increasing interest in comparative anatomy and the physiological relationship of human beings with other animals, particularly primates.[54] These developments placed the issue of the relationship of humans to the wider animal kingdom and, therefore, the nature of human physical differences, more prominently on the intellectual agenda by the late seventeenth century.

In addition to the growth of comparative anatomy, the treatment of human beings as subjects of natural history gradually became acceptable practice in the early eighteenth century. This occurred most significantly in the work of Carl Linnaeus, one of the most influential eighteenth-century naturalists. Linnaeus's *Systema Naturae*, published in Leiden in 1735, was immediately successful, going through ten editions in Linnaeus's lifetime. His inclusion of the human species in his natural history was controversial and, indeed, forms part of the increasingly secular and scientific treatment of human beings in early modern science.[55] But his division of humanity into four groups must not be read anachronistically as a modern racial classificatory system. In the first edition of the *Systema naturae*, humanity is divided into four groups representative of Galen's medical philosophy of the four humors: "red people were choleric, white sanguine, yellow melancholic, and black phlegmatic."[56] Thus, Linnaeus can also be seen as a transitional figure, since humanity is unquestionably a part of natural history, and he utilized skin color in his classificatory scheme but adapted these elements to ancient ideas of human difference. Against this tradition, which focuses on human diversity and difference, there was also a powerful early modern tradition that emphasized human equality, to which I now turn.

The Equality of the Sexes and Natural Law
in the Seventeenth Century

Christian natural law has deep roots in medieval Europe, but it arguably took on a renewed importance in the wake of the Protestant Reformation because of the absence of religious consensus.[57] Seventeenth-century natural law theorists sought new grounds for political obligation in an investigation of something more fundamental than shared religious beliefs and practices that bind society together. Unlike medieval thinkers, early modern natural law theorists had to confront the bewildering cultural diversity of humankind reported in the burgeoning travel literature of the period if their theories were to maintain credibility as descriptions of universal elements of human nature. One theme that recurred in much of this travel literature was that of equality: Europeans described societies with few social distinctions and little material inequality. Additionally, by the seventeenth century, the idea that New World peoples occupied an early stage in an evolutionary trajectory of societal development was firmly secured in European intellectual culture, finding expression in the work of some of the century's most influential thinkers, including Hugo Grotius, Thomas Hobbes, Samuel Pufendorf, and John Locke. Thus, equality was associated with Edenic and classical golden-age myths of truly egalitarian societies, as well as with non-European, particularly American, societies.

Early modern Europeans used equality with either a positive valence, relating it to a virtuous stage of man's innocence or, in a more negative tone, pertaining to man's primitive simplicity.[58] Adam Smith would capture the latter perspective in his concise assertion: "Universal poverty establishes there [among hunters and gatherers] universal equality."[59] Michèle Duchet has remarked that the reality of the "savage world" was constricted by a "network of negations" that allowed the construction of alternative models among Enlightenment thinkers: sometimes, early modern writers contemned New World peoples because of their lack of history, writing, technology, manners, and other hallmarks of "civilization"; at other moments, the philosophes envied these very same people for lacking priests, laws, masters, and vices.[60]

Continuing a tradition from antiquity, all early modern natural law theorists asserted the natural equality of human beings. In Grotius's *Commentary on the Law of Prize and Booty,* he takes from Aristotle's politics the need for social virtue and connects it to the "social good" of equality.[61] He refers to inequality as a "great evil." In his most influential work, *On the Laws of War and Peace,* Grotius distinguishes between three understandings of natural law and lays down the minimal morality that is the foundation for social life, arguing that natural law is separate from Christian law.[62] He writes that the first element contained in the concept of "Right" is "a Power either over our selves, which is term'd Liberty; or over others, such as that of a Father over his Children, or a Lord over his Slave."[63] Grotius argues that people could make use of their natural right to self-preservation in extreme situations by selling themselves into slavery; thus, he did not consider the inequalities of slavery to be in violation of his notion of natural right or equality.

Hobbes appropriated many of Grotius's main insights. He wrote that every person would prefer to be his own master, and from this he deduced his "ninth law of nature": "*That every man acknowledge other for his Equall by Nature.*"[64] As Kinch Hoekstra has demonstrated, Hobbes was not at all unique in postulating the natural equality of human beings, contrary to the assertions of Hobbes himself and many Hobbes scholars. But what makes Hobbes's contribution to equality so important is that he argued that whether or not we are *really* naturally equal or unequal, human nature is such that we *feel* ourselves to be equal to one another, and affronts to equality can easily lead to violence: "It is less a matter that we are equals because we can destroy one another if we are so inclined, and more that we must acknowledge one another as equals because we will otherwise be inclined to destroy one another."[65] Equality was of course a central concept of contestation in the English Civil War, and the conflict brought into sharp relief the emergence of a new conception of the individual and society.[66]

Grotius, Hobbes, and other seventeenth-century natural law theorists deduced basic principles about social and political life from what they considered to be a shared human nature, and natural equality was an important principle in their philosophical systems. Thus, what remained consistent between equality in the medieval Christian tradition and that of the early modern natural law theorists was that the idea was conceived of as part of human beings in a "natural state" and that inequality was a (usually less than ideal) human contrivance. What changed between these traditions was that while for most medieval Christian thinkers, social hierarchies were most often viewed as divinely ordained—a necessary consequence of humanity's fallen state—the advent of the autonomous individual in early modern thought put pressure on the conceptualization of the corporate structure of society.[67] In addition to the intellectual revolution associated with the canonical seventeenth-century thinkers, this transformation was linked to many long- and short-term social and cultural developments in early modern Europe—from changes in architecture that allowed for more privacy, such as the study and chamber, and increasing literacy rates, to the rise of portraiture and listening to theatre and opera in silence.[68] All of these developments reinforced the view that each individual is autonomous and has rights to bodily inviolability.

Samuel Pufendorf was one of the most influential natural law theorists of the second half of the seventeenth century and sought to bring together elements of Hobbesian and Grotian theory. Hobbes's psychology made it difficult to see how human nature could have made social relations possible at any point in the course of human history. Grotius's "realism," understood as his argument that transgressions against natural rights are so inherently wrong that not even God could make them acceptable, was seen as a relic of scholasticism.[69] Pufendorf argued that although self-preservation is a trait common to all human beings, man is naturally sociable and that Hobbes's state of nature is a chimera.[70] Contrary to Hobbes, who theorized that mental and physical abilities are approximately equal across the human species, Pufendorf argued that God had distributed capacities unequally such that human beings excelled at various functions to make society prosper.[71]

Nonetheless, Pufendorf postulated two elements of the equality of human beings: we are equal in that we all have the obligation to obey natural law and in that we innately possess duties which we all owe toward one another. Like Hobbes and Grotius, Pufendorf rejected Aristotle's idea of the natural slave. He conceived of a ubiquitous human nature and inherent dignity in the ontological status of man, writing, "[the] second of the duties of every man to every man is held to be: that each man value and treat the other as naturally his equal, or as equally a man."[72] Anthony Pagden has argued that Pufendorf's appeal to the "natural" instincts of human beings to be benevolent and to recognize their fellows as human beings marked a crucial turn in moral philosophy that would have major consequences for eighteenth-century theorists.[73] Eighteenth-century thinkers would call these instincts "sentiments," and this would become central to Enlightenment thinking on equality and common humanity. Pufendorf drew from Cicero and other ancient thinkers the idea that some persons are naturally suited to govern and others to be governed. Although Pufendorf brought human sentiment and benevolence back into moral philosophy, one must recognize that he did not apply his conception of equality to criticize colonialism, slavery, or other social and political inequalities. On the contrary, he even lamented that slavery had been abolished in Europe, viewing bondage as a suitable condition for some human beings, whether European or non-European.[74]

Along with Grotius, Hobbes, and Pufendorf, John Locke transformed the concept of equality in the context of Christian natural law. Jeremy Waldron has argued that "we have in Locke's mature corpus as well worked-out a theory of basic equality as there is in the canon of political philosophy."[75] Locke confidently asserted, in a similar vein as Hobbes and Pufendorf, that the state of nature is "a *State* also *of Equality*, wherein all the Power and Jurisdiction is reciprocal, no one having more than another."[76] We will see that all of the encyclopedists I analyze were immensely influenced by Locke, and so I examine the ways in which Chambers, Diderot, De Felice, and their collaborators appropriated his ideas in the relevant articles. There is a very large body of scholarship on the controversial topic of Locke's place in the history of liberalism and his contribution to slavery and racism. One of the most important recent interventions emphasizes the fact that slavery developed in the context of arguments for political absolutism and the divine right of kings, which Locke firmly rejected.[77]

These seventeenth-century Protestant natural law thinkers are often placed in a progressive narrative detailing the origins and ultimate triumph of human rights. However, we must recognize that their contributions to political philosophy often, though certainly not always, stemmed from a morally conservative worldview and that their actual political involvement was often to maintain the hierarchical status quo, a theme to which we will return in Chapter 4.[78] As we will see, eighteenth-century intellectuals transformed thought on natural or human rights in crucial ways, giving equality an appeal and impetus it lacked in the great tomes of the seventeenth-century thinkers.[79] We should understand that for many of the early modern thinkers who asserted the natural equality of all human beings and then went on to deny equality to myriad groups, they were not reasoning inconsistently. Rather, they did not believe that some groups, such as women, propertyless men, and some non-Europeans, were capable of autonomy, thus rationalizing their disenfranchisement.[80] Positing the basic moral equality of each individual and querying inequality's social origins—rather than anchoring it in God or nature's plan—meant that eighteenth-century thinkers had to deal with a question that ancient and medieval philosophers never did: How can social inequality be just or legitimate if it is not rooted in nature or providence?[81] By examining how Enlightenment thinkers came to believe that certain others are capable of autonomy and therefore that basic moral equality has real political and social consequences, we can better understand what makes equality so important in present-day political philosophy.

As discussed in the introduction, Siep Stuurman has made a seminal contribution to the history of the idea of equality with his intellectual biography of François Poulain de la Barre (1647–1723). Analogously to Benjamin Constant's famous comparison of ancient and modern liberty, Stuurman argues that in the seventeenth century, there emerged "modern equality" in European philosophy.[82] Poulain's theorization of equality is formulated in terms that precede and transcend any political or social institution. He wrote three Cartesian-feminist treatises between 1673 and 1675, in which he argued that "the two sexes are equal, that is, that women are as noble, as perfect and as capable as men."[83] Enlightenment, for Poulain, was primarily an intellectual and moral attitude, a state of openness to instruct and to be instructed by others, and one in which we recognize "no authority apart from the authority of reason and of sound judgment."[84] Stuurman has demonstrated that seventeenth-century debates on women's equality went into the making of the Enlightenment, contributing the modern, universalist concept of equality and the public contestation of gender to that intellectual movement.[85] Renaissance and early modern feminists, such as Lucrezia Marinella, Marie de Gournay, and Anna Maria van Schurman, drew from Platonic, Stoic, and Christian philosophical traditions to argue that "the mind has no sex."[86] Feminist arguments spread to elite society in the seventeenth century, as evidenced by the many feminist treatises of the 1660s carrying dedications to Nobles of the Robe as well as to members of the Académie française. We should thus not conceive of modern feminism as the result of the belated application of Enlightenment philosophy to gender but rather recognize that the criticism of the naturalness of patriarchy went into the making of the Enlightenment itself.[87]

Early modern feminists made a crucial contribution to Enlightenment thinking about equality, contesting the significance of male-female bodily differences that could easily extend to questioning the significance of racialized bodies in the eighteenth century. Poulain also saw the connection between his feminist argument and the prejudices commonly held against non-Europeans when he wrote, "It is commonly believed that the Turks, the barbarians and savages are not as capable of study as the peoples of Europe. However, it is certain that if one saw five or six of them who had the ability or the title of doctor—which is not impossible—one would . . . admit that these people are men just like us, are capable of the same things and that, if they were instructed, they would be equal to us in everything."[88] Gender thus permeated both egalitarian and racial discourses of the early modern period.

Another important contribution to equality in early modern philosophy can be discovered in the anthropological turn associated with travel literature. The anthropological turn is a metaconcept that Siep Stuurman uses in his *longue durée* history of equality and which postulates two basic tenets: that other cultures have a different order and rationality than one's own, rather than a lack of order or rationality, and that one looks at people in another culture the same way that people in another culture look at oneself.[89] Herodotus's famous formulation of cultural relativism—in which he demonstrates that a given culture finds another's treatment of the remains of the dead abhorrent—could have an "equality effect," in that all human beings are equal in the way they relate to their own culture.[90] Herodotus's cultural relativism was put to use in feminist debates in the seventeenth-century Académie des Orateurs.[91] Additionally, in his famous essay "On Cannibals," Montaigne advanced a powerful formulation of cultural relativism that is an exemplary demonstration of the inversion of the gaze: "I do not believe, from what I have been told about this people [the indigenous inhabitants of Brazil], that there is anything barbarous or savage about them, except that we all call barbarous anything that is contrary to our own habits."[92] Elsewhere, he castigates those Europeans who deny the Native Americans equal intelligence as Europeans: "Its people were in no sense our inferiors in natural clarity of understanding and cogency."[93]

While texts employing the noble savage trope often aimed to criticize European society, the non-European peoples and societies cast in the mold of noble savagery were conceived of as closer to a state of nature. As Sankar Muthu has insightfully argued, this tradition was ultimately dehumanizing in that it promulgated an image of New World inhabitants as "natural," exotic, and less than fully rational, to the point of living in an animallike state.[94] The eighteenth-century philosophes developed a more robust anthropological vindication of cultural pluralism. From Jean-Frédéric Bernard and Bernard Picart's fascinating investigation into the religious impulse across all cultures to the inversion of the gaze so powerfully employed by Montesquieu and Voltaire, Enlightenment thinkers "sought to understand . . . people in their own social and cultural contexts, that is, anthropologically."[95] Thus, feminist, natural law, and anthropological traditions, in addition to Cartesian philosophy, all contributed to the invention of modern equality—the idea that all peoples are fundamentally equal based on membership in the human species. As we turn our attention to how eighteenth-century thinkers transformed these conceptions of human sameness and difference, it is crucial to appreciate that it was often the same set of Enlightenment thinkers who advanced *both* a politically puissant understanding of equality *and* the new racial taxonomies of humanity embedded in natural history. Contrary to what many scholars assert, to say that race served as a justification for inequality is only part of the story than can be told about the concept.[96] Race is more complex than those scholars maintain.

"Nature," Race, and Slavery

Modern racial classification depends upon conceiving of human beings as part of the natural world, as a species that can and should be classified alongside all other living organisms. Although this had been observed long ago,[97] scholars engaged with the cultural analysis of race are not always sufficiently attuned to the significance of this insight. Jean Feerick, in her astute analysis of the idea of race in Renaissance England, argues that the early modern idea of race followed a different social logic than the modern one, namely, in its ambiguous relationship to skin color. The crux of her analysis is that the modern idea of race depends "on defining the realms of nature and culture in opposition to one another, construing racial features as inalterable ascriptions of nature."[98] She focuses on Richard Ligon's *True and Exact History of the Island of Barbados* (1657) and Henry Neville's *The Isle of Pines* (1668) to pinpoint a moment of transition in the course of the seventeenth century. Ligon fits into an intellectual world where race was associated with nobility and bloodlines, regardless of color, whereas modern conceptions of race depend on an understanding of differences in *kind* between human beings based on skin color, among other physical markers, which comes to the fore in nascent form in Neville's work.[99]

Eighteenth-century thinkers further developed the distinction between the cultural and the natural. Johann Friedrich Blumenbach pointed out that it was only in the eighteenth century that Europeans realized "that man is also a natural product, and consequently ought at least as much as any other to be handled from the point of natural history according to the difference of race, bodily and national peculiarities, etc."[100] Justin Smith remarks that modern racial classification can be understood as an "overextension" of biological classification more generally.[101] He traces the decline in Christian and Cartesian conceptions of mind/body dualism across the early modern period, which gave impetus to the study of human beings as natural entities and thus also racial thinking. These scholars' insights can be extended to thinking about the Enlightenment as an intellectual movement to make sense of the tension between an increasingly politicized notion of natural equality and a Eurocentric racial classification.

Due to the highly racialized nature of the transatlantic slave trade, the question of the role of slavery in the development of modern racial theory is particularly contentious. Three elements in this debate deserve close attention: the monogenism/polygenism debate over human origins, the legal construction of race in laws that regulated the slave trade and slavery, and the writings of racial theorists themselves on slavery. Monogenism is the theory that all human beings share a common origin and are of the same species, whereas polygenists postulate that various human populations or "races" have separate and distinct origins. As we have seen, the biblical creation myth bequeathed a strong monogenetic tradition to Europe, but polygenetic accounts increased with the intellectual challenge posed by the discovery of the New World and the waning of scriptural authority. While the words "polygenism" and "monogenism" were first coined by members of the anthropological school of Philadelphia in 1857, the history of the concepts goes back at least to Paracelsus, Giordano Bruno, and, perhaps most important, to Isaac La Peyrère and his controversial *Prae-Adamitae*, which was published in Latin in 1655 and translated into the major European vernaculars.[102] These early speculations on polygenism mainly involved biblical criticism, and La Peyrère's work was deeply embedded in an eschatological worldview. But by the eighteenth century, defenders of polygenism such as David Hume and Voltaire engaged in a more secular historical criticism.[103] Polygenism remained a minority discourse in the eighteenth century but, with support from such illustrious figures as the leading lights of the Scottish and French Enlightenments, it was far from insignificant.[104]

No longer simply a question of theological and philosophical curiosity, the debate on human origins took on acute political and cultural urgency in the eighteenth century as the nascent but expanding abolitionist movement called into question the legitimacy of Black slavery.[105] While not all

polygenists supported slavery (Hume and Voltaire again serve as significant examples), the polygenetic account of human origins could more easily
lead to the dehumanization of Blacks and justification of their enslavement,
soothing the consciences of European slaveholders.[106] Eighteenth-century
abolitionists exerted considerable effort to defend the common humanity of
Blacks, as they were aware that concepts of the natural rights of humanity
or the rights of man would be impotent if Blacks were thought to be something other and lesser than human.

One of the most fruitful avenues of historical research into the invention
of race in the early modern period has been investigations of the genesis and
development of legal apparatuses that regulated hereditary slavery, and
thereby created race, in New World colonies. All of the laws that institutionalized slavery in the English colonies date from the period of the restoration
of the Stuart monarchy and after.[107] Scholars generally agree that at the beginning of English colonization, White indentured servants and enslaved
Blacks or Amerindians were treated similarly, with colonists such as Richard Ligon observing that English servants were treated even worse than enslaved Blacks.[108] In England's most profitable colony, Barbados, whether the
shift from White indentured servants to Black slave labor occurred gradually or suddenly between the 1640s and 1680s is a matter of dispute, but it is
undeniable that the shift occurred, with significant consequences for how
the seventeenth-century English, both in the colonies and the metropole,
thought about race.[109] Servitude came to be identified with blackness, and
the New World planters developed draconian laws to discipline a rapidly
growing population of enslaved Africans. The first slave code in an English
colony, "An Act for the Better Ordering and Governing of Negroes,"
which was passed by the Assembly of Barbados in 1661, referred to enslaved Africans as being "of barbarous, wilde and savage nature, and such
as renders wholly unqualified to be governed by the Laws, Customs and
Practices of our Nation" and thus reified an essentialist African "nature"
that was so wholly debased as to be outside the realm of customary legal
practices.[110]

Religion played an important role in these developments, as planters
went from identifying predominantly as Christian to White, especially from
the 1680s onward.[111] Europeans generally agreed that it was unlawful to en-
slave fellow Christians, and, as Rebecca Goetz has demonstrated in the case
of colonial Virginia, the conversion of enslaved Black peoples to Christianity instigated the creation of racial divisions, in that a notion of "hereditary

heathenism" developed to ensure that conversion to Christianity did not threaten the slave system.[112] We should not, however, see this development as a change in the justification of slavery from religion to race, as Winthrop Jordan explains: "No such justifications were made. There seems to have been, within the unarticulated concept of the Negro as a different sort of person, a subtle but highly significant shift in emphasis."[113] Indeed, when Protestant missionaries were shocked to find that many planters resisted their efforts to convert enslaved peoples, they developed a perspective that argued that conversion to Christianity would make better, more obedient slaves.[114]

Developments in the French colonies in the same period present a contrasting case. Unlike in the English colonies, Louis XIV's infamous Code Noir (1685) focused much attention on Christian conversion. It banned Jews from the French colonies, demanded the baptism of all enslaved peoples in the Catholic religion, and provided many stipulations concerning sexual relations between masters and slaves.[115] Unlike eighteenth-century French laws concerning slavery and freedom, the Code Noir did not distinguish between peoples of different skin color and ancestry ("mulattoes," "quadroons," etc.) but rather between those born free and those manumitted. As Yvan Debbasch has noted, "In 1685, the positive law does not admit the criterion of color; at most, a tendency emerges for a distinction, which is not based on ethnicity, between those who became free and those born free."[116] Debbasch demonstrates that a more segregationist ideology developed in the course of the eighteenth century, as, for example, laws began to lump together all Black peoples, whether enslaved, born free, or emancipated, a process that intensified especially in the wake of the Seven Years' War. John Garrigus has deepened Debbasch's perspective with extensive archival work concerning France's most important colony, Saint-Domingue, and has demonstrated a relative lack of concern with color or "racial" categories in census and social life more generally up to 1760. Until the second half of the eighteenth century, free people of color and Whites often intermarried, because the logic of social class trumped the logic of race. Extending Debbasch's argument concerning the importance of the Seven Years' War as a turning point, Garrigus demonstrates that an ideology of whiteness enabled the French to shore up planter support for French colonial defense against their English rivals and maintain a monopoly on trade.[117]

In her important work on legal cases in which enslaved peoples sued for their freedom in eighteenth-century France, Sue Peabody has also demonstrated the fundamental role that the law played in the creation of race. The *parlement* of Paris failed to register the first French laws regulating slavery within metropolitan France—the Edict of 1716 and the Declaration of 1738—and the enslaved won in every case brought before the Paris Admiralty Court because of a deep-rooted idea that "there are no slaves in France."[118] From the first case of an enslaved person suing for his freedom at the Admiralty Court, that of Jean Boucaux in 1738, to the surge of cases from the 1750s onward, Peabody establishes that "racial" considerations— namely, a focus on blackness—became issues of central concern. Slave status was emphasized in court cases above any mention of physical features in most court cases in the first half of the eighteenth century, whereas after 1750, ordinances were issued concerning the control of all Black peoples in France, whether enslaved or free.[119]

Although the creation of race as a category in laws governing slavery is undoubtedly an important element in the history of the concept, we should also be careful not to exaggerate its impact. John Garrigus has offered one of the best studies of slavery, race, and the law in Saint-Domingue and observes that "because enslaved African people and their children were the blood-and-muscle of Saint-Domingue's economy, many students of the colony have overestimated the rigidity of racial categories, over time."[120] While it is generally agreed that across the eighteenth century race solidified into a more rigid concept that linked physical features and genealogy to psychological and moral traits, it is only in the postrevolutionary world of nineteenth-century European empires that race became an all-encompassing category of being. In an insightful study of household relations across lines of race in eighteenth-century Saint-Domingue and France, Jennifer Palmer successfully shows that "studying day-to-day life within the household complicates narratives of race as a solidifying category by demonstrating that individuals habitually crossed racial lines throughout the ancien régime."[121] For Palmer and other scholars, the late eighteenth-century Atlantic revolutions mark a crucial turning point in the history of race, as the unprecedented act of declaring basic equality and freedom in state constitutions necessitated justifications beyond inchoate prejudices, and race came to serve such a function.[122]

Additionally, in some cases the practice of slavery among Native Americans and Europeans conflicted with the reification of race across the early modern period. Brett Rushforth has demonstrated that the enslavement of Amerindians, as opposed to Africans, remained the dominant form of slavery in New France until the Seven Years' War, as the Native allies of the French traded their enslaved enemies to solidify bonds of alliance. Because certain Native groups carried out slave raids on other Native groups, there was resistance to the creation of an all-encompassing "race of Natives" in French discourse in the seventeenth and eighteenth centuries.[123]

Many historians have overstated the role of the Enlightenment in the development of racism and, correspondingly, the role of racial theory in debates on slavery. George Mosse wrote that "eighteenth-century Europe was the cradle of modern racism."[124] Kenan Malik also gave primacy to the eighteenth century: "The concept of race emerged . . . as a means of reconciling the conflict between the ideology of equality and the reality of the persistence of inequality. Race accounted for social inequalities by attributing them to nature."[125] However, recent scholarship has nuanced this monolithic interpretation of Enlightenment racial theory.[126] I would argue that the hardening of racial categories particularly followed from the eighteenth-century Atlantic revolutions and that, in the thought of the philosophes, race was not primarily used to justify existing inequalities.[127] To take the example of slavery, the most common justifications for slavery in the early modern period—when justifications were offered at all—were religious, legalistic, or economic, rather than racial or naturalistic.[128] Additionally, rather than race being used to reconcile European hypocrisy with the rise of Enlightenment values, the rise of those values itself can partially be explained as a reaction against the extremities of slavery and other inhumane practices. As Seymour Drescher has argued, the sheer inhumanity of the growing slave system may have helped to "sharpen the meaning of human rights."[129]

Race and Eighteenth-Century Natural History

Related to but distinct from debates concerning slavery, the discourses and practices of natural history were an important context in the development of race in the eighteenth century. Given the great prestige of Buffon in the Enlightenment and the reliance on his work by all of the Francophone encyclopedists I have studied, a brief sketch of the main dimensions of his anthropology may be useful. Buffon's *Histoire naturelle*, published in thirty-six volumes between 1749 and 1788, was the third most common work in private

French libraries in the second half of the eighteenth century.[130] The nature of Buffon's contributions to the development of modern racial classification is a particularly vexed issue. He is variously ushered in either as a quintessential defender of the universalist Enlightenment values of equality and freedom or as representative of the intellectual movement's consolidation of a Eurocentric racial classificatory system. Thierry Hoquet, Pierre Rosanvallon, and Jacques Roger all emphasize Buffon's defense of the unity of the human species, the power of climate and culture to shape character, and the egalitarian implications of his physical anthropology.[131] For Louis Sala-Molins and Michèle Duchet, on the other hand, Buffon is indictable for a blatant and apologetic Eurocentrism.[132] The crux of the matter is that both positions are defensible and valid.[133] What I think is important to appreciate is that underneath the Eurocentric conception of racial difference lies a new understanding of humanity's place in nature. That does not excuse Buffon from the charge of Eurocentrism but can help to delineate the distinct strands of Enlightenment thought that are often confounded by various scholars.

Although theories of the influence of the natural environment on living species in general and on human beings in particular go back to antiquity, Buffon was at the center of a transformation in the understanding of nature during the eighteenth century in what Phillip Sloan has called the "Buffonian revolution."[134] Buffon revived Descartes's interest in the deep history of the cosmos and the earth, and, thanks to his work, "re-established [at mid-century] was the concept of nature as a substantive, causal agency."[135] This revolution in the understanding of nature had important implications for understanding humanity. Most significant, Buffon argued that physical differences between human populations must be explained primarily by the force of the natural environment acting on bodies to instigate changes that could become hereditary.[136] A role was also reserved for culture, and here Buffon's prejudices come to the fore, as he postulated that a non-European climate and a nomadic lifestyle had a negative impact on a people's physical features. According to Buffon, humanity's original and most beautiful color was white, and all nonwhite peoples degenerated from this primeval homogeneity.[137] Buffon nonetheless held to a materialist defense of monogenism, asserting the unity of humanity based on the observation of the production of fertile offspring across "racial" lines.

Buffon's inclusion of the race concept within his natural history was in fact quite novel. The first edition of the dictionary of the Académie française defines race as a "line of descent, lineage, extraction, all that comes from the same family" and offers this example: "He is from a good race, from an illustrious, ancient race,"[138] revealing the connections between race and nobility.[139] To add to the confusion, numerous eighteenth-century authors used the word "race" interchangeably with such diverse terms as "people," "nation," "variety," and "species." Nicholas Hudson writes that Buffon elevated the term "to a new, eminent status in scientific nomenclature" and points out that his use of the term stressed the transience of various racial features and confirmed the fundamental unity of the human species.[140] Buffon used the concept of race to refer to peoples who share the same phenotype and a common origin, as when he explained the relationship between the Tartars, Chinese, and Russians: "This Tartar blood is mixed on one side with the Chinese and on the other with the eastern Russians. This mix did not make the traits of that race completely disappear, as there are many Tartar faces among the Russians."[141] The slipperiness of Buffon's use of "race" becomes clear when he writes that it is necessary to divide Blacks into two different races, the "Nègres" and the "Cafres" and subsequently refers to "these two *species* [espèces] of black men."[142] In general, it is a combination of physical and cultural resemblance attached to ideas of patterns of inheritance that lies at the basis of Buffon's concept of race.

Claude-Olivier Doron has argued that Buffon's concept of race "pertained to a genealogical style of reasoning which was largely extraneous to natural history before the middle of the eighteenth century."[143] He contrasts this genealogical style of reasoning with the logical/classificatory style that dominated most natural histories up to and including Linnaeus. While he cogently demonstrates that Buffon used the concept of race to refer to a level of classification different from the species or variety, he is not entirely convincing when he argues that race was a more important concept for monogenists than for polygenists.[144] Of the eighteenth-century polygenists, Doron focuses mostly on Voltaire, stating that the patriarch of Ferney does not present an exception of any significance to his argument that race was a concept of more importance to the monogenists. Other influential polygenists, such as John Atkins and Henry Home, Lord Kames, used the term "race" to describe the distinct ancestral lineages that trace their origins to separate acts of creation.[145] The term "race" was simply too multivalent in the eighteenth century for Doron's argument to hold water.

Nonetheless, Doron's focus on the novelty of the genealogical style of reasoning in natural history from mid-century onward is immensely important for making sense of the transformation of race in the Enlightenment.[146] This style of reasoning contrasted not only with that of Buffon's main rival, Linnaeus, but also with the ancient tradition of linking Blacks to Noah's cursed son Ham.[147] While the curse of Ham is also a genealogy, Enlightenment thinkers rejected it because it depends upon supernatural presuppositions of God's actions in the world. As the twentieth-century's most prominent Buffon scholar, Jacques Roger, has noted, Buffon's main concern in the controversial chapter "Varieties in the Human Species" was to explain, not just to describe, humanity's physical diversity.[148] Buffon refused the fixity of any of the "races" he described, and his survey of human physical diversity served, first and foremost, to place the human species within the ambit of a natural historical development.

As he stated in his *Preliminary Discourse*, "The first truth which issues from this serious examination of nature is a truth which perhaps humbles man. This truth is that he ought to classify himself with the animals, to whom his whole material being connects him. The instinct of animals will perhaps appear to man even more certain than his own reason, and their industry more admirable than his arts."[149] And his concluding remarks to the chapter "Varieties in the Human Species" are worth reiterating: "Everything thus contributes to proving that humankind is not composed of essentially different species; on the contrary, there was originally only one species of men, which, having multiplied and spread itself over the entire surface of the earth, underwent various changes resulting from the influence of climate, of differences in food, of lifestyle, of epidemic diseases, and also from the infinitely varied mixture of more or less similar individuals."[150] While Buffon maintained a Cartesian distinction between mind and body, he was the first major naturalist to include humanity in a history of nature formulated outside of the biblical framework.

To outline the main contours of the transformation of race across the eighteenth century, we must consider the various methods used by racial classifiers, the changing uses of racial language, and significant national differences. Regarding methodology, nearly all naturalists before the second half of the eighteenth century relied on travel literature to understand the physical diversity of humanity. Buffon had a collection of preserved human specimens, including the heads of two Africans, and he observed an albino boy from Angola in Paris in 1744. But the majority of his exposure to non-Europeans was through travel literature, as was the case with most of his contemporaries.[151] In the final decades of the eighteenth century, Petrus

Camper and Johann Friedrich Blumenbach, among others, gave impetus to the primacy of the direct observation, measurement, and anatomical investigation of human beings. Many historians argue that the 1760s and 1770s were decisive years in the development of modern racial theory, partially due to this transformation in the methodology of racial knowledge production.[152]

Camper, a renowned professor of medicine who worked at numerous Dutch universities throughout the eighteenth century, invented the concept of the facial angle, the idea that different types or races of human beings can be distinguished from one another by the angle formed when an imaginary line is drawn from the base of the nose to the forehead. He presented his work to the Amsterdam Drawing Academy in 1770, but it was not published until 1791. He wrote, "The two extremities . . . of the facial lines are from 70 to 100 degrees, from the negro to the Grecian antique; make it under 70, and you describe an ourang or an ape; lessen it still more, and you have the head of a dog."[153] Camper subscribed to the Buffonian, environmentalist explanation of racial difference but more readily accepted clear racial demarcations based on continental divides. His influence reached across Europe: Diderot read his work while in the Dutch Republic, and so too did numerous anthropologists of the late eighteenth and early nineteenth century.[154] With his invention of the facial angle, Camper initiated a shift in racial thought and "practice," as anthropologists increasingly looked to measurable bodily differences to carve up the human species into finite groups. Although Camper was a pious Christian and Cartesian dualist, conceiving of race as a malleable category of being, the facial angle was later taken up by anthropologists to argue for the fixity of race and even for the polygenetic origins of different varieties of human beings.

Blumenbach's contributions to racial theory in the late eighteenth century demonstrate the increasing importance of anatomical investigation and measurement in the developing field of physical anthropology. In his highly influential 1775 account of the natural history of humanity, *The Natural Variety of Mankind* (*De generis humani varietate nativa*), he distinguished between five races—Caucasian, Mongolian, Malayan, Ethiopian, and American (Amerindian)—each linked to the skin color of, respectively, white, yellow, brown, black, and red. While Blumenbach's races appear in list form and, at first glance, seem more fixed than Buffon's presentation of racial divisions, he actually echoed Buffon in arguing for the primacy of climate and "civilization" in determining racial composition and was a vociferous supporter of monogenism. He wrote that his five varieties of human beings cannot be clearly demarcated one from the other, as they "all do so run into one another, and that one variety of mankind does so sensibly pass into the other."[155] In *The Natural Variety of Mankind*, Blumenbach was responding to important polygenetic theses that had been published since mid-century, namely Griffith Hughes's *The Natural History of Barbados* (1750), Oliver Goldsmith's *A History of the Earth and Animated Nature* (1774), and Henry Home, Lord Kames's *Sketches of the History of Man* (1774).[156]

Blumenbach had a collection of eighty-two skulls that, in addition to his anatomical investigations into hair, fetuses, and other prepared specimens, were instrumental in his studies on race.[157] Nicholas Hudson remarks that Blumenbach transformed the meaning of race, because his concept refers to peoples sharing a similar color and physiognomy, regardless of whether they share a common stock.[158] Considering Blumenbach's defense of the common origin of humankind and his environmentalism, it is ironic that his work contributed to the essentializing of race at the end of the eighteenth century. He explicitly spoke out against those who held that non-Europeans are inherently less intelligent than Europeans: "It has been asserted that the negroes are specifically different in their bodily structure from other men, and must also be placed considerably in the rear, from the condition of their obtuse mental capacities. Personal observation, combined with the accounts of trustworthy and unprejudiced witnesses, has, however, long since convinced me of the want of foundation in both these assertions."[159] His use of skulls in racial classification was also a significant innovation; if racial divisions could be seen at this level of human anatomy, some naturalists argued that race indelibly marked the individual, thus further contributing to the hardening of race.[160]

In any case, as Londa Schiebinger argues, Blumenbach's emphasis on the malleability and fluidity of racial types bucked the wider trend of most late eighteenth-century European naturalists to entrench racial differences.[161] Even Blumenbach, however, held that humanity was originally white, all other races having degenerated from this original, and that going from a dark complexion to a lighter one was significantly more difficult than the other way around. The methods Blumenbach employed to investigate racial variation were used by racial determinists to argue against his core values. In Blumenbach's work, we also see the importance of aesthetic considerations that were integral to the development of modern racial classification in the eighteenth century.[162] He considered peoples indigenous to the Caucasus to be the most beautiful in the world, and this, along with the myth of Noah's ark having landed on Mount Ararat, partially contributed to his argument that the human species originated in this region.

Despite the convergence of numerous factors that contributed to the development of a more fixed and reified idea of racial difference at the end of the eighteenth century, scholars sharply disagreed on the nature of the physical diversity of humankind. In the midst of a growth in antislavery publications in the 1760s and early 1770s in Britain, for example, the colonial administrator and planter Edward Long published his *History of Jamaica*. He argued that Africans are essentially different from and naturally inferior to Europeans. Long was a polygenist and wrote that Africans "are void of genius" and "have no plan or system of morality."[163] In malicious prose, he associated Africans with the animal world in order to justify their enslavement. While Long's work fits with the hardening of racial categories in the late eighteenth century, his theories gained remarkably little traction in British literate society.[164] For example, a selection of letters discussing the slave trade was published in the *Morning Chronicle* in 1788, and the opponents of the trade outnumbered the supporters eight to one.[165] Seymour Drescher writes that in late eighteenth- and early nineteenth-century Britain, "neither in the press nor in the Parliament was there an indication of preoccupation with theories of racial inferiority, much less acceptance of them."[166]

Coeval developments in France suggest that its government authorities were more concerned with "racial purity" and miscegenation than were their British counterparts, in that the French government passed a law in 1764 restricting the entrance of Blacks into the metropole as well as barring mixed-race people from practicing medicine and surgery in the colonies.[167] No such law was ever introduced in England, despite the number of Blacks as a percentage of the population being about ten times higher in England than in France during this period.[168] While this indicates the racist posture of French authorities, the law's preamble betrays an indication of the social acceptance of Blacks as marriage partners among the autochthonous population: "The Negroes are multiplying every day in France. They marry Europeans, the houses of prostitution are infected by them, the colors mix, the blood is changing."[169]

Metropolitan debates concerning slavery reveal that enlightened French opinion on the question of racial divisions was also divided, at least until the Haitian Revolution, which marked a turning point in French thinking on race. Voltaire represents one "extreme" of racialist Enlightenment thought, since he was a polygenist and argued that nature produced a fixed racial hierarchy: "Nature has subordinated to this principle these different degrees of genius and these characters of nations that one rarely sees change. It is because of this that *negres* are the slaves of other men."[170] But while Voltaire is often taken as the prime example of a racist Enlightenment, and indeed we can find many examples of anti-Semitism and other prejudices in his writings,[171] his world histories began with China, thus calling into question the self-congratulatory stance of most of his contemporaries' scholarship.[172] We also see an evolution in his writings. His *Remarques sur l'histoire* (Observations on history, 1742) displays a confidence in historical progress, both moral and material, driven by European colonialism. But this confidence is partially sapped by the 1750s, demonstrated by his criticism of slavery and the excesses of European colonialism in his *Essai sur les mœurs* (*Essay on the Manners of Nations*, also translated as *An Essay on Universal History*, 1756) and his later addition of a chapter harshly condemning slavery in *Candide*.[173]

Going against Voltaire's relatively fixed racialist worldview, Claude-Adrien Helvétius produced two radically materialist and egalitarian texts: *De l'esprit* (*On Mind*; 1758) and *De l'homme* (*On Man*; 1773). Helvétius denied any links between human physiognomy and intelligence: "It would however be easy to perceive that the exterior difference that one notices, for example, in the physiognomy of the Chinese and of the Swedish cannot have any influence on their minds; and that, if all of our ideas arrive to us by our senses, as Locke has shown, northerners, having no greater number of senses than the Orientals, have by their physical structure equal mental capacities."[174] The views of Voltaire, a deist and anti-materialist, and Helvétius, a materialist, reveal that although materialism could encourage a view of the fixity of racial differences, this was certainly not always the case. And criticisms of racial prejudices even found their way into the French government. In 1784, the finance minister to King Louis XVI, Jacques Necker, wrote a scathing attack on slavery in his *Traité de l'administration des finances de la France* (Treatise on the financial administration of France) in which he minimized racial differences: "We pride ourselves on the greatness of man and we rightly see this greatness in the surprising mystery of all the intellectual faculties. However, a small difference in hair or in the color of skin is enough to change our respect into contempt and to make us rank beings similar to us on a par with unintelligent animals."[175]

The establishment of the Society of the Friends of Blacks in Paris in 1788 demonstrates that a significant segment of elite opinion rejected the argument, mainly emanating from the colonies, that Africans formed a fundamentally separate and inferior race. In the preamble to "Rules for the Society of the Friends of Blacks," penned in 1788, the Marquis de Condorcet wrote, "We deprive the Negro of all his moral faculties and then declare him inferior to us, and consequently destined to carry our chains."[176] To find near contemporaneous expressions of essentialist views of race, however, one only has to look at some of the anatomical investigations into blackness, such as Claude-Nicolas Le Cat's *Traité de la couleur de la peau humaine* (Treatise on the color of human skin; 1765), in which he argued that sub-Saharan Africans possess a peculiar fluid, which he dubbed *oethiops*, that indelibly differentiates them from the rest of humankind.[177]

We are thus faced with an Enlightenment with diverse and divergent views on race, as these eighteenth-century debates on human physical and cultural diversity contributed to "defining a discourse that was simultaneously universalist and relativist, Eurocentric and cosmopolitan."[178] While the sources reveal a general trend toward the fixity of racial categories near the end of the century, it was by no means uncontested, and many important voices maintained the fluidity of human physical diversity and its irrelevance to social and political issues. We should also be careful not to conflate everything that was said about human diversity in the eighteenth century with the Enlightenment, as some historians have done.[179] Thus, the discriminatory laws of the French crown should not be seen as a political expression of Enlightenment values.

Unlike the history of race in the eighteenth century, which has been the subject of an extensive and continually growing secondary literature, histories of the idea of equality are relatively rare, which is quite remarkable considering the importance of equality during the Atlantic revolutions and in the subsequent development of modern Western thought.[180] Although Sanford Lakoff's 1964 *Equality in Political Philosophy* presents a useful overview of the idea from antiquity to the twentieth century, he uses an outmoded method in the history of ideas in seeking to discover three "unit ideas" of equality. Doing so leads to anachronistic readings of texts, which are revealed when he writes that there exist "concepts [of equality] which are present in their essential elements from earliest times but which are only made explicit and propounded in opposition to each other in the course of modern history."[181] He distinguishes between liberal, conservative, and socialist positions

on equality, each of which has ancient roots. Regarding the Enlightenment, he argues that the philosophes were more concerned with abolishing
extreme inequalities than with instituting a truly egalitarian society. And,
as we have seen, Harvey Chisick argues that equality served to "infuse good
feeling" into the society of orders.[182] While both authors are certainly correct
that many mainstream Enlightenment thinkers placed important restrictions on the application of equality in civil society and politics, they are too
hasty in their summation of the impuissant nature of the idea of equality in
Enlightenment thought.

In contrast to these assessments, André Delaporte argues that the
golden-age myth of a propertyless, egalitarian society drawn from classical
sources and travel literature lay at the base of Masonic societies and was one
of the most powerful tropes of egalitarian thought in the Enlightenment and
Revolution.[183] But Delaporte brings such disparate thinkers as Voltaire and
François-Noël Babeuf together and accuses them of subscribing to an "egalitarian anarchy."[184] I argue that both of these perspectives—accusing Enlightenment thinkers of not rising to a given egalitarian standard and holding
them accountable for the violence that would become associated with
egalitarianism—are misguided. Rather, it is important to appreciate that the
invention of modern equality in the Enlightenment was a "world-historical
turning point": "Henceforth equality enjoyed the benefit of the doubt, while
inequality stood in need of rational justification. That is, inequality had to
be justified in the language of Enlightenment human science."[185]

That equality gained greater traction among a diverse set of Enlightenment thinkers is thus uncontroversial, but explaining *why* this is the case and
what consequences it would have are less straightforward matters. Jonathan
Israel essentially views political equality as a logical consequence of the philosophy of the radical Enlightenment—egalitarianism simply follows from
philosophical monism, if one reasons correctly.[186] Contrary to Israel, Richard Rorty completely divorces commitment to equality from Enlightenment
rationalism. He famously asserted that there were in fact two Enlightenment
projects: one political and one philosophical, with the primary aim of the
former being to create "a world without caste, class, or cruelty" and the
only one worthy of our continued commitment.[187] In Rorty's view, there
simply is no connection between commitment to equality and the Enlightenment's rationalist philosophical program: "The association between Enlightenment egalitarianism and Enlightenment rationalism is as accidental
as the association between Jesus, the preacher of brotherly love, and Christ,

the divinity who will, at the Last Judgment, condemn sinners to eternal torture."[188]

Somewhere between these two extremes lies the most fruitful perspective for understanding the transformation of equality in the Enlightenment. Many commentators have pointed out that Israel's argument elides the lack of coherence of the values that he purports constituted the radical Enlightenment—Spinoza omitted women from political participation in his imagined republic, Paul-Henri Thiry, Baron d'Holbach was an atheist materialist but supported constitutional monarchy, and Rousseau was the era's most trenchant critic of inequality but certainly not a straightforward atheist-materialist thinker in Israel's mold. Meanwhile, Rorty's stark cleavage of Enlightenment egalitarianism from the movement's rationalism ignores the fact that early modern views of nature were inextricably linked to the way people understood the social and moral order. As Margaret Jacob explains, "It is not accidental that Spinoza was both a republican and a pantheist," but she also remarks that the connection between atheistic or pantheistic philosophical visions and republican political stances could disintegrate, as can been seen in the work of Julien Offray de La Mettrie and d'Holbach, among others.[189] It is hard to imagine human beings as equal in rights, indeed as having rights of any consequence at all, if one thinks of the species as corrupted by original sin. Indeed, the idea of the Fall was long used as a justification for temporal inequalities, and the rejection of original sin and rehabilitation of human nature are hallmarks of Enlightenment thought.[190]

If both Israel and Rorty fall short of the mark, how should we make sense of the transformation of equality in Enlightenment thought? It seems to me that both of their positions are to a certain extent correct and that they may not be diametrically opposed to one another. I argue that Israel misses the importance of the transfer of sacrality from the otherworldly to the human realm and the momentous consequences this had for thinking about morality in general and equality in particular.[191] Meanwhile, Rorty overlooks the importance of Enlightenment rationalist criticism of supposedly divinely sanctioned social hierarchies and entrenched prejudices. Both of these developments—the transfer of sacrality, with an attendant affective revolution, and the critique of orthodox religious defenses of hierarchy and obedience—contributed to the modern concept of society to describe the interdependence inherent in human relationships, which consequently opened the space for theorizing equality as a value of which there should be more.[192] Rather than ensuing from any single early modern philosophical or religious school of thought, a variety of intellectual and cultural developments coalesced during the Enlightenment to contribute to the destabilization of inequality as a natural given.

The philosophes posited the reality of the individual and thus adhered to a logic that conflicted with the contemporary reality of a hierarchy of bodies or corporations. Admittedly, the "individuals" around which Enlightenment thinkers constructed their theories almost always turned out to be property-owning, male heads of families, but their philosophies contained a logic that threatened traditional justifications of hierarchy and obedience. Louis Dumont argues that the philosophy of individualism is a distinctive feature of Western modernity. He asserts that prior to the Reformation and the Wars of Religion in Europe, the whole (social) or political body took precedence over the individual human element.[193] Keith Michael Baker follows Dumont's lead, arguing that the state took the place of the Church as the sovereign institution in Western Europe and modern natural law theory collapsed "*universitas* into *societas*, dissolving all corporate existence into an association of individuals. *Societas* was the sign under which the traditional logic of the organic whole was subverted by the modern logic of individualism."[194] Baker argues that while there is a necessary interdependence in human relations, it can be construed in many different ways, and the one that has dominated in the West since the eighteenth century—under the concepts of society and the social—is a result of the Enlightenment thinkers' response to a set of epistemological, ethical, religious, and political crises. Crucial for our discussion, accepting the ontological primacy of the individual leads to important political and philosophical consequences, namely, that accepting individual autonomy implies at least a basic acceptance of equality.[195]

In this book, I expand on the existing historiography by investigating the links between racial and egalitarian thought in the Enlightenment. To date, most historians have presented race as responses to, or justifications of, the creation and maintenance of inequality, whether inside or outside the system of slavery. I argue that this view is only partially correct. It explains the hardening of racial categories in the late eighteenth and nineteenth centuries but ignores important developments in racial and egalitarian thinking before the Age of Revolution. Ideas of natural equality and race depended on notions of human sameness and difference, respectively, and it is in the epistemology of the human that one can discover deeper links between these ideas in Enlightenment thought. With the emergence of the secular human sciences, of which interest in the sentiments was an integral part, the Enlightenment philosophes developed a new understanding of human nature and society. Natural equality and racial classification were part of the emerging, secular human sciences, and many eighteenth-century thinkers were unaware of either the political uses to which equality would soon be put or of the dehumanizing potential of a racialized worldview. This is part of the legacy of the Enlightenment with which we are still grappling, elements of which we find in one of the most important eighteenth-century English reference works, Ephraim Chambers's *Cyclopaedia*.

CHAPTER 2

Chambers's *Cyclopaedia* and *Supplement*: The Growth of the Natural History of Humanity

"The Whole intended as a Course of Antient and Modern Learning." I take this phrase to be a key part of the long title of Ephraim Chambers's masterpiece, which earned him a place in the Royal Society of London and burial in Westminster Abbey. His *Cyclopaedia: Or, an Universal Dictionary of Arts and Sciences* was published in two volumes in 1728 in London.[1] Within twenty years of publication, it went through five editions, an Italian translation was published, and a French translation was begun. Although it is a disputable claim, one historian maintains that Chambers's *Cyclopaedia* was "the father of the modern encyclopedia throughout the world."[2] What *is* indisputable is that Chambers himself conceived of his work as being part of, and contributing to, a distinctively ebullient "modern age." "A Course in Antient and Modern learning" is significant for two reasons. First, it indicates Chambers's goal of providing an educated person with a comprehensive overview of the contemporary state of knowledge, because it was a *course* of learning. Here, "course" may refer to onward movement on a particular path, the path being the circle that circumscribes a well-rounded education, which was the original meaning of the word "encyclopedia."[3] Second, it bespeaks the importance of the antiquity/modernity divide so prominent in the philosophy and science of the early Enlightenment.[4] Given the impact of Chambers's *Cyclopaedia* on subsequent eighteenth-century encyclopedias and on the European Republic of Letters more generally, it is worthwhile to query how Chambers engaged with questions of human sameness and difference. To appreciate the significance of Chambers's magnum opus, in this chapter I first investigate how, by whom, and for what purposes the *Cyclopaedia* might have been read. I then explore how Chambers presents cultural and ethnic differences, and how and in what ways he was committed to cross-cultural equality. Where relevant, comparisons to other encyclopedias and dictionaries of the era will be drawn.

Publishing and Reading the *Cyclopaedia*

Chambers's work was a great commercial success and had a significant impact on the European Republic of Letters. The *Cyclopaedia* was sold by subscription, a method of bookselling pioneered by seventeenth-century English publishers. The first edition of the *Cyclopaedia* had 375 subscribers, slightly more than the median number of 245 found by historians from a sampling of eighteenth-century subscription lists.[5] The first edition sold far more than 375 copies, however, and subsequent editions did not require a subscription list, as booksellers were certain of their sales. Chambers's work fed the growing demand among the educated public to have accessible and comprehensive overviews of the advances that had been made in natural philosophy in the seventeenth century. Considering the primacy of Newtonian science in Chambers's *Cyclopaedia*, his work certainly reflected and fed into this public appetite.[6]

Richard Yeo, the leading scholar on Ephraim Chambers and his *Cyclopaedia*, contrasts Chambers's work with earlier encyclopedias, particularly those of the Middle Ages, arguing that rather than being a confident summary of established knowledge, the *Cyclopaedia* responded to a crisis—specifically, to a "knowledge explosion."[7] This is only partially correct, because Chambers was indeed responding to what he and many of his contemporaries viewed as a crisis, but Yeo overlooks the role of the perception of "crisis" in earlier times. Jacqueline Hamesse has demonstrated that the emergence of late twelfth- and early thirteenth-century reference works was also a response to what scholars perceived as a "literary explosion," and Ann Blair has examined how sixteenth- and seventeenth-century scholars dealt with the phenomenon of there being "too much to know" following the invention of moveable type print.[8] What arguably made Chambers's work different was the incorporation of the most significant breakthroughs of the "new philosophy" of the seventeenth century. In this sense, Chambers's work fit into the dominant intellectual trends of his day, taking the side of the moderns in the "Battle of the Books" and both responding to and promoting the insatiable public appetite for the "new science."[9] Benjamin Franklin must have been exposed to the *Cyclopaedia* during his visit to London in the 1720s, because he included some of Chambers's entries in his *Pennsylvania Gazette* from 1729 onward.[10] This is unsurprising when we consider the social worlds within which Franklin and Chambers circulated: both were Freemasons.[11] And Laurence Sterne drew primarily from Chambers's *Cyclopaedia* for the medical knowledge that appears in *Tristram Shandy*.[12] In short, we see that Chambers's *Cyclopaedia* commanded significant authority among, and was widely read by, the educated classes in Europe and at least some of its colonies, responding as it did to the most significant intellectual and cultural transformations of the day.

Notwithstanding the personal motives, monetary or otherwise, that drove Chambers and his publishers to produce the *Cyclopaedia*, an egalitarian ethos can be discerned in the very makeup and goals of the encyclopedia. In his preface, Chambers explains the broad appeal he believes and hopes his book will have: "No body that fell in my way, has been spared; Antient nor Modern, Foreign nor Domestick, Christian, nor Jew, nor Heathen: Philosophers, Divines, Mathematicians, Critics, Casuists, Grammarians, Physicians, Antiquaries, Mechanics, all are served alike. The Book is not mine, 'tis every body's; the mix'd Issue of a thousand Loins."[13] The fact that Chambers states that his book will be of use to "mechanics" is significant, because the inclusion of the mechanical arts in general reference works signaled an important change in what was viewed as worthy of inclusion in a compendium of knowledge. While some historians disregard such passages as empty rhetoric typical of the Enlightenment, others stress that these sentiments reflect deeper structural changes in European society in the eighteenth century. For example, James Van Horn Melton's analysis of the rise of the public in the eighteenth century focuses on the growth of the vernacular in the widening literate classes. Of the six thousand books held in the Bodleian Library around 1600, only thirty-six were in English, with the vast majority in Latin.[14] By 1700, a Latin encyclopedia was almost unthinkable as a publishing venture in much of Europe.[15] Chambers's *Cyclopaedia* also fits into the trend of the decline of religious works and the growth of other literary genres during the eighteenth century. The *Cyclopaedia* cost four guineas, the equivalent of the monthly income of a modest middle-class family.[16] In theory, then, the *Cyclopaedia*'s readership was probably restricted to the upper echelons of society. Yet books began to be read in different ways in the eighteenth century by a broader cross section of society in a variety of new venues, from public libraries to coffeehouses, so his book may have reached beyond the wealthiest few.

Chambers and other editors and publishers of reference works in the eighteenth century generally imagined two types of readers: the educated reader, who would use the *Cyclopaedia* as a commonplace book to prompt their memory and to explore fields of knowledge outside their own expertise, and the "less scholarly" reader, who would use the *Cyclopaedia* as a single point of reference, accepting the authority of the author.[17] Regarding the former type of reader, Yeo writes, "We know this notion was in vogue because authors of reading guides for undergraduates at Cambridge in the early 1700s cited the dictionaries of [John] Harris and Chambers."[18] The nature of Chambers's work also reflects the growth of the public both as an increasingly large and cosmopolitan Republic of Letters and as arbiter in addition to reader.[19] Chambers was co-editor of the short-lived periodical *The Literary Magazine: Or, the History of the Works of the Learned* in 1735 and 1736. In the preface to the first volume of this periodical, Chambers writes, "We conceive it the duty of a *Journalist* to give a faithful account of the books which come into his hands. . . . When he affects the air and language of a censor or judge, he invades the undoubted right of the *Public*, which is the only foreign judge of the reputation of an author, and the merit of his compositions."[20] Indeed, the invention of public opinion was the authority to which eighteenth-century intellectuals most often appealed.[21] Yet this public was clearly a *European* public interested in the new science developed by the illustrious thinkers in its own intellectual tradition. Chambers's *Cyclopaedia* thus offers a fascinating opportunity for the researcher to explore how human cultural and ethnic diversity were treated in the early Enlightenment.

Cultural and Human Diversity in the *Cyclopaedia*

As mentioned in the introduction, the opening paragraph of Chambers's dedication to the king reveals the centrality of notions of European cultural and societal advancement in the early Enlightenment, as he asserts that knowledge of the arts and sciences is what separates Europeans from the indigenous peoples of America and Africa.[22] The explicit juxtaposition of "his Majesty's Subjects" to the "Savages of Canada, or the Cape of Good

Hope" reveals a notion that had become common currency by the early eighteenth century: that societies pass from barbarism or savagery to civilization incrementally over time, and it was Europeans who proudly stood at the summit of that societal advancement. The dedication appears immediately after the title page in the *Cyclopaedia*, demonstrating the prominence of this idea for Chambers, since self-evident or generally accepted notions are usually presented in dedications and prefaces. As we saw in Chapter 1, this idea was already expressed in inchoate form in the sixteenth century by José de Acosta and Michel de Montaigne, among others, and can be found in the work of all of the major seventeenth-century political philosophers, from Hugo Grotius and Thomas Hobbes to Samuel Pufendorf and John Locke. Specifically relating to the arts and sciences in the era of the new science, Thomas Sprat wrote of the importance of spreading the "mechanic genius" to the rest of the world, particularly those parts of it that "continue in the rude state of nature."[23]

The juxtaposition of the "rude state of nature" and the civil state was central to how seventeenth- and eighteenth-century Europeans made sense of their place in the world. Roxann Wheeler has demonstrated that among eighteenth-century Britons, particularly in the first half of the eighteenth century, "older conceptions of Christianity, civility, and rank were *more explicitly* important to Britons' assessment of themselves and other people than physical attributes such as skin color, shape of the nose, or texture of the hair."[24] Indeed, in many European pictorial representations of the continents, the half-naked female figures representing America and Africa are often paired, juxtaposed to the pairing of fully clothed Europe and Asia. In these allegorical images, cultural trappings such as elaborate clothing, cultivated fields, and large buildings with ornate architecture figure more prominently than physical features such as skin color or physiognomy.[25]

Further evidence of the unfavorable moral judgment of the "savage" state in the *Cyclopaedia* can be found in the articles "Savages" and "Barbarian." Savages are described as nomadic peoples who live without religion, law, or policy, and the article states that a great part of America is populated with savages, many of whom are also cannibals.[26] Chambers relates that "Barbarian" first simply referred to "foreigner" in ancient Greece and Rome but says that it now carries a certain "odium."[27] These descriptions served as a justification of European colonialism, and codes of courtesy and civility were intended to keep intact the subtle behaviors that lay at the basis of the complicated structures of social hierarchy.[28] As we saw Margaret Hodgen and

Ronald Meek have demonstrated, the ignoble savage trope is far more common than the noble savage variety in the Western tradition, particularly from the Renaissance onward, and Chambers is no exception.[29] In this period, bringing "the Arts and Sciences" to the "less civilized" was used as an argument to defend slavery, even by those who otherwise defended the basic rights of slaves against oppressive masters. For example, in a parliamentary proposal drafted in the late 1680s or early 1690s by one of Robert Boyle's amanuenses, Robert Bacon, the basic civil rights of enslaved people, particularly Christians, are proclaimed but the institution of slavery is defended: "It [proselytization] being a means to better these people, and likewise have influence on these they sell as Slaves to the English to persuade them, that by their Slavery, their Condition wilbe better'd by their accesse to knowledge, Arts and Sciences."[30] The denigration of non-European others, particularly those deemed "uncivilized," also fit Chambers's regime of temporality, in which the arts and sciences had progressed within Europe, leading to what he perceived as the auspiciousness of his contemporary moment. As we saw in the introduction, Chambers argued that eighteenth-century Europe surpassed the achievements of ancient Rome.

While the regime of temporality that emphasizes the achievements of seventeenth- and eighteenth-century Europeans is a prominent discourse of inequality in Chambers's *Cyclopaedia*, there are also powerful notions of common humanity and equality that permeate the work. As we will see, Chambers's treatment of religion and toleration is quite remarkable, placing him alongside many leading figures of the early Enlightenment who transformed toleration into a positive value and sought secular explanations of social changes.[31] Equality of rights is an important part of his defense of religious toleration. Regarding non-Europeans, the coverage is rather scanty: Chambers presents very little anatomical or natural historical information concerning human varieties. He was critical of slavery, and assertions of a universal human nature are scattered throughout the work.

One of the few articles that specifically mentions skin color in the *Cyclopaedia* is the article "Negro's." This article begins, "A Kind of Slaves, which make a considerable Article in the modern Commerce."[32] It is significant that the first quality that is mentioned is the social and legal status of the "Negro," that is, enslavement. Beginning in the late seventeenth century in the British colonies, "Negro" and "slave" were starting to become synonymous.[33] Chambers mentions skin color only once, when he says, "The Origin of *Negro's*, and the Cause of that remarkable Difference in Complexion from the rest of Mankind, has much perplex'd the Naturalists; nor has anything satisfactory been yet offr'd on that head." This statement demonstrates Chambers's monogenism, as he clearly positions Blacks under the ambit of "Mankind," although whiteness serves as the norm from which blackness deviates. Chambers is critical of the slave trade: "This Commerce, which is scarce defensible on the foot either of Religion, or Humanity, is now carried on by all the Nations that have Settlements in the *West-Indies*."[34] Although one cannot call Chambers an abolitionist, these comments are remarkable in that very few European voices spoke out against slavery in the period of New World slavery up to 1750, and those who did were normally radical Quakers.[35] The rest of the article is morally ambiguous, as Chambers focuses on the geographical origins of enslaved people and the prices at which they are purchased in Africa and the American colonies. He remarks that they are enslaved in Africa in one of four ways: some sell themselves to avoid famine, others are prisoners of war, others are captured by "petty princes" to be sold as slaves, and some sell even their own family members into slavery "for a few bottles of brandy, or a bar of iron."[36]

Aside from its usage in the entry "Negro's," the word "Negro" appears seventeen times throughout the two volumes. Of these, ten instances occur in the context of commerce and trade and seven in the context of anatomy. Chambers fits quite well into the manner in which the slave trade was generally discussed in the early to mid-eighteenth century, because "the language of commerce still predominated over the languages of humanity and justice."[37] Chambers's misgivings about slavery in the article "Negro's" excepted, none of the other articles raises any of the moral quandaries surrounding the issue. Thus, it is clear that commercial and anatomical questions dominated the discussion of Africans in the *Cyclopaedia*, reflecting the importance of Africans as commodities or chattel in the British empire at this time. The British forcibly transported a steadily increasing number of enslaved Africans to the Americas from the 1650s until reaching its apex in the 1760s, except for a brief dip in the 1740s (see Table 1). By way of example, Great Britain brought around 71,000 enslaved Africans to the Americas in the 1670s compared with more than triple that number—226,000—in the 1720s.[38] Thus one might qualify Roxanne Wheeler's argument that considerations of Christianity and civility were the most important markers of difference between Europeans and non-Europeans in the eighteenth century. In the case of Africans, as James Walvin has argued, the English increasingly viewed African peoples as commodities in the course of the seventeenth century.[39]

Table 1. Number of Enslaved People Transported from
Africa to the British Colonies Between 1651 and 1780,
Excluding Those Taken to the Thirteen Colonies.

Years	Number of transported enslaved people
1651–1660	26,720
1661–1670	67,469
1671–1680	71,689
1681–1690	112,193
1691–1700	116,495
1701–1710	151,877
1711–1720	167,409
1721–1730	226,192
1731–1740	243,929
1741–1750	175,232
1751–1760	255,346
1761–1770	360,785
1771–1780	301,323

Source: "Estimates," Voyages: The Trans-Atlantic Slave Trade
Database, accessed January 14, 2020, http://www.slavevoyages
.org/assessment/estimates.

The economic realities of slavery began to be expressed in English law from
the late seventeenth century onward; for example, in 1677, the solicitor general declared "that negroes ought to be esteemed goods and commodities
within the Acts of Trade and Navigation."[40] Chambers's comments reflect
the harsh reality of the growing dependence of British global economic
power on the labor of enslaved Africans.

While black skin is only mentioned in passing in the entry "Negro's,"
Chambers wrote more detailed accounts of the anatomical differences between Europeans and Africans in some entries on the anatomy of human
skin, reflecting the growing prominence of skin as an object of investigation
and experimentation that began in the late sixteenth century, with a particular focus on pigmentation.[41] In the article "Cutis," Chambers writes that this is
a body of vessels immediately under the cuticle that contains a liquor responsible for the pigmentation of the skin.[42] Even the very mention of skin color
is remarkable in this relatively short article, since the same article in John
Harris's *Lexicon technicum*, a popular dictionary upon which Chambers
relied extensively, does not mention pigmentation.[43] Chambers references
Marcello Malpighi (1628–1694), the famous Italian anatomist who in his *De*

externo tactus organo (1665) was the first to suggest that pigmentation resides in a separate layer within the skin (now known as the Malpighian
layer).[44] In the article "Reticular," Chambers explicitly compares black skin
to white skin: "These Vessels contain a mucous Liquor, from the Tincture
whereof Malpighi imagines the Color of the Skin to be derived; founding
his Conjecture on this, that the Cutis as well as Cuticle of Blacks, is white;
*and that they differ in no other Circumstance than those of Europeans, but
in this particular.* See NEGRO."[45] Chambers thus sees blackness as literally being only skin deep, albeit a "peculiarity" that deviates from the
implicit white standard. This is significant because the drive to associate
skin color with an inner, innate character intensified with the growth of
transatlantic slavery.[46]

While the increased interest in pigmentation was undoubtedly connected to the expansion of European colonialism and race-based slavery,
whether conscious or not in the minds of anatomists and other researchers,
the case of Chambers demonstrates that anatomical investigations of pigmentation did not necessarily lead to a racist position. Given that Chambers
held antislavery views and defended the unity of the human species, the
connection between scientific interest in human varieties and slavery only
goes so far. Craig Koslofsky emphasizes the importance of looking at
"broader cultural forces" rather than the conscious intentions of historical
actors.[47] While these wider cultural trends are undoubtedly important, they
do not fully explain the intellectual shift that occurred to make a racialized
worldview possible. Chambers's work stands at a crucial moment in which
thinking about human and natural varieties was transitioning from sacred
history to natural history.[48] Chambers clearly believed that naturalists
could contribute to the understanding of why some peoples have dark skin
and, presumably, why others have light skin.

The very idea that naturalists could contribute to this debate points to a
significant intellectual shift—namely, the idea that human beings were also
a part of nature as it was newly conceived in the seventeenth century. Chambers's encyclopedia is interesting because it registers the subtle shifts taking
place in conceptualizing human sameness and difference at this time; older
notions of European civilizational superiority were complemented by the
emergent anatomical and natural historical interest in human physical diversity. Contrary to what some historians hold, however, the shift from a
civilizational/barbarian discourse to an anatomical one was not necessarily

accompanied by the dehumanization of non-European others. This partially explains why Chambers could express misgivings about slavery while at the same time being interested in anatomical and natural historical questions of human diversity.

In addition to using the word "Negro," Chambers also uses the common "black-more" to refer to African peoples. While there is no entry with the headword "black-more," Chambers's entry "Trope" gives the example "to *wash the Black-more white, for a fruitless Undertaking.*"[49] "Wash the blackmore white" was a stock expression among Elizabethan dramatists.[50] In his study *Tropicopolitans*, Srinivas Aravamudan has used Chambers's entry for stimulating reflections on the issue of colonialism and agency in English literature from the long eighteenth century.[51] While Aravamudan positions himself within the legacy of the Enlightenment in a Foucauldian vein,[52] his book sometimes overreaches what his sources are able to provide, such as when he uses Chambers's quote to claim that Black people came to represent "unchangeable uselessness," a perspective that is belied by a more extensive analysis of the rest of Chambers's work.[53]

In his analysis of science and superstition in eighteenth-century encyclopedias, Philip Shorr concludes that Chambers's *Cyclopaedia* lies "in the middle" on many points between ancient and medieval superstition and modern science.[54] Without wishing to fall into the Whiggish story that Shorr tells of the advancement of science, it becomes clear that there are not only distinctive elements from the new science with which Chambers was intimately familiar but also lingering elements of much older theories, such as humoralism. Roxann Wheeler remarks that the persistence of humoral theory into the eighteenth century "reveals the ways in which old modes of thinking were not abandoned in the face of the new science associated with the Enlightenment but coexisted with it and were partially reworked."[55] Craig Koslofsky also notes that in a slow process across the early modern period, "the colors of the humoral body (red, white, yellow/brown, and black) very slowly transformed into polarized skin colors: white for European Christians, dark for others."[56] Chambers's *Cyclopaedia* captures this transition from humoral to anatomical theory. In the article "Complexion," Chambers matter-of-factly outlines the "four general and principal complexions in man," these being the sanguine, phlegmatic, bilious, and melancholic, although he does add the proviso "according to some philosophers."[57] This article is cross-referenced to the entry on each individual humor, in which Chambers uncritically presents the classical definition of the humor.

Chambers was nonetheless skeptical about the authority of humoralism, as evidenced by the article "Humour," in which he writes of "the *four Humours* so much talk'd of by the ancient Physicians," adding "but the Moderns do not allow of these Divisions."[58] On the "modern" side of the scientific enterprise of the period is Chambers's inclusion of the anatomical investigation of skin color, which we have seen in the articles "Cutis" and "Reticular." Furthermore, one may add Chambers's comments on contemporary research into the role of skin in touch and sensation. Early modern Europeans inherited from Aristotle the view that touch was located below the skin, as a property of the flesh.[59] This view slowly changed across the seventeenth and eighteenth centuries, and the investigations of touch in the developing field of microscopic anatomy are registered in the *Cyclopaedia*.[60] Chambers cites Nicolas Steno (1638–1686) in claiming that the cutis is "the Organ of Feeling" as a result of the innumerable nervous fibers that form what is called a "parenchyma."[61]

Chambers's articles on reproduction and inheritance summarize the most widely held and respected theory of the day: the animalculist version of preformation.[62] In the article "Generation," he cites the most important advancements made in research on generation in the new science, including that of Harvey, Malpighi, Regnier de Graaf, and Leeuwenhoek, as well as the most succinct summary of all this new information, George Garden's 1691 essay, "A Discourse Concerning the Modern Theory of Generation."[63] The animalculist theory held that the preformed germ was the spermatozoon, a position backed by the new microscopic evidence. As Joyce Chaplin has demonstrated, the final intellectual work that needed to be done for the modern theory of race to develop was a convincing explanation of the mechanism of inheritance, and this was slowly put in place from the mid-seventeenth century onward.[64] The anatomical/natural historical understanding of human varieties and theories of inheritance were synthesized in a slow process across the eighteenth century, and it would not be until the late eighteenth century that the idea of racial difference being "fixed in nature" would gain broader acceptance. Chambers's *Cyclopaedia* demonstrates not only the confidence in theories of generation developed by the new science but also the lack of a synthesis within research on human varieties. The anatomical articles demonstrate that to Chambers and most anatomists and naturalists of the period, racial difference was literally only skin deep. These differences were overshadowed by the preoccupation with "civilizational" and religious diversity.

Ideas of Toleration and Equality

Equality as a political concept forms a significant subtext in the *Cyclopaedia*. Chambers's political ideas were broadly shared by the subset of thinkers associated with the early Enlightenment, showing that Chambers's *Cyclopaedia* was both reflective of, and contributed to, wider social, political, and philosophical trends. While there is a large body of literature on toleration in early modern Europe, few historians have analyzed how the advent of theories of toleration was linked to questions of equality as a political concept. A significant exception here is Martha Nussbaum, who, in *Liberty of Conscience: In Defense of America's Tradition of Religious Equality*, argues for the central role that equality played in establishing religious toleration in the seventeenth- and eighteenth-century English colonies, particularly during the American Revolution. She focuses on Roger Williams's *The Bloudy Tenent of Persecution* (1644) to argue that the Stoic conception of equality, predicated on the notion of the inherent dignity of every human being, was the most prominent philosophical current behind Protestant defenses of toleration in the early modern period.[65]

Regarding eighteenth-century political developments, Nussbaum follows Gordon Wood's lead in arguing that equality was the most powerful ideological force in the American Revolution.[66] She convincingly connects the Founding Fathers' rejection of a state church to their concern for, and commitment to, basic equality. Nussbaum shows that some seventeenth- and eighteenth-century thinkers inherited from the Stoics the idea that "everyone has inside something infinitely precious, something that demands respect from us all, and something in regard to which we are all basically equal."[67] For the ancient Stoics, this was the capacity for moral striving or choice because all human beings partake in the cosmic logos of the universe. Although the implications of this theology with regard to equality are ambivalent, Stoicism could be and certainly was used to defend various forms of political or social equality since antiquity.[68] Chambers demonstrates such concern for equality in his defense of religious toleration. The impact of Stoic/Ciceronian ideas more generally on Chambers is demonstrated by the fact that "Cicero" appears 256 times in Chambers's *Cyclopaedia* and *Supplement*. That this is a high frequency can be demonstrated by the fact that "Newton" appears 293 times, and promotion of Newtonian science was one of the central aims of the entire work. I will demonstrate that Chambers's defense of religious toleration is underpinned by an argument for the basic equality of autonomous individuals.

In his impressive study of toleration in early modern Europe, Benjamin Kaplan demonstrates that toleration was practiced in various ways throughout Europe long before Pierre Bayle, Locke, and Voltaire defended it philosophically. Regarding equality, many cities throughout Europe practiced "parity" before and after the Peace of Westphalia, which meant that cities had either a de facto or official arrangement in which equal numbers of Protestants and Catholics sat on important governing bodies.[69] But these kinds of practical tolerationist arrangements differ markedly from a defense and theorization of toleration. Some Enlightenment thinkers would transform how we view and understand toleration, as Kaplan remarks: "The practice of toleration did not await the Enlightenment. What the latter did was change the attitude of powerful groups, who adopted in the eighteenth century a new creed, a belief in the positive value of toleration."[70] From the new and flourishing coffeehouses, to the theater, libraries, and Masonic lodges, Europeans developed and had available to them an unprecedented number of centers around which social life would turn. Margaret Jacob has also demonstrated that the new science of the seventeenth century encouraged new forms of sociability, furthering the development of a nascent cosmopolitanism in parts of Western Europe.[71]

Although we lack a thorough biography of Ephraim Chambers, from knowledge of his social network we can establish that he was firmly embedded in a group of literate, urban men and women who were active both in the emergent civil society and in promoting the new science. Margaret Jacob even describes the *Cyclopaedia* as a "Masonic project," because Chambers belonged to the Richmond Lodge and was its master for a time.[72] Chambers apprenticed for the globemaker, engraver, and bookseller John Senex, who was among the leadership of the early Grand Lodge, along with John Theophilus Desaguliers, the Reverend James Anderson, and Francis Sorrell. Senex's shop was just two or three doors down from the Marine Coffee House, where John Harris and James Hodgson gave free public lectures on mathematics and Newtonian mechanics.[73] E. G. R. Taylor highlights the importance of the social network in which Chambers found himself, particularly the role of John Senex, who was a subscriber to Harris's *Lexicon*, and Chambers must have been exposed to that work while apprenticing at his shop.[74] Thus, we see that Chambers was part of the urban, literate, and mobile social class that propagated the ideals of the early Enlightenment. This makes the question of how Chambers treats religious matters and toleration in his encyclopedia particularly interesting and, as we shall see, presents revealing contrasts with other encyclopedias of the period.

Let us begin with the entry "Religion" itself. Chambers defines religion as "that Worship or Homage due to God, considered as Creator, Preserver, Redeemer, etc. See 'God,' 'Theology,' etc."[75] He then divides religion into "natural" and "revealed." Regarding natural religion, Chambers states that this is what is arrived at using natural reason, whereas revealed religion results from God's actions through, for example, prophets. He privileges natural religion above revealed religion, stating: "The first [natural religion] we ordinarily call Morality, or Ethicks; because immediately conversant about the Manners and Duties of Men towards one another; and towards themselves, considered as Creatures of that Being, see 'Morality,' 'Ethics,' etc." Although the Christianized Aristotelian tradition took natural religion and reason as the foundation of the political and moral order, the controversies surrounding deism, freethinking, and the new science in the wake of the English Revolution politicized the issue of the relationship between morality and religion.[76]

The linking of morality and ethics to natural religion as opposed to revealed religion was far from a neutral stance at the time and suggests that Chambers believed that any human being, using their natural reason, could lead a morally upright life. Revealed religion, Chambers writes, "supposes an immediate Mission from God himself," and the article is cross-referenced to the entry "Miracle," in which Chambers is very skeptical that such a thing is possible. Chambers uses the entry "Religion" as an opportunity to celebrate the diversity of the human religious experience, as he writes, "The Siamese hold the Diversity of Religious, i. e. the different Manners of honouring God, to be pleasing to him; inasmuch as they have all the same Object, all tend to the same End, though by different Means. *Claude.* The Sentiment of these Idolaters is doubtless more just than that of our Zealots, who hold all but those of their own Religion odious to God."[77]

Chambers's use of the example of a non-Christian people to criticize European practices of intolerance is clearly a relativistic stance. The "Claude" whom Chambers cites is undoubtedly Jean Claude, the French Protestant scholar who was forced to flee to The Hague in 1685 following the revocation of the Edict of Nantes. Claude argued that the Catholic position on transubstantiation had changed over time and thus held that this doctrine was not necessary for true

Christian faith. His argument was a source of inspiration to the authors of one of the most radical works on religion during the Enlightenment, Bernard Picart and Jean-Frédéric Bernard's *Cérémonies et coutumes religieuses de tous les peuples du monde (Religious Ceremonies and Customs of all the Peoples of the World).*[78] Chambers's article is also clearly indebted to the Cambridge Platonists, who developed the idea of religion as a category of thought and as a set of social practices that can be studied "from the outside" and, in their work, natural religion was favorably juxtaposed to revealed religion.[79]

The controversial status of Chambers's definition of religion, particularly the subtext of toleration, is made clear by contrasting it with what appears in another popular encyclopedia of the period, Louis Moréri's *Le Grand dictionnaire historique*, first published posthumously in 1683 in Lyon. Moréri's encyclopedia had gone through seventeen editions by 1725. Various individuals of differing religious persuasions edited the editions, so the religious opinions "changed with each new set of editorial hands," going from a defense of Catholicism to Protestantism and back again.[80] Following the revocation of the Edict of Nantes, in 1685, toleration could not be openly defended in these French encyclopedias. Unsurprisingly, the article "Religion" in each successive edition was particularly prone to revision. In the twentieth edition (1759), for example, religion is defined as "the service one renders to God in a legitimate manner." The author continues, "Although this word only properly applies to the legitimate worship of the true God, one nonetheless applies it to worship of idols and false gods, and to illegitimate and false worship of the true God, like to Mahommetism and to diverse heresies."[81] "Heresies" refers to all non-Catholic Christian denominations, in that he unequivocally states that Catholicism is the true religion. The contrast with Chambers's position could hardly be starker. Indeed, Lawrence Sullivan argues that of the nine most notable seventeenth- and eighteenth-century predecessors to Diderot's *Encyclopédie*, all supported religious orthodoxy except for Pierre Bayle's *Historical and Critical Dictionary* and Chambers's *Cyclopaedia*.[82] Thus, we can see that the religious views Chambers expounded in the *Cyclopaedia* were unique compared with other contemporary encyclopedias and that he took a stance that must be positioned within the early Enlightenment.

Other articles reveal that Chambers's views both reflected and promoted an open-mindedness in religious matters typical of early Enlightenment thinkers. While these views were more widely shared by urban and literate classes in early eighteenth-century English society, particularly in London, their novelty and controversial status should not be underestimated. As

Mark Goldie remarks, "It is mistaken to suppose that the practice of intolerance betokened mere unthinking bigotry. On the contrary, a fully developed ideology of intolerance was articulated in countless treatises and sermons and was upheld by Protestants and Catholics alike."[83] Of additional significance is the fact that Chambers's *Cyclopaedia* gives considerably more attention to the natural and applied sciences yet subtly advances a freethinker's political and religious views. Even though his main purpose was not to advance a wholesale criticism of the political and social status quo, contentious religious questions were nevertheless tackled. This serves to remind us that Chambers was writing at a time when religion was developing as a separate category of thought.

It is likely that Chambers was a deist, as the article "Deists" unambiguously declares the reasonableness of this position. Chambers writes, "The Deists hold, that, considering the Multiplicity of Religions, the numerous Pretences to Revelation, and the obscure, precarious Arguments advanced in Proof thereof; the best and surest Way is, to return to the Simplicity of Nature, and the Belief of one God, which is the only Truth agreed to by all Nations."[84] He also claims that the number of deists in England is steadily rising, particularly among "Men of Speculation and Letters," suggesting that he is among their number. Chambers defines "Liberty of Conscience" as "a Right or Power of making Possession of any Religion that a Man sees fit. This seems to be a natural Right; it is vigorously opposed by the generality of the Romanists, and even by many of the Reformed, tho' it seems as if the Reformation could scarce subsist without it."[85] Describing freedom of conscience as a natural right demonstrates Chambers's concern for the equal respect and dignity of all human beings. His article "Toleration" even connects support for toleration to correct reasoning, as he writes, "All who have reason'd consistently from the Principles of the Reformation, have been for Toleration."[86] In his coverage of Judaism and Islam, Chambers is generally respectful, mainly focusing on the histories of these religions, the basic tenets of their beliefs, and what they hold in common with Christian believers.[87] It should be noted, however, that he refers to the Quran as a "detestable work," so there were limits to his toleration. Chambers is critical of "enthusiasm" in religious matters, arguing that unrestrained religious fervor is simply "the ungrounded Fancies of a Man's own brain."[88] In short, Chambers propagated the central tenets of early Enlightenment views of religion—the virtues of a rational, natural religion, the importance of freedom of conscience, and the promotion of toleration as a positive value.

What is often overlooked in histories of the advent of toleration is that a notion of equality of rights underpinned Enlightenment theories of toleration. Indeed, the culmination of Locke's *Letter Concerning Toleration* is essentially a call for the equality of the rights of all citizens. He writes, "The *Sum of all we drive at is, That every Man may enjoy the same Rights that are granted to others.*"[89] Locke's radical claim that "there is absolutely no such thing, under the Gospel, as a Christian Commonwealth," among other social and cultural factors, set in motion a change in worldview in which the sacral community and the civil community came to be seen as separate entities.[90] Establishing and promoting the equality of the rights of all individuals in the latter constitutes one of the primary goals of Locke's political thought.[91] While not explicitly invoking Locke in the entries on religion and toleration, equality of rights underpins Chambers's defense of toleration as well, which is unsurprising given the overwhelming influence of Lockean philosophy on Chambers's thought.[92] There are further references to a shared humanity in Chambers's *Cyclopaedia*; for example, regarding human nature, where he states, "meaning all Men together that possess the same Spiritual, Reasonable Soul."[93]

Furthermore, Chambers explicitly connects natural rights to equality in his argument against primogeniture: "The *Right of Primogeniture* seems to be an unjust Prerogative, and contrary to natural Right: For since 'tis Birth alone gives Children a Title to the paternal Succession, the Chance of *Primogeniture* should not throw an Inequality among them."[94] This criticism of primogeniture fits with a wider trend Randolph Trumbach observes in eighteenth-century England, what he calls "the rise of the egalitarian family."[95] Trumbach argues that not only did relations among men of aristocratic families become more egalitarian, but so did those between men and women, particularly husbands and wives. While he makes a convincing case, this trend is not wholly reflected in Chambers's *Cyclopaedia*. In the article "Wife," for example, Chambers states, "In the Judgment of the Law [a wife] is reputed to have no Will, as being supposed entirely under, and subject to that of her Husband," and he goes on to uncritically present the strict English laws that bind wives to their husbands.[96] While he remarks that many foreigners consider English laws to be harsh on women, he concludes by citing Tertullian to argue that women should not aim to please by their beauty because it can lead to loose morals. In the article "Woman," the issue of the equality of the sexes is central, as he states, "'Tis a point much controverted, how far, Learning and Study become the Sex."[97] He notes that Erasmus and Juan Luis Vives have contributed answers to the problem but that

Anna Maria van Schurman "has gone beyond 'em both." He asserts that many women who are renowned for their learning have also distinguished themselves for their "want in conduct," mainly because of their early preoccupation with books filled with "gallantry and intrigue." He writes that the close study of metaphysics, mathematics, logic, physics, and criticism would establish "the virtue of continency" in women. This article is rather ambiguous, since the criticism of the moral conduct of learned women is certainly not a pro-woman position, yet his advocacy of a typically male educational program for women is remarkable.

In the more expressly political entries of the *Cyclopaedia*, Chambers's political views are difficult to discern. Most of the articles are factual and he is more reticent than in the articles on toleration. For example, in the article "Democracy," he explains that it is "a Form of Government, wherein the Soveraignty, or supreme Authority, is lodged in the People, who exercise the same by Persons of their own Order, deputed for that Purpose."[98] He states that ancient Athens and Rome had flourishing democracies and that the modern states of Venice and the Dutch Republic are actually aristocracies rather than democracies. He refrains from making evaluative statements. In the entry "Monarchy," Chambers explains that "some are Absolute and Despotic, where the Will of the Monarch is uncontrollable; as *France*, etc.; others limited, where the Prince's Authority is restrained by Laws, and part of the supreme Power lodged in other hands; as in *England*."[99] This indeed seems to be a slight to France's absolute monarchy, yet Chambers goes on to cite Hobbes's *De Cive* and matter-of-factly states that since the people transfer their natural rights to the monarch, he can do no injury against his subjects. While Locke's epistemology would seem to lend itself to an egalitarian position, given that environment and experience determine a person's character and knowledge, Caroline Robbins has shown that even for eighteenth-century Commonwealthmen, that was not necessarily the case. While many of these thinkers emphasized the importance of education and the possibility, or even the justice, of upward social mobility, they took a stratified social sphere and the uneducated masses largely for granted.[100] Chambers does report rather favorably on the newly founded charity schools, which offered an education to poor children, though we should not assume that such an education was intended to offer these children equal opportunity, because many of these schools had as their mission the creation of "useful servants," respectful of authority.[101] Lael Ely Bradshaw argues that Chambers favored the limited monarchy of England, and indeed there is weak evidence to support this.[102]

Chambers offers a fairly evenhanded assessment of the Tories and Whigs in the article "Tories."[103] He seems to think little of these party politics, stating in the article "Faction" that this is a "Cabal, or Party, form'd in a State to disturb the publick Repose" and that the Whigs and Tories in England are among the most celebrated factions in the world.[104] In "Tories," he stresses the reasonableness of the moderate position of each side and toward the end of the article, one can detect slight Whig leanings, as he writes that the leaders of the Whigs "conduct themselves on fix'd Principles, proceed to their End gradually, and without Violence" and that "they maintain a good Cause, *viz.* the Constitution of the Government as by Law establish'd." Chambers's support for limited monarchy is unsurprising given his philosophical and scientific outlook. Margaret Jacob has shown how Newtonian science was wedded to a particular political and social ideology in late seventeenth- and early eighteenth-century England, when early modern Europeans assumed that a direct relationship existed between the natural world and the political or social world. She writes of the Newtonian viewpoint: "The social structure is sanctioned by God; it is singularly perverse to attempt its alteration."[105] It is in the thought of the more radically republican tradition from the English Civil Wars that an egalitarian political philosophy was wedded to a pantheistic and materialistic understanding of nature in the late seventeenth century.[106] Chambers supported Newton's theistic conception of the universe, and thus his political views aligned with his natural philosophy; in short, he was a thinker of the moderate Enlightenment.

Chambers was acutely aware of the theological controversies stirred up by the new science and of the rise of a materialist and atheistic strand in the new philosophy of the seventeenth and eighteenth centuries. In the preface, he explains that atheism arises from making a philosophical error, specifically from not distinguishing between causes and occasions.[107] His opposition to materialism is made clear in the article "Soul," where he writes, "All the Motions of Plants and Brutes plainly discover an Intelligence; but the Intelligence does not reside in the Matter thereof, as is that which ranged the Wheels of the Watch, is distinct from the Watch itself."[108] While Chambers was certainly not an atheist, he was strikingly respectful in his coverage of Epicureanism and Spinozism, commonly though sometimes incorrectly associated with atheism. His articles "Epicureans" and "Epicureanism" are essentially a rehabilitation of a controversial philosophy, in that Chambers states that Epicureans have been disparaged throughout the ages for being hedonists. He says that they actually promoted contentment or tranquility of mind rather than hedonism, and "this Opinion seems just, and well grounded."[109] In "Spinosism," Chambers impartially describes Spinoza's philosophy and offers a brief biography of the man. In terms of critical commentary, he simply states that "there have been abundance of Answers made to this Work of *Spinosa*; but all exceedingly weak, except what we have in *Clark*'s Sermons at *Boyle*'s Lecture."[110]

That Spinoza's philosophy was important in this period is demonstrated by the fact that it is one of the few philosophical entries updated in the subsequent editions of the *Cyclopaedia*. The original entry "Spinosism" is only approximately half a column (one-quarter of a folio page), whereas the same entry in the third edition (published in Dublin in 1740) is about five times as long, at one and a quarter pages in length.[111] Unlike the original, the updated entry uses the words "naturalism" and "pantheism" and expands upon the sources from which Spinoza drew his ideas. Additionally, the bibliography of works that responded to Spinoza's philosophy is updated. Chambers speculates as to what may have led Spinoza to formulate such a radical philosophy and admits that his philosophy has resolved certain difficulties, but he remains unconvinced by it: "But it is certain, if the new system rescues us from some difficulties, it involves us in others much greater." He goes on to outline the principal reasons why Spinoza's philosophy is flawed, maintaining that it insults God to equate Him with matter and that Spinoza's monist metaphysics is philosophically untenable because he takes it as obvious that the universe contains different substances.

In conclusion, while Chambers does not offer extensive explications of equality as a political concept, there is a discernible and significant egalitarian subtext, mainly in the form of religious toleration and a cosmopolitan ethos that undergirds some of the ethnographic information in the encyclopedia. Nonetheless, the juxtaposition of "civilized" Europeans to "savage" Americans and Africans is a fundamental distinction for Chambers, as the "arts and sciences" are viewed almost exclusively as a European achievement, with the possible exception of the Asian tradition, which receives very little attention. The enterprise remains almost entirely a Eurocentric one, a state of affairs that did not change in the *Supplement* to Chambers's work, which was published twenty-five years later.

The *Supplement*

In 1753, Thomas Longman and other London-based publishers brought out *A Supplement to Mr. Chambers's Cyclopædia: Or, Universal Dictionary of*

Arts and Sciences. This was primarily the work of the mathematician George Lewis Scott (1708–1780), who had been a pupil of Abraham de Moivre and became the subpreceptor to Prince George (later George III).[112] The *Supplement*, also published in two folio volumes, drew on the success of the original work, expanding and updating the entries in what we would call science and technology: "Anatomy, surgery, chemistry, mineralogy, agriculture, medicine, and other analogous subjects."[113] Most readers were unsatisfied with the *Supplement*, and Thomas Longman soon began to scout for contributors to an entirely new and expanded edition of the *Cyclopaedia*.[114] Despite its commercial failure and relatively low impact on learned society, the *Supplement* offers the intellectual historian the opportunity to analyze how ideas of race and equality evolved from the original to the *Supplement*, or, as far as these works can be taken as representative of broader opinion, from early to mid-eighteenth-century intellectual concerns.

The editors singled out natural history as a field that was especially improved upon in the *Supplement*. The anonymous author of the preface describes the importance of authors who worked in the years following the publication of the original encyclopedia, explaining, "By their help considerable additions have been made to the work, particularly with regard to natural history."[115] That was primarily due to John Hill's participation in the enterprise. Hill was an English botanist and journalist who contributed some eighty works to botany between 1746 and 1775.[116] The *Supplement* fit with the wider trend of the popularization of natural history in England around mid-century.[117] This popularization, along with other social and political developments, had significant consequences for the thinking about human differences that one finds in the *Supplement*.

Changes to the article "Negro" between the *Cyclopaedia* and *Supplement* provide striking evidence of the impact of these developments. While the original article "Negro's" in the 1728 edition mentions the "dark complexion" of Africans only in passing and discussed no further physical differences or potential causes of those differences, the entry in the *Supplement* is entirely devoted to a lengthy discussion of the causes of black skin. The entry begins: "Mr. Boyle [Robert Boyle] has observed, that the heat of climates cannot be the true cause of the colour of *negroes* For though the heat of the sun may darken the colour of the skin, yet experience does not show that heat is sufficient to produce a true blackness, like that of *negroes*."[118] The author relied on the work of two significant investigations into human varieties in the 1740s: *Dissertation sur la cause physique de la couleur des nègres*

(Dissertation on the physical cause of the color of negroes; 1741), by Pierre Barrère, and, most extensively, "An Essay upon the Causes of the Different Colours of People in Different Climates" (1744), by John Mitchell, the Virginia-born and Edinburgh-educated physician and anatomist. Both publications were in fact responses to a competition announced by the Académie royale des sciences de Bordeaux in 1739 in the *Journal des sçavans* for essays to answer the questions "What was the physical cause of blackness and African hair, and what was the cause of their degeneration?"[119] Mitchell communicated his paper to the Royal Society in London, and it was published in its *Philosophical Transactions*, thus reaching a wide audience.[120] The cases of Barrère and Mitchell demonstrate the increasing scientific interest in human varieties, blackness in particular, around mid-century, as two leading European scientific academies took up interest in the topic.

Mitchell's essay was unique in its combination of anatomical research with Newtonian optics to explain skin color, attributing the cause of dark skin to the opacity and smallness of the particles of African people's skin, which prevented the transmission of light. He performed experiments on black skin of enslaved peoples in the Americas, and though his work was later taken up by abolitionists, some historians argue that his essay served to subtly justify the colonial order.[121] The encyclopedist quotes Mitchell to specifically refute Chambers's explanation of the cause of darker skin, thus denying the existence of a black humor or liquid component of the skin. The entry concludes by remarking, "We cannot pretend to follow the author [John Mitchell] in all the detail of his observations on this subject" because he relies too much on climatic causes of variations in skin color and thus cannot account for the differences in skin color of various populations at similar latitudinal lines, which Robert Boyle had remarked upon. The author observes that Mitchell's ideas could be further reinforced by observing whether white peoples taken to Africa would become darker over time.

The transformation of the article "Negro" between these publications can be explained by both intellectual and political developments of the first half of the eighteenth century: the inclusion of humanity in the study of natural history, the growing importance of African slave labor to the Atlantic economy, and the subsequent desire to understand the "nature" of blackness. Regarding the intellectual developments, the place of humankind in nature received increasing attention in the early Enlightenment following the publication of Edward Tyson's anatomy of a chimpanzee in 1699 and, most important, in reaction to the inclusion of the human species in two of the most significant works of eighteenth-century natural history: Carl Linnaeus's *Systema Naturae* (first ed., 1735) and George-Louis Leclerc, Comte de Buffon's *Histoire naturelle, générale et particulière* (Paris, vols. 1–3, 1749), both published after the *Cyclopaedia* but before the *Supplement*. In the most important seventeenth-century natural histories, such as John Ray's *The Wisdom of God Manifested in the Works of the Creation*, humanity was not included in the order of apes, or in any of the natural orders, for that matter.[122] Linnaeus in particular achieved almost instant popularity, and the implications of that for understanding humankind's place in nature were significant, as Gunnar Broberg has remarked: "The fact that man is an animal was no secret in 1735, when Linnaeus published the first edition of *Systema Naturae*. The innovation lay in expressing this view without reservation, as a fact of natural history."[123] The novelty and importance of including humanity as a subject of natural history is confirmed by Chambers, when he explains that "the Philosophers comprehend Man under the Species of Animals; and define him, a reasonable Animal: though among Naturalists, etc. Animals are usually restrain'd to Irrationals."[124] The modern concept of race depends on conceiving of the human species as part of nature and thus susceptible to the same taxonomical systems as other living beings.[125]

The border between the human and simian species became an issue of pressing concern in the Enlightenment, as anatomical investigations of both humans and the higher apes became increasingly common.[126] Chambers's original encyclopedia did not contain any mention of chimpanzees or other higher apes, but the *Supplement* contains the entry "Chimpanzee." In this entry, the author explains that this is an animal "very much approaching the human figure, but of a fierce disposition, and remarkably mischievous."[127] The association of simian species with Africans, a European trope that long predates the eighteenth century,[128] is made clear when the author writes that these animals "often set upon, and ravish the negro women when they meet them in the woods." In addition to Tyson's 1699 publication on the anatomy of a higher primate, a chimpanzee brought to London in 1738–39, known as Madame Chimpanzee, caused a sensation as throngs of people went to observe the animal, which Sir Hans Sloane, president of the Royal Society, declared to be "the nearest to the Human Species of any Creature."[129] Silvia Sebastiani has found that the great apes were brought to Europe by the same trade routes as enslaved peoples, and Madame Chimpanzee in fact came to Europe via the New World on a slave ship.[130] Madame Chimpanzee and other episodes demonstrate increased scientific interest in the boundaries between the human and animal species in the eighteenth century, as reflected in the *Supplement*.[131]

Comparing the 1728 and 1753 "Natural History" entries demonstrates the expansion of natural history and the increasingly common trend of including human beings in the discipline at this time. Chambers's 1728 entry does not mention the natural history of humankind. He wrote that natural history is the study of the natural products of the earth, water or air, including "Beasts, Birds, Fishes, Metals, Minerals, and Fossils." Chambers divided the study of natural history into two main parts: that of particular things (such as the history of shells) or that of particular "Countreys or Provinces" (such as the history of the Antilles).[132] By contrast, the entry on "Natural History" in the *Supplement* is over twice as long as the original entry. The section addressing the study of the earth states that the inhabitants of the earth should be considered, "and in particular their stature, colour, features, strength, agility or defects of these; and their complexions, hair, beauty and the like; their diet, inclinations and customs, so far as they are not owing to education: the fruitfulness or barrenness of the women."[133] This passage is lifted directly from Robert Boyle's 1666 article "General Heads for a Natural History of a Countrey, Great or Small," in the *Philosophical Transactions* of the Royal Society.[134]

At the basis of the increased scientific attention paid to human diversity lay, at least in part, European colonial expansion and the transatlantic slave trade. As discussed in the introduction, there is a substantial historiography that traces the connection between the exigencies of a new colonial order and "scientific" interest in human variety. For example, Cristina Malcolmson shows that several members of the Royal Society who performed research on or who were interested in varieties of human skin color were also members of the Council for Foreign Plantations, both societies having been established in 1660.[135] Robert Boyle is probably one of the most important thinkers in this regard, given his prominence in English science and the publication of his influential tract *Experiments and Considerations Touching Colours* in 1664.[136] He encouraged English travelers to collect data on the physical appearance of the indigenous peoples of non-European lands; thus, science and colonialism were intimately connected in the early modern period.

Specific political developments within England in the first half of the eighteenth century may also partially explain the changing gaze of natural history, particularly its preoccupation with blackness. In 1729, the Yorke-Talbot decision (named after Philip Yorke, then attorney general, and Charles

Talbot, solicitor general) decreed that enslaved people brought from the West Indies to Great Britain or Ireland would not be freed nor would conversion to Christianity confer manumission.[137] Yorke confirmed this decision once again in 1749 in the judicial case of *Pearne v. Lisle,* in which the declaration of the status of enslaved Black people as chattel no matter where they find themselves in the British Empire is unequivocal: "I have no doubt but trover will lie for a Negro slave; it is as much property as any other thing."[138]

Discussions of the morality of slavery and the slave trade were also raised in the British press in the 1730s and 1740s. For example, the *Gentleman's Magazine,* a popular monthly London periodical, published the speech of an "old free Negro" in 1735 in which the freeman purportedly prevented the English from recapturing an escaped slave. In this speech, he argued for the basic equality of Europeans and Africans, stating "that Education and Accident, not Difference of Genius, have been the Cause of this Superiority, that bids a *White* Man, despise and trample on a *Black* one."[139] This was followed five years later by "A Letter to the Gentlemen Merchants in the Guinea Trade," signed Mercator Honestus, in which the author expressed shock at the manner in which enslaved people were treated by traders and owners, employing a natural rights argument to call slavery into question: "I take it to be undoubtedly true, that all Mankind are brought into the World with a natural Right to Liberty, and that a Man cannot forfeit his Right to Liberty, but by attempting to take away the Property of another unjustly, in which I include his Life, Liberty, and other Valuables."[140] This article prompted an anonymous defense of slavery published in the *London Magazine* in which the author argued that the Africans who are taken to the Americas are in a worse state of slavery in their indigenous lands and thus they become freer in the colonies, particularly after converting to Christianity.[141] Additionally, in 1744, the African Company petitioned the House of Commons for financial aid in the upkeep of trading posts in West Africa, and the company received twenty thousand pounds instead of the customary ten thousand that had been paid to it annually since 1730.[142] This amount reflects the growing importance of slavery and slave-produced products, particularly sugar and tobacco, to the economic health and consumer demands of the metropole.[143] While the slave trade and slavery would come directly into the spotlight from 1770 onward in Great Britain, these political developments demonstrate that the issues raised by slavery periodically surfaced in the pre-1770 period.

Thus, the growth of the natural history of humankind and the increasing political and economic importance of the slavery of Black Africans goes a long way in explaining the changes we have noticed between Chambers's *Cyclopaedia* and the *Supplement*, from early to mid-century intellectual and political concerns.

Conclusion

Chambers's *Cyclopaedia* and *Supplement* can be approached as windows onto the culture from which each emerged. As we have seen, the *Cyclopaedia* captures quite well the political and religious debates of the early Enlightenment. The promotion of religious toleration was a central element in the network of ideas that formed the Enlightenment narrative in the late seventeenth century, which would be intensified in the eighteenth. Concerning the scientific and political concerns of Chambers's work, the *Cyclopaedia* can be meaningfully placed in the moderate as opposed to the radical Enlightenment. His primary concern was to promote Newtonian science, and while he offered respectful treatment of other natural philosophical systems, he remained opposed to a materialistic conception of nature. His politics reflected his conception of the natural order: he offered a subtle defense of England's constitutional monarchy and no thoroughgoing criticism of the social or political norms of the period, except of religious intolerance and torture.[144] Yet Chambers's political and social views should not simply be written off as a defense of the status quo, since his promotion of religious toleration was grounded in a conception of the basic equality of all human beings. Chambers's vindication of religious toleration can be interpreted as the anthropological vindication of cultural pluralism, an important part of Enlightenment discourses of equality. The references to common humanity and the criticism of bigotry stem from Chambers's view that the religious impulse can be found among all peoples and that one manner of worshipping the deity is no more correct than any other.

Alongside the anthropological perspective, however, runs the idea that Europe is the most "civilized" part of the world, distinct because of its achievements in the arts and sciences. Perhaps the most revealing aspect of Chambers's coverage of non-European peoples is its scantiness; we will recall that he considered his book a "Course in Antient and Modern Learning." However, it should also be noted that Chambers explicitly excluded geography and history from his *Cyclopaedia*, because these subjects were left to the separate genre of historical dictionaries.[145] Chambers ignored the rich and ancient traditions of learning across the world, particularly in China, that were widely reported in the travel literature with which Chambers was undoubtedly acquainted. Only Western knowledge traditions were deemed worthy of coverage. Chambers's claim that his book was a "Universal Dictionary of Arts and Sciences" is quickly found wanting, mainly for its Eurocentrism. Noticing such a shortcoming is certainly important, but it should not obscure the subtext of egalitarian ideals that can be found throughout the *Cyclopaedia*. Charles Withers's assessment of Chambers's *Cyclopaedia* as emblematic of an "Enlightenment project" that seeks to subdue the natural world and non-European human worlds through its "masculinist gaze" thus obscures more than it illuminates.[146] Chambers's cultural and ethnic prejudices are indeed important to acknowledge, but a more thorough analysis of the *Cyclopaedia* reveals a tension between a Eurocentric view of the progress of knowledge and an egalitarian subtext that affirms basic equality and common humanity.

The *Cyclopaedia* and *Supplement* register the changing views of human physical diversity in the first half of the eighteenth century. The civilization/barbarism binary is prominent in Chambers's work, but the growth of the anatomical and natural historical interest in physical forms is also conspicuous. We have seen that this interest reflects the harsh economic and political circumstances of the enslavement of sub-Saharan Africans in that a "scientific" exploration of blackness is particularly prominent, although the growth of the field of the natural history of the human species cannot be reduced to these political and economic concerns alone. This trend is intensified in the *Supplement*, as registered in the more thorough coverage of natural history in general and the natural historical perspective on human diversity in particular. As we turn to Diderot and d'Alembert's *Encyclopédie*, we will find that humanity is firmly placed within a natural historical framework and that both discourses of racial inequality and cross-cultural equality are intensified in this key publication of the Enlightenment, capturing the ambiguities of Enlightenment anthropology.

CHAPTER 3

Diderot and d'Alembert's *Encyclopédie*: A New Human Science

Equality as a political concept takes on a salience in Diderot's *Encyclopédie* that markedly differentiates this French encyclopedia from its English predecessor. Perhaps owing to the encyclopedists' unique situation in mid-eighteenth-century France—with an intolerant Catholic Church and an absolutist political establishment—equality simply mattered more to Diderot and many of his fellow contributors than it did to Ephraim Chambers. The encyclopedists were careful to defend themselves against the charge of supporting absolute equality, but they grounded their attacks on royal absolutism in a defense of individual rights and an attendant political equality. Keith Michael Baker has shown that we must position the *Encyclopédie* within the political battles between the Crown, the *parlements*, and the church hierarchy in the 1750s, when Louis XV failed to impose his authority in the strife between the *parlements* and the church hierarchy.[1] Who should have the authority to define crucial political and social terms? Diderot argued that this authority lies with a society of men of letters, which cares intimately about the public good. If we appreciate that "social and political changes are themselves linguistic," then the encyclopedic project itself, particularly as conceived by Diderot and d'Alembert, becomes part of the political conflicts of the ancien régime.[2]

In addition to this direct political context, we should also place the political ideas defended in the *Encyclopédie* in a longer history of deeper social and cultural transformations in eighteenth-century Western Europe and of profound changes in religious beliefs and practices. While Diderot and a handful of other contributors to the *Encyclopédie* were atheists, we will see that even for the more pious contributors, a defense of the social function of religion—the idea that religion should facilitate the smooth functioning of society—subtly emerges in a number of articles. This subordination of the religious to the societal was a, perhaps *the*, significant shift in worldview in the Enlightenment that had powerful egalitarian consequences that are reflected in the *Encyclopédie*.[3] The rise of society as the fundamental ground of human interdependence, a transformation that intensified in the second half of the eighteenth century, particularly in the Francophone world, helps to explain why equality was more widely discussed, debated, and occasionally defended in French Enlightenment texts. As Yair Mintzker has shown, Diderot and Rousseau were among the first to use "social" to refer implicitly to society itself, changing the originally English term in the process.[4] Taking interactions of autonomous individuals as its basis, the autonomous human order that is society threw the justice of the hierarchical corporate structure of society into doubt. Partially as a result of the rise of this new, secular way of understanding human interdependence, Enlightenment thinkers no longer viewed inequality as an inevitable feature of humanity's fallen state.

This is not to say that the *Encyclopédie* expounds a revolutionary political philosophy or that the work (and its many offspring) led in any simple or direct way to the French Revolution. Indeed, the work contains a diverse chorus of voices, ranging from staunch defenses of Catholic orthodoxy and political absolutism, to moderate suggestions for political and social reform, to more radical anti-Christian and anti-absolutist ideas.[5] As Daniel Brewer argues, "It would be incorrect and . . . reductive to read the *Encyclopédie* either as simply a manifesto of proto-capitalist bourgeois ideology, on the one hand, or as the heroic expression of a timeless humanism, on the other."[6] Brewer demonstrates that, at times, the *Encyclopédie* advances a universalist, Enlightenment humanism while at others it reflects a Euro- and male-centric knowledge and politics. While the uniformity of the work should not be exaggerated,[7] one can perceive many recurrent themes in politics and philosophy that are reflective of the core concerns of the men and women of the Republic of Letters in the Enlightenment—namely, defenses of toleration and freedom of the press, the separation of Church and state, freedom of conscience, and some measure of political equality and liberty are all liberally distributed throughout the work. Dorinda Outram and many others are right to construe the Enlightenment as "a series of interlocking, and sometimes warring problems and debates,"[8] but only if one qualifies this statement by adding that within these debates, a cluster of ideas connected to the new science and human betterment emerges. After all, certainly every historical epoch is marked by warring problems and debates. In other words, the Enlightenment—among all of the recent discussion of a radical versus moderate Enlightenment, a religious versus secular Enlightenment, a national versus European or colonial Enlightenment, and many more in between—can still be viewed as a movement possessing a thin but meaningful coherence that is reflected in the *Encyclopédie*.[9]

This idea was expressed by Diderot himself in the immensely important entry "Encyclopedia," where he wrote that "everything must be examined, everything must be sifted, without any exceptions and without restraint," emphasizing the quintessential *esprit de critique* of the Enlightenment in general and of the *Encyclopédie* in particular. But Diderot also stated that the work had an additional aim: "To change the common mode of thinking."[10] The idea that the common mode of thinking should be changed implies that Diderot had some idea of what direction this change should take, and indeed, in his correspondence, we see that he had just that: "Over time, this work will certainly produce a revolution in minds, and I hope that the tyrants, the oppressors, the fanatics, and the intolerant will not win. We will have served humanity."[11] The work was certainly not steeped in Spinozist philosophy, as Jonathan Israel has claimed to bolster his contention that the radical Enlightenment lies at the foundation of modernity, but instead captures the diversity and controversies characteristic of the Enlightenment.[12]

I stress the thin coherence of the Enlightenment in order to make sense of the diversity of perspectives one encounters in the *Encyclopédie*, which contains ideas and philosophies running the gamut from radical to counter-Enlightenment. The idea of a thin coherence will help us to determine the relationship of the Enlightenment to the politicization of equality and the development of a racial classificatory system. As we will see, slavery is tacitly defended in a few *Encyclopédie* articles, but to conclude that because this defense appears in the *Encyclopédie*, it must be representative of the Enlightenment as a whole would be misguided. The *Encyclopédie* can be equated with the Enlightenment as a whole only to the extent that it reflected and contributed to "a series of debates." But to find the core political, philosophical, and ethical ideas central to the movement, we have to be more specific. As Jean Ehrard argues, "The fact is that the *Dictionnaire Raisonné* never aimed to propose a body of doctrine about anything, but rather to get people thinking. The *Encyclopédie* is at once a data bank and a debating platform. Its most useful role in the formation of the anti-slavery movement was certainly to have made an unspoken malaise into an open confrontation."[13] As we will see, it was those thinkers from within the fold of Enlightenment philosophy who were at the forefront of condemning slavery and the slave trade in eighteenth-century France.

Analyzing the encyclopedists' treatment of the cultural and physical diversity of humanity is of great present-day import given the charges laid against the Enlightenment as a whole for being implicitly or explicitly Eurocentric or even racist. What I hope to demonstrate in this chapter is that, for those encyclopedists committed to Enlightenment philosophy, the charge of racism does not hold. While they were certainly Eurocentric, to stop there is to miss the innovativeness and diversity of Enlightenment thinkers' contributions to nascent physical and cultural anthropology. I follow Siep Stuurman in distinguishing between a vulgar Eurocentrism and one that is reflexive and self-critical, as we find both in the *Encyclopédie*.[14] The Enlightenment was quite literally unthinkable without the discovery of the New World, as eighteenth-century observers themselves noted. In the introduction to his best-selling *Histoire des deux Indes* (*History of the Two Indies*), Raynal wrote, "There has not been an event as interesting for the human species in general, and for the peoples of Europe in particular, as the discovery of the New World and the passage to the Indies by the Cape of Good Hope. Thus commenced a revolution in commerce, in the power of nations, in their customs, industry, and the government of all peoples."[15] Or as Voltaire stated, "We subjugated a new world, and ours is completely different."[16] The nascent human sciences took root in the quest to make sense of the bewildering diversity of humanity with which the philosophes were confronted and their realization that a new world system had taken root since the fifteenth century. Enlightenment thinkers realized that they must understand human diversity in order to understand their own humanity.[17]

When it comes to the indigenous peoples of the Americas, the encyclopedists' politicization of equality meant that these peoples and their societies could serve as positive examples that highlighted the gross inequalities, corruption, greed, and overall miserable state of European society in contrast to the alleged equality, freedom, and tranquility of Amerindian societies. In other words, the noble savage is certainly prominent in the *Encyclopédie*, serving to cast Europe in a negative light. At the same time, as a result of the pedagogical authority that occasionally characterizes the philosophes' self-understanding, in which they positioned themselves as the enlightened few above the unenlightened many (European or not),

Native Americans are judged to be superstitious and irrational compared with the "superior" standard of enlightened Europe.[18] There are a handful of genuinely culturally relativist articles in which Native Americans are shown to possess the rational and imaginative capacities to construct peaceful and well-organized societies, and I will analyze these articles closely, because they were, and are, of great importance. In any case, however, whether portrayed positively or negatively, the discussion of Native Americans primarily reflects European political and philosophical concerns. Additionally, the inclusion of humanity within natural history is a remarkable innovation in the *Encyclopédie* compared with its English predecessor, and the physical features of Native Americans are often commented upon. But I will demonstrate that the political or philosophical significance that Amerindians had for European debates overshadowed the natural historical or racial consideration of Native Americans. Thus, while Native Americans are only the primitive, savage Other in Chambers's *Cyclopaedia*, they take on a renewed political and natural historical significance, both "positively" and "negatively," in Diderot's *Encyclopédie*.

Similar to Native Americans, the encyclopedists' sub-Saharan African is often either the debased savage Other or the enlightened, Epicurean Man of Nature. But, crucially, the physical features of Blacks are of much more immediate concern than those of Native Americans, reflecting the growing importance of race-based slavery that gave black skin and other physical features an unprecedented salience. Indeed, in certain articles, slavery is all but defended and sub-Saharan Africans are assessed based on their utility as enslaved people. But the *Encyclopédie* also contains the most radical condemnation of slavery in French thought published up to that date, and, in numerous articles, slavery is vehemently condemned as a violation of natural rights. The reader is thus confronted with a profound ambiguity on the status of Blacks and slavery. While one encyclopedist, the engineer and colonial administrator Jean-Baptiste-Pierre Le Romain, claims that the "animal nature" of Blacks justifies the institution of slavery, more prominent and prolific encyclopedists fervently denounced the institution with impassioned appeals to a shared humanity aimed to elicit an emotional reaction in the reader, to stimulate the reader's empathy for the immense human cost of the slave trade and slavery. Slavery is problematized in a way unseen in reference works published before the *Encyclopédie*, including that of Ephraim Chambers. For example, in the immensely important Jesuit *Dictionnaire de Trévoux*, upon which Diderot and his collaborators relied heavily, the entries "Slavery" and "Négre" are blithe reports of the enslave-ment of Blacks, emphasizing their "laziness" and their idolatrous religion or lack of religious sentiment altogether.[19] While Diderot's *Encyclopédie* has been taken to task for not being sufficiently antislavery, when we place it in the context of other seventeenth- and eighteenth-century dictionaries and encyclopedias and of the antislavery debate more generally, the picture be-gins to look different. True to Diderot's aims, and thanks mainly to Jaucourt's articles on slavery, the encyclopedists were instrumental in mobilizing the secular French antislavery movement.

The *Encyclopédie*'s treatment of China reveals the exploitative practices that lay at the basis of interest in the physical differences between Europeans and non-Europeans, as the encyclopedists did not racialize the Chinese to the same extent as Native Americans and Africans. The philosophes were primar-ily interested in Chinese history, philosophy, and culture because Europeans deemed the Chinese "civilized." Chinese traditions of learning had already had a great impact on European thought by the mid-eighteenth century, lead-ing one historian to call Confucius the "patron saint of the Enlightenment."[20] The *Encyclopédie* captures the complexities of Enlightenment debates on China, since both Sinophilic and Sinophobic voices can be heard. Taking the *Encyclopédie*'s treatment of Native Americans, Africans, and Chinese to-gether enables us to see how the philosophes laid the foundations for the modern human sciences as they carved out new, secular pathways for better understanding humankind in all its physical and cultural diversity.

Natural Equality and Rights in the *Encyclopédie*

What is most remarkable about the concept of equality in the *Encyclopédie* is the very fact that it appears as a political concept at all. In the major refer-ence works that precede the *Encyclopédie*, encyclopedists primarily treated equality as a mathematical or logical concept. Regardless of Jaucourt's as-sessments and judgments of equality, the very presence of his article "Natu-ral Equality" indicates a significant shift in the development of political philosophy in the Enlightenment. Jaucourt opens his entry by stating, "Natural equality is that which is among all men solely by the constitution of their nature. This equality is the principle and the foundation of liberty. Natural or moral equality is thus founded on the constitution of human nature common to all men, who are born, grow, live, and die in the same way."[21] While present-day political theory stresses the tension between equality and liberty, Jaucourt and most other prerevolutionary theorists of equality viewed it as the necessary counterpart of liberty. Rather than being an oversight on the part of Enlightenment philosophers, Pierre Rosanvallon has insightfully explained that the philosophes' theorization of equality was intimately connected to the advent of the autonomous individual in early modern political philosophy.[22] As a result, liberty was seen not as adversarial to equality but as its necessary partner, expressed most succinctly in Rousseau's dream of a society characterized by the "reciprocity of free consciousnesses."[23] The advent of the autonomous individual in Enlightenment thought was indeed central to the development of the idea of human rights and equality as a political concept and will be explored more thoroughly below.

Jaucourt states that several consequences ensue from natural equality but that he will highlight just four principal ones. First, all men are naturally free, and reason dictates that they can only be dependent on another for their own welfare. Second, "that despite all of the inequalities produced in political government by the difference in conditions, by nobility, power, wealth, etc., those who have risen the most above others must treat their inferiors as being naturally equal to them." Third, whoever has not acquired a right that grants him preferential treatment, must not claim more than others. Last, anything that is a universal right must be universally enjoyed. He refers to equality as an "incontestable principle" from which is derived "all of the duties of charity, of humanity, and of justice which all men are obliged to practice toward one another." He leaves it up to the reader to derive additional consequences that follow from the principle of natural equality but adds, "I will only remark that it is the violation of this principle which established political and civil slavery. Because of this, in the countries subjected to arbitrary power, the princes, the courtiers, the principal ministers, those who control the finances possess all the wealth of the nation while the rest of the citizens only have the necessities and the great majority of people groan in poverty."[24] The subtle indictment of Jaucourt's contemporary French society would certainly not have been lost on eighteenth-century readers.[25]

Jaucourt subsequently warns readers that they should not do him the injustice of accusing him of being a supporter of "that chimera of absolute equality." He states, "I know all too well the necessity of different conditions, grades, honors, distinctions, prerogatives, subordinations that must prevail in all governments" and, following Montesquieu, argues that society forces people to lose their equality, which can only be restored by the law.[26] While it is important to recognize the limitations that eighteenth-century thinkers placed on a potentially radical idea, the fundamental change in worldview that the idea of equality both reflected and shaped should not be over-looked.[27] Jaucourt's use of Montesquieu is significant, because Montes-quieu's analysis of the three different types of government dissociates power from any higher purpose, whether associated with divine or natural law, and thus, even though *The Spirit of the Laws* can be viewed as a monarchist tract, his analysis opens up power differentials within society to the most devastating of criticism.[28] To argue, as Chisick does, that Jaucourt "refrains from condemning the old regime" is to miss the significance even of the presence of an article that expounds the logic of natural equality and, by referring to the absence of a condemnation of the "old regime," belies the postrevolutionary standard to which he holds prerevolutionary thinkers.[29]

Jaucourt also called inequalities between men and women into question, no doubt owing much to his experience as a pupil of one of the great femi-nist thinkers of the early Enlightenment, François Poulain de la Barre.[30] In his article "Wife," Jaucourt argues that while most countries grant authority to the father or husband of a family, this is only a convention resulting from positive law and can thus be transformed: "First of all, it seems that it would be difficult to demonstrate that the authority of the husband comes from nature because this principle is contrary to the natural equality of men."[31] This also demonstrates that the phrase "the natural equality of men" was indeed sometimes interpreted in truly universalist fashion, what we would call "the natural equality of human beings." He begins the article by stating that governing authority must rest with one person and this is often the male, owing to his "greater strength of body and mind," but the rest of the article calls this assumption into doubt. He argues that men do not always have stronger bodies or sharper intellects than women and cites examples of capable female rulers throughout history, which, he states, proves that women can be the head of a family.

However, Jaucourt's article is only one of four articles with the headword "Femme" and is the most egalitarian (this article should be translated as "Wife," whereas the others are better translated as "Woman"—"*femme*" means both in French). Joseph-François-Edouard de Corsembleu de Des-mahis's article "Woman" (Morality) presents us with a startling contrast to Jaucourt's entry, as he emphasizes the "natural differences" and inequalities between the sexes that education must reinforce, as men are naturally more rational and courageous, whereas women are more delicate and graceful, he claims.[32] Voltaire in fact complained to d'Alembert about the frivolity of this article and in his *Confessions*, Rousseau remarked that Desmahis did not show women proper respect.[33] Lieselotte Steinbrügge demonstrates that this article was primarily a critique of the *femme du monde*—a woman active in the French salons—and a rationalization of the ideal of confining women to the private sphere.[34] Antoine-Gaspard Boucher d'Argis's article "Woman" (Law), is generally supportive of the status quo, because he also mentions the natural inequalities that exist between men and women, a perspective he repeats in his article "Husband."[35] Paul Joseph Barthez's article "Woman" (Anthropology) has an egalitarian subtext, as he states that given the lack of education girls receive, it is surprising to find so many learned women in Europe.[36] Additionally, Jaucourt's article "Paternal power" discusses the rights of both fathers and mothers over their children, in fact transforming these "rights" into a set of obligations that parents have to their children, and rejects the idea that the authority of the state stems from paternal authority.[37]

Historians disagree as to how we should assess the position and treatment of women and gender in the *Encyclopédie*, as in the Enlightenment more generally. There were only two recognized female contributors to the encyclopedia, only one of whom we know by name: Madame Delusse, who contributed "Lute Making" to the fifth volume of plates.[38] A number of women engraved plates for the *Encyclopédie*.[39] Additionally, Glenn Roe has demonstrated that the great eighteenth-century savant Émilie du Châtelet's work on physics was copied, often unacknowledged, extensively in the *Encyclopédie*.[40] Many scholars argue that the *Encyclopédie* lacks a pro-woman position, since women are primarily discussed in the *Encyclopédie* only in relation to men,[41] but as Lieselotte Steinbrügge argues, looking at other eighteenth-century encyclopedias throws the *Encyclopédie* into a different light, because the *Dictionnaire de Trévoux* was almost completely misogynistic, demonstrating the importance of Jaucourt's and others' more egalitarian interjections.[42] While the *Encyclopédie* can rightfully be criticized for falling far short of a truly feminist, egalitarian philosophy and politics, it is also certainly the case that the work fits into the flurry of treatises on women's education in the second half of the eighteenth century.[43] In other words, looking at the work contextually gives a different impression than looking at it through the gloss of the twenty-first century.

Not only was Jaucourt's article "Wife" the most far-reaching in its advocacy of women's equality, but we also find a distinctly more egalitarian voice than what is to be found in the sources he drew from for his articles in other areas of political philosophy, as Céline Spector has argued.[44] For example, in the article "Democracy," while Jaucourt opens the article by stating that he does not believe that democracy is the most practical or stable form of government, he goes on to assert this powerful qualifying sentiment: "The natural equity that is among us, says Plato when speaking of his homeland Athens, makes us seek in our government an equality that conforms with the law, while at the same time we submit ourselves to those among us who have the most ability and wisdom."[45] As Spector explains, even though Jaucourt relied heavily on Montesquieu, he altered the spirit of the original text: "Contrary to Montesquieu, Jaucourt thereby refers to 'natural equity,' the principle of participation in communal affairs by all."[46] Although he devotes a lot of attention to democracy in antiquity and explains that the large territories of modern monarchies such as France pose obstacles to democratic government, he gives the distinct impression that modern republics are admirable. After all, Jaucourt lived and studied in Geneva and in the Dutch Republic.[47] We find an encomium to Geneva in Jaucourt's article "Republic," where he explains, "In Geneva, one feels only happiness and liberty."[48]

All of this is not to imply that Jaucourt recommended the implementation of a democracy in France or anywhere else in the world. He followed Montesquieu in arguing that democracies fall apart when citizens lose the spirit of equality or, alternatively, when they clamor for extreme equality which, Montesquieu and Jaucourt argue, leads to despotism.[49] But what is clear is that he had unmistakable sympathies for democratic forms of government, which come to the fore in numerous articles in the *Encyclopédie*. Compared to Chambers, who laconically and indifferently describes democracy, Jaucourt dwells on its pros and cons, one of the very few prerevolutionary eighteenth-century thinkers to do so. What is without doubt the central concern in the political philosophy of Jaucourt, Diderot, and many other encyclopedists is countering the legitimacy of absolutism and despotism. Political authority must not be arbitrary or cruel and must guarantee the welfare and happiness of the majority of the people. This does not mean, however, that the encyclopedists, Diderot included, were critical of monarchical government as such. Indeed, they lavished Great Britain's constitutional monarchy with praise. Istvan Hont has argued that one of the most exciting developments of eighteenth-century political philosophy was the treatment of the modern monarchy as a res publica.[50] While the attack on absolutist royal authority peppered throughout the *Encyclopédie* has been thoroughly studied,[51] what has been overlooked is how equality as a political concept figured in the encyclopedists' attacks on royal absolutism and the society of orders. I argue that, in countering absolutism, the philosophes utilized equality as a political concept and thus turned it into a foundational concept; once they incorporated equality into their attack on despotic government, they were forced to argue about the consequences and limitations of equality in the political sphere.

This politicization of equality to counter royal absolutism is evident in the article that caused the greatest stir in the early years of the *Encyclopédie*: Diderot's "Political Authority."[52] John Lough has demonstrated that this article was singled out for its radicalism and impiety again and again for at least the first twenty years after its appearance.[53] Jesuits, Jansenists, and anti-philosophe writers such as Elie Cathérine Fréron poured venom on Diderot and the *Encyclopédie* as a whole because of this article. Diderot's central argument is that no person receives the power to rule from nature. Each individual is free and equal to each other individual, and legitimate political authority must come from the consent of the people and must be exercised in such a manner as to benefit society at large. Even though Diderot placed restrictions on the people's right to rebellion, the thrust of the article, and the attention from critics and sympathizers alike, fell on this radical proposition: "In a word, the crown, the government, and the public authority are goods of which the body of the nation is owner and of which the princes are the beneficiaries, ministers, and custodians."[54] The discussion revolves around the consent of free, autonomous, and *equal* individuals who voluntarily enter into society and submit themselves to certain laws and a ruler (or rulers) for their own good.

In the last ten volumes, published all at once in 1765, the most critical stance against absolutism is taken in four anonymously authored articles: "Power," "Property," "Protection," and "Sovereigns." Equality as a political concept is of central importance in the longest of these articles, "Sovereigns." The anonymous author traces the development of humanity from the state of nature to complex civil society. As was commonplace in early modern political thought, the author argues that humanity in the state of nature enjoys a state of equality and liberty: "Man, in the state of nature, knows no sovereign; each individual is equal to another and enjoys the most perfect independence. There is no other subordination in this state than that of children to their father."[55] He assumes that the subordination of children to their father is natural and thus, tacitly, also wives to their husbands. But crucially, the equality of the state of nature is used to place clear limits on political authority: "One sees that their [the sovereigns'] power and their rights are founded only on the consent of the people; those who establish themselves by violence are only usurpers. They become legitimate only when the consent of the people has confirmed the rights the sovereigns seized."[56] This politicization of equality within natural law and natural rights discourse is a remarkable feature of the *Encyclopédie*. As is well known, the encyclopedists relied heavily on seventeenth-century natural law theorists, primarily Hugo Grotius, Thomas Hobbes, Samuel Pufendorf (especially through the work of Jean Barbeyrac and Jean-Jacques Burlamaqui), and John Locke.[57] Equality features prominently in the work of all of these thinkers, yet none opposed slavery outright.

Many of the encyclopedists would transform the ideas they inherited from seventeenth-century natural law thinkers, such as equality, by expanding their purview. For example, although Pufendorf theorized extensively on the consequences of the natural equality of human beings, he did not invoke the concept to call into question entrenched legal and social inequalities; as we have seen, he lamented the abolition of slavery in Europe. But the philosophes transformed the language and philosophy of natural law by putting it to new uses.[58] In relying on Pufendorf for the article "Citizen," Diderot criticizes the philosophy of this eminent professor of natural law:

> Puffendorf [*sic*], in restricting the name citizen to those who founded the state by an initial assembly of families and to their successors from father to son, introduces a frivolous distinction on which his work sheds little light, and which can cause a lot of trouble in a civil society by distinguishing original citizens from naturalized ones based on a mistaken idea of nobility. Citizens in their capacity as citizens, meaning in their societies, are all equally noble; nobility comes not from ancestors, but from the common right to the first ranks of the magistracy.[59]

It is thus precisely relative to the equality of citizens that Diderot criticizes Pufendorf.

In "Government," Jaucourt relies on Locke and Montesquieu to make a case for the restriction of sovereign power and the respect political authorities must have for equality and liberty. Céline Spector argues that Jaucourt radicalizes Locke and Montesquieu by invoking both the laws of nature and reason and by using them to discuss perfecting the science or art of politics and government in the best regime, rather than primarily focusing on restricting power in the worst regime.[60] Equality is, once again, of primary importance to Jaucourt: "All public governments obviously seem to have been formed by deliberation, by consultation, and by agreement. Who doubts, for example, that Rome and Venice were not started by men free and independent of one another, between whom there was neither natural superiority nor subjection, and who agreed to form a society of government?"[61]

Jaucourt argues that all governments must work to make their citizens happy and provide them with peace, security, and the necessities of life.[62] It should be noted that in many of the articles analyzed thus far, where absolutist authority is called into question and equality is politicized, Montesquieu and Locke were the main sources. Dan Edelstein, Robert Morrissey, and Glenn Roe have demonstrated that Jaucourt and other encyclopedists employed a strategy of non-citation, since the political works of certain authors, such as Locke and Helvétius, were either officially banned or only allowed to be published with *permission tacite* in France.[63] When David Mazel, a Huguenot refugee resident in London, first translated Locke's *Two Treatises of Government* into French in 1691, it was primarily meant to provide French readers with an anti-absolutist critique of the Bourbon monarchy.[64]

Whether power is concentrated in the hands of one or in the hands of an elite or is held by the people, Jean-François de Saint-Lambert, in his well-known article "Legislator," or "Law Giver" (*législateur*), opens with an uncontroversial maxim: "Every law giver must ensure the security of the state and the happiness of the citizens." He argues that the state of nature has two advantages—equality and liberty—and two disadvantages—fear of violence and lack of assistance. Human beings only agree to enter into society if as little of their equality and liberty as possible is lost and if they can live in more peaceful and supportive circumstances. Cultivating an egalitarian spirit is a prerogative of all governments, in all times and places: "So that men feel as little as possible that they have lost the two advantages of the state of nature—equality and independence—the legislator, in all climates, in all circumstances, in all governments, must propose to change the spirit of property into the spirit of community."[65]

On the whole, the main thrust of many of the political entries is a biting criticism of absolutism, expressed most cogently by Diderot in the article "Oppressor, Oppress": "Term pertaining to the misuse of power. We oppress, we merit the name oppressor, we make one groan under oppression, when the weight of our authority leans on our subjects in a manner that crushes them and renders their existence unbearable. One renders existence unbearable by invading liberty, exhausting wealth, hindering opinions, etc."[66] But we cannot conclude from these criticisms that Diderot or most of the other encyclopedists were republican political thinkers. While Diderot's political thought would transform significantly in the years after the publication of the *Encyclopédie*,[67] in the period from 1751 to 1765, he, like many of his contemporaries, believed that a constitutional monarchy was best suited to govern a large, modern country and that this form of government could best guarantee the freedom of its citizens, a position most elaborately theorized and defended by Montesquieu and expounded in Nicolas Antoine Boulanger's article "Political Economy."[68]

But the crucial point for our discussion of equality is that the concept became politicized in the encyclopedists' criticism of absolutism, as the freedom and equality of autonomous individuals were ushered in to defend citizens' rights against an overbearing monarchical and ecclesiastical establishment. Upon comparing the political philosophy of Diderot's *Encyclopédie* with Ephraim Chambers's *Cyclopaedia*, one is immediately struck by the scantiness and nonpolemical nature of Chambers's work compared with its successor. Political philosophy is both more fully developed by Diderot and his collaborators, and it is more polemical, in fitting with the philosophes' aims of spreading enlightenment by, in Diderot's words, "teaching men to doubt," by bringing all topics to the table for open and vigorous discussion.[69]

Society, Toleration, and Equality

The intellectual history of equality cannot be separated from the social experiences of the thinkers who theorized and transformed the concept. One of the reasons that equality came to the fore in Enlightenment thought was as a result of structural changes in eighteenth-century society—in particular, the growth of the public sphere and new forms of sociability.[70] Literacy rates increased over the course of the eighteenth century in France, from 29 percent at the beginning of the century to 47 percent toward the end for men, and from 14 percent to 27 percent for women.[71] Additionally, there was an increase in the proportion of the population that owned books and in the size of their libraries. New forms of sociability were connected to the rise of the public sphere, as men and women of varying ranks mingled in the growing urban centers that boasted an increasingly large number of coffee-houses, taverns, salons, public libraries, Masonic lodges, and literary socie-ties.[72] Intimately connected to these developments, and particularly from the 1750s onward, public opinion as a political force grew in importance.[73] In many of these new spaces, traditional distinctions of status were tempo-rarily suspended, making civic equality both thinkable and acceptable to a growing number of people from all levels of society.[74] A new vocabulary developed that described and shaped these changes, in particular with the coining of the word "sociability" in the early eighteenth century.

In *Citizens without Sovereignty*, Daniel Gordon defines sociability as "egalitarian interaction among individuals with different corporate stand-ing" and argues that in the period from about 1670 to the French Revolution, there developed a new standard of polite conversation among equals in the new social space that was opening up.[75] As his title indicates, he argues that this sociability was nonpolitical in nature and so can help to explain the invention of "the social" as a category in the eighteenth century. Since men and women of letters were excluded from the official political process in France, they carved out their own space where the arbitrary distinc-tions of rank were of no import. Antoine Lilti has revised this focus on a sphere of egalitarian interaction, pointing to the hierarchical, aristocratic codes of behavior and networks upon which the salons rested.[76] Though Lilti presents a convincing argument, it remains the case that the cultural logic of individualism that gained ground during the Enlightenment nonetheless conflicted deeply with the rigid hierarchical structure of the ancien régime.

The stress on the autonomy of the individual led to the theorization of the culture and practice of "sociability," a term that was coined in the early eighteenth century.[77] The concept of sociability was in fact first used in France by absolutist political thinkers such as Jacques-Bénigne Bossuet, who argued that there is a latent sociability in human nature such that humans need to live in society, but because of the unruly nature of the human passions, they require a sovereign to institute that society.[78] As Daniel Gordon remarks, "The Enlightenment . . . may be viewed as the process through which sociability was defined not as a latent feature of human na-ture but as an active and operating principle of human life."[79] In the texts of Enlightenment thinkers, sociability would be reworked as a principle of humanity with distinct egalitarian aspects, as demonstrated by Jaucourt's account of the concept.

Jaucourt argues that sociability is the disposition to treat others respectfully and to subordinate one's own interests to the general interest. He connects the advent of sociability not only to the advances in the study of humankind associated with the Enlightenment but also to God's will: "The more we study ourselves, the more we will be convinced that this sociability conforms with God's will."[80] He argues that three principles follow from sociability as an ethical standard. First, men must place the common good above their individual interests. Second, the spirit of sociability must be universal. And third, that we treat one another as equals: "Reason tells us that creatures of the same order, of the same species, born with the same faculties to live together and to share in the same advantages, have in general an equal and common right. We are therefore obligated to regard one another as naturally equal and to treat one another as such; it would contradict nature by not recognizing this principle of equity (that legal scholars call *oequabilitatis juris*) as one of the main founding principles of society."[81]

Even though the salons were not spaces of egalitarian social interaction, the cumulative effect of a thickening social space in eighteenth-century Paris led some thinkers, such as Jaucourt, to claim that equality ought to be a foundational principle. Elsewhere, Jaucourt doubts whether the ancient Roman festival of Saturnalia, in which social norms were overturned and masters served their slaves, would have really taught masters and slaves anything because the institution of slavery was too gross a violation of the principle of equality: "There is only sweet equality, Mr. Rousseau says very well, which can reestablish the order of nature, form an instruction for some, a consolation for others, and a bond of friendship for all."[82]

As mentioned in the introduction and at the beginning of this chapter, the invention of society as the ontological frame for our collective existence had significant consequences for how Enlightenment thinkers theorized equality, particularly their conceptualization of society as an aggregate of autonomous individuals. Not only are the egalitarian consequences of the modern understandings of society and the social present in the *Encyclopédie* but, as we will see in Chapter 4, equality is more extensively theorized within the discourse of society and the social in the *Encyclopédie d'Yverdon*. I contend that the advent of individualism and the invention of society as our shared frame of reference might help us to make sense of the bewildering multiplicity that now characterizes the study of the Enlightenment. I would like to suggest that we can move beyond the at-times anachronistic distinction between the radical and moderate Enlightenment or the religious and secular Enlightenment by focusing on this shift in worldview that involved religious thinkers, deists, and atheists alike.

The anonymously authored article "Society" presents us with a striking contrast to Chambers's entry and with ample evidence that this concept indeed had egalitarian political and social consequences. Chambers defined society as "an Assemblage, or Union of several Persons in the same Place, for their mutual Assistance, Security and Interest. Of *Societies* we have a great many kinds, distinguished by the different ends proposed by them: Civil Societies, Trading Societies, Religious Societies, etc."[83] Chambers's definition clearly conceives of society only as a voluntaristic association, as he goes on to explain the various mercantile and religious societies that have been established for the purposes of trade or evangelism. When we turn to the *Encyclopédie*, we see that the shift has been made to an understanding of society as a necessary association, the essential domain of human interdependence. The author opens: "Men are made to live in society; if it were God's intention that each man should live a solitary life, separate from others, then he would have given each individual the necessary traits for this type of solitary life."[84] He is of course responding to the debate raging in the aftermath of the ideas of Hobbes, Locke, Pufendorf, and, perhaps most important in the 1750s and 1760s, Rousseau, as to whether human beings are naturally sociable, and takes an anti-Rousseau stance. He argues that proof that God intended human beings to live in society can be found in the capacities unique to human beings, namely speech and empathy. While not using the word "empathy," a twentieth-century neologism, his description fits modern definitions of empathy remarkably well: "This marvelous mechanism that ensures that the passions and the impressions of the soul communicate themselves so easily from one brain to another."[85]

The author argues that ethical principles follow from the simple proposition that each human being desires happiness but also lives in society and thus must work together with others in a reciprocal way to ensure that all can achieve happiness. He asserts that all of the laws of society follow from the principle of sociability. The egalitarian consequences of his ideas are powerful and clear: "The natural equality between men is a principle that we must never lose sight of. In society, it is a principle established by philosophy and religion. Whatever the inequality that the difference in conditions seems to place between members of society, it was introduced only to make them more effectively reach their common purpose according to their present state, which is to be happy as much as this mortal life allows."[86]

It is important to acknowledge the limitations the author places on equality, as he approves of the ranks and orders in society and argues that subordination is necessary in society. But the author is careful to circumscribe the hierarchy inherent to society, writing, "But if the public good demands that subordinates obey, the same public good expects that superiors preserve the rights of those who are subject to them and govern them only to make them happier."[87] The author argues that the principles of ethics would be impotent without religion, but Locke is then invoked to argue that salvation is neither the cause nor the goal of society, and the author defends toleration. Keith Michael Baker argues that "this article reveals quite clearly the centrality of the Enlightenment engagement between society and religion. Neither could be thought without reference to the other: the institution of society as the conceptual frame of human collective existence required (indeed, it found its ultimate logic in) the displacement and reworking of the prior claims of the divine."[88]

What is important to remark in this regard is that imagining autonomous individuals uniting in society where salvation is neither cause nor goal opened up the intellectual space for theorizing and defending equality. This is at the root of the aversion to the system of privileges and the society of orders one finds in the article "Privilege," probably by Diderot himself, in which he states, "The only legitimate privileges are those that accord with nature. All others can be regarded as injustices committed against all men for the benefit of one."[89] We see here that the philosophes substituted one form of inequality—that based on birth—for another—that based on natural talent. This was also bound up with a new anti-aristocratic conception of labor, as the philosophes condemned the idleness of the nobility and praised work that serves social utility.[90] Given the dominance of sensationist theory in the Enlightenment, which held that knowledge comes from the senses through experience, everyone should have, in theory, equal potential to achieve, rendering inequality problematic to an unprecedented degree. These issues were central in the disagreement between Diderot and Helvétius, as Helvétius took Lockean empiricism to its logical conclusion: If the mind results from experience alone, give people equal experiences, and one will create equal minds.[91] Diderot countered Helvétius's posthumously published *De l'homme*, arguing that if organization makes the difference between humans and animals, as Helvétius admits, then subtle differences in the organization of the brain between individual human beings must have some impact on differences in intelligence and aptitudes.[92] Beyond the

egalitarian or inegalitarian conclusions that each thinker drew, the significance of this debate lies in the fact that inequality has become fundamentally unstable and open to debate.

This intellectual transformation also opened up space for cultural relativism and the secularization of virtue, captured most vividly in Pierre
Bayle's argument that a society of virtuous atheists is possible and Diderot's
radical separation of morality from religion in the article "Irreligious."[93]
Diderot explains that the label "irreligious" is completely dependent upon
context, since there is a fabulous diversity of religions within Europe and
around the world. But morality is universal: "It is the universal law that the
finger of God has engraved in all hearts. It is the eternal precept of sensitivity and of common needs. Immorality and irreligion should therefore not be
confounded. Morality can exist without religion and religion can exist, even
often does exist, alongside immorality."[94] And, in the famous article "Philosophe," the author makes the transfer of sacrality from an otherworldly
realm to the human, "social" realm explicit when he writes: "Civil society is,
so to speak, a divinity on earth for him [the philosopher]."[95] The author goes
on to emphasize that this ideal philosophe is imbued with an egalitarian
ethos that he acts upon: "Our philosopher, who knows how to divide himself between seclusion and the commerce of men, is full of humanity. He
is Terence's Chremes, who feels that he is a man, and whose humanity
alone makes him interested in the fortune of his neighbor, whether good
or bad."[96]

The mingling of ranks in the new social venues of the eighteenth century
perhaps also fostered a more wide-ranging egalitarian ethos that could extend down the social ladder, in that numerous encyclopedists rejected the
gross social and economic inequalities endemic in Europe.[97] In his article
"Fortune," d'Alembert's ire is clearly directed at exorbitantly wealthy members of his contemporary French or wider European society: "The means of
enriching oneself can be morally criminal, although permitted by the laws;
it is against natural law and against humanity that millions of men should
be deprived of necessities, as they are in certain countries, to feed the scan-
dalous luxury of a small number of idle citizens."[98] Diderot and Jaucourt
express similar sentiments, countering the argument that subjects must be
poor in order to be docile and decrying the injustice of a large gap between
rich and poor.[99] Jacques Proust has demonstrated that while some historians have portrayed Diderot as a socialist avant la lettre, this is in fact misguided because the "social problem" and social classes were concepts alien

to the prerevolutionary world, making it anachronistic to formulate the question of Diderot's "socialism," even though he was committed to the equal moral equality of all peoples throughout his life.[100] Crucially, the philosophes rejected the traditional Christian view of a divinely ordered, hierarchical society, although they accepted hierarchy as an inevitable and a potentially useful feature of a complex society.[101]

I argued in the previous chapter that Enlightenment defenses of religious toleration engendered a nascent defense of equality as a political concept, which we found in Chambers's *Cyclopaedia*. Fascinatingly, the *Encyclopédie* both expands and restricts the toleration Chambers expounded in the *Cyclopaedia*. The orthodox thinker Abbé Mallet, who was appointed chair of theology at the University of Paris in 1751,[102] was the main author of the intolerant entries in the *Encyclopédie*, although a significant number were written anonymously. It is likely that Diderot was pleased to have Mallet as a contributor, because his articles proved that the *Encyclopédie* was not a thoroughgoing atheistic or deistic diatribe.[103] Given the overbearing presence of the ecclesiastical and royal censors, it is unsurprising that the articles dealing explicitly with religion are often the most orthodox.[104] Meanwhile, the more severe criticisms of Christianity, theology, and superstition are often, though not always, cleverly hidden. Diderot, Jaucourt, and others formulated impassioned and radical defenses of toleration that were more elaborate and far-reaching in their consequences than anything found in Chambers.

Although the article "Religion" was one of the most radically tolerant articles in Chambers's work, the tolerant vision of the same article in Diderot's *Encyclopédie* is significantly contracted. The anonymous author begins with a close but unacknowledged translation of Chambers's article, stating that religion is knowledge of the Divinity and of the worship that is His due. He also divides religion into two parts—natural and revealed—and connects morality to natural religion. But whereas Chambers goes on to praise the Siamese for celebrating religious diversity and condemns the fanaticism and religious intolerance of certain Christian sects, the Parisian encyclopedist leaves this out entirely and instead argues for the necessity of revealed religion for teaching humanity the true nature of God and upright morals.[105] Even more strikingly, Mallet's article "Deists" offers a faithful translation of Chambers's article but makes subtle additions to distance himself from deism, such as using "they say," whereas Chambers's article was more firmly grounded in personal conviction.[106] Following the translation of Chambers's article, Mallet adds a lengthy section in which he argues that Jacques Abbadie successfully refuted deism with the sole weapon of reason in his *Traité de la vérité de la religion chrétienne* (*Treatise of the Truth of the Christian Religion*).[107] Mallet then relies on the Abbé de la Chambre's *Traité de la véritable religion* (Treatise on the true religion) to argue for the insufficiency of natural law, and the necessity, truth, and divinity of revelation, all to denounce deism.[108] But Mallet and Chambre had more than just deism in mind in their defense of religious orthodoxy, as revealed by the full title of Chambre's work: *Traité de la véritable religion: Contre les athées, les déistes, les païens, les juifs, les mahométans & toutes les fausses religions* (Treatise on the true religion: Against atheists, deists, pagans, Jews, Muslims, and all false religions). And in numerous other articles where Chambers rejected the possibility of miracles and defended biblical criticism, anonymous encyclopedists in Diderot's circle defended an anti-Enlightenment position on both accounts.[109]

The overarching concern, however, when it comes to religion in the *Encyclopédie* is to defend toleration and attack fanaticism, superstition, and clerical authority. Diderot and d'Alembert in particular took the secularization of knowledge the farthest, in that they rejected their predecessors' separation of "divine learning" and "human learning" and subjected both to the critical gaze of reason.[110] The individual's right to freedom of conscience is affirmed against the demands of religious conformity to a group, thus opening up the space for theorizing and defending the equal rights of all. This development is related to the subordination of the religious to the societal as discussed above, and we see that even in cases where certain groups are denied toleration—atheists, for example—the stability and prosperity of a society of equals is paramount. The Protestant minister Jean-Edme Romilly's lengthy defense of toleration in the article "Toleration" is grounded in the separation of church and state, a position perhaps most influentially formulated by Locke in the seventeenth century: "The state or the republic has as its goal the conservation of its members, the guarantee of their liberty, their life, their peace, their possessions, and their privileges. The Church, by contrast, is a society in which the goal is the perfection of man and the salvation of his soul. The sovereign is concerned above all with the present life; the Church is concerned above all and directly with the life to come."[111] Like Locke, Romilly does not extend toleration to atheists, in this case because they deny the divine sanctity of society's laws.[112] Despite these restrictions, it is remarkable that Romilly prefers a civil religion, quoting directly from "the author of the *Social Contract*" to argue for the importance of a religion that teaches sociability, as well as a love of justice and humanity.[113]

Other encyclopedists expound an even more radical defense of toleration than Romilly. Jaucourt's article "Superstition" scathingly condemns religious fanaticism even to the point of a qualified defense of atheism in the tradition of Plutarch: "Even atheism (and this says everything) does not destroy natural sentiments, does not violate the laws or morals of the people; but superstition is a despotic tyrant that makes everything yield to its chimeras. Its prejudices are superior to all other prejudices. An atheist is interested in public peace out of love of his own rest. But fanatical superstition, born of a disordered imagination, overthrows empires."[114]

Jaucourt refers the reader to Alexandre Deleyre's radical article "Fanaticism," which presents the most severe indictment of religious intolerance in the *Encyclopédie*.[115] Jaucourt's article "Jew" is remarkably respectful and tolerant, as are most of the various articles touching upon Jews and Judaism in the *Encyclopédie*. Just how unique this was is revealed by comparing Jaucourt's entry with the discriminatory entry in the dictionary of the Académie française, where the authors state that "we do not place this word here as the name of a nation, but because it is used figuratively in some phrases of the language. Thus one calls a Jew a man who practices usury or who sells exorbitantly expensively."[116] The articles reveal the importance of the encyclopedists' engagement with Jewish culture, as this engagement was bound up with their interest in such central issues as the rise and progress of civilization and human perfectibility.[117] Counter-Enlightenment thinkers severely condemned all of these articles, even the "moderate" defenses of religious toleration, demonstrating the contentious nature of this subject at mid-century.[118] Unsurprisingly, the encyclopedists who defended religious toleration were generally either Protestants, such as Jaucourt and Romilly, or philosophers firmly within the fold of Enlightenment philosophy, such as Diderot and Deleyre. The discussion of toleration was not only relative to debates internal to Europe; it also extended to Europe's relations with the extra-European world. While voices critical of European actions in the Americas were not new in the eighteenth century, some of the philosophes did make a novel move by expanding the purview of toleration to assert that

Native Americans have a right to difference and to resist European encroachment.

Native Americans: Between Nobility and Ignobility, Natural History and Politics

As is evident from our discussion of the *Encyclopédie*'s political philosophy, natural equality became a foundational concept in the reference work, an essential element in the encyclopedists' criticism of absolutism and an important element in Enlightenment sociability. Given the prominence of natural equality, it is not surprising that the encyclopedists offer extensive deliberations on Native American peoples and societies, who were widely held to "still" be living in a state of equality. By the mid-eighteenth century, the idea that Native Americans were closer both to the beginning of history and to nature was firmly entrenched in European culture. Locke most famously expressed this idea when he wrote, "Thus in the beginning all the World was *America*, and more so than that is now."[119] This statement appears in his discussion of the role of money in modern societies, where he argues that money indicates a tacit consent among peoples to the unequal distribution of land and wealth. Early modern Europeans thus positioned the "savage" not only in space but also in time, a perspective that would become theorized as the four stages theory in the 1750s and 1760s most famously by Anne Robert Jacques Turgot and Adam Smith.[120] In early modern Europe, "savage," "Oriental," and "ancient" were in dialogue with one another, evolving in such a way as to come to transform what it meant to be "modern" and "European."[121] Most important, the ignoble savage certainly dominated early modern European texts on the New World and sub-Saharan Africa.[122] We will see that the encyclopedists variously employed tropes of elevation and debasement.

The most important article to deal with humanity as an object of natural history is Diderot's "Human Species," a resume of Buffon's influential chapter "Varieties in the Human Species" of the *Histoire naturelle*. The very presence of this article, just like the article "Natural Equality," is, once again, of considerable significance. The increasingly widespread acceptance of humankind as a species that can be legitimately included in a natural history required no less than a revolution in worldview. Philipp Blom's assessment that

this article is "the least well informed in the entire work" is far from accurate
and is based mainly on his surprise to find such aesthetic and moral judgments mixed with what we would now consider more "serious" biological
and anthropological information.[123] Hailed as a literary masterpiece, Buffon's
Histoire naturelle was also the most important work in the eighteenth-
century Francophone world to revive historical cosmology, synthesizing a
theory of the origins of the world and natural history. Although Buffon did
not contribute any articles to the *Encyclopédie*, Buffonian natural history is
by far the most prominent in the work, mainly due to the contributions of
Buffon's collaborator Louis-Jean-Marie Daubenton to the *Encyclopédie* as
well as the general congruence between Buffon's natural history and Enlightenment philosophy more generally.[124] As a short summary of "Varieties
in the Human Species," the article places more emphasis on the fluidity of
human physical differences than the original and portrays the mixing of
various races in a distinctly positive way.[125]

Diderot describes Native Americans as being of "one race," excepting the
Inuit of the far north. As with all other human "races," Diderot's description
of Native Americans is centered on physical features but is colored by pater-
nalist and Eurocentric aesthetic and moral judgments. Surveying the continent from north to south, Diderot often describes the natives as being "well
made," robust, and agile. He also considers their hair color, facial features,
bodily form, and height. He maintains that the skin color of these peoples
generally darkens as one descends farther south, beginning with the "tanned
complexion" of the Native Canadians and describing those who live between
Florida, Mexico, and Peru variously as "swarthy," "olive," "copper-colored,"
"red-copper tan," or "color of yellow or orange copper." Interestingly, he distinguishes between the color of Native Americans and those of "mulattoes,"
stating, "The Indians of Chili are of a swarthy reddish copper color, but not
one of mixed white and black like the Mulattoes born of a white man and a
black woman or of a white woman and a black man."[126] It is in Diderot's discussion of Native Americans that he argues that white is the original color of
humankind, thus all non-Europeans degenerated, in the vocabulary of Buffon
and Diderot, from this primeval homogeneity. He bases his argument for
whiteness as humanity's ur-color on the fact that more darkly pigmented
people occasionally give birth to white babies. The phenomenon described is
clearly what we now know to be albinism, but it was widely used by eighteenth-
century European thinkers to argue both for the unity of humanity and as
evidence for the argument that white is humankind's primeval color.[127]

Diderot concludes his discussion of Native Americans by remarking that there is only one race of Amerindians, which is more or less dark-skinned and which issues from the same stock, just as all Europeans issue from the same stock. He then concludes that, as one sees similar changes in the physical form of human beings from north to south on all continents, we can conclude that humanity does not consist of different species but rather that the difference between lightly and darkly pigmented peoples comes "from the food, customs, habits, and climates."[128] Thus race is conceptualized as not only something mutable, dependent upon factors that can be altered, but also as something that is heritable, in that Diderot describes Europeans and Americans as having distinct lines of descent, though ultimately all humans share a common origin.[129] As in his discussion of humanity more generally, Diderot's discussion of Native Americans takes the adult male to be the universal racial subject, which can be discerned from the fact that he often mentions facial hair when discussing a particular peoples and, after describing any given people, he sometimes adds comments on "*their* women."[130]

More generally throughout the *Encyclopédie*, the ethnographic information concerning Native Americans is rather scarce, partially because this information was most often placed in the laconic geographic entries. Although in his article "Human Species" Diderot argues that Native Americans form a single racial group (Inuit excepted), the individual entries on specific Native American nations do not stress a common Amerindian phenotype. Rather, the encyclopedists generally offer a short description of their mode of subsistence and way of life, the nature of the contact they have had with Europeans (whether they still live independently or have been subjugated), their forms of religious worship, and occasionally their physical features. But it should be emphasized that the articles do not follow a standard format and thus differ greatly in the amount and type of information they offer. In any case, there is no overarching racial discourse on Native Americans, though comments upon certain physical features do recur, such as skin and hair color and bodily stature. Diderot wrote many of the geographic entries in the first few volumes until Jaucourt took over from volume 5. What is remarkable is that Diderot frequently commented upon the customs and religious life of non-Europeans and only rarely on their physical features, whereas Jaucourt more often remarked upon Amerindian physiognomy.

Diderot clearly used these ethnographic descriptions as an opportunity to reflect on broader philosophical and political issues of the day, such as whether "natural atheists" existed. This issue was one of the most fiercely debated among seventeenth- and eighteenth-century European thinkers. Joseph-François Lafitau's *Mœurs des sauvages amériquains comparées aux mœurs des premiers temps* (*Customs of the Native Americans Compared to the Customs of Primitive Times*) was both an impressive ethnographic study that would be used by later cultural anthropologists as a model and also a forceful argument against atheism based on the *consensus gentium* of a belief in God.[131] Diderot was obviously unconvinced by this thesis, such as when he describes the Aricouri of South America as a people who "hardly show any sign of religion."[132] Like most Enlightenment philosophes, Diderot used the travel literature of his day with a critical eye and carefully distanced himself from European reports of cannibalism. Regarding the Amerindians of Brazil, he writes, "The interior of the country is inhabited by savage and idolatrous people who disfigure the face to appear more formidable to their enemies: *one purports that they are cannibals*."[133] Given that this is about Brazil, it is also likely indicative of the influence of Montaigne on Diderot's humanism.[134] We will see a similar circumspection as well as approbatory comments on the philosophy and religion of sub-Saharan Africans from Diderot's pen in the next section.

Jaucourt generally describes the Natives Americans as a robust, "well made," and agile peoples. The significant exception is the Inuit, about whom Jaucourt has nothing positive to say: "They are the savages of the savages and the only ones in America that we have never been able to tame; small, white, fat, and real cannibals. One observes humane though extraordinary manners among other peoples, but among these people everything is ferocious and nearly unbelievable."[135] The use of the verb *apprivoiser* (to tame) reveals the power of the early modern European association of some Native Americans with a wild, animallike nature. Though as Françoise Le Borgne points out, even these most "savage" of people possess the technical skill that allows them to live in their environment.[136] Jaucourt attributed what he viewed as the northern indigenous people's "shortcomings" to the climate, as he expressed similar sentiments in his description of the Native Canadians around Hudson's Bay as well as of the Laplanders.[137] He even quoted passages from Voltaire's *Essai sur l'histoire universelle* (*Essay on Universal History*) that strongly suggest polygenism: "They seem a particular species made for the climate that they inhabit, which they like, and which only they could like. . . . It seems that the Lapps are a new species of men."[138] Whether Jaucourt actually held a polygenist position is doubtful, because this is the only instance that I have been able to find of polygenism in all of his contributions to the *Encyclopédie* and also because of his radical condemnation of slavery, which was grounded in the argument that certain political rights follow from our common humanity. A more likely explanation for the inclusion of these polygenist arguments in this article is the sheer scale of his contribution to the *Encyclopédie* and his use of disparate material to complete as many articles as quickly as possible.

More salient than these aspects of prejudiced and racialist thought concerning the *Encyclopédie*'s coverage of Native Americans is the role that these peoples and their societies played in Enlightenment political and philosophical debates. From the perspective of political philosophy, by weighing Amerindian societies against Europe, the latter was often found wanting. For all the faults of a more "primitive" and "simple" lifestyle, the egalitarianism, freedom, and tranquility that supposedly reigned in much of the New World proved very enticing to thinkers who found the restrictions and vast inequalities of Europe troubling. It was undoubtedly, at least in part, reading about or experiencing firsthand the more egalitarian and free New World societies that awakened some European thinkers to the possibility of a different and more just social and political order. For example, Jaucourt invokes the Americas in his article "State of Nature" to support his argument that political society has its origin in a voluntary contract, concluding that political authority is only legitimate when it is based on the consent of the people.[139] He argues that the state of nature is a state of liberty and equality, though not one of license, because the laws of nature still hold even when there is no formal political structure. René Hubert uses this article and many others to argue that we can find the rudimentary elements of social science in the *Encyclopédie*, in that the encyclopedists used the comparative method and did not accept the travel literature at face value, but rather sought underlying patterns and connections between politics, religion, and customs.[140] While Hubert demonstrates that the encyclopedists were aware of increasing societal complexity across time and the relationship between modes of subsistence and societal customs and norms, his reading is sometimes anachronistic, in that he judges the encyclopedists' perspective to be less theoretically sophisticated than that of the nineteenth-century thinker Emile Durkheim.[141]

Jaucourt extols the state of nature only in so far as it is a state that grants considerable autonomy to individuals. One still finds such a state in much of the Americas, explains Jaucourt, where "there is no question of a king, of community, or of government."[142] People decide to form a society governed by laws because of three crucial elements that the state of nature lacks:

established laws upon which everyone agrees, an impartial judge, and a re-
straining power to carry out executive orders. While Jaucourt emphatically
denies that the state of nature is a Hobbesian state of war, he writes of the
"human depravity" that renders the civil state an attractive option in order
to better maintain law and order.[143] Nonetheless, the liberty and equality of
the state of nature are construed by Jaucourt as "natural rights" that impose
limitations upon all governments: "These same men [those who punish the
violation of laws in the state of nature], by entering a society, are only remit-
ting to society the powers that they had in the state of nature. Therefore, the
legislative authority of all governments can never extend beyond what the
public good demands."[144] Jaucourt expresses similar sentiments in the radical article "Government," in which he argues that sovereignty must emanate
from the free consent of the people. He describes Native Americans who do
not live under the domination of Peru or Mexico as societies exemplary of
the preservation of liberty.[145] The myth of a primitive, egalitarian, and
peaceful society that was equated with most of the Americas in the European imagination thus offered Jaucourt and many other philosophes am-
munition in the Enlightenment debate concerning the nature, origins, and
legitimacy of sovereign authority.

While "America" served as shorthand for the set of ideas contained
within the noble savage myth in these articles, in other entries, Jaucourt and
the other encyclopedists acknowledged the great diversity of New World
societies and peoples. In general, the coverage of North American indigenous peoples is scarce, despite the importance of the French presence there.
This is probably reflective of the power of the myth of a uniform "savage"
firmly planted in the French imagination by the mid-eighteenth century.[146]
Beyond the noble/ignoble savage tropes, the encyclopedists sought an explanation for the differences in ways of life and the technology of New World
societies outside of the providentialist perspective of "corruption" and
"heathenism." Jaucourt argued that the more "advanced" state of European
technology and civilization is due to geographical factors: the supposed
need to cultivate European land versus the natural bounty of American
soil.[147] Jaucourt was also more discriminating when it came to the peoples of
Central and South America, and, unsurprisingly, the powerful Aztec and
Incan empires in particular. Jaucourt described Tenochtitlan (Mexico City)
before European contact as "offering to the eyes the most beautiful monument of American industry."[148] His prose evokes a vivid picture of a thriving
commercial center, replete with the fruits of advanced technology. Not only

did Jaucourt laud the arts and sciences of this civilization, he also praised their moral principles, as the Mexican Emperor Moctezuma built palaces that served as centers to care for the physically disabled and less fortunate, as well as one for the cultivation of medicinal plants.[149] And in the article on the Mexican Empire, Jaucourt wrote of their "wise and humane civility," excepting their "barbarous" custom of sacrificing prisoners of war to the God Vitztzilipuzli.[150]

In other articles, the encyclopedists moved beyond the noble savage myth by giving Native Americans the agency to create and sustain a prosperous society. As Sankar Muthu has argued, envisioning all human beings as possessing the rational, emotive, and imaginative capacities to establish and transform social institutions and cultural practices is a remarkable feature of a strand of Enlightenment political thought that enabled a novel and robust anti-colonialist argument to develop.[151] This perspective is clearly present in Jaucourt's treatment of the Aztec civilization discussed above but also appears in certain political entries. For example, Jean-François de Saint-Lambert extolls the wise policies of the Peruvian leaders:

> The laws of Peru aimed to unite the citizens by the bonds of humanity. And, as in other legislations, they forbid men from harming one another, but in Peru they also constantly ordered them to do good. These laws, by establishing the community of goods (as far as this is possible outside of the state of nature), weakened the spirit of property, source of all vice. In Peru, spring days and holidays were the days when one cultivates the fields of the state, the field of an elderly person, or that of an orphan. Every citizen worked for the mass of citizens. He deposited the fruit of his labor in the storehouses of the state and, as a reward, he received the fruit of others' labor.[152]

While this is certainly not the dominant discourse concerning Native Americans in the *Encyclopédie*, it is nonetheless a significant one.

Yves Benot has argued that there is a marked shift in how the encyclopedists discuss colonialism if one compares the first seven volumes, published between 1751 and 1757, and the last ten published in 1765.[153] The importance and usefulness of colonies is more or less taken for granted in the first phase of the *Encyclopédie*, whereas more arguments are presented against colonialism in volumes 8 to 17, a phenomenon that Benot attributes to the crushing defeat of France during the Seven Years' War. The overall significance of new ways of fighting and understanding war has been squarely brought within the field of Enlightenment studies by Christy Pichichero's important work.[154] The centrality of the Seven Years' War in the transformation of Enlightenment political thought as a whole has been underestimated, and the *Encyclopédie* demonstrates that it was of fundamental significance in changing attitudes toward colonization and war, awakening the philosophes to the growing interconnectedness of peoples across the world.[155] It is worth noting that in the entry "Colony," François Véron de Forbonnais, an expert on economics, argues that the European colonies in the New World were established by and for the metropole and that they must therefore remain directly dependent upon it. He is blithely indifferent to the fate of the indigenous inhabitants, writing that these colonies were established for both commerce and agriculture and "consequently, it was necessary to conquer the territory and to chase away its former inhabitants in order to import new ones."[156] For Forbonnais, European commerce and agriculture render the rights and even lives of Native Americans completely dispensable, subsequently providing justification for the transatlantic slave trade. Benot remarks that this article would continue to be cited in the nineteenth and twentieth centuries to support European colonialism around the world. But many other encyclopedists developed a powerful anti-colonial perspective, such as Etienne-Noël Damilaville in his article "Population," where he argues against colonies not only from the standpoint of a prudential politics—colonies may weaken the metropole by depopulating it—but also from a morally principled position, maintaining that liberty is an inalienable right of humanity.[157] Benot's conclusion regarding the right to colonize in the *Encyclopédie* is similar to my principal argument regarding equality: the existence of both callously colonial and fervently anti-colonial voices in the text is what is most interesting.[158]

Jaucourt's antislavery sentiments will be discussed in the next section, but it is also noteworthy that Diderot's workhorse grew to despise Spanish atrocities in the New World. Jaucourt's remarks fit into a longer history of the notorious Black Legend of Spain, which sprang from Las Casas's indictment of the Spanish colonizers' actions in the Americas and was further developed by northern European Protestants. While his remarks clearly show an anti-Spanish bias, what is significant is that they expound an argument that applied to the rest of Europe. His criticism of Spanish colonialism grew at least partly from his aversion to religious fanaticism, which he did not only associate with Spain or Catholicism more generally, for that matter.[159] As we have seen, Jaucourt fervently defends religious toleration in his article "Superstition" and elsewhere but did not connect fanaticism only to Catholics, instead holding fanaticism to be "any excess of religion in general."[160] But Spain was particularly indictable for its intolerance, as Jaucourt defends the Japanese decision to banish Spanish missionaries from their country due to the intolerance that these same missionaries demonstrated in the Americas.[161] Elsewhere, Jaucourt rejects the principle that religious difference, or "idolatry," is sufficient grounds to justify war. After stating that it is unjust for a people to move to more fertile land using force, he says that "it is not less unjust to attempt an armed attack on the liberty, the lives, or the territory of another peoples, such as Native Americans, under the pretext of their idolatry."[162] The general formulation of this argument is obviously not just directed at the Spanish but also at all of the European powers who used religion as a pretext to wage war on the Native Americans. Jaucourt also speaks out against the greed of Europeans, and the Spanish in particular, which stands at the root of a shockingly inhumane history of death and slavery. He writes of the depopulation of the Lucayan Archipelago of the present-day Bahamas as a result of the "gruesome fury [of the Spanish] to enrich themselves."[163] Elsewhere, Jaucourt emphasizes the universality of moral principles, such as when he explains that underneath the superficial differences between European and Japanese religious and ethical principles lies a fundamental similarity: "Their principal commandments, which they call *divins*, are also ours; lying, lack of self-restraint, theft, and murder are forbidden. It is natural law reduced to positive precepts."[164]

By far the most striking instance of cultural relativism in the *Encyclopédie* is Abbé Jean Pestré's article "Canadians, Philosophy of the."[165] Pestré primarily relies on the immensely popular travelogue of the "baron de la Hontan," which he cites.[166] Louis-Armand de Lom d'Arce de Lahontan was a soldier who served in New France for many years and wrote a travelogue that contains a (supposedly real) dialogue between him and a Huron named Adario in which the relative merits of "civilized" and "savage" society are compared, with Adario gaining the upper hand in the argument. Following a brief description of the nature of Lahontan's work, Pestré clears up some confusion, stating that rather than being very hairy, as Europeans might suppose "savages" to be, Native Canadians are in fact hairless except on their heads and they are "born white, like us" and only become tanned as they age because they go about naked, grease themselves with oils, and paint their bodies with various colors that the sun burns into their skin. He also describes them as being generally taller than Europeans and well proportioned. Following these physical descriptions, he introduces Native Canadian customs with the clear intention of encouraging European readers to engage in some critical self-reflection:

> Upon seeing these savages at first glance, it is impossible to make a positive assessment of them because they have a fierce look, a rough comportment, and a manner so simple and reserved that it would be very difficult for a European who doesn't know them to believe that this behavior is a type of civility in their own fashion, which they maintain among themselves just as we maintain ours among ourselves, which they find rather ridiculous. They are not very amorous and show little affection. But notwithstanding this, they are kind and friendly and approach strangers and the less fortunate with a charitable hospitality that puts all the nations of Europe to shame.[167]

This culturally relativist standpoint formed part of the growth of what Siep Stuurman has called "global cross-cultural equality" in the Enlightenment, which was grounded in the anthropological vindication of cultural pluralism.[168]

Asserting that the Native Canadians are charitable, hospitable, and polite "in their own fashion" probably evokes an egalitarian sentiment in the reader; Native Canadians deserve to be respected. Pestré does not, however, uncritically praise Native Canadians, as he goes on to state that they are fickle, lazy, and vindictive. While they possess many virtues, they are nonetheless described as leading a "primitive way of life." Counterbalancing such harsh judgments is Pestré's laudatory assessment of Native Canadian philosophy, a concise summation of deistic principles. Although his summation is clearly a comment upon European philosophical concerns, the very act of attributing such ideas to non-Europeans enables Pestré to call into question the supposed superiority of Europeans in philosophical debate, as he remarks of the Native Canadians' philosophy: "All of this [the tenets of Native Canadian philosophy] is not so savage."[169] Walter Rex notes that while Diderot and d'Alembert were probably happy to accept Abbé Mallet's orthodox contributions in order to appease the censors, Abbé Pestré demonstrated a firm commitment to ideas central to the Enlightenment in the few articles he contributed to the *Encyclopédie*.[170]

But the pendulum could just as easily and swiftly swing the other way, from culturally relativist to Eurocentric or from the noble to the ignoble savage, not only when it came to those Native Americans who were hostile to the European presence on their territory, but also when the encyclopedists judged the actions of Native Americans to be superstitious. Even Jaucourt occasionally denigrated Native American peoples and societies; for example, when he writes of the Iroquois religion as being composed of nothing but "puerile superstition, to which their customs correspond."[171] Perhaps such animosity is to be expected from the foremost enemies of the former New France, but Jaucourt was also derogatory when it came to France's most important Native Canadian ally in the New World (until France's defeat in the Seven Years' War), the Hurons: "The language of these savages is guttural and very poor because they only know very few things."[172] Sometimes, the encyclopedists used this unflattering portrait of the New World to argue for the corrupting power of a priestly class in all times and places, revealing an anticlerical position typical of the philosophes. This is particularly prominent in d'Holbach's contributions to the *Encyclopédie*. In numerous ethnographic entries on Native American and African peoples, d'Holbach paints a picture of corrupt and cruel priests who take advantage of the credulity of the masses.[173] The parallels with contemporary Catholicism were more or less obvious. For example, in the entry "Michabou," defined as the name that the Algonquins and other Native Americans give to the Supreme Being, d'Holbach writes, "Nothing is more ridiculous than the ideas that these savages have of the divinity."[174] He continues to say that the Native Canadians believe the primeval mother had two sons, one of whom killed the other, and that they believe a universal flood destroyed all of humankind—comments clearly meant to stimulate self-reflection and doubt in the Christian reader. Although he uses this as a rhetorical device to attack Christian sensibilities, the reader is left with an image of the Canadian peoples as superstitious, naïve, and irrational.

Surveying all of these perspectives on Native Americans, we are presented with a multilayered image of New World peoples and societies. On the one hand, we have seen that the encyclopedists do not present a coherent picture of Native Americans as a distinct "racial" group. Aside from the article "Human Species," there are very few statements that link New World populations together based on what we would consider "racial" characteristics, and the encyclopedists only occasionally remark upon Native American physical features. This confirms the general consensus in the secondary literature that race in the eighteenth century was a concept in flux, transitioning from the dominant theological and environmentalist paradigm to a more "biological" and natural historical one. The encyclopedists' dominant concern is with Amerindian cultural characteristics. The tropes of the noble and ignoble savage frame the encyclopedists' descriptions of Amerindians, though of course these were not dichotomous positions in early modern thought. But the encyclopedists also grant agency to the Native Americans, particularly the Aztecs and Incas, reflecting the commonly held bias of sedentary societies against nomadism.

What is striking is that European superiority operates in the *Encyclopédie* in two ways, broadly speaking: for the more orthodox contributors, Native Americans are steeped in idolatry and barbarism and can only be saved by entering the fold of Christendom, while for the more secular encyclopedists, the Native Americans suffer from superstitious and cruel cultural and religious practices. For the latter group of writers, however, cultural relativism informs some of their entries on the New World, and they argue for the separation of morality and religion. They admire the cultural achievements of the Aztecs and Incas and use New World societies to buttress support for new social and political perspectives on humanity that were part of Enlightenment human science. While the encyclopedists certainly used Native Americans to make polemical points in the distinctively European philosophical, religious, and political debates of their day, we should not underestimate the importance and novelty of their attempt at an honest engagement with Amerindian cultures and peoples and the role that this engagement played in the development of secular theories of humanity and society. The significance of this perspective is made all the more relevant when we remember that Chambers did not deem the Native Americans worthy of any sustained attention in the *Cyclopaedia*, and when they did appear, it was as a monolithic whole representative of the primitive and savage. The greater prominence of Native Americans in the *Encyclopédie* probably resulted from the growing importance of philosophical history around mid-century. The *Encyclopédie* is fascinating precisely because it contains not only a much older and reductive view of the noble and ignoble savage, as well as of the idolatrous Other, but also a culturally relativist assessment of what the Amerindians can tell us about humans as religious, social, and cultural beings.

Sub-Saharan Africans: Natural History, Slavery, and Natural Rights

We will see many of the same themes in the encyclopedists' treatment of sub-Saharan Africans and the African diaspora as we saw in the previous section on Native Americans, but with one crucial difference: Africans were racialized in a much more thoroughgoing way than Native Americans. As we shall see, this racialization owes much to the transatlantic slave trade and chattel slavery. Interestingly for our discussion of equality, the philosophes' opposition to slavery helped to crystallize the idea of natural rights and politicize equality in a more radical way than arguably would have happened if the transatlantic slave trade and New World slavery had not expanded as rapidly as they did in the seventeenth and eighteenth centuries.[175] Thus we see that both racial classification and equality as a political concept were bound up in complicated ways with slavery in the early modern period. This is not to say that racial classification developed only as a justification for slavery, but rather that the institution gave skin color a salience it arguably would not otherwise have had.

There are four articles with the headword "Negre[s]" in the *Encyclopédie*. The first two articles, "Negre" (Natural History) and "Negres blancs" (Natural History), concern Blacks from the perspective of natural history, reflecting and entrenching the more highly developed racial discourse of the mid-eighteenth century. The last two articles concern the institution of slavery: "Negres" (Commerce) and "Negres, considérés comme esclaves dans les colonies de l'Amérique" (Negroes, considered as slaves in the colonies of America) [Unclassified].[176] We saw both elements—natural historical and socio-legal—in Chambers's article "Negroes" in the *Cyclopaedia*, but the institution of slavery was much more important to Chambers. In the Parisian successor, these elements are explicitly separated and more intricately developed, both as a result of the larger size of the *Encyclopédie* as a whole and because of the general growth in "scientific" interest in blackness around mid-century. As we have seen in Chapter 2, the Académie royale des sciences de Bordeaux launched a competition on the nature of blackness in 1739, of which Pierre Barrère's *Dissertation sur la cause physique de la couleur des nègres* (Dissertation on the physical cause of the color of nègres), published in 1741, was the most influential response.[177] It is certainly not coincidental that Bordeaux is a port city that became one of the most important hubs of colonial trade by the 1740s.[178] The Academy of Pau proposed a competition in 1743 to answer the question "Does the difference in climate where men are born contribute to that between their minds?"[179] And the Royal Society published John Mitchell's "An Essay upon the Causes of the Different Colours of People in Different Climates" in 1744.[180] Additionally, Pierre-Louis Moreau de Maupertuis's immensely popular *Vénus physique*, Abbé Prévost's synthesis of many different African travelogues, and the first three volumes of Buffon's ground breaking *Histoire naturelle* all appeared in the 1740s.[181] These developments help to put the *Encyclopédie*'s discussion of sub-Saharan Africans in relief.[182]

Johann Heinrich Samuel Formey, a descendant of Huguenot refugees in Germany, a member of the Academy of Berlin and the Royal Society, and the author of a number of books popularizing the philosophy of Christian Wolff, wrote the article "Negre" (Natural History).[183] The article is permeated by a language of difference, in that Formey states that Africans differ from all other men not only in the color of their skin, but also in "all of their facial features, the large and flat nose, the big lips, and the wool instead of hair." He states that they "seem to constitute a new species of men."[184] He goes on to compare the physical features of Africans with other principal populations of human beings, holding to the climatic explanation of physical difference. Upon seeing a Danish woman with white skin and blonde hair, Formey remarks that an observer "would not believe that the object he is seeing and the African he has just seen are both women."[185] He lifted significant sections from Maupertuis's *Vénus physique*, the most popular philosophical investigation that responded to the sensational visit of Mapondé, an albino boy of African descent to Paris in 1744.[186]

While Maupertuis was a monogenist who believed humanity's original color to be white, Formey only quoted the parts of *Vénus physique* that can easily be interpreted as polygenist.[187] He alludes to the monogenist/polygenist debate when he asks, "All of the people that we have just seen, such a diversity of men, did they all come from the same mother? We are not permitted to doubt it."[188] Formey seems to have been attracted to polygenism as an explanation for what he sees as the bewildering diversity of humankind and perhaps only stopped short of fully accepting it due to his Christian piety.[189] He also accepted slavery and attacked the leading philosophes in a number

of publications from 1749 onward.[190] Formey then surveys anatomical literature to defend the idea that black skin results from an enigmatic process in
the livers of Africans. White skin serves as a "colorless" standard, and blackness presents itself as a peculiarity that must be explained. The anonymous
author of "Negres blancs" (Natural History) struggles to understand the
cause of what we now know to be albinism, considering but rejecting the
theories that albinism results from a pregnant woman's stricken imagination, a kind of leprosy, or "commerce" between Black peoples and "large
monkeys." The author concludes by remarking that all of the peculiarities of
nature are not yet known, and neither is the interior part of Africa, where an
as yet unknown "species" (of men) may reside.[191]

The article "Negres, considered as slaves in the colonies of America" by
Jean-Baptiste-Pierre Le Romain, an engineer and colonial administrator in
the French colony of Granada, contains some of the most disparaging comments on Africans in the entire encyclopedia. He refers to Blacks as living
an "animal life" and remarks that they are "for the most part inclined to
libertinage, vengeance, theft, and lying," laying bare his prejudices as a colonial administrator.[192] He describes what practical tasks each nation of Africans excels in, demonstrating the centrality of slavery in the racialization
of Africans in early modern European culture. He essentially presents a
manual for slave owners, stating, for example, that "the Mines *negres* are
vigorous and highly adept at learning crafts," while "we employ . . . [the
Congolese] as house servants since they are often attractive."[193] As Michèle
Duchet has remarked, even for naturalists like Buffon, descriptions of enslaved people in New World colonies were central to their natural histories,
making their ethnologies just as useful to slave traders and owners as to
scholars interested in the natural history of the human species.[194] Le Romain ends his discussion with a summary of the infamous Code Noir, a
decree passed by Louis XIV in 1685 to govern the conditions of slavery in
French colonies, concluding a chilling article which, as Andrew Curran argues, divides Black peoples "by ethnicity into a typology of practical domination."[195] Last, the anonymously authored article "Negres" (Commerce)
refers to slavery as "odious" and "contrary to natural law" but focuses on the
history of the Atlantic slave trade, the ways in which Africans become enslaved, and the prices at which Europeans buy and sell them. Disregarding
the moral issues raised by slavery that opened the article, the author concludes, "Their hard nature demands that one does not treat them with
too much leniency but neither with too much severity."[196] Upon consulting

these articles, a reader could reasonably conclude that, due to their physical differences, Africans may form a distinct species from the rest of humankind and that their moral deficiencies render their enslavement comprehensible, perhaps even justifiable.

Antoine-Gaspard Boucher d'Argis, the austere legal expert of the *Encyclopédie*, contributed articles concerning the place of slavery in French law. In the article "Slave," Boucher d'Argis opens by stating that natural law declares that all peoples are free and that personal servitude results from the law of nations. He traces the history of slavery from ancient times, starting with the Spartans and Assyrians, with whom he speculates it may have originated, but dwelling particularly on slavery in ancient Rome. He acknowledges that slavery continued to be practiced under Christianity in the Middle Ages and contrasts this period with his contemporary France, promulgating the widespread notion of the "free soil" principle: as soon as slaves enter France and become baptized, they become free, not because of a formal law but because of a custom that has acquired the force of law.[197] The rest of the article contains a detailed explication of the Code Noir and of the Edict of October 1716, which regulated the entry of slaves into France. He covers all of this material in a dispassionate, uncritical manner. As discussed in Chapter 1, the Code Noir is remarkable when compared with later laws regulating slavery for *not* explicitly dealing with ethnicity or race. The Edict of October 1716 is arguably no more "racial" than Louis XIV's 1685 ordinance, but it had a paradoxical effect in that it extended the legality of slavery to metropolitan France at the same time that it provided a formal means for enslaved people to sue for their freedom.[198]

Diderot treats sub-Saharan Africans as a distinct racial group in his article "Human Species," but contrary to what we have seen in the previous articles, he denounces the institution of slavery. Following Buffon, he divides sub-Saharan Africans into two principal races or kinds, "Negres" and "Cafres," but considers both subdivisions to be part of "the race of blacks" (*la race des noirs*).[199] This "race of blacks" is juxtaposed to the "white race" of Europeans, and Diderot argues that within each race, one finds the same degree of physical diversity. As with the rest of humanity, Diderot's survey of all of the different sub-Saharan African ethnic groups is a combination of "biological" and aesthetic considerations. He attributes the cause of black skin primarily to the effects of climate and secondarily to customs and lifestyle. Diderot presents us with both the disquieting aspects of the racial theory of the Enlightenment and the germ of the movement's more progressive ethical goals: "Although in general, *negres* have little intelligence, they do not lack feeling. They are sensitive to good and bad treatment. We have reduced them, I won't say to the condition of slaves, but to that of beasts of burden; and we are reasonable! And we are Christians!"[200] Both equality and inequality went into the making of this article.[201]

A clear indication of the rising interest in blackness as an object of "scientific" investigation is the presence of an entire article devoted to the subject: Jaucourt's article "Skin of *negres*."[202] Jaucourt runs through the principal anatomists who have investigated the subject, first asserting that blackness resides in the reticular membrane between the epidermis and the skin proper, as established by Malpighi. He rejects the idea that the blood of Black peoples is dark, almost approaching black, as contrary to empirical evidence. He devotes considerable attention to Barrère's experiments, which held that blackness results from an abundance of black bile, but Jaucourt finds this explanation unsatisfactory, because the bile of Europeans is no different than the bile of Africans. Jaucourt gives the greatest credence to Buffon's perspective on the subject: a combination of the effects of climate, diet, and lifestyle produces variations in skin color, and he postulates that these traits can become heritable. The result is that Jaucourt, following Buffon, quite forcefully defends monogenism from a biological-materialist perspective: "According to this system, the human genus [*le genre humain*] is not composed of species essentially different from one another. Rather, there was originally only one species of men that multiplied and spread itself across the face of the earth, underwent various changes due to the influence of climate and differences in food and lifestyle."[203] In response to the objection that the equatorial Amerindian population is not as darkly pigmented as sub-Saharan Africans, Jaucourt argues that this is because this area of the world is not as hot as equatorial Africa; blackness is not just an effect of the sun but also of excessive heat in general. He acknowledges that experience proves that black people's children are as darkly pigmented as their parents even when they are born in a more temperate climate but postulates that the lightening of the skin is a very slow, almost imperceptible process. The fact that Barrère conducted his research on the black skin of deceased slaves in the French colony of Cayenne, which Jaucourt mentions, attests to the importance of the institution of slavery even in such "scientific" treatises on the subject of blackness and pigmentation. Nonetheless, the emphasis on external and alterable factors as the cause of blackness renders dark skin a relatively insignificant physical variation in a diverse but fundamentally unified human family.

In the articles on specific indigenous African populations, we find the same themes as those concerning the Native Americans: only occasional remarks on physical features and more lengthy descriptions of their cultural and religious practices. Once again, we find a mixture of noble and ignoble "savage" characteristics, often dependent upon the encyclopedist's assessment of contemporary Europe. In the first few volumes, Diderot contributed many articles in which he paints a portrait of entire nations following the dictates of natural religion, for example, of the Beninese: "These people practice no worship of God; they assert that this being, inherently good, does not require prayers or sacrifices"[204] And while he devotes a considerable amount of space to proving that Ethiopian philosophy ultimately derives from the older and more venerable ancient Egyptians, he praises their reasonableness in a thinly veiled attack on the excesses of Christianity: "Truth has nothing in common with the terror of the magical arts nor with the imposing apparatus of miracles and wonders. Temperance is the foundation of virtue. Excess strips man of his dignity."[205]

In addition to the "Negre" articles, the encyclopedists racialized sub-Saharan Africans more often than they did Native Americans. For example, the anonymous author of "Hottentots, The" explains that "the author of *Histoire naturelle* rightly says that the Hottentos are not *negres*. They are *Caffres*, who would only be tanned if they did not blacken the skin with fat and lard, which they mix to smear themselves with. They are olive-toned and never black."[206] The Khoekhoen are described as living in "awful filth" and as having a large and flat nose that results from the mother's flattening of the baby's nose shortly after birth. He describes a "deformity" that many of the women were afflicted with: a growth of skin from the pubic bone down to the middle of the thighs. By focusing on the "filth" and "odd" physical features of the Khoekhoen, the encyclopedist presents the reader with a portrait of an essentially bestial peoples. In the article "Samoyedic peoples, the" ("Samoyèdes, les, ou Samoiedes"), Jaucourt makes this connection explicit when he writes that "the races of the Samoyeds and the Hottentots appear to be the two extremes of our continent. And if one pays attention to the black breasts of Samoyed women and the overgrown pubic 'apron' that nature has given to the Hottentots, which extends to the midpoint of their thighs, one will have some idea of the varieties of our animal species."[207] The extremities of the continent seem to correspond with the extremities of the human species as they approach animals, in that Jaucourt presents the Samoyedic peoples of the far north of Russia, and thus also the Khoekhoen, as possessing an extreme simplicity, unable to form abstract concepts. Despite some redeeming moral qualities that they may possess, such as being strangers to murder and other vices, one is presented with a stereotypical image of the unthinking savage: "feeling alone guides them."[208]

In general, the geographical entries are very short and contain limited ethnographical information, but often a rather unflattering portrait of sub-Saharan Africans emerges. For example, in the article "Guiney," Jaucourt describes the natives as "idolatrous, superstitious, and living very dirtily, they are lazy, drunk, deceitful, unconcerned about the future, and insensitive to happy or unhappy events that please or upset other peoples."[209] Jaucourt also bestializes their appearance, or at least their hair: "Their skin is very black, their hair is real wool, and their sheep sport hair." D'Holbach, as we saw in some of his articles on Native Americans, in criticizing the superstition of such "primitive" peoples, also denigrates certain sub-Saharan Africans: "If one believes the unanimous testimonies of many travelers and missionaries who have frequented the Jagas, no nation has ever taken cruelty and superstition so far. In effect, they present us with the strange phenomenon of the most atrocious inhumanity that is authorized and even commanded by religion and by law."[210] The trope of the ignoble savage combined both the image of an unthinking peoples as well as a depraved, inhumane cruelty and can be found in various articles on sub-Saharan Africans in the *Encyclopédie*.

As we have seen in Diderot's article "Benin," the encyclopedists also used African societies to promote their own philosophical and political agendas. Contrary to the image of the near-total savagery of the Khoekhoen we have just seen, d'Holbach argues that the Khoekhoen have an enlightened political tradition. In the article "Kraals," he describes the mobile villages in which the nomadic Khoekhoen live. He writes that the leader of the "Kraals" is a heritable position, but the leader cannot change the established body of laws, thus the article serves as a hidden defense of constitutional monarchy. This time, the perspective of an enlightened and free Europe versus an unenlightened and despotic Other is reversed: "That is why one sees Hottentots living under a very prudent and wise government, whereas some people, who believe themselves to be much more enlightened than them, groan under oppression and tyranny."[211] In describing the sovereign rulers of a vaguely described "nation of Africa," d'Holbach indicts the self-serving

French monarchy but belies the common association of excessive heat and despotic government in Enlightenment thought: "Unlike ordinary kings of these climates, he governs with the greatest moderation, his laws seem dictated by love for the public good and he is, so to speak, only the voice of his nation."[212] While clearly positioned within European political and philosophical debates, the encyclopedists occasionally granted indigenous sub-Saharan African peoples the agency to create and sustain prosperous societies.

As with the issues of equality as a political concept and colonialism, the *Encyclopédie* does not present a unified view on the slave trade and slavery. Jean Ehrard has examined forty-eight articles in which slavery or the slave trade could be reasonably assumed to be mentioned, ranging from obvious candidates such as "Slavery" and "Negres" to articles concerning slave-produced products central to the European economy, such as tobacco and indigo. Of the articles he samples, fifteen do not mention slavery, twenty mention it neutrally, ten condemn it more or less vigorously, and three support it.[213] We have already discussed the most important articles that support the institution. Jaucourt contributed the most fascinating and forceful articles condemning slavery, serving, as he so often did, as the compassionate humanist of the *Encyclopédie*.[214]

We see, in fact, a remarkable transformation in Jaucourt's thought between these articles, since "Slavery" was published in 1755 whereas "Slave Trade" ("Traite des negres") appeared a decade later. In the first article, Jaucourt relies primarily on Montesquieu's *The Spirit of the Laws*, taking the reader through a history of slavery that begins with a conjectural reconstruction of the primeval past and moves through Biblical times, ancient Greece and Rome, and the Middle Ages and finally discusses colonial slavery. The tone of the article is set early on: "All men are born free; . . . nature had made them all equal."[215] Given the overwhelming reliance on Montesquieu, one must keep in mind that Montesquieu was arguably the most important thinker to put slavery on the agenda of the philosophes from mid-century onward, representative of the beginning of the philosophes' unease with the issue. But Montesquieu presents a contradictory image of slavery, declaring it to be both against nature and natural: "As all men are born equal, one must say that slavery is against nature, although in certain countries it may be founded on a natural reason, and these countries must be distinguished from those in which even natural reasons reject it, as in the countries of Europe where it has so fortunately been abolished."[216] He struggled with the issue, and his unease was a necessary step in the transition of some Europeans' attitude from one of indifference to one of outrage against the institution.[217] It is remarkable that in his private notes on the institution of slavery, he was markedly more antislavery than anything that can be found in his published works, because he refers to the war of slaves in ancient Rome to acquire their freedom as "the most just that has ever been undertaken, because it meant to prevent the most violent abuse of human nature ever engaged in."[218]

As we saw with Jaucourt's transformation of Montesquieu's political philosophy, he reconstructs chapter 15 of *The Spirit of the Laws* to make the condemnation of slavery even more emphatic than in the original.[219] Jaucourt argues that slavery cannot be established by the laws of war, acquisition, or birth because it violates the inherent dignity of human beings: "Thus, everything favors leaving to man the dignity which is natural to him. Everything cries out to us that we cannot take away that natural dignity which is liberty. The rule of the just is not based on power but on that which conforms with nature. Slavery is not only a humiliating state for he who is subjected to it, but for humanity itself, which is degraded by it."[220] As in Montesquieu's opposition to torture, the opposition to slavery is grounded in the argument of the self-evidence of the freedom and equality natural to humanity.[221]

The concept of natural equality is vested with real political consequence: "Whatever great injuries one has received from a man, once one has reconciled with him, humanity does not permit reducing him to a condition where there no longer remains any trace of the natural equality of all men and, by consequence, to treat him as an animal of which one is the master to use as he pleases."[222] While Jaucourt's article forcefully condemns slavery, it should be noted that the article contains a similar tension as in Montesquieu's original between arguing that the institution is more explicable and more "natural" in certain places, though it still goes against nature: "Notice that in despotic states, where one is already under political slavery, civil slavery is more bearable than elsewhere ... but although slavery in these countries is, in a manner of speaking, founded on natural reason, it is nonetheless true that slavery is against nature."[223] Nonetheless, as Dan Edelstein has shown, before following Montesquieu here, Jaucourt distances himself from the Baron de La Brède.[224] In response to the question "are there no cases or places where slavery derives from the nature of things?," Jaucourt assertively states "there are none," which we do not find in Montesquieu.[225]

Jaucourt's 1765 article "Slave Trade" immediately establishes a more rad-ical tone that he sustains throughout the article: "Slave trade is the purchase of *negres* that Europeans make on the coasts of Africa to employ these un-fortunates in their colonies as slaves. This purchase of *negres* to reduce them to slavery is a negotiation that violates religion, morality, natural laws, and all the rights of human nature."[226] Gone is the awkward and inconsistent argument regarding the naturalness of slavery in certain climates. He ar-gues that slavery violates the "laws of humanity and of equity" and, most fundamentally, it corrupts humankind's inalienable right to liberty. Jau-court translated almost all of these passages from the work of the relatively obscure Scottish thinker George Wallace.[227] In Wallace's original, the con-cept of political equality is central to his attack on slavery, when he declares that "inequality . . . is derived from political and arbitrary institutions alone."[228] The idea of common humanity grounds Jaucourt's argument against slavery: "It is thus an obvious inhumanity on the part of the judges in the free countries where he [the slave] is transported not to immediately emancipate him by declaring him free, because he is their fellow human, having a soul like them."[229] This appeal to the inner similarity of Africans, indeed of all human beings, became central to the nascent idea of human rights in the post-1750 period.[230] Jaucourt, following Wallace, even goes on to argue that the European colonies in the Americas should be destroyed because of the human suffering they cause. He was thus the first French thinker to make the step from antislavery to anti-colonialism, and equality lies at the center of his argument.[231]

In addition to the politics of slavery, another intellectual matter was cen-tral to the encyclopedists' discussion of sub-Saharan Africans, and that is how to account for physical differences within humanity in a theory of gen-eration and inheritance. In Buffon and Diderot's thought, race served, first and foremost, to place humanity within nature's purview as a species that possesses a long history, susceptible to the effects of climate. Race was important in Enlightenment life science because it incorporated new under-standings of heredity, generation, and deep time into the study of human-kind. The preexistence strand of preformationism was the dominant theory of generation in the late seventeenth and early eighteenth century, but this theory, if taken to its logical conclusion, necessitated a polygenist account of the varieties of the human species, which conflicted with the Bible. Formey advanced the preexistence theory in his article "Negre" (Natural History), asserting that a (white) Eve contained all of the eggs of all future human beings and that providence would have intervened at a certain moment to initiate the creation of more darkly pigmented peoples.[232]

As Phillip Sloan remarks, it is no coincidence that the two most prominent thinkers in the 1740s to reject preexistence, Maupertuis and Buffon, were also the thinkers who advanced an explanation of human varieties using a naturalistic account.[233] Maupertuis, Buffon, and the other philosophes who followed in their footsteps rejected preexistence because the theory necessitated divine intervention to explain human diversity and because it failed to account for the resemblance between parents and offspring.[234] Unlike Maupertuis and Diderot, Buffon did not advance an epigenetic theory of reproduction; he rejected preexistence and postulated that each species is the product of an "interior mold," and reproduction a result of the combination of "organic molecules" spread throughout an organism.[235] Once the Enlightenment philosophes rejected preexistence (and some even embraced epigenesis), the road was open to speculating that the environment had acted on species, including humanity, to introduce changes that might have become hereditary. Precisely how this worked remained nebulous, since rigorous theories of inheritance would not be introduced into the life sciences until the merging of Mendelian genetics with Darwinian theory in the early twentieth century. But debate on generation, vitalism, and materialism intensified from the 1740s with observations of the regenerative abilities of the freshwater polyp and experiments on heredity conducted by Maupertuis, among others.[236]

The issue came down to how far a given thinker was willing to take materialist monism. Diderot altered Louis-Jean-Marie Daubenton's article "Animal" to include Buffon's materialism: "The living and the animate, instead of being a metaphysical degree of beings, is a physical property of matter."[237] In such a worldview, all living forms, including human forms, must be situated historically and there are no fixed and eternal races. However, reducing life to matter in motion and complex organization meant that some thinkers adopted naturalistic explanations for inequality: some peoples are less highly developed because of a less complex organization of cerebral matter.[238] These contradictions in Enlightenment thought would go on to underpin similar tensions in nineteenth- and early twentieth-century atheists' writings on race, when some irreligious writers used Darwinian theory to argue that the races are separately evolved and form a hierarchy, while other atheists argued that we all share a common ancestor and races are impermanent, superficial adaptations.[239]

We must also position these debates on heredity and generation within new understandings of time and history. Darwin's *On the Origin of Species* (1859), Charles Lyell's *The Geological Evidences of the Antiquity of Man* (1863), and John Lubbock's *Pre-historic Times* (1865) constitute what has been called the mid-nineteenth-century "time revolution."[240] But these nineteenth-century naturalists and geologists were continuing the work of their eighteenth-century predecessors, particularly Buffon, who coined the phrase "the dark abyss of time."[241] In his article on fossils, d'Holbach remarked that perhaps no other phenomenon in natural history occupied the attention of naturalists as much as the discovery of fossils of marine life that can be found in great quantities on the tops of mountains and in the depths of the earth.[242] Paolo Rossi's brilliant study demonstrates how such evidence combined with non-European histories and chronologies in the seventeenth and eighteenth centuries to cast doubt on a literal interpretation of the Bible, Genesis in particular, as the true history of the earth and humanity.[243] Buffon was perhaps the most influential Enlightenment thinker to integrate these various cosmological, geological, biological, and historical questions into a new "human science."[244] Although Buffon's chapter "Varieties in the Human Species" and Diderot's summary of it are unmistakably Eurocentric, their chief significance lies in the fact that they place humanity within a history of nature alongside animals that eschews the rigid classifications of Linnaean natural history.[245] Jacques Roger eloquently explains the importance of Buffon's accomplishment: "Buffon did not yet possess the modern concept of 'populations,' but he was at least rid of the old logical categories of classification and creationism that they assumed, which underlay all naturalist thought at the beginning of the eighteenth century."[246] We must also position the Enlightenment concept of race within an intellectual revolution that eschewed biblical creationism and genealogies, and placed humanity in the ambit of nature.

China: Venerable Civilization or Despotism?

Compared with sub-Saharan Africa and the African diaspora, China and the Chinese occupied a very different realm in the imaginative geography of the Enlightenment. In the brief entry "China," Diderot states: "The Chinese are very industrious. They love the arts, sciences, and commerce: the usage of paper, printing, and gun powder were known there long before we knew of them in Europe."[247] This tone of veneration and respect is a well-known feature of European discourse on China in the early modern period. But it was contested. Particularly in the second half of the eighteenth century, an increasing number of thinkers began to question the status of China as an advanced civilization. The *Encyclopédie* captures both perspectives. The ancient civilization is at times exalted as a society of virtuous citizens ruled by philosopher-administrators and emperors who have long cultivated the arts and sciences; at other times, the empire is scorned as a despotism of slavish and lazy subjects who, despite some past achievements, have succumbed to the forces of inertia. Regarding the concepts of race and cross-cultural equality, what is most remarkable in the encyclopedists' treatment of China is that the philosophes more readily considered the Chinese as fully cultural beings, and thus fully human, compared with their treatment of Native Americans and sub-Saharan Africans. This reflects the long-standing bias of sedentary societies against nomadic and seminomadic peoples rather than the force of a proto-racial worldview, as evidenced by the acknowledgement of the sophistication of certain Native American and African civilizations.[248] The civilization-barbarism-savage divides were more salient in the minds of the Enlightenment philosophes than racial groupings or racial determinism. Nonetheless, the encyclopedists racialized Native Americans and, especially, sub-Saharan Africans more often than they did the Chinese. By this, I mean that the encyclopedists more often described and explained the physical traits of Native Americans and Africans than those of the Chinese. In the shorter geographic entries on countries or regions of Africa and the Americas, the encyclopedists occasionally described the physical features of the indigenous inhabitants, whereas entries on specific regions or cities in China rarely contain any mention of physical traits. I will elaborate on this point below.

Although the Chinese are "less racialized" than Native Americans or Africans, the encyclopedists nonetheless do consider the Chinese as a racial group on at least two occasions in the work. Diderot, in "Human Species," describes the Chinese as follows: "The Chinese have well-proportioned limbs, are tall and fat with a wide and round face, small eyes, large eyebrows, raised eyelids, a small and flat nose, and a sparse beard. Those who live in the southern provinces are brown and of a darker complexion than the others. The inhabitants of the middle of the empire are white. Elsewhere, these characteristics vary, but in general these people are meek, peaceful, lazy, superstitious, submissive, slaves, and ceremonious."[249] As with other racial groups, the implicit focus is on men—indicated by the mention of the beard—and more than purely physical or biological factors go into the making of the Chinese as a racial group.

The most significant example of the racialization of the Chinese in the *Encyclopédie* can be found in Guillaume d'Abbes's article "Face," which is an exposition on the aesthetics of the human face. His main concern is with the relativity of beauty, and he uses "Chinese" facial characteristics to demonstrate his point:

> Do you see that Chinese woman? She is more beautiful than her country could ever imagine; the rumor of her charms reverberates across an empire as civilized and more powerful than any other. You demand large, well-shaped and wide-open eyes, and this one has very small ones, extremely far apart from one another, and her eyelids cover the greatest part of them. In your opinion, the nose should be well made and elevated, notice how short and crushed this one is. You demand a round and chubby face, while hers is flat and square; small ears, but she has tremendously large ones; a slim and pleasing waist, but she has a heavy and bulky one.[250]

Elsewhere in this article, d'Abbes is culturally relativist, stressing that a French person in China, or a Chinese person in France, would be considered a curiosity but rarely beautiful. But he then goes on to assert that the natural and original human form is the European and that Chinese physical features result from human intervention, a surprisingly common trope in the eighteenth-century understanding of human physical diversity.[251] The place of women in d'Abbes's article is significant: eighteenth-century men often commented upon women's beauty, which fits into the privileging of the physical over other features in a novel classificatory system.[252] D'Abbes's Eurocentrism is clear, but he takes the idea of aesthetic relativism seriously, as he doubts the possibility of achieving an objective, universal standard. Additionally, after presenting a racialized picture of the Chinese, he remarks "Do not go on to retort that these are barbarians. The Asians, and among them the Chinese, are not barbarian at all."[253]

Aside from these articles, what is, on the whole, remarkable about the encyclopedists' treatment of China and the Chinese is the relative lack of concern with the physical features of this population and thus the absence of a racialized discourse. The main concern of the encyclopedists, and that of the philosophes more generally, was to assess the cultural and intellectual achievements of this ancient civilization, which rivalled Europe in its "sophistication" and longevity. The *Encyclopédie* captures both the dominant Sinophilism of mid-century and the rise in criticism of this perspective that would dominate from the 1770s and 1780s onward, though the reference work is unique in that it was one of the few to privilege China above Europe.[254] The Sinophiles were fascinated by Chinese history, law, and ethics, partially because this ancient civilization challenged Christian arrogance in all of these fields, thus providing European freethinkers with material for their criticism of religious and political authority.[255]

In his article "China," Diderot uses China in a thinly veiled criticism of despotic (French) kings. Perhaps the most important use of China in enlightened critical thought was to demonstrate that morality and virtue were not the special reserve of Christians. This idea was most famously expressed by Pierre Bayle, when he argued that a society of virtuous atheists was possible and may in fact really exist in China and other parts of Asia.[256] Diderot's appropriation of Bayle's ideas concerning "Asian" philosophy is manifest in the article "Asians, Philosophy of the Asians in General."[257] Saint-Lambert furthers the secularization of virtue advanced by early Enlightenment thinkers, such as Bayle, in the *Encyclopédie* in his discussion of honesty: "Manco Cápac and Confucius were also legislators and they rendered men more moderate and more humane. They formed honest citizens. The love of order and of the fatherland were a way of being for their disciples, a habit confounded with nature and, in some circumstances, an active passion. In the span of five hundred years, there were more honest and happy men in China and Peru than there were in the rest of the world since its birth."[258] By emphasizing the rationalism and high ethical standards of Chinese civilization (Confucianism in particular), the Jesuits had unwittingly provided heterodox Enlightenment thinkers like Diderot, Saint-Lambert, and d'Holbach with fuel to feed a secular and atheistic flame.[259]

In addition to venerating Confucian morality, the encyclopedists held a deep respect for the ancient Chinese tradition of learning and the cultivation of the arts and sciences. The anonymous author of the article "Library" is unwavering in his praise: "It is certain that all the nations cultivate the sciences, some more and others less; but there is none where knowledge is more esteemed than among the Chinese."[260] In addition to praising Chinese intellectual culture, many philosophes greatly admired the Chinese meritocratic system of state examinations. The anonymous author of the article "Literary or Spiritual Nobility" stressed this point, contrasting the hereditary

nobility of Europe to the Chinese meritocratic system: "In China, one recognizes only men of letters as truly noble. But this nobility is not hereditary;
the son of the highest-ranking officer of the state remains among the masses
if he does not have personal merit to support him."[261] Many of the encyclopedists praised what they believed was a general level of enlightenment that
may even have surpassed that of Europe, owing mainly to a superior system
of general education. The merchant and man of letters Joachim Faiguet de
Villeneuve adopted this perspective in his article "Studies," in which he argues that only the Ancient Spartans and the Chinese have managed to do
what many of his contemporaries believed to be theoretically impossible: the
creation of a philosophical people.[262] Drawing on the educational treatise of
Charles-Irénée Castel, Abbé de Saint-Pierre, Villeneuve argues that they have
achieved this by instituting a meticulous educational system that moves beyond the ignorance of past ages, questioning the authority of tradition. Many
of the encyclopedists thus used Chinese history and philosophy to criticize
Europe, arguing that a natural religion that fostered a humanist ethical system could produce a virtuous and prosperous society.

As is well known, however, the period of Sinophilism terminated before
the century's end and some Sinoskeptic voices can be heard in the *Encyclopédie*. In his elegant study *Machines as the Measure of Men*, Michael Adas
convincingly argues that even though many Enlightenment thinkers en-
thusiastically praised many aspects of Chinese civilization, the era's most
fervent Sinophiles were skeptical about one thing: their scientific and
technological achievements.[263] Even the Enlightenment's most important
agitator and defender of the "cult of China" in Europe, Voltaire, argued
that China was centuries behind Europe in astronomy, chemistry, and
mathematics. The encyclopedists venerated the scientific and technological
achievements of the ancient Chinese but, true to Adas's assessment, they
argued that the Chinese had stagnated and now lagged behind Europe in
science. D'Alembert and Johann Heinrich Samuel Formey, in their article
on astronomy, remark with a certain admiration that astronomy has been
practiced in China since time immemorial, but they go on to state that the
Jesuits, particularly the accomplished mathematicians among them, doubt
the accuracy of Chinese astronomy. The authors say that astronomy in
China has been secured on a more solid footing after the Jesuits' involvement in Chinese intellectual life than it previously had been.[264] The transition from Sinophilism to a more distant and skeptical attitude is reflected
in Jaucourt's articles.[265] In his article "Punishment," Jaucourt praises the

Chinese justice system for its humaneness and rationality due to two factors: the precision of degrees of punishment and the principle of determining the punishment based on the severity of the crime.[266] Yet in Jaucourt's discussions of Chinese religious beliefs and practices, he disparages them as superstitious and irrational, for example, in his discussion "'Fe, Fo, Foé' (Buddha)," whom he states is the idolatrous God of some of the Chinese, Japanese, and Tartars. He describes the worship of this God as "ridiculous" and "thus the most fitting for this people."[267]

Perhaps the most important article on China in the entire *Encyclopédie* and the one that captures the diversity of viewpoints of the work as a whole is Diderot's entry "Chinese, Philosophy of the." Diderot was, on the whole, skeptical of the reverence that many of his contemporaries had for China and would become more firmly "Sinophobic" in his later life. Although the balance of Diderot's article on Chinese philosophy certainly tilts toward the Sinophobic, Huguette Cohen's argument that whatever praise Diderot has for China in this article was only to fool the censors is a bit too simplistic.[268] Given Diderot's own humanistic ethics, there is no reason to doubt his sincerity when he writes of Confucian morality: "This school was very numerous. From it came a mass of skilled men and honest citizens. Its philosophy was more in action than in discourse."[269] Diderot is indeed critical of Chinese natural philosophy and metaphysics, but he lauds Confucius's ethical teachings, because among Confucius's principal aims were "that love of the truth and of virtue strengthen in the heart and that conduct toward others be decent and honest."[270] But, similar to d'Alembert and Formey in the article "Astronomy," Diderot doubts the current state of Chinese artisanal and scientific skills. While he grants that they have a very long history of impressive inventions and manufactures, "they do not have the genius of invention and of discovery that shines in Europe today."[271] He describes the "Oriental mind" as being "calmer, lazier, more preoccupied with base needs" than its Western counterpart. The result, as Diderot sees it, is a stadial theory of human progress through history where Europe has come to dominate: "The sciences and the arts demand a more vigorous activity, a curiosity that does not tire of searching, a kind of inability to be satisfied. We are more suited to this and it is not surprising that although the Chinese are more ancient, we have so far surpassed them."[272]

While such entries reveal the Eurocentrism that was often part of the philosophes' analysis of non-Western societies, the picture of China that emerges from the *Encyclopédie* as a whole is more complex than one of simple Sinophobia or Sinophilism. Nor can this picture be reduced to a one-dimensional will to dominate, as influentially described by Edward Said.[273] The encyclopedists' engagement with Chinese philosophy, history, and science conforms better to the more nuanced position of J. J. Clarke, who argues that, while knowledge of the East must be understood within the framework of the history of colonialism and domination, it cannot be reduced to that history either. He argues that "in the Western context it [Orientalism] represents a counter-movement, a subversive entelechy, albeit not a unified or consciously organized one, which in various ways has often tended to subvert rather than to confirm the discursive structures of imperial power."[274] While the philosophes' engagement with China, like that of the Jesuits, the Franciscans, or the Dominicans, reflects European concerns above all, to stop there would be to miss the significance of the cultural encounter between West and East. As David Allen Harvey notes, "Whatever the specific image of China a particular Western observer came away with, the very fact of China's existence, and the great antiquity and refinement of its civilization, posed a challenge to Europe's sense of its identity and place in the world."[275] China presented Europeans with social forms that they recognized as a civil society proper to humankind's nature. Imagining cross-cultural equality thus arguably came more readily in the case of the Chinese than with the image of nomadic or semi-nomadic American and African peoples that dominated the European imagination, even if this did not often accord with reality.

Conclusion

The perceived commensurability between the civil societies of East and West meant that these were placed on a par with each other, in contradistinction to the more "savage" peoples and lands of Africa and America. It is interesting to note that even before the hardening of racial categories in the nineteenth century, we see that Europeans were more interested in the physical features of Native Americans and, especially, of Africans than of the Chinese. This is very revealing, as it demonstrates the centrality of power differentials in the generation of racial theory. The encyclopedists took note of physical differences between Europeans and East Asians, but the focus in numerous geographic entries is on cultural themes. As Michael Keevak has noted, describing non-Europeans as "white" was as much evaluative as descriptive, and Europeans ascribed the label "white" to East Asians as a marker of their perceived level of civilization.[276] Diderot described the Chinese living in the south of the empire as "brown and of a darker complexion than the others" while those from the middle of the empire were "white."[277]

The idea of a civilized-savage divide that exists in both space and time, and the inequalities associated with this divide, are clearly present in the encyclopedists' engagement with China, Africa, and the Americas. In his article "Galles," which is on a nomadic peoples bordering the Ethiopian civilization, Jaucourt explains that the sedentary-nomadic frontier is something to be found throughout history in many places of the world: "As soon as they feel the weakest, they retire with their livestock to the bottom of the country and place a desert between them and their enemies. It is like this that the Huns, the Pannonian Avars, the Goths, the Vandals, and the Normans were formerly seen spreading terror among the civilized nations of Europe, and the Oriental Tartars made themselves masters of China."[278] In the article "Japan," Jaucourt relies primarily on Voltaire's *Essai sur les mœurs* to describe how Europe has progressed and the East has stagnated: "The peoples of the Orient were once superior to our Western peoples in the arts of the mind and of the hand. But how we have won back lost time, Mister Voltaire adds! . . . I say that these [European] countries have become the foremost countries on earth. At the present, Oriental people are only barbarians or children in the fine arts despite their antiquity and all that nature has done for them."[279] What we see, then, is what I call "soft" Eurocentrism, in which Europe is theorized as the culmination of progress in history, but "soft" because this was not yet a racialized idea—other peoples were believed to possess the capabilities of becoming more like Europeans. China was perhaps the most powerful reminder to eighteenth-century Europeans that Europe was one civilization among many and that other ways of life can be as reasonable and virtuous as the European or Christian way. But the upshot is that the nations of the world were unequally divided along the arrow of time.[280]

I began this chapter by noting that equality as a political concept mattered more to Diderot and his circle than it did to Ephraim Chambers. Yet, we have also seen that a reader of the *Encyclopédie* would have found in Le Romain's articles a practical guide for trading and owning slaves. With well over one hundred contributors, such contradictory viewpoints within the *Encyclopédie* mainly reflect the nature of the work as a debating platform. This style of presenting information would have reinforced one of the central tenets of Enlightenment philosophy—that each individual must decide for him or herself what is most reasonable or ethical given the current state of knowledge. Yet the fact that by the 1760s and 1770s the term *"encyclopédistes"* became synonymous with those supportive of Enlightenment philosophy betrays where the sympathies of many of the contributors lay, particularly the most prolific encyclopedists, such as Jaucourt and Diderot. Some present-day scholars take the Enlightenment as a whole, and the *Encyclopédie* specifically, to task for its Eurocentrism and its failures in light of what we have learned from the ethical and epistemological teachings of postcolonialism. But when we position the work within the struggles for freedom of expression and conscience, and within the Enlightenment program of humane reform more generally at mid-century, the picture takes on a different hue.

Approaching this encyclopedia from the general reader's perspective, we can discern a number of recurring themes that are distinctive of Enlightenment thought more generally. First, many of the encyclopedists transformed equality into a foundational concept. In Jaucourt's influential article "Natural Equality" and in numerous others, we have seen that the encyclopedists brought the idea of equality in both the political and social spheres to the center of discussion of what a good and just society might be. While we should be aware of the limits the encyclopedists placed on the concept, their engagement with and commitment to a certain form of egalitarianism helped break the "absolutist mold of politics" that characterized French history after 1750.[281] Second, cross-cultural equality takes center stage in numerous articles by a diverse group of contributors. From the articles praising the sage laws of precontact Central and South America to those lauding the profound humanity of the Chinese, Europe is at times decentered from her position as the locus of all that is just and virtuous. There are also significant differences between how the encyclopedists wrote about the Native Americans and Africans, both of whom were widely considered "savage" or "barbarian" by eighteenth-century Europeans. In general, Diderot and his collaborators recognized the great diversity of Native American societies in terms of modes of subsistence in contrast to African societies, which were more uniformly described as "savage" (either noble or ignoble). This is rather surprising, given that Europeans had to respect local African political and cultural authority throughout the entire early modern period and that they were aware of the great traditions of learning in Ethiopia and Timbuktu, for example.[282] This difference between European perspectives on the Americas and Africa can perhaps partially be explained by the dominance of African-based slavery by the mid-eighteenth century and the fact that European ethnographies of African peoples were most often based on the diasporic communities of enslaved Africans in the New World.[283]

Last, the encyclopedists were instrumental in entrenching racial classification in Enlightenment thought, thus reinforcing the trend that began in earnest at the beginning of the century of including human beings in natural history. There were clear inegalitarian sources and consequences of this intellectual innovation, as the encyclopedists racialized those groups they deemed inferior, such as the Native Americans and, above all, sub-Saharan Africans, in contrast to the venerably "civilized" Chinese. It is undeniable that the salience of physical features grew as a result of the expansion of the transatlantic slave trade. Yet the Enlightenment philosophes most firmly committed to an egalitarian politics, such as Diderot, also contributed to racial classification. This was but one piece that went into forming the puzzle of modern race thinking. The naturalization of the human species was also a necessary part of the development of racial classification, and it seems that this goes part of the way in explaining how eighteenth-century thinkers who were committed to a set of egalitarian Enlightenment values could contribute to a body of thought that would go on to have disastrous consequences.

The article "Race," like all dictionary or encyclopedia entries on the concept before the nineteenth century,[284] does not offer a recognizably modern definition, defining race as "extraction, lineage" and connecting it to the nobility in particular.[285] Jaucourt actually uses this article to offer a subtle criticism of the inegalitarian principle that lies at the heart of premodern racialist thinking: "It is a happy present of fortune to have a beautiful name, but one must know how to wear it."[286] He then quotes from Plutarch's *Moralia* the story of Harmodius's insulting Iphicrates for his lowly birth, to which Iphicrates responded, "My family history begins with me, but yours ends with you."[287] Nobility also results from noble deeds, not just noble birth.

The *Encyclopédie* was coeval with Buffon's masterpiece *Histoire naturelle,* and as we have seen, Diderot and other encyclopedists relied heavily on Buffon not only for incidental articles but also for the epistemology that underpins the view of nature that dominates in the *Encyclopédie.*[288] The Buffonian revolution of a truly historical understanding of nature impacted how some of his fellow philosophes understood not only the history of the earth but also the history and psychology of humanity, traces of which can be found in the *Encyclopédie.*[289] And we have seen that explaining both humanity's unity and diversity using epigenesis to attack preformationism was an important part of a strand of Enlightenment life science. D'Holbach made a significant contribution to the mid-century shift in the understanding of the history of the world and of humanity in which nature exists in time and presents us with structures that may appear constant but are in fact incessantly changing.[290] In the article "Fossils," D'Holbach notes the inadequacy of the most common explanations for the existence of fossils: the theory of "plastic forces" (that God or nature created fossils in the shape of animals or plants) and the Noahic Flood.[291] It should be noted, however, that a coherent theory bringing together geological time, fossils, and the natural history of the human species remained elusive in the eighteenth century.[292]

This fits with the picture we have of the radical role that the concept of nature could play in the Enlightenment, as philosophes committed to naturalizing the human species and thus racializing it as well, often, though not always, denounced the profound social and political inequalities of their societies. But a striking result of what we have analyzed is that the encyclopedists were less likely to racialize those they deemed more "civilized," especially the Chinese. When the encyclopedists revered the cultural and scientific achievements of a given peoples, they were more inclined to consider their minds rather than their bodies. But we should also remember that the presence of such articles as "Canadians, Philosophy of the" and "Ethiopians, Philosophy of the" signaled a decisive shift in what Europeans considered to be worthy of serious philosophical consideration. Thus, real and imagined inequalities went into the making of racial classification, but justification of inequality was not sufficient for the development of the modern idea of race.

Regardless of the extent to which the encyclopedists did or did not support equality, the *Encyclopédie* advanced equality by asserting its role as the voice of public opinion and its service to the public good. While we should not be under any illusions that the *Encyclopédie* reached the majority of Europeans, given its prohibitive costs, its elevation of artisanal knowledge to the same level as the more traditionally revered philosophical knowledge was of immense importance.[293] Additionally, as Dena Goodman has argued, the *Encyclopédie* was at the center of the transformation of the Republic of Letters at mid-century and this newly constituted Republic of Letters, separate from the academies and the universities, embodied the principle of equality: "It [the Republic of Letters] was to retain the same principles of equality and reciprocity among its members on which the academies stood, but instead of gathering people together in the interests of knowledge, it would gather knowledge together in the interests of humanity."[294] The encyclopedists thus expanded the purview of equality by asserting that everyone, not just an educated or a social elite, should be served by the knowledge they were collecting. Goodman also connects the *Encyclopédie* to the "project of Enlightenment," which she argues consisted of the interrelated goals of making people both less ignorant and making them ethically better.[295] The idea of a "project of Enlightenment," a term mainly used by critics of the intellectual movement, has generally fallen out of favor of late.[296] Already for quite some time, the dominant trend in Enlightenment studies has been its pluralization. Sankar Muthu has suggested that in the wake of this fragmentation, the only coherence that remains may be a negative one; what united the philosophes was what they were against, namely political absolutism and the most orthodox interpretations of religious dogma.[297] While this may be the case, we may add that an egalitarian ethos undergirded the flurry of literary activities of the philosophes, which was elegantly captured by Diderot in his article "Encyclopedia" when he described the goals of the work: "That the works of past centuries will not be useless for succeeding centuries; that our descendants, becoming more educated, may at the same time become more virtuous and happier and that we will not die without having served humanity."[298] Although we should not forget the Eurocentric limitations of the *Encyclopédie*, our enduring engagement with it in our contemporary cosmopolitan context surely stems from the fact that the work brushes up against the historical constraints that bounded it.

CHAPTER 4

De Felice's *Encyclopédie d'Yverdon*: Expanding and Contesting Human Science

In crucial respects, Fortunato Bartolomeo De Felice's *Encyclopédie d'Yverdon* fits so perfectly into Jonathan Israel's moderate Enlightenment, as opposed to the radical and counter-Enlightenments, that the term could have been invented by him.[1] In the revised article "Philosophe," one of the most important contributors to the *Encyclopédie d'Yverdon*, Gabriel Mingard, explains that the word "philosophe" has become associated with eighteenth-century atheist thinkers who do not, in fact, deserve the title they have acquired: "Such being the philosophers popular today, do not be surprised if in this dictionary we have often referred to them by the title philosophists [*philosophistes*], more suitable to their moral character and to the nature of their works."[2] Mingard maintains that only those thinkers willing to accept that there are certain truths, namely, those associated with liberal Protestant theology, that are beyond reason can lay claim to the title of philosophe.

Yet following Mingard's introductory defense of the necessary symbiosis between Christian theology and philosophy, he goes on to reproduce nearly the entire text of the famous article "Philosophe" from Diderot's *Encyclopédie*, which included such radical statements as, "Civil society is, so to speak, a divinity on earth for him [the philosopher]." This amalgamation of viewpoints is characteristic of the *Encyclopédie d'Yverdon* as a whole. On the one hand, one finds that De Felice and his collaborators were uniformly opposed to the atheism, materialism, and irreligiosity characteristic of some of the leading French philosophes. On the other hand, one also finds ample support, sometimes verging on the radical, for key Enlightenment causes and concepts, such as social contractarianism, toleration, the scientific method, and natural rights. In this chapter, I explore how De Felice and his circle

transformed the concepts of equality and racial classification that I analyzed in Diderot and d'Alembert's *Encyclopédie* and what these transformations mean for our understanding of the Enlightenment as an intellectual
movement.

In the *Encyclopédie d'Yverdon*'s preface, De Felice obsequiously acknowledges his debt to the Parisian predecessor upon which his encyclopedia was based.[3] He explains the system he used to indicate to the reader
where changes have been made to Diderot and d'Alembert's *Encyclopédie*:
completely new articles are indicated by "(N)" after the headword and revised articles by "(R)." Occasionally, a new paragraph or section has been
added to an otherwise intact article, and this is indicated by an asterisk at
the beginning of the additional section.[4] So, if no "N," "R," or asterisk is present, then the article is identical to the original. What De Felice fails to mention is that some sentences or paragraphs were omitted from numerous
articles without any notice to the reader. For articles central to my research,
I have thus carefully compared the Yverdon entry to the original. For the
most part, however, De Felice implemented his scheme consistently. As
Christian and Sylviane Albertan have noted, the fact that such a system
worked demonstrates that De Felice and his collaborators shared much in
common with their Parisian predecessors.[5]

I demonstrate that the Yverdon encyclopedists advanced the transformation of "society" and "social" that we saw in Chapter 3. Like the Parisian
encyclopedists, De Felice and his collaborators helped to bring the rights-
bearing individual to the center of political philosophy. But the primacy
given to autonomous individuals in this new conceptualization of society
was not the only factor that gave equality greater currency in Enlightenment
thought. Defending equality also depended upon empathic identification
with other autonomous individuals, and we see that this affective element in
the new egalitarian ethos is expanded in the *Encyclopédie d'Yverdon*. For
example, in the article "Sensitivity" (R), De Felice describes sensitivity as a
"tender and delicate disposition of the soul" that is a universal attribute of
humankind. He argues that cruel and inhumane actions result from the obstruction of this natural sensibility, which grows from "the feeling of equality": "It is mainly the similarity of men, *the feeling of their natural equality*
that gives birth to benevolence and humanity. Anything that makes this
similarity and equality disappear weakens natural sensitivity and can render man inhumane."[6] The articles "Sociability" (R), "Man" (R), "Convention" (R), and "Sensitivity" (R) contain explicit discussion and defenses of

natural equality in the Yverdon encyclopedia, whereas the concept is largely absent from these same articles in Diderot's encyclopedia, demonstrating the increased traction of equality by the 1770s. We will see that this empathic identification plays a central role in the robust antislavery stance of the *Encyclopédie d'Yverdon*.

Even though De Felice's predilection for elective aristocracy is immediately apparent, making him a decidedly inegalitarian thinker in crucial respects, it is remarkable that equality receives the benefit of the doubt in the *Encyclopédie d'Yverdon*; all human beings are fundamentally equal, and while the encyclopedists argue that societal inequalities are both necessary and inevitable, these must now be justified. Inequality is not something God-ordained but must fit within a political framework that aims to ensure the happiness of all: "This dependence is that which we call subordination, political or civil, without which it is clear that there can be no society. But this power being established only for general happiness, it is itself subordinated to this end, and must act only to lead men who are subject to it."[7] At times, the Yverdon encyclopedists stress the usefulness and even naturalness of inequality, while at others they celebrate and defend equality, thus presenting us with a deep ambiguity. This underlines the transformation of equality into both a foundational and an essentially contested concept in Enlightenment political thought. In the article "Inequality" (R), the anonymous author follows Rousseau in arguing that "the inequality of conditions is a purely human establishment."[8] Yet, in the article "Political Equality" (N), De Felice states: "I also consider it a mistake to think that nature wanted men to be equal: we cannot ascribe intent to a blind nature."[9]

Rather than signaling the lack of importance of equality, such inconsistencies in fact point to the concept's essentially contested nature. Inequality must now serve some sort of social purpose and is thus opened up to criticism in Enlightenment thought. Opponents of this development reveal just how controversial it was in the eighteenth century. For example, in the article "Inequality" in the popular Jesuit publication *Dictionnaire de Trévoux*, the author writes, "A certain inequality between men, which maintains order and subordination, is the work of God."[10] The Dominican historian and biographer Antoine Touron expressed a similar sentiment in even more trenchant terms: "If all men had the same proportion of wealth and of status, there would be neither master nor subjects among them and this equality would absolutely destroy all government. This would open the door to crime and impunity. [Inequality] serves to fulfil the wise designs of Providence."[11]

Louis-Mayeul Chaudon's *Dictionnaire anti-philosophique* takes aim primarily at Rousseau's conjectural history of the origin of inequality, beginning the article "Equality" by stating "only religion enlightens us on the inequality of conditions," which is followed by a defense of divinely sanctioned social hierarchy.[12] From these perspectives, criticism of social hierarchies is not only politically dangerous but also blasphemous and thus demonstrates the ways in which reactionary political viewpoints occasionally overlapped with orthodox religious and philosophical positions during the Enlightenment. The examples of *Trévoux*, Touron, and Chaudon also demonstrate the importance of determining the framework within which equality and inequality were discussed or defended. They demonstrate that the discussion of equality and inequality in the *Encyclopédie d'Yverdon* belongs within the framework of the Enlightenment, because society and social utility provide the groundwork for interpreting (in)equality, not religion.

Before analyzing these concepts in detail, it would be helpful to contextualize the *Encyclopédie d'Yverdon* to better understand the milieu from which it emerged. With the *Encyclopédie d'Yverdon*, De Felice tapped into the expanding European market for Francophone reference works in the late eighteenth century. The high-minded goal of spreading enlightenment notwithstanding, there was a substantial market for an updated and more affordable encyclopedia in the wake of Diderot and d'Alembert's monumental but expensive work. While the Parisian *Encyclopédie* was published in folio format, the *Encyclopédie d'Yverdon* was produced in the cheaper quarto size and thus competed with the other quarto reeditions of the original *Encyclopédie* published in the 1770s and 1780s in various western European cities.[13] The editor of the *Encyclopédie d'Yverdon*, Fortunato Bartolomeo De Felice, was born in Rome in 1723 and studied under Fortunato da Brescia, the savant well known for introducing Newtonian physics to Italy.[14] He taught mathematics and philosophy in Rome and Naples before fleeing to Bern, Switzerland, in 1757 following a romantic scandal involving an Italian noblewoman. His escape was made possible by the international connections he had established while working as a scholar in Naples. He was able to secure the support of the leading Bernese intellectuals Albrecht von Haller and Vincent Bernard Tscharner, who entrusted him with the establishment of a *café littéraire* and two journals.

As Clorinda Donato has remarked, the reason for their trust in his abilities must be sought in his connections within enlightened Neapolitan circles.[15] Two of the most important Enlightenment intellectuals in mid-century

Naples—Raimondo di Sangro, Prince of Sansevero, founder of a Masonic lodge; and Antonio Genovesi, the first professor of political economy at a European university—were close to De Felice.[16] Together with Tscharner, De Felice co-edited two journals in Bern beginning in 1758: the *Estratto della letteratura europea*, which introduced European literature to an Italian readership, and the *Excerptum totius italicae nec non helveticae litteraturae*, which focused on Swiss and Italian literature for a European-wide Latin readership.[17] Due to his conflict with the Neapolitan authorities, De Felice's publications were banned in the territory, and even correspondence with him was prohibited, but the *Estratto* was very well received in northern Italy, particularly in Milan. For example, the important Milanese Enlightenment intellectuals Pietro Verri and Cesare Beccaria were pleased with the *Estratto*, and De Felice began corresponding with Beccaria.[18]

De Felice moved to Yverdon in 1762 after becoming acquainted with two of the city's deputies and set up a publishing house there.[19] In the early years at Yverdon, De Felice wrote notebooks on philosophy, mathematics, physics, and natural law. He became particularly well versed in the natural law tradition, in the course of finding one of Burlamaqui's unpublished manuscripts and using it to augment the famous law professor's masterpiece *Les principes des droits de la nature et des gens* (*The Principles of Natural and Political Law*).[20] We should keep in mind that in addition to Burlamaqui, two of the other most influential eighteenth-century natural law professors, Jean Barbeyrac and Emer de Vattel, were also Swiss, partially accounting for the prominence of natural law in the *Encyclopédie d'Yverdon*. In 1768, De Felice acquired Diderot and d'Alembert's *Encyclopédie* with the aim of studying it closely. He claimed to have been shocked by the number of errors in the work and aimed to publish a corrected, up-to-date edition. This was the first of three encyclopedic projects that De Felice would lead. He edited the *Dictionnaire géographique, historique et politique de la Suisse* (Geographical, historical, and political dictionary of Switzerland) in 1775 and the so-called *Code de l'humanité* (Code of humanity), published in thirteen volumes between 1777 and 1778.[21] For the revised *Encyclopédie*, De Felice secured the support of the important bookseller Pierre Gosse in The Hague, who purchased two-thirds of the approximately sixteen hundred copies that were printed at Yverdon.[22]

The contributors to the *Encyclopédie d'Yverdon* formed a more homogenous group than the contributors to its French predecessor.[23] Nearly all of the contributors were Protestant and many of them were Swiss. The four most prolific contributors were De Felice, Élie Bertrand, César-Alexandre Chavannes, and Gabriel Mingard. Bertrand was a naturalist and Protestant minister who contributed 170 articles on theology, philosophy, ethics, and the natural sciences.[24] Chavannes was an orthodox minister and professor based at Lausanne who wrote almost 300 articles on theology and sacred history, in addition to serving as the censor of the encyclopedia. The Lausannois Mingard is one of the most intriguing contributors to the *Encyclopédie d'Yverdon*, because he was responsible for revising some of the most important and controversial articles on philosophy, theology, anthropology, and natural history, writing nearly 400 articles. He was one of the founders of the *Société littéraire de Lausanne* in 1772 and a member of the *Société économique d'Yverdon*. Mingard hailed from a long line of Calvinist ministers and became one himself, spending the late 1750s and early 1760s as the minister at the Walloon Church in Breda in the Dutch Republic.[25] Because many of his contributions concern politics and society, it is important to note that he corresponded with one of the leading "Italian lights" of the period, Pietro Verri, and De Felice published Mingard's French translation of Verri's *Meditazioni sulla felicità* (Thoughts on happiness) at his publishing house at Yverdon in 1766.[26] De Felice informed his readers that unnamed authorities accused Mingard's theological articles of being too heterodox, and so for the more controversial articles, Mingard changed his signature from the usual "G. M." to "M. D. B." for the last volumes of the encyclopedia.[27] As we will see below in a more in-depth look at Mingard's contributions, he was a strong opponent of atheism and materialism and fervently defended the compatibility of reason and Christianity. Indeed, the two are inseparable in his mind. While clearly a moderate in religious and philosophical terms, he was also deeply committed to such enlightened causes as toleration, education, and political reform. His articles on psychology and anthropology are also strikingly original and contributed to the development of the secular human sciences.

Regarding equality as a political concept, the most remarkable difference between Diderot's *Encyclopédie* and the *Encyclopédie d'Yverdon* is the influence of the mature political philosophy of another Swiss thinker, Jean-Jacques Rousseau, particularly his *Social Contract*, on the *Encyclopédie d'Yverdon*. While De Felice was certainly not a champion of republicanism, his wholesale copying of extensive sections of Rousseau's *Social Contract* for key articles in political philosophy result in some surprisingly radical egalitarian statements. At the same time, however, De Felice and other contributors did not hide their enthusiasm for aristocracy and their belief in the necessity of inequality. One of the most interesting lines of inquiry that I will trace in this chapter concerns the rise of the language of sentiment and sensibility and how it relates to equality and the Enlightenment as an intellectual movement. As Helena Rosenblatt argues, the adoption of the language of sentiment was a key feature of the Christian Enlightenment from mid-century onward.[28] Rather than arguing for the reasonableness of Christianity, as had been of paramount concern in the first half of the eighteenth century, Christian Enlightenment thinkers emphasized Jesus's appeal to the heart and to sensitive souls. Both the idea of a Christian Enlightenment and an Enlightenment of Sensibility fit the *Encyclopédie d'Yverdon* well, and we find that the political implications of this transformation are contradictory.[29]

The context of eighteenth-century Swiss politics helps to explain many of the arguments that we encounter regarding equality and toleration. Yverdon was in Bernese territory, and Bern was a "patrician canton," where a small oligarchy had come to monopolize power by the eighteenth century.[30] Many Swiss cities, including Bern, had a *grand conseil*, whose members were elected by tradesmen and artisans, and a *petit conseil*, which only admitted elite patricians by co-optation. Political power was vested in the *petit conseil*, and many Swiss cantons witnessed political unrest throughout the eighteenth century as democratic thinkers reasserted the political rights of the petty bourgeoisie and artisans. These tensions nearly boiled over into civil war in Geneva in 1707 and 1734 and resulted in revolution in 1782; Bern also experienced much unrest. The lower Bernese bourgeoisie petitioned for the opening of positions in government administration in 1744, but they were unsuccessful. Samuel Henzi, one of the main agitators behind the petition, was exiled from Bern for five years and, upon his return, organized the so-called Henzi plot in 1749. Henzi and about sixty to seventy other petty bourgeois citizens aimed to overthrow the patrician government. Government officials were warned about the plot, however, and Henzi was executed shortly thereafter.[31]

Such events would have been fresh in the minds of De Felice and his fellow encyclopedists, helping to explain the mixture of support for both aristocracy and democracy that we find throughout the *Encyclopédie d'Yverdon*. That toleration is vigorously defended in the encyclopedia is not surprising, given that a more open, liberal form of Protestantism had come to dominate Swiss urban centers by mid-century.[32] Many eighteenth-century Swiss theologians and other intellectuals distanced themselves from the strict Calvinism of the Formula Consensus of 1675. An intellectual genealogy can be traced from Jean-Alphonse Turrettin, Jean-Robert Chouet, and Marie Huber, who criticized orthodox Calvinism in the early eighteenth century, to Jacob Vernet and the Yverdon encyclopedists at mid-century, who promoted religious toleration.[33] Vernet, one of eighteenth-century Geneva's most prominent theologians, sought to reconcile Christian theology and the core Enlightenment philosophical principles of toleration and reason.[34] But he consistently maintained a conservative position in Genevan political crises, arguing that inequality and subordination are grounded in divine providence and natural law, and his influence demonstrates the extent to which toleration had been incorporated into a conservative political stance by mid-century.[35]

Reflecting the "hardening" of racial categories in the second half of the eighteenth century, one finds key articles in the *Encyclopédie d'Yverdon* that assert that a natural gulf separates Europeans from non-Europeans, particularly Native Americans and sub-Saharan Africans. We will see that this is a remarkable difference, setting racial discourse in the Swiss encyclopedia apart from its Parisian predecessor. Also in sync with a broader European trend of the late eighteenth century, De Felice and his collaborators propound an image of China as a stagnating civilization. Yet we also find notable defenses of cultural relativism from the Parisian encyclopedia reproduced at Yverdon, in addition to a more coherent and forceful antislavery stance. For their treatment of racial classification and the colonial world, De Felice and his collaborators relied heavily on two best sellers of the period: Cornelius De Pauw's *Recherches philosophiques sur les Americains* (Philosophical research on the Americans) and Raynal's *Histoire des deux Indes* (*History of the Two Indies*). The use of these texts helps to explain the contradictory views of non-Europeans that we find in the *Encyclopédie d'Yverdon*. But before we delve into the natural history of the human species, let us look at how our Swiss encyclopedists understood their political and social worlds and the place they gave to equality.

Equality and Rights in the *Encyclopédie d'Yverdon*

De Felice altered Jaucourt's powerful affirmation of the natural equality of human beings in interesting ways.[36] The article "Natural Equality" is more than double the length of Jaucourt's original. De Felice accepts Jaucourt's definition of natural equality, opening the article with Jaucourt's phrase: "Natural equality is that which is among all men solely by the constitution of their nature." Following this identical opening, he heads in a different direction than Jaucourt, stating that natural equality lies at the basis of the demands of sociability and, by consequence, of equity. Jaucourt did not mention sociability, whereas De Felice relies on the work of Jean-Jacques Burlamaqui to explore the relationship between equality and sociability. As we have seen, De Felice was well versed in the natural law tradition and, throughout the article, he relies on Jean Barbeyrac and Burlamaqui's popular natural law textbooks to explore the nature and meaning of natural equality.[37] De Felice stresses the universality of human nature and explains that we all possess reason, share the same faculties, and pursue the same goal. He then states that there are more "popular reasons" one can cite to illustrate "the natural equality of men": that humankind shares a common origin and the same fragile material constitution. He underscores the artificial character of differences in wealth: "That the rich and the poor, the great and the small, are all conceived in the womb of their mother and enter the world in the same way."[38] He continues to rely on Pufendorf by way of Barbeyrac to examine how Christianity also teaches us that human beings are equal, stressing that worldly possessions and power do not matter in the eyes of God. This is a striking addition to Jaucourt's original entry, because Jaucourt made no mention of Christianity or scripture. De Felice's reflections on Christianity and equality underscore the centrality of liberal Protestant theology in the *Encyclopédie d'Yverdon* as a whole and in its political philosophy in particular.

In addition to the inclusion of the religious dimension of natural equality, De Felice's article is remarkable in that it also employs the language of sensibility to buttress support for equality. He writes, "Everything that hurts the least fortunate irritates us and drives us to a last resort. The reason is that *we all feel that human nature, being the same in all men, also deserves for all the same respect*, the same consideration."[39] The reason we must treat one another as equals is because we feel that we share a common human nature. He follows Burlamaqui in explicitly stating that he is arguing against Hobbes's conception of equality: the equality that De Felice is writing about is one of right ("une égalité de droit"), and not one of fact or of strength.[40] De Felice writes that the kind of equality he is concerned with is of a different sort: one that can harmonize relations among the infinite diversity of bodies and minds. In other words, given the reality of the inequalities between peoples, equality ensures the smoothing over of these real differences. De Felice explains that even the poorest, most unfortunate people in society have the right to demand equal treatment in certain respects; namely, they have a right to share in the "common rights of humanity."[41] De Felice concludes the article by arguing that all human societies are, by their nature, societies of equality because all members enjoy an equality of liberty and each individual is independent vis-à-vis other individuals.

This leaves the question of the political implications of De Felice's rendering of natural equality open and vexed. On the one hand, the demands of natural equality impose a set of boundaries that cannot be crossed—namely, equality before the law and recognition of the equal moral autonomy of all human beings. This is why De Felice condemns slavery, ending this article with a cross-reference to the antislavery articles "Slave" and "Slavery" and with the assertion that the ancient idea of natural slavery runs contrary to "the natural state of man." De Felice thus clearly recognized certain political and social consequences of natural equality. On the other hand, rather than calling the social and economic inequalities of contemporary European society into question, equality is defended by De Felice as a means to an end: to smooth over and mollify the very real (and necessary, in De Felice's opinion) inequalities between human beings. He explains, "Thus as in a highly civilized republic, every citizen equally enjoys liberty, even if one is more highly regarded or wealthier than another."[42] While De Felice severely circumscribed the purview of equality, the greater length of the article "Natural Equality" compared with its Parisian predecessor attests to its growing importance and contestation in Enlightenment political philosophy. The pithy and succinct nature of De Felice's account of natural equality, which collects Jaucourt, Barbeyrac, and Burlamaqui's reflections on the subject, results in a powerful affirmation of human equality. Even if the political and social consequences of this affirmation are unclear, the affirmation in itself demonstrates the increasingly contested nature of hierarchy.

A further demonstration of the increasing contestation of equality in Enlightenment philosophy, if not of its thoroughgoing defense, can be gleaned from the addition of a new article by De Felice, "Political Equality." This article is a lengthy justification of the necessity, usefulness, and justice of political and social *in*equalities. He opens the article by defining political equality as "the equal sharing of wealth among the citizens of a civil society."[43] He states that a "metaphysical sentiment" has led many thinkers to imagine that instituting equality is an important aspect of public justice. He uses the example of the reform of agrarian legislation under the Gracchus brothers, as well as other examples from antiquity, to argue that instituting such policies is impractical and invariably leads to bloodshed. Additionally, he argues that policies that impose equality stifle humanity's creativity and industriousness and run counter to human flourishing and happiness. In stark contrast to the preceding article, "Natural Equality," De Felice argues that there is a basic inequality between human beings that is both natural and just: "I also consider it a mistake to think that nature wanted men to be equal: we cannot ascribe intent to a blind nature."[44] He then devotes the rest of the article to explaining what a just distribution of wealth would be between the clergy, the nobility, and the rest of the people, given that inequality is necessary but too much inequality is destabilizing.

In stark contrast to Jaucourt's corpus of articles in the *Encyclopédie*, where his sympathies for equality are abundantly clear, we see that De Felice supported aristocracy. Although De Felice copied liberally from Rousseau's *Social Contract* and defended the idea that sovereignty lies with the people, Charly Guyot has demonstrated that "in reality, he is hardly favorable toward democracy."[45] In the article "Democracy," for example, De Felice reproduced only part of Jaucourt's original article, omitting the opening two paragraphs in which Jaucourt had praised democracies for elevating the minds of all its participants. He included the more anodyne list of the basic features of democratic government and added a section in which he assesses the advantages and disadvantages of this form of government, concluding that the liabilities of democracy outweigh its benefits. He argues that popular government takes on the character of the people, a small number of whom are wise and a great many of whom are ignorant. He argues that democracies are the weakest form of government and are destined to degenerate. One of their faults is that they suppose an equality of human beings that does not exist in reality and people are expected to take on roles that they are not fit to fulfil. He states that the inequalities that naturally exist between people are at the basis of society. In this way, De Felice could posit equality but also circumscribe the reach of the concept: "We must therefore not interpret the equality that should form the basis of democracy as an absolute equality, but rather as relative to the degrees of received qualities. And these qualities had to vary to accord with the diversity of society's needs."[46] This conservative take on the subject derives from Burlamaqui's natural law texts.

While the natural law tradition is quite often associated with "progressive" political developments in Western history, one must look carefully at how the concepts within natural law were used in a given context. One of the leading scholars on natural law in the early modern period, Knud Haakonssen, argues that prominent seventeenth-century natural law theories, such as those of Grotius, Pufendorf, and Burlamaqui, fit into a morally conservative worldview.[47] Helena Rosenblatt's analysis of natural law in the Genevan context helps to explain De Felice's arguments: "The famous natural law theorists, Jean Barbeyrac and Jean-Jacques Burlamaqui, were openly committed to the Genevan government's side: they lent their reputation and theories to the oligarchical cause. Natural law theory was part of a concerted effort by those in power in Geneva to depoliticize the bourgeoisie."[48] De Felice praises the elective aristocracies of the Swiss cantons in the article "Government," stating that this is the only true aristocracy and that it is the "the means by which integrity, enlightenment, experience, and all other reasons of preference and public opinion are so many new guarantees that one will be wisely governed. See Bern, Basel, Zurich, etc."[49]

Just as with the articles classified as "political," the natural rights articles in the *Encyclopédie d'Yverdon* also present us with a deep ambiguity. On the one hand, the encyclopedists used the defense of natural rights to call oppressive religious and political power into question. On the other hand, the encyclopedists remained firmly committed to the idea that hierarchy is natural and necessary in society. It is difficult to argue that one or the other— either a politically consequential or a muted equality—carries more weight in the encyclopedia, since one finds a diverse array of positions across numerous articles. For example, in the revised article "Sovereign," De Felice argues that sovereignty essentially rests with the people, who have an "incontestable right" to resist tyranny.[50] He explains that the people are not obliged to obey a ruler who violates fundamental laws and cites the Dutch Revolt against the Habsburg monarchy as a just revolt. But in Mingard's article "Authority" (R), one finds a powerful apology for hierarchy and the legitimacy of a "natural authority" that can be found among human beings. The contrast with Diderot's controversial article "Political Authority" (which does not appear in the *Encyclopédie d'Yverdon*) could hardly be starker.

Mingard argues that human beings are unequal in their ability to direct their desires and their fears, which is necessary to achieve happiness. In a polemical statement that is undoubtedly directed at Rousseau and Hobbes, he argues that society is natural to man and that being in close contact with one another, human beings in a primitive state would have immediately recognized that certain individuals have a more powerful intellect than others.

This serves as the basis of "natural authority": "The favorable judgment that our reason bears on the superior merit of a person is thus the real foundation of natural authority."[51] He writes that many writers have argued that dogmatic authority is contrary to the most precious rights of humanity but that this has often been confounded with "simple authority," which he defines as the judgment by which a man of common sense recognizes the validity of expert knowledge. He argues that this type of authority is indeed grounded in nature and argues that most people unthinkingly rely on "dogmatic authority," making it important to establish a legitimate and upright dogmatic authority in society. While Mingard makes much of "natural authority," Diderot takes a strikingly different stance: "If nature has established some authority, it is paternal power, but this paternal power has its limits. And in the state of nature it would terminate as soon as the children would be in a state to behave themselves. All other authority comes from another origin than nature."[52] These reflections on equality reveal that it was a much more dangerous concept to the Swiss encyclopedists than to their Parisian predecessors, because De Felice and his circle were closer to the governing elite.

A similar traditionalism can also be found in the *Encyclopédie d'Yverdon* if we look at sex and gender. We saw that Jaucourt incorporated a strong critique of patriarchy in his article "Wife," and while his article is reproduced in the Yverdon encyclopedia, it is with a lengthy addition in which De Felice explains how women are essentially different from and, without using the word, *lesser* than men. He explains that "men, by the prerogative of their sex and by the strength of their temperament, are naturally capable of doing all kinds of employments and tasks; whereas women, because of the fragility of their sex and their delicate nature, are excluded from many functions and incapable of certain tasks."[53] Again in contradistinction to Jaucourt, De Felice transformed the article "Paternal Power" in a more patriarchal direction. He states that in the state of nature, the husband/father holds sovereign power over his children and his wife, though he does qualify this by stating that the mother shares in some of the parental authority.[54]

But one does not have to look far to find much more radical political positions among these Protestant encyclopedists. We will see that the encyclopedia's opposition to slavery is as radical as any mounted in the prerevolutionary period and that equality was an integral part of the encyclopedists' antislavery posture. The more egalitarian political orientation of the *Encyclopédie d'Yverdon* is partially owing to De Felice's use of Rousseau's *Social*

Contract for many key articles concerning politics. For example, most of the article "Legislation" (R) is taken verbatim from book 2, chapter 11 of Rousseau's *Social Contract*.[55] Kathleen Hardesty Doig has compared Rousseau's famous treatise and De Felice's article and found that De Felice removed the first footnote of the chapter and integrated it into the main text, in addition to removing the second footnote entirely.[56] This chapter includes one of the most important reflections on equality in the entire *Social Contract*. Rousseau and, following him, De Felice, explain that the greatest goal of any system of law can be reduced to two objects: freedom and equality. He explains that equality is not the complete leveling of material wealth, but instead the concept should imply that "[power] stop short of all violence and never be exercised except by virtue of rank and the laws."[57] Significantly, the footnote that De Felice brought into the main body of text is a strong condemnation of extreme inequalities in society, with Rousseau arguing that such inequalities bring political instability. Furthermore, this article contains one of Rousseau's most insightful remarks on how legislation relates to equality: "This equality, they say, is a chimera of speculation which cannot exist in practice: But if abuse is inevitable, does it follow that it ought not at least be regulated? It is precisely because the force of things always tends to destroy equality, that the force of legislation ought always to tend to maintain it."[58]

De Felice then follows Rousseau in arguing that these general objectives must be adapted in specific ways to meet the particular situation of a given nation, such as the fertility of the soil. Rousseau states that if the territory is barren, one may look to manufacturing to foster trade and acquire the natural resources one needs. But Rousseau had included a footnote stating that foreign trade "brings only an illusory advantage." As Patrick Riley notes, Rousseau's focus here on how particular cases conform to general principles follows Montesquieu but, contrary to Montesquieu, Rousseau "cannot bring himself to praise a commercial nation" and he thus relies upon but also quietly departs from *The Spirit of the Laws* in this chapter.[59] Significantly, De Felice removed this second footnote entirely. This is because De Felice, along with many of his Swiss compatriots, disagreed with Rousseau concerning the possibility of a virtuous commercial society. De Felice and many of his fellow encyclopedists were politically moderate in the sense that they found themselves in between, on the one hand, the Bernese and Neuchâtelois magistrates who had banned Rousseau from their territories on July 1, 1762, and, on the other, those more radically democratic thinkers who criticized aristocracy, on the other. For example, in the article "Intolerance" in the *Supplément* to the *Encyclopédie d'Yverdon*, the anonymous author castigates Swiss authorities for banishing Rousseau: "If the ministers of Neuchâtel, accusers of Rousseau, were born Athenian or Jewish, they would thus most certainly have hunted Socrates or Jesus. Oh! Eloquent Rousseau, may the favor of the great prince who protects you against such fanatics avenge you well for their insult!"[60]

De Felice's use of Rousseau's political writings follows the general pattern of the reception of Rousseau in eighteenth-century Switzerland, where he was avidly read and greatly admired but also pointedly criticized.[61] Béla Kapossy has assiduously studied the most important Swiss-German thinker to systematically confront Rousseau's thought, Isaak Iselin, and many of his insights apply equally well to the place of Rousseau in the *Encyclopédie d'Yverdon*.[62] De Felice and his circle were impressed by Rousseau's examination of politics but were clearly uncomfortable with Rousseau's religious views and his naturalistic account of the origins of morality. Perhaps most contentious was Rousseau's deep pessimism concerning the possibility of a virtuous commercial society, something to which the Swiss encyclopedists were firmly committed. For example, in the article "Sovereignty," De Felice follows Burlamaqui in arguing that sovereignty originally lies with the people and advocates the anti-Rousseauist position that though it owes much to human conventions, it is grounded in divine law just as much as it is in human law.[63] In the article "Legislator" or "Law Giver" ("Législateur"), De Felice copies book 2, chapter 7 ("On the Law Giver") of Rousseau's *Social Contract* verbatim. This chapter contains some remarkably radical ideas that were essential aspects of Rousseau's political philosophy, namely, his subscription to the idea that human nature is shaped by politics: "Anyone who dares to institute a people must feel capable of, so to speak, changing human nature; of transforming each individual who by himself is a perfect and solitary whole into part of a larger whole from which that individual would as it were receive his life and his being."[64] But in a telling alteration, De Felice deleted the last paragraph of this chapter. After explaining that in order to make people follow the law without coercion or violence, founders of nations must appeal to the divine, Rousseau explains: "One should not from all this conclude with Warburton that among us politics and religion have a common object, but rather that at the origin of nations the one serves as the instrument of the other."[65] As Doig explains, this argument opposes one of the ideas fundamental to the enterprise of the *Encyclopédie d'Yverdon*—that primordial religious principles lie at the foundation of human society and historical development.[66]

De Felice adapted Rousseau's *Social Contract* to fit a favorable judgment of the political system of his adopted homeland.[67] But that does not mean that the *Encyclopédie d'Yverdon* was a thoroughly moderate encyclopedia. For example, in the article "Virtue," De Felice advocates the separation of religion from morality in a statement typical of many Enlightenment reflections on the topic: "The difference in religion is not an obstacle to virtue. Natural religion is one among all men; the demands to be fulfilled are the same for a pagan, for a Turk, for a Christian. Thus, I can and I must be virtuous in any religion I find myself in."[68] Guyot's assessment of the *Encyclopédie d'Yverdon* is particularly apt: the articles oscillate between defenses of the natural conscience or sentiments of humanity that form the basis of morality, on the one hand, and the uniquely important role that Christianity plays in fostering these sentiments, on the other.[69] Specifically regarding the place of Rousseau's political philosophy in the *Encyclopédie d'Yverdon*, he remarks, "If the *Encyclopédie d'Yverdon* owes a lot to the political theories of the *Social Contract*, it parts from the Rousseau of the *Discourse on Inequality*."[70] And one might add that the Yverdon encyclopedists separated themselves from the Rousseau of the *First Discourse* as well. This assessment is accurate with regard to at least two themes: (1) the issue of the possibility of reforming modern society to create a virtuous commercial republic; and, relatedly, (2) the place of natural law in the political philosophies of Rousseau and the encyclopedia.

Regarding the first theme, De Felice was close to members of various Swiss reform societies, most notably the Bernese Vincent Bernard Tscharner, one of the leading Swiss intellectuals of mid-century who was active in the Helvetic Society, the Economic Society of Bern, and the Patriotic Society.[71] All of these societies were predicated on the idea that enlightened reform is a feasible enterprise. De Felice relied on publications by various members of these societies, using, for example, the *Traités sur divers sujets intéressans de politique et de morale* (Treatise on various interesting political and moral subjects) of Georg Ludwig Schmid, a member of the Economic Society, in the article "Project" (N) to argue that projects in science, religion, and government have contributed to improving the lot of humankind.[72] One sees similar sentiments expressed in Mingard's newly added article "Perfectibility"

(N), the headword having been first recorded in Rousseau's writings.[73] "Perfectibility" and "civilization" were newly coined terms in the 1750s, and it is around these terms that the political and scientific structures associated with modernity would be built.[74]

Regarding the second theme, although many Swiss thinkers in enlightened circles, including most of the contributors to the *Encyclopédie d'Yverdon*, admired Rousseau's thinking, one of the main points of disagreement between them and Rousseau concerns the issue of the natural sociability of humanity specifically and the topic of natural law more generally. Rousseau's relationship to the natural law tradition continues to generate scholarly controversy.[75] Robert Wokler asserts that "Rousseau's idea of natural right in the *Discours sur l'inégalité* is established from a combination of *amour de soi* and *pitié* alone, rather than from any notion of natural sociability,"[76] and on this point, De Felice and his collaborators certainly disagreed with Rousseau. As previously mentioned, De Felice was trained in the modern natural law tradition, having supplemented Burlamaqui's famous work.

In numerous articles, De Felice and his collaborators affirm the naturalness of society based on humankind's natural sociability. In the article "Natural Law" (R), Mingard states that natural law has two meanings: first, it relates to the actions of rational beings that are well directed, meaning that they take into account the nature, state, and goal of these beings. Natural right in this sense is fixed and constant, he argues, rooted in the nature of things. And second, natural law is the science that teaches us to effectively judge the actions of rational beings.[77] One must know the nature and capacities of humankind in order to know their natural rights. In this regard, Mingard takes aim at Rousseau, arguing that Rousseau's solitary "man of nature" is a chimera: "Thus we will never suppose in natural law that man was like wild and solitary animals, abandoned to itself, with no interaction with his fellows, without any dependence on any other, without parents, and absolutely isolated from the moment of his birth."[78] De Felice relied heavily on Jean-Jacques Burlamaqui's writings on natural law and thus disagreed sharply with Rousseau, arguing for the natural sociability of humanity and the naturalness of society.[79] The state of nature in the *Encyclopédie d'Yverdon* generally follows Burlamaqui's line of thought, where it is portrayed as a state of equality, liberty, and general harmoniousness, although with some disadvantages, contrary to the arguments of Hobbes and Rousseau.[80] The transformation of the concepts of society, social, and sociability are such an important part of Enlightenment thought generally and fundamental to the politicization of equality specifically that we will now turn to a more detailed analysis of these concepts.

Society, Toleration, and Equality

In Chapter 3, we saw that the transformation of the concepts of society and social were crucial elements in bringing the concept of equality to the fore in Enlightenment political thought and that this transformation was both reflected and intensified in Diderot and d'Alembert's *Encyclopédie*. De Felice and his collaborators followed the lead of Diderot, Rousseau, and others in using "society" and "social" in a modern way, and partially as a result of this transformation, these Enlightenment thinkers contributed to establishing equality as a foundational concept in political philosophy. I propose that beyond the very real philosophical and religious divisions that characterized the Enlightenment, we can find a measure of coherence in the commitment of nearly all of Diderot and De Felice's circles to a secular vision of an irenic society shaped by laws aimed at ameliorating the human condition. While certain Enlightenment thinkers were indeed irreligious, it seems that a more fruitful way to make sense of the intellectual movement as a whole is by viewing it as one that pushed forward the transfer of sacrality from the otherworldly to the human realm and the interiorization of religious beliefs.[81] This development created the conditions for a more robust defense of equality—individuals could now be seen as autonomous, rights-bearing persons equal to other rights-bearing persons. I will elaborate on these themes throughout this section.

While Diderot's *Encyclopédie* had announced that "social" was "a word newly introduced into the language," the *Encyclopédie d'Yverdon*—published within a decade of the last volumes of the Parisian original—reveals the speed at which the concept gained currency in Enlightenment thought. The word "social*"[82] occurs more than three times as often in the *Encyclopédie d'Yverdon* than in its Parisian predecessor, occurring sixty times in Diderot's *Encyclopédie* versus 188 times in the *Encyclopédie d'Yverdon*. In the article "Society," the Parisian original did not contain the word "social" at all, whereas its rewritten Swiss successor contains the word thirty-five times. My research has confirmed Yair Mintzker's argument that Diderot and Rousseau were crucial in transforming and popularizing these concepts.[83] We have already seen Rousseau's immense influence on the *Encyclopédie d'Yverdon*, and even when it comes to Rousseau's critics, the power of his thought is revealed in the way that they inadvertently adopted his language.

This is nowhere more revealing than in De Felice's reworking of the article "Society" (R),[84] in which he defines society as "the union of one or more families, under subordination to a leader, to safeguard, by his protection and his care, the happiness to which we naturally aspire."[85] First, inequality is an integral part of how he views society, as he argues that the existence of society necessitates "subordination." Second, happiness is a crucial element in his theorization of society. He begins his lengthy article by explaining that the natural needs and inclinations of human beings pushed them to unite together and to work to achieve happiness for the larger group and even for humanity as a whole. Inequality is both a part of the nature of humanity and a necessary component in the creation and functioning of society: "But nature does not create men with equal strengths, or with the same dispositions and talents for the functions that can contribute to the happiness of others."[86] This passage and many others are taken verbatim from Abbé Pluquet's *De la sociabilité* (On sociability), published in 1767 as a refutation of Rousseau's *Second Discourse*.[87]

Although Pluquet's work critiqued Rousseau's *Second Discourse*, the two thinkers in fact agreed with the argument expressed in the previous quotation, as Pluquet describes what one might call "natural inequalities." Rousseau distinguished between two types of inequality: "natural or physical," on the one hand, and "moral or political," on the other.[88] The natural inequalities between human beings are of no consequence in the state of nature. It is only with the development of civilization that such inequalities begin to matter.[89] From here, their positions begin to diverge sharply. De Felice, following Pluquet, has a sanguine view of the development of societies from the state of nature to "civilization." Contrary to Rousseau, he argues that nature made humanity weak and therefore humans naturally dependent on one another: "Subordination was his first habit."[90] Although De Felice argues that submission to a governing power is natural to humanity and necessary for society, he introduces the important qualification that this subordination must only occur with a view to achieving happiness. He argues that an original and immutable law of nature and of society is "general and shared happiness."[91] His main argument is that society is based upon humankind's natural sociability and thus directs himself against the theories of Hobbes, Bernard Mandeville, and Rousseau. Following Pluquet, De Felice argues that human beings do not naturally love independence or dominance but rather have natural sentiments, such as social virtues, benevolence, and sensitivity engraved in their hearts. The *Encyclopédie d'Yverdon*, by way of Pluquet's *De la sociabilité*, advanced the novel perspective that society itself is natural and thus attempted to move beyond those who equated solitariness with the natural state and society with human artifice.[92]

There is a tension in this article, as subordination, obedience, and attendant inequalities are presented as both natural and necessary, while natural equality is simultaneously vindicated: "It seems that nature has created men with the same dispositions, the same talents, the same inclinations, and therefore in a state of perfect equality." De Felice explains that even though a person may possess a particular talent, other individuals are more talented than that individual in other areas. His conclusion is that "nobody has the right to believe himself naturally superior to another man."[93] It seems that De Felice takes a similar position as Jaucourt, who defended the natural equality of human beings and invested the idea with political consequences but also affirmed the need for social distinctions and inequalities.

What is remarkable about the transformation of the entry "Society" is that in the hands of a thinker of the Christian Enlightenment, primacy is given to the peaceful functioning of the human collectivity, and issues of salvation and religious worship take a secondary role. De Felice affirms his belief that all societies must pay homage to God, but this comes after a conjectural history of humanity's development from the rude state of nature to refined civil society that is formulated outside of the biblical framework. And most important of all, religion is ultimately justified in the name of society: "Attack fanaticism and superstition that are contrary to the glory of the Supreme Being and detrimental to the happiness of societies. But with your enlightenment and your genius, with a heart blessed with the gentlest, most compassionate, and most generous humanity, love and respect a religion that teaches morality that is the most suitable to generating and perfecting all of the principles of leniency, gentleness, kindness, and all of the social virtues."[94] Society serves as the ground of meaning, and religion is necessary insofar as it facilitates the smooth functioning of society.[95] Even for the more pious contributors to the *Encyclopédie d'Yverdon*, such as the Calvinist minister Élie Bertrand, religion is deemed necessary for its ability to facilitate social cohesion. In the article "Religion" (R), Bertrand writes, "Because religion teaches us these duties [the obligations we owe to our fellow human beings], religion is necessary for the man living with his fellows.

It is not religion that established these relations, it is nature; but the existence of these relations establishes the duties that religion teaches and prescribes us."[96] While Diderot and some of his collaborators would have disagreed with Bertrand's conclusion of the necessity of religion, all of these thinkers contributed to the process whereby society displaced religion to become the ground of meaning. Thus, notwithstanding the disagreements between Rousseau, Diderot, and De Felice and his collaborators, they were part of the same intellectual transformation that invented the modern concepts of society and the social as part of a multifaceted set of the religious, political, and cultural transformations characteristic of the Enlightenment.[97]

Enlightenment thinkers invented (or discovered, depending on one's point of view) our modern conceptualization of society by reworking prior claims about the divinely instituted nature of human collectivities. Despite De Felice's misgivings about democracy and social leveling, his concept of society rests on the assumption of it being an association of naturally equal individuals. He presents a list of nineteen laws that all societies must follow, one of which is a defense of the idea of equality as a political concept: "The esteem, goodwill, and kindness of citizens, so necessary for the maintenance and happiness of society, has as a foundation the natural equality of men, and so any distinction in ranks and conditions that destroys this natural equality is contrary to the principles of sound politics."[98] The invention of the modern concepts of society and the social was thus bound up with the transformation of equality into a foundational concept in Enlightenment political philosophy.

The issue of toleration reveals the tension running through the *Encyclopédie d'Yverdon* between its privileging of society as the groundwork of human collective existence and its simultaneous commitment to the fundamental truth of Protestantism. In the article "Toleration" (R), the unknown contributor offers a lengthy and impassioned defense of toleration, but the purview of the concept is restricted from the outset to diversity within Christianity.[99] While he argues that all religious organizations must obey the laws of the state, he considers religion to be necessary for the maintenance of morality and public order. This is his grounds for excluding "atheists who dogmatize" from the ambit of toleration.[100] The place of other non-Christians in this article is unclear. As noted, the dominant framework of the article is toleration of the various Christian denominations, reflecting the legacies of the sixteenth- and seventeenth-century Wars of Religion. The author mentions Jews and "pagans" only once, when he argues against the proposition that the sovereign has absolute authority in matters of faith. This article demonstrates the issue that Protestant defenders of toleration faced: they argued for the primacy of public peace and harmonious social relations across confessional divides at the same time that they wished to promote Protestantism as the true religion. Depending on where one looks in the *Encyclopédie d'Yverdon*, one finds the accent variously placed on one or the other.

The *Encyclopédie d'Yverdon* switches allegiances, variously siding with the atheistic philosophes against the anti-philosophes and, at other times, defending a Protestant position against deists and atheists alike.[101] For an encyclopedia committed to liberal Protestant theology, some remarkably radical criticisms of religion can be found in the reference work. For example, Alexandre Deleyre's vitriolic denunciation of religious fanaticism in his article "Fanaticism" is reproduced in full, as is Jaucourt's qualified defense of atheism in the article "Superstition."[102] Additionally, the article "Jew" incorporates Jaucourt's remarkably tolerant article into an augmented consideration of Jewish history and philosophy.[103] De Felice could be quite harsh in his criticisms of orthodox Protestants: "One is not mistaken if one regards the bigoted as the most dangerous plague of society. They abound among the Catholics, and Protestants do not lack them either."[104] And, in the article "Atheist," Mingard quotes Voltaire: "I agree with you that fanaticism is a monster one thousand times more dangerous than philosophical atheism. Spinoza did not commit a single misdeed."[105] Clorinda Donato has shown that De Felice defended the encyclopedists against the attacks of such "anti-philosophes" as Abraham-Joseph de Chaumeix and favorably reviewed books by openly materialist thinkers like Helvétius.[106] And even the more conservative minister Élie Bertrand condemned Calvin's persecution of "heretics."[107]

But the middling or moderate position of the *Encyclopédie d'Yverdon* in matters of religion becomes clear in how the encyclopedists viewed the Bible. For example, Mingard argues that Scripture should serve to combat the "bad faith" and "ignorance" of "modern philosophers . . . [who] portray the evangelical doctrine as absurd, Jesus Christ's morality as fanatical, and the entire Gospel as a monstrous illusion."[108] And on the doctrine of resurrection, Mingard argues that one must simply admit ignorance: "One can ask, first, in what manner did this resurrection occur? A modest 'I do not know anything about it' is the only response to give."[109] Whether intentional or not, the reader is presented with a profoundly ambiguous picture of religion and morality in the *Encyclopédie d'Yverdon*. In this sense, we encounter a similar phenomenon as in Diderot and d'Alembert's *Encyclopédie*, where strikingly contradictory positions are put forward on any given topic depending on which articles one consults, this being reflective of the Enlightenment encyclopedia as a debating platform and the diversity of viewpoints among the various contributors. While we cannot deny the more uniformly Protestant nature of the *Encyclopédie d'Yverdon* compared with its Parisian predecessor, the divergences in the arguments concerning various religious, philosophical, and political topics in this Swiss reference work point to the quintessential *esprit de critique* of the Enlightenment.

That the *Encyclopédie d'Yverdon* should be included in the fold of Enlightenment philosophy is most conspicuously demonstrated by De Felice and his collaborators' concern for the happiness of all members of society and their suggestions for social reform. Commitment to ameliorating the human condition in this world has long been taken as a hallmark of Enlightenment thought, and it is notable that discussion of happiness is more prevalent in the *Encyclopédie d'Yverdon* than in its Parisian predecessor.[110] Mingard's French translations of Pietro Verri's *Meditazioni sulla felicità* (Thoughts on happiness) and his *Meditazioni sull'economia politica* (*Reflections on Political Economy*) were published in 1766 and 1773, respectively. According to Franco Venturi, Mingard's introduction to the latter work was "one of the most important and best-informed pictures of Italian intellectual and moral life to be drawn in those years."[111] Unsurprisingly, many of these reflections on the importance of happiness found their way into the *Encyclopédie d'Yverdon*. For example, in the article "Natural Law," Mingard incorporates happiness into his very definition of the term. Natural law is taken to mean that which is well directed in intelligent beings, which entails that it contributes "to their perfection and to their happiness."[112] Throughout the article, Mingard explains that we must understand "man's nature" in order to understand the possibility for achieving happiness in this world, which is framed as a natural right. While Diderot argued that happiness is part of the "general will" of humanity that frames natural rights, Mingard moves it to the heart of the discussion of natural rights.[113] We also see that De Felice and his collaborators incorporate happiness into their political philosophy to a greater extent than in its Parisian predecessor; political power and policies must be designed to ensure the happiness of all. Pietro Verri and Cesare Beccaria developed the idea of the greatest happiness of the greatest number, and De Felice and his collaborators took up their arguments in many articles.[114]

As an example of the increased attention paid to happiness in the *Encyclopédie d'Yverdon* compared with its predecessor, "happiness" is mentioned 13 times in the article "Society" in Diderot and d'Alembert's *Encyclopédie*, while De Felice mentions it 130 times in his revised article. Darrin McMahon states, "If there was a central concern that animated the Enlightenment's many questions, it was how to make life better," and the *Encyclopédie d'Yverdon* certainly fits this assessment.[115] Criminal justice reform emerged as a crucial aspect of human and societal improvement in the Enlightenment, most famously with Beccaria's work. De Felice incorporated Beccaria's recommendations for penal reform in his encyclopedia. In the article "Punishment" (R), for example, he explains: "Punishment will be all the more just if the sovereign will preserve greater individual freedom and at the same time public liberty will remain more inviolable and more sacred. The first consequence of these principles is that it is for the laws alone to determine the punishment of crimes and that the right to make penal laws can reside only in a legislator who represents all of society united by the social contract."[116] Not only is the goal to create a happier and more just society, but the argument depends upon the new understanding of the social world that Enlightenment thinkers ushered in. The previous quotation and most of De Felice's article is lifted directly from Beccaria's *Traité des délits et des peines* (*Treatise on Crimes and Punishments*), though he does not cite the work.[117] De Felice's use of the *Treatise on Crimes and Punishments* demonstrates that Beccaria's insights and arguments made their way into Enlightenment reference works. Beccaria's treatise is most well known for presenting powerful arguments for penal reform, but crucially, it was also an egalitarian text. As Beccaria explains, "To be legitimate, every distinction whether of honor or wealth presupposes an antecedent equality based on the laws, which treat every subject as equally subordinate to them."[118] Beccaria's tract also presented powerful arguments against the use of judicial torture, which were grounded in the recognition of the inner similarity of all human beings. This recognition of inner similarity was fundamental to the politicization of equality in the Enlightenment, and the *Encyclopédie d'Yverdon* both reflected and contributed to this development.

We have seen that De Felice and his collaborators both expanded and contracted the purview of equality compared with its Parisian predecessor. So far, we have mainly dealt with this topic as it related to debates internal to Europe. But what impact did the new conceptualizations of religion, society, and the social have on how the Yverdon encyclopedists viewed the extra-European world? Interestingly, we will see a similar paradoxical phenomenon—both the deepening of a culturally relativist perspective and the growth of a more hardened, inegalitarian concept of race—in the articles concerning the peoples and cultures of America, sub-Saharan Africa, and China. Let us now turn to the treatment of Native Americans and Pacific islanders in the *Encyclopédie d'Yverdon*.

The Americas and the South Pacific

For the articles concerning Native American peoples and cultures, the encyclopedists drew variously from Guillaume Thomas Raynal's *Histoire des deux Indes*, which contains a powerful egalitarian strain of thought, and Cornelius De Pauw's *Recherches philosophiques sur les Américains*, which is almost uniformly inegalitarian. The first edition of Raynal's bestseller was published in 1770 in Amsterdam, and Raynal acted more as editor than sole author, since other philosophes such as Diderot and Jean de Pechméja contributed significantly to the work.[119] The Yverdon encyclopedists drew variously from this edition and from a reissue also published in Amsterdam, between 1772 and 1774.[120] The starkly disparate sources of De Pauw and Raynal partially account for the conflicting perspectives that the *Encyclopédie d'Yverdon* offers on Native Americans. Additionally, the use of these sources indicates the growing importance of the colonial world in the consciousness of the philosophes in the second half of the eighteenth century, particularly following the Seven Years' War.[121] Similar to my focus in the previous section on the deep ambiguity of equality as a political concept in the *Encyclopédie d'Yverdon*, I will demonstrate that these Swiss encyclopedists present us with an inconsistent picture of Native American peoples and cultures: from noble to ignoble savage, from a hardened notion of Native Americans as a "race" distinct from and lesser than Europeans, to an anthropological vindication of cultural pluralism, the reader of the *Encyclopédie d'Yverdon* was presented with the full range of early modern perspectives on Native Americans. The crucial question, then, is which of these perspectives is part of the Enlightenment? All of these discourses of equality and inequality must be seen as part of the Enlightenment. This diversity of perspectives—the combination of discourses of modern equality and modern inequality in both Francophone encyclopedias—serves to remind us that "all that is modern is not Enlightened," as Darrin McMahon has memorably stated.[122]

The anonymously authored article "America" is, as with many of the other geographic and ethnographic entries, considerably lengthened in the *Encyclopédie d'Yverdon* compared with its predecessor.[123] The writer opens with basic information concerning the location and size of the continent, its discovery by Christopher Columbus, an assessment of the fertility of the soil, and brief comments on the absence of the large domesticated animals of the Old World. He also describes the natural resources that abound in the various parts of the continent. Regarding the indigenous peoples, he states that America is not very densely populated and describes the hunter-gatherers as being all "in the same circumstances": they are divided into numerous sparsely populated nations, wage cruel wars against one another, and they eat their enemies. He states that there were also great Native American nations—the Mexican and the Inca—and, as was common in early modern sources, these nations receive more favorable treatment than the hunter-gatherers: "They were more humane and more sociable than most other people are. They do not know most of the arts of Europe yet they had found a means of doing without them, the invention of which implied almost as much genius as the arts of which Europeans are proud."[124] Their craftsmanship, while different from its European variant, is nonetheless held in equally high regard. He presents two perspectives on New World religions: one anonymous author maintains that the Native Americans believe in the existence of God as the creator and judge of the universe; other authors, on the contrary, assert that the inhabitants lack a coherent concept of the deity. He does not pass judgment on this, going on to state that, in general, "these people are well built and very robust, sufficiently disposed to living in peace with those who have not harmed them."[125] He goes on to describe the geography of the continent in more detail, including mentioning particular Native American nations and their location. In his discussion of the origin of Native Americans, he takes it for granted that they descended from one of Noah's sons and speculates that a land bridge in the north enabled crossing from Asia.[126] This article offers a concise summary of commonplaces regarding the Americas that a European audience found useful—information about natural resources, a generalizing ethnography that pays relatively little attention to specifics, and a short history of the region that takes for granted that Native Americans only really entered history with the arrival of Europeans.

In the article "Canada," Paul-Joseph Vallet writes disparagingly of the indigenous population: "The savages know very little of the world or of the arts and sciences. That is why they are cruel, boastful, and liars, but they demand that we always tell them the truth. Those who trade with them must always explain events in a way that can be interpreted to their advantage, without appearing to lie."[127] One of the reasons for his contempt seems to be his outrage at their continued "heathenism" despite their familiarity with Christianity: "Currently, all of the savages have an idea of the Christian religion but they are not moved to embrace it because they defend polygamy, divorce, drunkenness, theft, and homicide."[128] This reinforces Saliha Belmessous's conclusion that the French started to see Native Canadians as a race especially with the failure of their *francisation* policies.[129] Similar to the article "Canada," the entries that draw from Cornelius De Pauw's work present us with a very derogatory depiction of Native American peoples and culture. In the newly added article "Character of the Savages," De Felice copied De Pauw's remarkably derogatory prose: "Stupidity is unfortunately the common and original characteristic of all Americans."[130] In the course of the article, the character of these "savages" becomes more and more "savage." They are likened to children: "His reason does not age: he remains a child until death, foresees nothing, perfects nothing, and lets nature degenerate before his eyes and under his hands, without ever stimulating it and without it pulling him from his lethargy."[131] Eventually, even the status of children is deemed too intelligent or noble for the Native Americans, because he subsequently likens them to animals: "Savage man, in whom all light is extinguished and all feeling obliterated, hardly strays from the level of quadrupeds and other animals left to their instincts."[132]

Because of such an offensive view of Native Americans, one might expect that De Pauw was a polygenist who asserted the fundamental difference and inequality of the races of humanity, or at least between Native Americans and Europeans. But he was in fact a monogenist who argued that it was the environment that caused the "liabilities" of Native Americans (as well as of Africans), and he was agnostic regarding slavery.[133] This perspective is confirmed in the *Encyclopédie d'Yverdon* as well, when De Felice draws from De Pauw to explain that the Native Americans' intellect and morals are negatively affected by their lifestyle and the climate in which they live: "Hunting, which is all that concerned Americans, provides only a precarious subsistence, familiarizes man's heart with carnage, and incites discord and ongoing wars. This state is thus the most unfavorable to which men can be reduced. And if so many ancient nations were cannibals, that was when they were still ignorant of the art of cultivating edible seeds, and when they had not domesticated any species of quadrupeds or birds, so that the hunters and the animals were equally savage."[134]

With such forceful denigrations of Native Americans, De Pauw and De Felice "hardened" the concept of race, departing significantly from the dominant Buffonian view of human physical diversity. As Michèle Duchet explains of De Pauw, "He pushes the idea of a degeneration of living beings in the New World to an extreme: because of a 'vice in their makeup,' the Native Americans are not a 'variety' in the species, but a *race*, and extremely inferior to others."[135] While Buffon argued that Native Americans had only recently settled on the continent and that these peoples and their lands were quite literally relatively "new," De Pauw maintained that they had long been settled there and, contrary to Buffon, that the climate of the New World prevented all life forms from flourishing.[136]

De Pauw's publication was widely read in the 1770s and 1780s throughout Europe, and his provocative work set off a storm of controversy, spurring some of his contemporaries to directly challenge him.[137] John Browning has argued that De Pauw's negative and inaccurate descriptions prompted a concerted attack by Spanish Americans to correct his portrayal of the New World.[138] This response mainly came from exiled Jesuits born in the Americas, most notably Francisco Javier Clavijero and Juan Ignacio Molina. Browning demonstrates that De Pauw's extreme theories contributed to the development of nationalist movements in the late eighteenth century, as the Creoles were prompted to explore their own history and vindicate their native lands.[139] Significantly, Buffon also attacked De Pauw's theses in the *Supplément* to his *Histoire naturelle* in prose that displays one of the very few moments in which one can detect anger in Buffon's text.[140] Interestingly, an attack on De Pauw's thesis even appears within the *Encyclopédie d'Yverdon* in the volumes of the *Supplément*, which are analyzed below.

De Pauw's ideas found their way into other articles concerning racial theory in the *Encyclopédie d'Yverdon*. In place of Jaucourt's article "Mulatto," De Felice added the new article "Metis and Mulattos." The anonymous author states: "The metis are a species of men born to a white, European man and an Indian woman. In all of Spanish America, they are referred to by the name mestizos, meaning metis. And those born to a white man and a black woman [*négresse*] call themselves mulattos in the colonies."[141] The gendered language is remarkable: in sexual relations between Europeans and Native Americans or sub-Saharan Africans, the European is assumed to be male and the non-European female. But the author then outlines the genetic mixing that produced "quadroons" and "octoroons" and writes of the mixing between European women and non-European men. The anxieties caused by "racial mixing" in the colonies is illustrated by the intervention of religious and political officials in the definition of the offspring of mixed parentage. He remarks that "Pope Clement XI even declared by bull that one must regard the quadroon race as already white."[142] The author speculates on the natural history of variations in skin color and relies on De Pauw's more reified concept of racial difference, stating, "I am convinced that the more men have a dark complexion, the more their semen is colored since in Peru, the face of the inhabitants is not as dark as in French Guiana. And on the shores of the Orinoco, it sometimes only requires two or three generations to produce individuals with a perfect whiteness, while it takes four generations in French Guiana to obtain the same effect."[143] The idea that a darker complexion affects the male reproductive fluid contributed to the hardening of the divisions between perceived "races."[144] In contrast to Jaucourt's article, where the focus lay on the difficulties that enslaved women face as a result of their masters' violation of Louis XIV's restrictions on racial mixing, the Yverdon article concentrates mainly on racial mixture as a question of natural history with an attendant reification of race. While not citing him, De Felice and his collaborators nonetheless drew verbatim from De Pauw's controversial book for numerous other articles on Native Americans in which they stress their immoral or even amoral character.[145]

The *Encyclopédie d'Yverdon* does not present us with a uniform racial theory, however. The article "Man" (Natural History), which combines and modifies Diderot's articles "Man" (Natural History) and "Human Species" (Natural History), contains a section entitled "Varieties in the Human Species," which draws extensively from Buffon. It follows similar lines as Diderot's "Human Species," simply adding Buffon's most recent additions to the topic, including more information about a greater number of ethnic groups across the world.[146] Emphasis continues to be laid upon the primacy of the climate, with food and lifestyle playing a secondary role, in altering the physical makeup of a once homogenously white humankind.

Largely owing to the use of Raynal's *Histoire des deux Indes*, the *Encyclopédie d'Yverdon* presents us with a contradictory picture of Native Americans. In the modified entry "Savages," following the reproduction of most of Jaucourt's original entry the author adds a lengthy section in which he compares the happiness of "civilized" and "savage" peoples, drawing verbatim from Raynal's *Histoire des deux Indes*.[147] He states that a potentially more interesting question than the origins and antiquity of Native Americans is "whether savages are more or less happy than civilized people." In passages reminiscent of Rousseau's state of nature, the author explains that the conveniences of life are cures to miseries that the "savage" does not feel. He remarks that while civilized people enjoy healthier, more refined food, this in fact pertains only to the elite in a civilized society. But one should not look to the elite to judge the overall happiness of a society; rather, "the people" should form the basis and the object of social policy. One sees little else other than tyranny and misfortune among the people of civilized states working hard under the heavy hand of oppressive landowners.

Crucially, the author argues that the primary reason that "savages" are happier than civilized peoples relates to equality. He explains: "There would still remain an infinite distance between the fate of civil man and that of savage man, a difference that is completely to the disadvantage of the social state: it is the inequality of wealth and especially of conditions."[148] The picture of the dark side of civilizational progression that Rousseau so powerfully painted loomed large over many enlightened minds. The author explains: "Habit, prejudice, ignorance, and work pointlessly brutalize the people to the point where they do not feel their degradation. Neither religion nor morality can close the people's eyes to the injustice of the distribution of the evils and the good fortunes of the human condition in the political order."[149] He states that many people suppose civilized life to be better than the savage state because of the numerous conveniences to which the civilized have grown accustomed, but he counters that these conveniences have rendered civilized man helpless rather than genuinely happy. In this author's balance of civilized versus savage societies, the former is clearly judged deficient.

While this article certainly contradicts the vulgar Eurocentrism of other articles, particularly those which rely on De Pauw, its conclusion reveals that whatever the author's intention may have been, the celebration of the "savage" state is rooted in a worldview that infantilizes the "primitive" hunter-gatherer. He explains: "To compare the savage state to that of children, does it not decide the question so vigorously debated between philosophers on the advantages of the state of nature and of the social state? Children, despite the difficulties of education, are they not in the happiest period of human life?"[150] This analogy reveals the power of a new discourse of inequality: the temporal framework of philosophical history.[151] When time is understood as linear progression or development, as it was by many Enlightenment thinkers, it entails inequality because some societies—most notably European society for our thinkers—have made progress from a more primitive to a more advanced state. The anonymous author of the article "Savages" makes the inequalities inherent in philosophical history explicit by referring to savages as children—they may reach the more technologically "advanced" stage of Europe someday, but in the present moment they are unequal. Given that the author argues that the "savage" person is almost certainly happier than the "civilized" person, we should keep in mind that scientific and technological progress did not entail moral progress for all Enlightenment thinkers. Nonetheless, even the Enlightenment's most famous critic of the morals of contemporary European society, Jean-Jacques Rousseau, still accepted the temporal framework of philosophical history.[152] This temporal regime and its attendant inequalities are more pronounced in the *Encyclopédie d'Yverdon* than in its predecessor, reflecting the importance of the 1770s in the history of Enlightenment thought.

Crucially, the regime of temporality did not privilege only Europe, because the encyclopedists praised the sophistication of the precontact Aztec and Incan civilizations, relying once again on the *Histoire des deux Indes*.[153] The encyclopedists' praise reveals that in the eighteenth century, while Europe was commonly regarded as first among "civilized nations," the concept of civilized was certainly not limited to Europe alone.[154] In the article "Mexico, Empire of" (R), the author reprimands the Spanish for their cruelty and ignorance, particularly their inability to see that although the Aztecs did not have an absolute monarchy or Christianity, they still possessed laws, religion, and morality. He describes the Aztec territory as mountainous, well cultivated, and populous and its habitants as very happy, before dryly pointing out the absurdity of the ignorance of the Spanish: "These are the men whom the Spanish did not deign to recognize to be of their species. One of the qualities that they despised most among the Tlascalteques was the love of liberty. They [the Spanish] did not find that they [the Aztec] had a government because they did not have government by a single man, nor a civilized order because they did not have that of Madrid, nor virtues because they did not have their religion, nor intellect because they did not have their opinions."[155]

In a telling passage, the author then goes on to praise the ingeniousness of the Aztecs. It is telling because it reveals what the European author considered to be ingenious and his assumptions about what causes ingenuity to develop in a society. He states that these people, even without iron, without writing, situated in a climate where nature offers everything, where they lack a very ancient history, and "where man's genius is not awakened by needs," even with all of these caveats, he declares that the Aztecs are still among the most ingenious people in the world.[156] The author thus genuinely admires Aztec society and culture, but from a Eurocentric perspective that privileges technological mastery. Once again, we see a reflexive and self-critical, rather than a vulgar, Eurocentrism.[157] Crucially, the factors that the author argues have contributed to European ingeniousness are not in any way innately European but instead result from external and largely accidental circumstances—namely, possessing iron and writing and being positioned in a climate that does not readily sustain human beings and thus would "awaken" genius.

The culturally relativist perspective that the author defends at the outset of this article is then complicated by a celebration of the Mexicans' adoption of European knowledge, particularly technical knowledge. As we saw with the discussion of the "civilized" versus the "savage," European knowledge and materials are praised as superior: "Our fruits, grains, and quadrupeds made their food healthier, more enjoyable, and more plentiful. Their houses are better built, better distributed, and better furnished."[158] He applauds the Mexicans for adopting the European crafts and high culture, such as a taste for theater, concluding: "With these details, we see what the Mexicans were capable of if they had had the good fortune to come under the domination of a conqueror who had had enough moderation and enlightenment to loosen the chains of their servitude instead of tightening them."[159] Although this perspective has been interpreted as evidence of the pro-colonial position that can be found in the *Histoire des deux Indes*,[160] a reading that more accurately reflects the thrust of the most prominent arguments of this text maintains that such arguments are Eurocentric but not inescapably imperialistic.

Given the robustness of Diderot's anti-colonial arguments in the *Histoire des deux Indes*, we can reasonably doubt whether such counterfactual scenarios were meant as serious suggestions; rather, they served to illustrate the destructiveness of the realities of European colonialism.[161] Such an argument works equally well for the *Encyclopédie d'Yverdon*, because De Felice and his collaborators relied heavily on the *Histoire*, including both more direct criticisms of colonialism and the counterfactual arguments illustrating how this history may have unfolded differently. For example, in the newly added article "Duties of Nations," De Felice draws from the Swiss political philosopher Emer de Vattel's masterpiece *The Law of Nations*, the most influential textbook on the subject in the second half of the eighteenth century, to argue that the pretext of civilizing and converting the Native Americans was not just grounds for the European colonization of the Americas: "These ambitious Europeans, who attacked the American nations and subjected them to their greedy domination to, they said, civilize them and to instruct them in the true religion; these usurpers, I say, were based on an equally unjust and ridiculous pretext."[162] It should be noted, however, that while De Felice only quoted the anti-colonialist passages, Vattel in fact defended the right to colonize "uncultivated lands," including all of North America, because he viewed the indigenous population as uniformly nomadic peoples who, because of their alleged nomadism, did not possess any land or cultural rights.[163] The "Americans" to whom Vattel refers in the previous quotation thus meant only those he considered sufficiently sedentary and civilized—the Aztecs and Inca. Additionally, De Felice kept one of the strongest defenses of cultural relativism in the Parisian *Encyclopédie*, Abbé Pestré's article "Canadians, Philosophy of the."[164]

The *Supplément* to the *Encyclopédie d'Yverdon* contains some explicit rejections of the more racialized and racist depictions of Native Americans that we have analyzed. Those disavowals demonstrate that Native American societies and peoples raised contentious moral, philosophical, and anthropological questions for the philosophes and that Enlightenment encyclopedias did not present a single viewpoint but instead captured these debates and controversies. For example, in the *Supplément* entry "America," the author writes that the continent's indigenous peoples "are not . . . as ignorant as M. de P. [Pauw] wants to make them. . . . I could cite many examples of the intellect, intelligence, and good sense of the savages but this article would then become too long. It is very certain that we have never met any Raphaels, Newtons, Lockes, Montesquieus, etc. there, where they would have been very useless. But the savages who want to apply themselves to learning something of the arts and sciences succeed sufficiently well. . . . When a savage has decided to learn something, he will learn it."[165] This passage is drawn from *De l'Amérique et des Américains: Ou Observations curieuses du philosophe La Douceur* (Of America and the Americans: or curious observations of the philosopher "The Gentleness"), one of many responses penned in reaction to De Pauw's vitriolic work.[166]

As we have seen, the article "Canada" in volume 7 of 1771 has nothing positive to say about the indigenous population. Interestingly, the revised *Supplément* article in volume 2 of 1775 contains both a more racialized perspective on the Native Canadians, in that the author comments extensively on their physical features, and also more respectful treatment of their culture.[167] This demonstrates that racial discourse was not necessarily diametrically opposed to imagining cross-cultural equality in the Enlightenment, contrary to nineteenth-century racial science. He writes that their "reddish" skin color results from the effects of the strong winds of their climate in addition to the oils and pigments with which they anoint their skin, relying upon the Jesuit historian Pierre-François-Xavier Charlevoix's popular history of New France.[168] While the author considers their tawny complexion ugly, he qualifies this judgment by adopting their perspective: "[It is] hideous in our eyes, but beautiful without a doubt, or at least tolerable, to their not very sensitive eyes."[169] He then describes the linguistic groupings of the native peoples and admires their eloquence, stating that their rhetorical skills surpass those of the greatest Greek and Roman orators.

In his discussion of forms of government among Native Canadians, the European author lauds their stability, freedom, independence, and upright moral character. One senses that he envies the Native Canadians, not least because of the egalitarian ethos that permeates their society: "He [the Native Canadian] never harms those two powerful instincts of nature, love of equality and of independence."[170] He then describes their marriage practices, religious beliefs and customs, and modes of subsistence, all in an extremely respectful manner that often places Europe in a negative light. He details the history of Canada after the arrival of Europeans and the complex relations between the English and French colonists and the various First Nations. This entire article is drawn verbatim (save for a few deleted paragraphs) from the *Histoire des deux Indes*.[171] Scholars have shown that Raynal and his collaborators presented a picture of Native Americans as "within the fold of nature," for the most part excising the negative comments on Native Canadians from the sources they relied upon to paint a picture of the familiar "noble savage."[172] While Michèle Duchet argues that the anti-colonialism of the philosophes in general and of the *Histoire* in particular is largely a myth, Sankar Muthu focuses specifically on Diderot's contributions to show that the *Histoire* was at times forcefully anti-colonial.[173] It is of primary importance to note that this very debate is made possible by an Enlightenment transformation, since Raynal's *Histoire des deux Indes* may be seen as the first philosophical and historical treatment of a "world-system"—that which was launched by the European oceanic empires.[174] Although the term "colonialism" had not yet been coined, it was arguably one of the first works to treat the European empires as a system and thus an object of critique and criticism.[175]

De Felice and his collaborators drew liberally from the *Histoire* so that here we also find a similar tension between a story of advancement thanks to the progress of European commerce and a story of the atrocities committed by European colonists around the world.[176] We find, then, a polyphony of voices in the *Encyclopédie d'Yverdon* and a relatively evenhanded mixture of criticisms not only of the brutal effects of European colonialism but also of the civilizing effects of international trade and cultural exchange. We cannot, therefore, conclude that the work is either straightforwardly pro- or anti-colonial but rather captures the extent to which European expansion became problematized in the late Enlightenment. De Felice's use of the *Histoire* also indicates that we cannot draw clear divisions between an atheistic, anti-colonial Enlightenment, on the one hand, and a moderate, Christian, and pro-colonial Enlightenment on the other. While it remains true that the most hard-hitting attacks on colonialism in the *Encyclopédie d'Yverdon* came from the pen of the atheist Diderot via the *Histoire*, De Felice's use of this material reveals that such criticisms of colonialism did not depend upon materialist philosophy. Even his commitment to the truth and value of Protestantism did not result in a defense of evangelism. Although he expressed a desire to see Protestantism spread across the whole world, he remarks that changing the religion that someone was raised in is not the work of man but of God, and until God himself spreads Christianity across the globe, "let us remain peacefully at our own home, strive to make ourselves useful to our homeland, and respect other nations who do not merit the law of nations, which is the sacred link of humanity, any less than us."[177]

De Felice kept abreast of the latest travelogues, since the Pacific—what has been referred to as "the eighteenth century's New World"[178]—was also covered in the *Encyclopédie d'Yverdon*. The newly added article "Tahiti" (N) describes the location of the island and its natural resources. The anonymous author relies upon Louis Antoine de Bougainville's famous *Voyage autour du monde* (*Voyage Around the World*), and his remarks on the natives reveal a lot about how race was understood in the 1760s and 1770s:

> The people of Tahiti are composed of two very different races of men, who nonetheless have the same language, the same customs, and who seem to mix together without distinction. The first, and it is the most numerous, produces men of the greatest height: one sees men

of six feet or more among them. I have never met better-built or better-proportioned men. To paint Hercules or Mars, one will not find equally beautiful models anywhere else. Nothing distinguishes their features from those of Europeans. And if they were clothed and if they lived less exposed to the bright sun, they would be as white as us. In general, their hair is black. The second race is of a modest height, has frizzy and tough hair like horsehair, its color and its traits differ little from those of mulattoes.[179]

Height, skin color, and hair type are particularly important factors that distinguish one race from another, but Bougainville's aesthetic judgments form a large part of his description. The more a given race resembles Europeans, the more favorably he judges it, while the hair of those with a darker complexion is likened to that of animals ("crin"). There is also an implicit distinction made between darker pigmentation that is reversible—a darker complexion resulting from exposure to the elements—and one that presumably runs deeper. He does not speculate further on the origins of these two separate races. While Bougainville's categorization of the Tahitians into two distinct races would later be incorporated by Blumenbach into his "Malay" and "Ethiopian" races,[180] Bougainville understands race in less essentialist terms here.[181] After all, he states that the two races have "the same language, the same customs, and seem to mix together without distinction."[182]

The encyclopedist then describes the society and culture of the Tahitians, depicting the island as nearly paradisiacal: the inhabitants are gentle, peaceful, and kind, and all of the necessary provisions of life are held in common. As the article goes on, however, we find out that Tahitians are superstitious and that the priests hold much power. The stereotype of the "unthinking savage" is also promulgated by the anonymous encyclopedist (following Bougainville), as he describes any sort of reflection as being "unbearable" to the Tahitians. But he qualifies this judgment: "I will not, however, accuse them of lacking intelligence. Their skill and industry in the few necessary instances of industry, which notwithstanding the abundance of the country and the beauty of the climate, would contradict this account. One is surprised by the art with which the fishing instruments are made."[183] He mentions that polygamy is widely practiced on the island but omits Bougainville's famous report of the Tahitians' sexual freedom that prompted what are perhaps Diderot's most penetrating philosophical and anthropological reflections.[184] Interestingly, the encyclopedist concludes the article by calling into doubt his earlier praise of the liberty and egalitarianism that Tahitians enjoy: "I was mistaken. The distinction of ranks is very noticeable in Tahiti and the disproportion cruel."[185] He describes a class of people, called Tatacinou, whom the higher-ranking individuals hold in virtual servitude and the Tahitian commoners only eat fruit and vegetables while the meat and fish are reserved for the elite. While Bougainville offers a sympathetic account of Tahitian peoples and society, we should not forget that the pretext for his entire voyage was the expansion of the French overseas empire in the wake of the losses France suffered during the Seven Years' War.[186] Overall, the article combines discourses of equality and inequality and thus offers a mixed picture of the Tahitians. It is noteworthy that when the encyclopedist, quoting Bougainville, describes the egalitarian ethos of Tahitian society, there is a palpable sense of envy.

De Felice and his coterie thus present us with an ambiguous picture of Native American and Pacific island peoples and cultures. On the one hand, we find a racialized discourse, sometimes a deeply disparaging one, particularly as a result of borrowings from Cornelius de Pauw's work. On the other hand, we also find in the *Encyclopédie d'Yverdon* some of the most robust defenses of cross-cultural equality in Enlightenment thought, mainly owing to the use of Raynal's *Histoire des deux Indes*. These discourses are not mutually exclusive, because some articles portray Native Americans as a homogenous racial group while also respectfully describing their societies. This finding supports the argument that racial discourse did not develop as a bulwark to temper egalitarian political momentum, at least in the prerevolutionary period. Additional evidence in support of this argument can be found in the *Encyclopédie d'Yverdon*'s conceptualization of sub-Saharan Africans, to which I now turn.

Africa and the African Diaspora

De Felice and his fellow encyclopedists adopted the same Buffonian perspective on sub-Saharan Africans as a racial group as we found in Diderot's *Encyclopédie*, but they excised many of the pro-slavery passages and advanced a more forcefully abolitionist argument. Their abolitionism was grounded in a compassionate understanding of natural equality and demonstrates that modern racial classification in Enlightenment thought was not inextricably tied to inegalitarianism. While we find the usual eighteenth-century Eurocentric biases in this racial discourse, it existed alongside the defense of basic equality and natural rights.

Jaucourt's article "Slavery" is reproduced with the addition of a short section from Rousseau's *Social Contract* that is emphatically antislavery. The part that De Felice adds contains Rousseau's assertion that slavery violates "the rights of humanity": "To renounce one's freedom is to renounce one's quality as man, the rights of humanity, and even its duties."[187] Additionally, while De Felice included Le Romain's article "Sugar Refinery," he deleted the racist remarks toward the end of the article, in which Le Romain had referred to Blacks as "naturally lazy," "cunning," and "extremely vicious."[188] In an even more fascinating alteration to the Parisian encyclopedia, De Felice replaced the three separate articles containing the headword "Negre(s)" found in Diderot's *Encyclopédie*, all of which were more or less pro-slavery, with one article that contains a powerful antislavery argument. The article consists of three main parts. It opens with Formey's article "Negre" from Diderot's *Encyclopédie*, followed by the section "Commerce of the *Negres*," which is a brief history and description of the transatlantic slave trade, and "Slavery of the *Negres*," an uncompromising criticism of slavery. One is thus presented with both a natural historical and anatomical investigation into blackness and an impassioned antislavery position, once again revealing the coeval development of the modern racial classificatory system and the politicization of equality in Enlightenment thought.

The article contains tension between a reformist and an abolitionist perspective on slavery. The section "Commerce of the *Negres*" presents a reformist agenda, making recommendations on how to render slavery more humane to ultimately keep the system intact.[189] From the beginning of the next section, "Slavery of the *Negres*," the tone is much more forceful and the author uncompromising in his opposition to slavery. He begins: "We will not degrade ourselves here to the point of adding to the ignominious list of those writers who use their talents to justify politically that which morality condemns. In a century when so many errors have been courageously unmasked, it would be shameful to conceal important truths from humanity."[190] The author then takes Montesquieu to task for not being sufficiently thoroughgoing in his opposition to slavery, even going so far as to condone a violent reaction on behalf of the enslaved against their masters: "Whoever justifies such an odious system deserves from the philosopher a silence full of contempt and from the negro a stabbing."[191] He references Clarissa from Richardson's epistolary novel to assert the right of everyone to defend their liberty: "If you put your hand on me, I will kill myself, said Clarissa to Lovelace, and I would say to the one who would attack my liberty, if you approach, I will stab you. And I would reason better than Clarissa because defending my liberty, which is the same as defending my life, is my principal duty. Respecting that of another is only the second. And all other things being equal, the death of a culprit is more in conformity with justice than that of an innocent."[192]

This is a remarkable reference bolstering Lynn Hunt's thesis regarding the role that epistolary novel reading played in expanding the purview of empathy across the eighteenth century and giving birth to the idea of human rights in the 1760s and 1770s.[193] Following his reference to Clarissa, the author then speaks in the first person from the slave's perspective: "I hold from nature the right to defend myself; therefore, nature did not give you the right to attack me."[194] He then refutes multiple pro-slavery arguments, using the first-person perspective of a slave and grounding his arguments in an emotional appeal to natural equality and inalienable human rights.

We find a similar tension between reformism and abolitionism in the *Supplément* article "Domingue, Saint," once again owing to borrowings from the *Histoire des deux Indes*. The author defends the right of slaves to rebellion and even predicts, and celebrates, the prospect of such a revolution. He says that as a result of the cruelty of "civilized" nations, there will emerge from a community of maroons a leader who will rise up and conquer the island, reestablishing the "rights of humanity."[195] As Daniel Gordon has argued, this perspective demonstrates that the *Histoire des deux Indes* and, by extension, at least parts of the *Encyclopédie d'Yverdon*, subvert the Eurocentrism that was so often associated with the newly coined term "civilization." Raynal and Diderot used the word in the usual fashion—as a reference to European commercial society—but they also disconnected it from its specifically European connotations and employed it with reference to a more just and humane order in general.[196] Much of the article, however, is devoted to a discussion of the best means to ensure peaceful relations between the French and the Spanish, the ruling European powers of the island, and how best to defend the colony against an English invasion. As Siep Stuurman has pointed out, Enlightenment egalitarianism admitted of both colonialist and anti-colonialist perspectives, both of which we find in this article.[197]

Given that the concept of race and racial categorization are so often positioned in narratives that tell the story of political disenfranchisement, it is striking that this politicized notion of equality existed alongside the development of a racial classificatory system in the *Encyclopédie d'Yverdon*. The racial classificatory framework utilized by De Felice and his fellow encyclopedists remains the same as we found in its French predecessor: it is predominantly Buffonian. However, it should be noted that one of the more famous contributors to the *Encyclopédie d'Yverdon* was Albrecht von Haller, the Swiss anatomist and naturalist who was a steadfast supporter of the preexistence theory of generation in the face of Buffon's critique of it.[198] Additionally, the article "Canaanites" was lengthened to emphasize that Africans descended from Noah's cursed son Ham, though the curse is not explicitly used to explain dark pigmentation.[199] The issue of varieties within the human species seems to be ignored in the articles that concern generation and inheritance, however. Arnulphe d'Aumont's article "Generation" is reproduced in full but with a few pages added to the end of the article in which Albrecht von Haller defends his preexistence theory, appealing to a variety of naturalists and physicians to support his case and the supposed empirical evidence that underpinned it: "It is certain that the fetus, or at least a part of the fetus, has been seen in the ovary."[200] In the article "Man," the section "Varieties in the Human Species" is about one and a half times longer than Diderot's article "Human Species." While Diderot had shortened Buffon's antislavery remarks to just two sentences, the Yverdon article copied Buffon's oppositional paragraph in full.[201] Otherwise, the same mix of biological, moral, and aesthetic considerations lies at the basis of the racial classificatory system propounded in this article.

In the *Encyclopédie d'Yverdon*, we find the same combination of laudatory and condemnatory perspectives on sub-Saharan African peoples and cultures as we found in the Parisian *Encyclopédie*. Many articles from the original reference work remain intact and the revised or newly added ones do not reveal any patterns that would indicate a clear design on the part of De Felice in the direction either of redeeming or condemning Blacks. In the article "Africa," one finds the Eurocentric perspective that Africa is not a well-cultivated or "advanced" continent, but the author explicitly states that this is because of a lack of education: "We accuse the Africans of ferocity, cruelty, perfidy, cowardice, idleness. If the accusation is not false or exaggerated, it seems that we must attribute this less to the climate than to the cause that we have just indicated [ignorance]. If nature creates the difference between geniuses and characters, I believe that education makes an even greater difference."[202] He doubts whether such negative stereotypes are even true before going on to attribute them to external and alterable factors—climate and, especially, education. Following a description of ancient Roman knowledge of Africa and of how the Romans divided the continent, the author makes a telling statement that indicates the "racialized" perspective of his contemporary moment as opposed to that of the ancients. He writes that the primary division of Africa among the ancients was into the large nations of Egypt, Libya, and Ethiopia. By contrast, "let us come to the division of the moderns: they divide Africa in two general parts, which are the countries of the whites and the countries of the blacks."[203] The "countries of the whites" comprise northern Africa while the "countries of the blacks" encompass sub-Saharan Africa. Although the author does not reflect any further upon the differences between the "modern" and "ancient" divisions of Africa, the racial dimension of the comparison is very telling to the present-day historian. It lends support to the argument that the use of skin color to divide humanity, particularly the white-black binary, took hold as the transatlantic slave trade intensified in the early modern period, though we should not exaggerate the Atlantic context either, given that the Arab slave trade began much earlier and lasted longer than its transatlantic counterpart.[204]

In the articles on individual sub-Saharan African countries or regions, we find a mixture of vulgar and self-reflexive Eurocentrism similar to that found in Diderot's *Encyclopédie*. For example, Diderot's description of the Beninese as a deistic people who do not display any signs of organized religious worship is copied verbatim by De Felice,[205] as is the respectful treatment of ancient Ethiopian philosophy.[206] Yet De Felice also reproduced the more racialized and condemnatory articles "Hottentots" and "Jagas."[207] Interestingly, De Felice added an additional article on the "Jagas" under the headword "Giagas, ou Jagas, ou Jagues" (R), in which he offers a short description of the origin of what he describes as their violent and barbaric culture in the policies of their first queen, Tembam-Dumba.[208] In the article "Guinea" (R), the author states that this West African population is part of a larger race—called *nègres*—about which he has nothing positive to say: "The *nègres* in general are all of such a deceitful nature that one cannot trust them. They do not miss any opportunity to cheat a European or to cheat one another. . . . Their idleness is the reason that we find few arts or skilled trades among them."[209] The encyclopedist who compiled this article culled the entire text from Antoine Auguste Bruzen de la Martinière's *Le Grand dictionnaire géographique* (Great geographic dictionary), which demonstrates that seventeenth- and eighteenth-century reference works often contributed to the stereotyping of sub-Saharan Africans.[210] While De Felice did not link such pejorative statements to a justification of slavery, as had Le Romain in Diderot's *Encyclopédie*, we nonetheless find denigrating racial stereotypes of sub-Saharan Africans in the *Encyclopédie d'Yverdon*.

As previously mentioned, a notable difference between the *Encyclopédie d'Yverdon* and its Parisian predecessor is the increased attention paid to the world system that resulted from European expansion, and this included Africa. The example of Madagascar is quite instructive, because Jean-Baptiste Colbert's effort to colonize the island in the 1660s failed and a renewed effort was launched by the French in the late 1760s. The anonymous author of the article "Madagascar" (R) states that the indigenous peoples "do not possess any other principles than those of nature" but nonetheless are quite superstitious.[211] As a result of the island's fertility and the native people's "simplicity," he has confidence that the French should be able to establish prosperous plantations by transforming the peoples' laws and customs to mold them into enthusiastic farmers under the tutelage of the French: "The islanders are intelligent and skillful. In the regions where the Arabs have not penetrated, they have the simple laws of nature and the customs of the first men. These laws and these customs are more favorable to agriculture than all of the sublime speculations, than the most complete treatises on the best practices, than all those means employed today to revive among us an art that our customs make us look at with contempt."[212] This passage and many others in this article were actually written by Pierre Poivre, who traveled widely in South and East Asia as an employee of the Compagnie des Indes in the 1740s and 1750s and who was "intendant" of the Isle de France (present-day Mauritius) from 1767 to 1773.[213] He published his memoires as *Voyages d'un philosophe* (*Travels of a Philosopher*) at Yverdon in 1768.[214] While Pierre Poivre was critical of the slave trade and slavery for both moral and economic reasons, he belonged to the physiocratic school and, like his peers, believed in the usefulness of global European empires, a viewpoint that De Felice reproduces here.[215] Additionally, although the *Encyclopédie d'Yverdon* adopts a more consistent antislavery posture than its predecessors, there are other articles that dispassionately describe the slave trade. For example, in the article "Juda" (N) (present-day Ouidah in Benin), the author states that the enslaved Black people who pass through this port are the best and the most expensive "because of their dexterity and their disposition to learn everything in little time."[216]

In contrast to these denigrating depictions of sub-Saharan African peoples and cultures, the Yverdon encyclopedists sometimes advance a vision of cross-cultural equality as well. In the article "Custom" (R), Mingard writes:

> From the first moment of his birth, the Samoyed baby breaths the humid and stale air of his parents' den or the icy cold of the arctic lands. From the moment he exists, the *negre* experiences the scorching effects of the equatorial air. For the one and the other, the state where they are born is natural, their constitution is that which they receive from nature, or at least they believe as such and cannot think differently. We regard as natural that which we have never known to be different from what we experience, and as unnatural that which differs from which we have experienced until now.[217]

This is a robust example of what Siep Stuurman has called the anthropological turn, the inversion of the gaze in particular.[218]

The Yverdon encyclopedists, Mingard in particular, in fact transformed anthropology and psychology into recognizably more modern scholarly disciplines. Anthropology, for example, was defined in Diderot's *Encyclopédie* as having either a theological meaning—the attribution of human characteristics to God—or as relating to the constitution of man, especially human anatomy.[219] The *Encyclopédie d'Yverdon* contains two articles with the headword "Anthropology," one designated as a revision of Mallet's theological article and another designated as a new entry and classified under many disciplines: philosophy, natural history, physiology, metaphysics, and psychology. Mingard wrote the latter article and defined anthropology as "this important branch of philosophical science, which makes man considered under all perspectives known to us, which can offer ideas to our mind, and become the object of our knowledge."[220]

Mingard made anthropology the center of human science and called for its further development. The subjects to be covered in this developing science include "the origin of man" and "the different states through which he passes."[221] In his study of the development of early modern psychology, Fernando Vidal compares the *Encyclopédie d'Yverdon* with its Parisian predecessor and argues that in the Enlightenment in general and the *Encyclopédie d'Yverdon* in particular, thinkers transformed the concept of anthropology into a field of knowledge whose object was a science of human nature, and psychology became a part of that broader science.[222] The impetus to understand the faculties and traits that are universal to humankind made possible a more sympathetic account of non-European cultures, even if the encyclopedists often fell short of this goal.

On the whole, then, we are presented with a variegated picture of sub-Saharan African peoples and cultures. The Yverdon encyclopedists incorporated some of the most radical antislavery sentiments of the late eighteenth century, grounding their arguments in novel understandings of the political consequences of equality and the inalienability of rights. Yet the encyclopedists also rehashed derogatory stereotypes of Blacks, dressed in the language of natural history and scientific taxonomy. As previously mentioned, it is noteworthy that these discourses exist alongside one another and sometimes the same encyclopedist advanced each of these perspectives, demonstrating that a single mind could hold both seemingly contradictory positions. I write "seemingly contradictory" because in the worldview of these and many other eighteenth-century thinkers, the equality of rights did not mean the equality of civilizations. For our encyclopedists, Europe represented the apotheosis of the development of that eighteenth-century neologism "civilization."[223] However, as we saw in the article "Africa," this concept was not yet exclusively equated with whiteness and even became dissociated from eighteenth-century Europe in the *Histoire des deux Indes* and in our encyclopedia, as other cultures were described as more humane than Europe or its colonies. Another explanation for the existence of this tension between a nascent racial classificatory system and the politicization of equality is that racial classification primarily involved a rethinking of the place of humanity within nature's deep history, particularly given that De Felice and his collaborators continued to rely primarily upon Buffon.

China

The coverage of China in the *Encyclopédie d'Yverdon* follows a pattern with which we have by now become familiar: it is, paradoxically, both more Sinophilic and more Sinophobic than what we found in Diderot's *Encyclopédie*. The Sinophilic elements of this encyclopedia focus on Chinese technological sophistication, their great antiquity, and their stable and just social and political systems. The Sinophobic elements come from voices that doubt Chinese achievement in all of these areas and, perhaps most importantly, focus on Chinese "stagnation." The *Encyclopédie d'Yverdon* thus captures the intensification of the controversy surrounding China in Europe in the 1770s. It is notable that the more skeptical commentators on China do not adopt a more "racialized" viewpoint in the *Encyclopédie d'Yverdon*.

The same admiration for the ancient Chinese tradition of learning and the cultivation of the arts and sciences that we saw in Diderot's *Encyclopédie* is, to a large extent, copied by the *Encyclopédie d'Yverdon*. The articles "Library," "Honest," "Mandarin," and "Literary or Spiritual Nobility" all repeat the same praise for Chinese customs and criticisms of European traditions that we have seen in Chapter 3.[224] Additionally, the physiognomic analysis of Chinese people that we saw in the article "Face" is reproduced in the *Encyclopédie d'Yverdon*.[225] Interestingly, De Felice removed many of d'Holbach's short articles on various aspects of Chinese religion and philosophy that present a thinly veiled defense of natural religion or even atheism. The perspective is broadened regarding Chinese technological skill. Numerous articles from Diderot and d'Alembert's *Encyclopédie* on the mechanical arts that did not mention Chinese artisans were altered at Yverdon to include them, usually by Paul-Joseph Vallet, the mechanical arts specialist among the Yverdon encyclopedists. The article "Artificial Canal" copies the Parisian original but contains an additional section by Vallet which praises China's extensive canal system. He likens the system to the circulation of blood in the human body, stating that it brings life, health, and happiness to the country.[226] Vallet also authored the additions to "Chamoiseur," which lauds the skills of Chinese leather manufacturers, and "Gazette," which praises the great antiquity of Chinese periodicals.[227]

As with most geographical entries in the *Encyclopédie d'Yverdon*, the article "China" (R) has been considerably lengthened. While Diderot had written one short paragraph on China, the anonymous Yverdon author wrote several paragraphs containing just basic information about the country's location, size, and principal cities. The author then devotes considerable attention to Chinese agriculture, culling entire sections from Pierre Poivre's *Voyages d'un philosophe*. Poivre admiringly describes the industriousness of the Chinese and their ability to sustain such a large population. He argues that China has the most impressive agricultural production in the world and that this cannot be attributed to superior technology but instead results from "its government, whose profound and unshakeable foundations were laid by reason alone, at the same time as those of the world; from its laws dictated by nature to the first men and safely conserved from generation to generation since the first age of humanity."[228] Significantly for our discussion of equality, one of the reasons Poivre believes that China is such an enlightened country is because of a general spirit of egalitarianism that has permeated the citizenry from the beginning of its history. He contrasts this egalitarianism with distinctions between nobleman and commoner, with an obvious nod to Europe, arguing that such distinctions based on birth "insult without thinking and degrade the entire human species."[229] His virulent attack on nobility is grounded in his commitment to the natural equality of all human beings, as he explains that the Chinese have always known that we are all fundamentally equal and respect this principle. He does, however, take the authority of the emperor for granted, referring to his subjects as his "children" who are equal among themselves but not equal to the emperor. The author also comments upon the physical features of the Chinese: "The Chinese are dark skinned and have an olive complexion. For them, beauty consists in being tall, large, and fat, in having a wide forehead, small and flat eyes, a short nose, large ears, a long beard, and black hair. They are clean and civil but extremely miserly and jealous."[230] This passage is taken from Martinière's *Grand dictionnaire*, demonstrating the recycling of material between dictionaries and encyclopedias across the eighteenth century.[231]

The article "China" contains a cross-reference to the article "Chinese (Philosophy of the)," which contains a fascinating alteration capturing the increasing traction of the idea of Chinese stagnation. Diderot's article is reproduced in its entirety with a short addition at the end of the article. As we have seen, while Diderot praised Confucian moral philosophy, he was critical of Chinese natural philosophy and doubted whether the Chinese were technologically and scientifically more advanced than Europe. The additional section takes it for granted that Chinese science is currently stagnating and offers an explanation for this retardation. The anonymous author explains that many people have argued that this stagnation has resulted from the primacy that the Chinese place on being trained in the law to become a prominent state official, which has inadvertently pushed scientific knowledge and enterprise to the side. He argues that this is an insufficient explanation and that, more important, luck has played a determinate role—specifically, the Chinese could not benefit from the heritage of the "genius" of the ancient Greeks. He explains: "If this genius often showed itself in China, there would have been, as in Europe, some men who neglected fortune, nearly content with the pure necessities, who would have given all their care to perfecting the sciences."[232] While the author advances the Eurocentric argument that the ancient Greeks made a unique and significant contribution to scientific knowledge, he maintains that the Chinese would be able to perfect science if they had access to this rich tradition. Generally, the Yverdon encyclopedists maintained that Chinese philosophical and scientific knowledge could be traced back to ancient Egypt, because they claimed that ancient China had been colonized by the Egyptians.[233]

Additionally, we find the new article "Astronomy of the Chinese" which, remarkably, contains very little information about Chinese astronomy. Written by the famous French astronomer Joseph-Jérôme Le François de Lalande, the article contains only about one column of information on Chinese astronomy while the other twelve pages focus on the history of European astronomy.[234] The opening sentence reveals why so little space was devoted to Chinese astronomy in an article that was purportedly dedicated to the subject: "Although astronomy was cultivated very anciently in China, it made little progress there and it seems that one sees the Chinese follow other nations step by step in their progress." Similarly, the article "Cheou-King" (N) describes the life of a thirteenth-century Chinese astronomer whose knowledge, De Felice claims, came from Westerners.[235] Thus, the Yverdon encyclopedists solidified the image of Chinese stagnation that was gaining currency particularly in the final quarter of the eighteenth century. As far as explaining this perceived stagnation, the newly added article "Chou-King" (Shujing, or Book of Documents) in the *Supplément* states that "their language, their writing, and their calculating machines were, are, and will be obstacles that will always prevent them from making progress in arithmetic, algebra, geometry, music, history, etc."[236] While from the perspective of science and technology, Enlightenment thinkers often negatively judged Chinese achievement, the constancy of Chinese history and culture was in fact lauded from a moralistic perspective. In the article "God," Mingard argues that the Chinese are a virtuous people because they have strayed the least from their ancient customs.[237] This view not only accords with the more widespread Protestant sensibility about the purity of the early church, but also advances a more secular and culturally relativist perspective that decoupled virtue from Christianity.

What is perhaps one of the most interesting changes in the Yverdon's discussion of China compared with those of older encyclopedias is that De Felice and his fellow encyclopedists use the concepts of society and social to analyze and understand Chinese as well as other non-European peoples. In developing a "science of human nature," the Enlightenment philosophes knew they could not limit themselves to European culture and history. And so, in the article "Society," De Felice refers to Chinese society to argue that neither absolute independence nor domination is a fundamental part of human nature. The entire article is essentially an anti-Hobbesian tract that holds that the cultivation of our own happiness and that of our fellow human beings is natural to humanity, in addition to being the most virtuous of actions. Such a commitment to cultivating others' happiness stems from the "social virtues," which De Felice argues the Chinese have cultivated since time immemorial: "These are the instructions, the meditations, the writings of the Chinese sages that for three thousand years have preserved the social virtues and happiness."[238] Furthermore, in "Man" (R), De Felice argues that respect for one's parents is the first, most natural, and strongest of the inclinations or habits of human beings. In this anti-Rousseauist argument, De Felice argues for the naturalness of an enduring parent-child bond that serves as the basis for the formation of larger communities, and he cites China as a particularly laudable example of a society that prospers because of filial piety.[239]

While the political implications of these articles are ambiguous, the use of China demonstrates the broader reach of the Yverdon encyclopedists in their engagement with non-Western societies. There are additional articles in which the Yverdon encyclopedists do not condemn or praise but instead try to understand Chinese customs on their own terms—that is to say, anthropologically. For example, the article "Bereavement" and the *Supplément* article "Honors Rendered to the Dead" respectfully describe Chinese funerary customs, along with those of other peoples, presenting rituals associated with the deceased as cross-cultural phenomena.[240] De Felice appreciated that any discussion of the moral dimension of humankind could not be limited to Europe if it was to be accurate and rigorous. The difference between Chinese as well as many other societies and Europe is not used as a marker of backwardness; rather, De Felice attempts to find common elements between many societies, past and present, and extrapolate from these to understand the human condition.

The *Encyclopédie d'Yverdon* presents us with a similar mixture of Sinophilic and Sinophobic perspectives as that found in its Parisian predecessor. As we have seen, the scale could easily tilt to one side or the other depending on which article one consults but it does not seem to be heavily weighted to either side. A striking difference between how De Felice and his circle used Chinese society and history compared with how their Parisian predecessors did is in what we could call the social sciences—or, in non-presentist terms, human science. This incorporation of non-European societies into a broader human science is widely taken to be a hallmark of the Enlightenment and demonstrates another perspective from which we may position the *Encyclopédie d'Yverdon* as an Enlightenment encyclopedia. While certain articles describe the physical features of the Chinese and construct a "Chinese race," their physical or intellectual "peculiarities" are never singled out as a cause of their perceived stagnation. Rather, the Sino-sceptics point to specific historical or cultural factors to explain the supposed inertia or decline of China.

Conclusion

The *Encyclopédie d'Yverdon* contains such a diverse array of perspectives on equality and human diversity that, at first glance, it is difficult to find coherence. We can nevertheless discern some significant patterns. First, De Felice and his collaborators transformed equality into a foundational concept. We have seen that De Felice was far from a committed egalitarian political thinker, but he nonetheless accepted that the formal equality of individuals lies at the basis of a just political and social order. Although inequalities are necessary and even desirable in society, a significant avenue of criticism was opened up because in this novel conception of the formal equality of individuals, equality receives the benefit of the doubt and inequality must now be justified. Inequality can no longer rest undisturbed as part of reverential tradition. Those traditions came under sharp scrutiny by the eighteenth century, as European travelers across two and a half centuries wrote widely of Edenic egalitarian societies in the Americas and, increasingly, in the Pacific, and as new understandings of the nature of the individual and society took root in the wake of the religious and political upheavals of sixteenth- and seventeenth-century Europe. The transformation of equality into a foundational concept was bound up with the advent of the individual in moral and political thought and with the invention of society as the grounds of our collective existence. We have seen that even the more convinced Protestant encyclopedists acquiesced to religion's function as a guarantor of a peaceful and stable social order, and vigorously defended toleration.

This shift in the understanding of human interdependence affected how eighteenth-century thinkers, including the Yverdon encyclopedists, made sense of and evaluated cultural diversity. While De Felice and all of his collaborators were convinced of the truth of Christian revelation and of the uniquely powerful role that Christianity can play in instilling upright morals, the triumph of secular understandings of society's history and function created space for the positive evaluation of non-European peoples and cultures. We have seen that these encyclopedists praised the morality and "social virtues" of many different peoples around the globe. Such praise does not depend upon an Enlightenment understanding of society and social, but this development certainly gave additional impetus to the appreciation of cultural diversity. The *Encyclopédie d'Yverdon* both expanded and contracted the purview of equality compared with Diderot's *Encyclopédie*, but beneath this paradox, we find that a fundamental shift in the conceptualization of human interdependence has taken place that gave equality its political teeth.

As with equality, we find an ambiguous discourse of racial classification in the *Encyclopédie d'Yverdon*. De Pauw's pejorative remarks concerning Native Americans as a vastly inferior "race" compete with the cultural relativism of Raynal's *Histoire des deux Indes*. The *Encyclopédie d'Yverdon* even incorporated some of the most pointed criticisms of De Pauw, and so the reference work captured the diversity and range of the controversy surrounding human diversity that was raging in the mid- to late eighteenth century. Compared to the Parisian *Encyclopédie*, we are presented with both a more racialized and racist worldview in some articles, and a more rigorous cultural relativism and even anti-colonialist perspective in others. It is crucial to recognize that De Pauw's denigration of Native Americans and other non-European peoples as innately inferior is not a premodern, atavistic perspective but rather a modern discourse of inequality, in that it depends upon the conceptual apparatuses of taxonomy and the natural history of humanity.[241] In opposition to this denigratory perspective, we have also seen that the Yverdon encyclopedists took a much harder line against slavery, grounding their abolitionist arguments in the nascent rights language that was growing in strength and popularity in the second half of the eighteenth century. The equal potential of non-Europeans is emphasized in some articles, as is their morally upright character, which serves as grounds to defend their right to a different, non-European culture. As we saw, the author of the article "Africa" doubted the veracity of the common stereotype of an utterly barbarous African peoples and argued that, in any case, education has the power to transform people's morals. Additionally, these Swiss encyclopedists adopted Rousseau's emphasis on human beings' innate malleability and the power of the laws and upbringing in shaping a people's character. For example, De Felice concludes his article "Climate" by stating "he who knows how to put to use all the forms that can be given to legislation will prove to the universe that there is nothing than cannot be conquered, and that no force can be compared to it."[242]

The fact that both of these discourses—one that emphasizes malleability in intellect and moral character, and one fixity—exist side by side, usually not in the same article but certainly in articles by the same author, gives us pause for thought. We cannot ignore the pressure De Felice was under to complete the encyclopedia as quickly as possible, which may have contributed to his use of such disparate sources. But given that oppositional viewpoints are presented in various articles, one may reasonably argue that this was a strategy adopted to communicate to the reader the diversity of viewpoints on a variety of issues. In any case, I think it is important to notice that the discourse of racial classification did not develop in any simple or straightforward way as a *response* to egalitarianism. This is important because, as explained in the introduction, many scholars continue to maintain this perspective. Although race would eventually be used to serve regressive and reactionary political purposes, the concept of race in the Enlightenment demonstrates that there were (and are) more issues at stake in the modern idea of race than the power and hegemony of a White ruling class.

Finally, what can analyzing the discursive fields of equality and racial classification in the *Encyclopédie d'Yverdon* tell us about the Enlightenment? First, contra Jonathan Israel, we cannot draw a sharp distinction between an atheistic and egalitarian Enlightenment, on the one hand, and a moderate, Christian, and anti-egalitarian Enlightenment on the other.[243] These Swiss Protestant encyclopedists are more forcefully antislavery than any of Diderot's contributors, and while some of their arguments certainly do originate in the minds and texts of radical atheists, the *Encyclopédie d'Yverdon*'s incorporation of these arguments demonstrates that the Christian Enlightenment could serve radical political ends. In any case, Diderot's support for the American Revolution and for slave revolts in his writings of the 1770s and 1780s owed more to his disillusionment with the efficacy of reform, rather than following directly from his materialism.[244] Second, I argue that the cluster of ideas of equality, toleration, individual freedom, and a secularly framed ethics allows us to construe a thin coherence of Enlightenment thought between and within these encyclopedias. Such coherence includes both the more forward-thinking defense of political equality and the novel racial discourse. There is thus a tension within Enlightenment thought between the more expansive and inclusive language of universal equality and that of the exclusionary and particularistic one of racial divisions. Crucially, race did not yet serve as the basis of a deterministically inegalitarian worldview. Contrary to those who argue that Enlightenment thinkers' criticisms of colonialism and slavery only served to hide an even more sinister Eurocentric and hegemonic agenda, we must remember that these thinkers advanced a robust defense of the rights that follow from our common humanity, which included recognition of cultural differences.[245] The *Encyclopédie d'Yverdon* demonstrates that these debates concerning the physical and cultural diversity of humanity extended across eighteenth-century Europe, as the global system resulting from European expansion was felt even by thinkers in countries without a colonial empire, such as Switzerland.

CONCLUSION

The Enlightenment is often held accountable for modernity's ills, such as racism, and praised for its accomplishments, such as egalitarianism. Attempts to prove that the movement was really one or the other—racist or egalitarian—inevitably fail because of the Enlightenment's polyphonic nature. This polyphony cannot be infinitely extended, however, because the Enlightenment was an intellectual movement that was greater than its individual parts; it had thin coherence. The philosophes sought to apply new tools and theories emanating from the new science of the seventeenth century to the study of humankind and society in order to make life better. A cluster of ideas characterizes the Enlightenment—we have seen that toleration, the problematization of inequality, the nature and value of progress, and the growing consciousness of Europe as a geopolitical actor in world history all came to the fore in Enlightenment debates. The philosophes did not agree on the answers to the questions that these issues raised, but this disagreement should not obscure a more fundamental transformation in the framework within which these topics were debated.

Perhaps no concepts are more indicative of this transformation than those of society and social. Enlightenment thinkers reworked Christian notions of community and benevolence into the secular concepts of society and the social virtues. They viewed the rights-bearing individual as the fundamental reality, and by mid-century, "society" and "social" took larger human collectivities to be a fact of existence, sidestepping the issue of whether or not humankind is sociable by nature.[1] We have seen that although many philosophes continued to defend the necessity of religion, they did so in the name of society. While recent scholarship is correct to point to the importance of religion in the Enlightenment,[2] that should not obscure the secularization of the concepts of society and social and the fundamental change in worldview that this reflected and reinforced.[3] The *concepts* became secular, even if not all or even most Europeans did. As Ernst

Cassirer has explained, "In eighteenth-century thought the intellectual center of gravity changes its position," as the various fields of knowledge shake off the dominance of metaphysics and theology.[4] This shift is revealed by the term "enlightenment" itself, which had long been an important theological term for divine light or a philosophical term referring to the light of reason. But by the second half of the eighteenth century, the plural term in French (*lumières*) was omnipresent and referred to something quite different: the possibility of the accumulation of knowledge by collective effort.[5] In addition to the more purely philosophical and theological background of these transformations, J. G. A. Pocock and David Bell have argued that a much more tangible and frightening legacy of the sixteenth and seventeenth centuries, namely that of religious civil war, lay behind calls for the separation of politics from religion and the strengthening of civil authority.[6]

This novel conceptualization of the interdependence of human relationships under the concept of society had far-reaching consequences, not least regarding egalitarian thought. For the philosophes, society no longer had transcendental foundations but instead acquired its legitimacy from within. And given the primacy of the autonomous individual that the Enlightenment concept of society assumed, traditional hierarchies based on birth and corporate membership became problematic.[7] In this new worldview, inequality now had to be debated and justified. This did not happen evenly or all at once, and many Enlightenment thinkers who did not already possess a noble title sought one.[8] But even Voltaire, hardly an egalitarian thinker, reveals the force that equality acquired by the mid-eighteenth century. He declared in *Le Fanatisme, ou Mahomet le prophète* (*Fanaticism, or Mahomet the Prophet*), "All mortals are equal; it is not birth but virtue alone that makes the difference."[9] And in his entry "Equality" in his *Dictionnaire philosophique* (*Philosophical Dictionary*), Voltaire writes, "Every man, in the bottom of his heart, is right to believe himself entirely equal to other men."[10] While he then goes on to defend the necessity of social inequalities, this entry reveals the force of an eighteenth-century revolution in worldview in which inequality could no longer be so easily justified in the name of providence or nature's plan.

One can find many examples of pre-eighteenth-century critics of worldly hierarchies, such as Blaise Pascal, who argued that the nobility is not naturally superior to others and that their privileges result from convention alone. But Pascal himself provides us with a telling contrast to many eighteenth-century thinkers in that while he affirmed basic human equality, he ultimately argued that the corporate structure of his contemporary society must be upheld for the sake of peace and prosperity.[11] There is a vast distance that separates this argument from Diderot's attack on privilege in the *Encyclopédie*, where he argues that "the only legitimate privileges are those that accord with nature."[12] For Enlightenment thinkers, tradition no longer served as the arbiter of justice or legitimacy and thus worldly hierarchies became problematic. Inequality now had to serve the general utility, a keyword in the Enlightenment lexicon.[13]

Few philosophes argued for a leveled society, but their arguments for inequality are much closer and understandable to us because they are couched in the language of political economy in an imagined meritocratic society, rather than being grounded in birth and privilege.[14] The significance of the philosophes' contribution to egalitarian thought is not that they were thoroughgoing egalitarians, but rather that they gave equality the benefit of the doubt and made inequality an object of criticism and study. The origin of the greater traction of the idea of basic or moral equality among eighteenth-century thinkers is difficult to discern. Multifarious factors coalesced in the eighteenth-century Enlightenment to give equality its political bite. Pierre Rosanvallon has isolated four important ones: the Christian legacy, theories of natural right, a conceptual revolution in anthropology that established a material basis for our common humanity, and a sociological revolution associated with the advent of the individual.[15] He correctly points out that none of these transformations on its own can explain what he calls the "revolution of similarity," because Christianity has been compatible with gross inequalities and ruthless exploitation throughout its history and so too have various theories of natural right.

A crucial element that should be added to Rosanvallon's list is the affective revolution that Lynn Hunt and others have traced to the mid-eighteenth century. Human rights, and the equality that is a fundamental part of the concept, gained traction because of the emotional chord that was struck in a growing number of individuals, transforming human rights into a "self-evident truth."[16] A number of eighteenth-century intellectual and cultural developments, the rising popularity of the epistolary novel and portraiture among them, established a new framework in which individual bodies were viewed as sacred in themselves and thus possessing inviolable rights.[17] From Jaucourt's identification with enslaved people in the article "Slave Trade" to De Felice's uncompromising condemnation of slavery in the article "Negre," we have seen that empathic identification with others lay at the basis of calls to treat others as our equals. In the case of the *Encyclopédie d'Yverdon*, which drew on Diderot's passages from the *Histoire des deux Indes*, even characters from Samuel Richardson's epistolary novel *Clarissa* are cited to add emotional force to the defense of the moral autonomy of every adult individual, including the enslaved.

Part of the power of Hunt's argument is that she demonstrates that human rights depend upon a cultural and intellectual framework that does not jettison the sacred, but rather one in which the sacred is transferred from the otherworldly realm to the mundane, human one.[18] She demonstrates that much of this history was the result of the unintended consequences of numerous developments that reinforced individual personhood and autonomy. But Enlightenment thinkers were important in this transformation because they sought to understand religion "from the outside," thus laying the groundwork for the comparative study of religion and the defense of freedom of religion as a human right.[19] Jean-Frédéric Bernard and Bernard Picart's *Cérémonies et coutumes religieuses de tous les peuples du monde* (*Religious Ceremonies and Customs of All the Peoples of the World*) was the most influential example of such an approach, transforming religion from the unassailable ur-category to one alongside politics, society, and culture.[20] Concomitant with this process was the transfer of sacrality from the divine to the human world, which helps us to make sense of the role of religion in the Enlightenment. Many Enlightenment thinkers remained personal believers but upheld the rights of all to arrive at their beliefs (or a position of nonbelief) freely and autonomously. In his recent book on the basis of human equality, Jeremy Waldron suggests that there are "possible grounds we might have for thinking that a religious foundation for basic human equality is necessary."[21] But it seems to me that this is only true to the extent that political authority depends upon a cultural frame that includes a sacred center, and so equality as a political concept is bound up with notions of the sacred, but certainly not tied to religion as such.[22]

The Enlightenment, Race, and Inequality

But how does race fit into the picture we have sketched of the interplay between concepts of equality, society, and religion in the Enlightenment? Most important, the concept of race was not usually used as a justification for inequality by Enlightenment thinkers. This is important because many scholars have the tendency to project the later nineteenth- and early twentieth-century history of race and racism back into the eighteenth century.[23] Racism would become an ideology only in the nineteenth century in the wake of the Atlantic revolutions and the growing antislavery movement, which necessitated, in the eyes of slave owners and other elites, a new and modern justification for the enslavement of Black peoples and the continued disenfranchisement of non-Europeans.[24] Race would become an all-encompassing category of being that entailed physical, moral, and psychological attributes. For those who see race as a purely political category invented to oppress non-Whites, there thus seems to be a paradox in Enlightenment thought: the thinkers who politicized equality and initiated the secular antislavery movement were also those who contributed to the nascent racial science. The crux of the matter is that if we analyze the concept of race contextually, the paradox largely evaporates.[25] The Enlightenment concept of race can best be understood as a process or a genealogy of difference, rather than as referring to a fixed object "out there" in nature. There is no doubt that race was a Eurocentric concept in the eighteenth century, since white skin and "European" facial features were almost always taken to be humanity's original and most beautiful form.[26] But looking at how the concept operated in these encyclopedias and in the most important work upon which the Francophone encyclopedias relied, Buffon's *Histoire naturelle*, we see that race is far from the master concept that it would become in the nineteenth century. Benjamin Disraeli's contention that "all is race" would have been alien to Enlightenment thinkers.[27]

The concept of race used by Enlightenment thinkers is best understood within transformations of the interpretation of the history of nature, heredity, and humanity's deep past. We have seen that Buffon's rejection of preexistence theory was bound up with his vision of humanity's place within a deep history of nature. While both Diderot and Buffon were materialists, Diderot took Buffon's speculations on the transformation of living forms across geological time even further than Buffon was willing to go.[28] Buffon argued that each species is characterized by an "interior mold," which can transform—he usually used the term "degenerate"—over time but cannot morph into another species.[29] Instead, Diderot argued that the living beings we observe, including humanity, are contingent, mutable forms and classifications only serve a human cognitive necessity to order the world.[30]

Diderot was even more daring in texts that were either published anonymously or left unpublished during his lifetime. In the *Pensées sur l'interprétation de la nature* (*Thoughts on the Interpretation of Nature*), for

example, published anonymously in 1753, Diderot imagines species growing, developing, mutating, and going extinct across geological time: "Just as
in the animal and plant kingdoms, an individual begins, so to speak, to grow,
to endure, to wither and pass away, would it not be the same for entire species? . . . The philosopher, left to his speculations, can he not conjecture that . . .
the embryo, formed from these [material] elements, has passed through an
enormous number of organizations and developments?"[31] Diderot advanced
the Buffonian revolution by taking Buffon's materialism to its logical conclusion: motion inheres in matter, and life, including human life, is simply a
particular form of highly organized matter.[32] The religious framework for
understanding the natural history of humanity and living forms broke
down, as Diderot dryly points out in his *Pensées*: "Religion spares us many
deviations and much labor."[33] Race formed part of the Enlightenment's engagement with humanity on a new explanatory axis that superseded a paro-
chial religious framework.

Nonetheless, my research into how eighteenth-century Europeans conceptualized similarities and differences between themselves and Native
Americans, sub-Saharan Africans, and Chinese has demonstrated that
there is a correlation between racialization and inequality. The more unequal a population was judged to be, the more likely they were to be racialized. The encyclopedists I have analyzed generally considered Chinese
civilization to be the most venerable outside of Europe and rarely dwelled
on physical differences between Europeans and Chinese. At the other end of
the spectrum, Enlightenment thinkers associated peoples of sub-Saharan
African descent with enslavement and debasement, their objections to the
institution of slavery notwithstanding. This discourse of inequality was accompanied by preoccupation with physical differences, and Enlightenment
naturalists often described sub-Saharan Africans as a "race" or "variety" of
humankind that possessed many undesirable characteristics. Native Americans fit somewhere in between these two poles, since there was a long tradition of interest in Native American societies and cultures that Enlightenment
thinkers advanced, but they nonetheless racialized Native Americans more
readily than they did the Chinese. Eighteenth-century European racial discourse was imbued with understandings of degeneration and the aesthetic
denigration of nonwhite skin color, two factors that militated against an
egalitarian perspective on human differences.[34]

Although race was an Enlightenment language of difference and sometimes of inequality, it did not yet serve as an *explanation* for inequality.

Arguably the most powerful framework of inequality in Enlightenment thought was conjectural history, which is distinct from but related to the concept of race. We have seen that the idea of development across time was already formulated in the sixteenth century, perhaps most famously by José de Acosta. The most influential seventeenth-century thinkers elaborated on this scheme, and by the end of the century, Bernard le Bovier de Fontenelle coined a phrase that would become central to the historical imagination of Enlightenment thinkers: "the progress of the human mind."[35] In the early eighteenth century, we find major studies, such as Joseph-François Lafitau's *Mœurs des sauvages américains comparées aux mœurs des premiers temps* (*Customs of the Native Americans Compared to the Customs of Primitive Times*), that explicitly linked the ancients of the Old World to the contemporary indigenous peoples of the New.[36] At mid-century, Adam Smith, Anne Robert Jacques Turgot, Jaucourt, Diderot, and Rousseau, among others, would add theoretical depth to this perspective. For example, Diderot stated that hunting was common to all peoples in early human history before the development of civilization.[37] Jaucourt followed Montesquieu in distinguishing between "savage" and "barbarous" peoples, arguing that the former are small groups of hunter-gatherers, whereas the latter consist of small nations that unite and subsist on pasturage.[38] Jaucourt also postulated that the invention of agriculture and the opportunities for technological advancement furnished by it resulted from geographical factors alone, arguing that the fertility of the soil in the Americas naturally provides sufficient nourishment, while Europe's soil necessitated more labor.[39] Turgot argued that Native American "stagnation" in world-historical terms could be explained by the absence of large, domesticated animals, which had increased agricultural productivity in the Old World.[40]

Turgot, Smith, and many other Enlightenment thinkers transformed stadial history into a "science of society" that, they argued, could explain the customs, psychology, religion, arts, and sciences of a given peoples as they progressed through the four stages: hunting, pasturage, farming, and commerce.[41] This theory was not racist, since all peoples were seen as capable of reaching the end stage, or *telos*, of historical development—commercial society—but it used a language and theory of inequality that would later be racialized. Even the most trenchant critic of the sanguine view of moral progress that often accompanied eighteenth-century conjectural history, Rousseau, accepted the basics of stadial theory, but he simply inversed the moral: Europeans had become more corrupt, not more virtuous, with the progress of the arts and sciences.

In short, Enlightenment philosophes rejected older justifications of inequality rooted in tradition or providence and invented new frameworks of inequality, of which conjectural history was the most prominent and enduring. The significance lay in the conclusions that various thinkers drew from the conjectural historical framework and the inequalities inherent in it. The dominant perspective among Enlightenment thinkers was that contingent factors had resulted in the technological preeminence of eighteenth-century Europeans. Given the sway of climatic theory, many philosophes held that there may be something special about the European climate, but not about Europeans themselves.[42] Faith in a universal human nature often worked against belief in inherent inequalities between populations.[43] Anyone could achieve what the Europeans had achieved if they were exposed to the same climate, food, and lifestyle of upper-class Europeans.[44]

And some thinkers even used Locke's idea of the mind as "white paper," or a blank slate, to cast climatic theory into doubt and to advance a more radically egalitarian perspective,[45] such as that of Claude Adrien Helvétius, a materialist who made basic equality the cornerstone of two major and controversial studies: De l'esprit (On Mind) and De l'homme (On Man). Regarding climatic theory, Helvétius wrote, "The climate that would generate such a [superior] people is as yet unknown. History demonstrates . . . that from Delhi to Saint Petersburg, all people have been successively stupid and enlightened."[46] In his article "Climate," De Felice argues for a balance between those thinkers who attribute nearly everything to the climate and those who attribute to it almost nothing. But the balance tips toward the malleability of humanity, to what De Felice refers to as the centrality of "customs" and "law" in shaping individual and group character.[47] Many Enlightenment thinkers thus viewed the equality of non-Europeans as something that existed in potentia—non-Europeans are capable of being equal to Europeans but are not "yet" there. Siep Stuurman has called this Enlightenment concept of modern equality "Janus-faced." To be equal means to adopt Enlightenment culture and become like those who already are equal; a less common but nonetheless powerful Enlightenment perspective held that equality entails the equal right to difference, to live life according to one's own lights.[48]

In order to defend human rights, including the right to difference, one requires a concept of culture that Christopher L. Hill calls a "relativizing universal," and such a concept developed in the Enlightenment. Hill distinguishes between "generalizing" and "relativizing" universals. Generalizing universals are those concepts that are used to describe any human community, in any time and place, such as civilization and society, which many non-Western peoples would adopt in the nineteenth century. Relativizing universals are used to describe phenomena that are inherently different in every situation, such as culture, where every place is viewed as having a culture, but every culture is different.[49] It is telling that many of the concepts that Hill traces in his transnational history of the nineteenth century were either eighteenth-century neologisms, such as "civilization," or were significantly reconfigured during the Enlightenment, such as "enlightenment" itself, but also "society" and "culture." While the philosophes did not use the term "culture" as we do, they certainly possessed the concept and occasionally defended its relativity.[50] As Diderot stated, "You can't condemn the ways of Europe in the light of those of Tahiti, nor consequently the ways of Tahiti in the light of those of your country."[51] European universalism would form an important part of nineteenth- and twentieth-century anti-colonial movements. As Hill remarks, however, the universalization of concepts occurred through their use across the globe, not through the inherent universality of a given European concept.[52]

Insights from Other Enlightenment Encyclopedias

A brief foray into some of the most prominent English- and French-language encyclopedias published after Diderot's *Encyclopédie* may help to put my central arguments into relief. Publishing magnate Charles-Joseph Panckoucke and other prominent Enlightenment publishers spearheaded the *Supplément* to the *Encyclopédie*, which aimed to correct some of the errors of the original and profit from the lucrative market for reference works.[53] Edited by Jean-Baptiste Robinet, the *Supplément* was published in four volumes in Paris in 1776. Having as its goal the perfection of the natural sciences, the *Supplément* differed markedly from Diderot's *"machine de guerre"* in that Robinet's contract explicitly barred him from including anything "against religion, good morals, and the government."[54] Robinet removed many of the directly political entries, exemplified by the article "Droit," which would normally cover issues of the law and rights but which was written by the anatomist and naturalist Albrecht von Haller and concerns leg muscles called *droit*.[55] Robinet highlighted geography as a section that was particularly improved, and the lengthier geographical entries generally reflect a similar tension between Eurocentric prejudice and anthropological curiosity as we found in the *Encyclopédie d'Yverdon*.

For example, Samuel Engel's article "America" contains two parts, one taken verbatim though unacknowledged from Cornelius De Pauw's treatise on the Americas and the other authored by Engel himself.[56] De Pauw's section is typically vituperative about Native American peoples and society and even directly challenges the positive treatment of Native Canadian/American philosophy found in Diderot's *Encyclopédie*, most likely the article "Canadians, Philosophy of the."[57] He states that Native Americans do not possess even the vocabulary to talk about metaphysical ideas or morality. This racist perspective is directly countered, however, in Engel's own section, where he states, "Are not reason and genius shared by all men?"[58]

Kathleen Hardesty Doig has demonstrated that the *Supplément* was reformist in many areas, such as criminal justice, and presents convincing evidence that the work promoted religious toleration within a politically moderate (monarchical) framework.[59] She shows that the work reflects the importance of the 1770s in the evolution of Enlightenment thought, because rather than promoting doubt, one of Diderot's central aims, the work aimed to provide moral lessons from history rather than religion.[60] Sometimes she pushes the case too far, however, such as when she claims that the mention of slavery in Robinet's article "Africa" is an "obvious criticism" of the institution.[61] This is far from the case, since Robinet refrains from defending or attacking the transatlantic slave trade or slavery and stays true to his nonpolitical stance.[62] This reticence shows how controversial the issue of slavery and the slave trade had become by the 1770s and that Robinet chose not to enter into the discussion. Overall, the work captures the polarization of public opinion in the wake of the *Encyclopédie*, as the *Supplément* encyclopedists primarily adopted an apolitical stance to stay away from controversy, as well as its responding to changing notions of the role of a reference work.

Breaking away from revising or adding to Diderot and d'Alembert's *Encyclopédie*, as the *Supplément* and *Encyclopédie d'Yverdon* had done, Pancoucke's ambitious *Encyclopédie méthodique* adopted a unique organization to confront the fragmentation of knowledge resulting from alphabetical ordering. The *Encyclopédie méthodique* was published in approximately 159 volumes of text and 47 volumes of plates from 1782 to 1832 and was organized into a number of specific subjects.[63] Given the many hundreds of contributors and half-century-long publishing span, it presents, unsurprisingly, a great diversity of viewpoints.[64] If we focus on equality, the *Encyclopédie mé-thodique* reveals how highly contested the concept had become by the 1780s. In the *Jurisprudence* dictionaries of the encyclopedia, the anonymously authored article "Equality" follows De Felice's entry very closely, relying on ideas from natural law and Christian theology to argue for the natural equality of human beings. The article takes a fascinating turn, however, when the author states that this equality entails the right every man possesses to society and to happiness but stops there: "Every other kind of equality is impossible and repugnant to the natural order, and we must not listen to the senseless complaints of almost all men, even some *so-called philosophers*, who, without paying attention to all the goods they enjoy, either physically or morally, constantly covet the things they do not enjoy."[65] De Felice and his collaborators had used the phrase "so-called philosophers" (*prétendus philosophes*) often in the *Encyclopédie d'Yverdon*, especially to criticize the irreligion of atheist-materialist thinkers. But this *Encyclopédie méthodique* entry reveals that commitment to a more broadly conceived notion of equality, whether accurate or not, had become associated with the philosophes. It also reveals that a broader cross section of society found inequality increasingly abhorrent by the second half of the eighteenth century.

The three editions of the eighteenth-century *Encyclopaedia Britannica* were the most prominent English-language encyclopedias of the period and can be seen, in some ways, as an anti-*Encyclopédie* project, particularly by the third edition.[66] The first edition of the *Britannica* appeared in weekly issues from 1768 to 1771 and in three quarto volumes in the same period in Edinburgh, published by the printer Colin Macfarquhar and engraver Andrew Bell, with William Smellie, who would later achieve some fame for his English translation of Buffon, as the project manager.[67] The second edition was also published in weekly issues and separate volumes between 1778 and 1784, but with additional support from a new group of publishers. The weekly installments and eighteen quarto volumes of the third edition were published between 1788 and 1797, becoming more politically and religiously conservative due to the reaction against the Terror during the French Revolution and the accession of the more orthodox George Gleig as publisher following Macfarquhar's death.

Like the evolution between Diderot's *Encyclopédie* and De Felice's *Encyclopédie d'Yverdon*, we see lengthier coverage of the extra-European world across the editions of the *Encyclopaedia Britannica* and a similar tension between the development of both a more racialized perspective and a more anti-colonial one. In her astute analysis of the treatment of American peoples, history, and society in the eighteenth-century *Encyclopaedia Britannica*, Silvia Sebastiani demonstrates that a conjectural history of New World peoples, particularly indebted to William Robertson, dominated the encyclopedia by the second edition only to be cast aside as an irreligious theory in the third.[68] This theoretical model of development that encompassed all times and places served to justify the European colonization of the Americas, as monogenists like Robertson and polygenists like Henry Home, Lord Kames, all agreed that the indigenous population only really entered history with the arrival of Europeans. The Mexican Creole and Jesuit scholar Francisco Javier Clavijero challenged many of Robertson and De Pauw's arguments regarding the stagnation of Native American peoples, society, and history and the harshness of the American climate with his *History of Mexico*, published in Italian in 1780–81 and in English in 1787. His work was incorporated into the *Britannica*'s third edition. As Sebastiani demonstrates, despite the third edition's reactionary stance in some areas of politics and religion, particularly in the wake of the Terror, the tools of Enlightenment criticism were being turned against one of the most important Eurocentric discourses of Enlightenment progress.[69] What we get is a similar tension as we found in the *Encyclopédie d'Yverdon* between the hardening of the race concept and the Enlightenment critique of empire.

The long shadow cast by Ephraim Chambers's *Cyclopaedia* is revealed by the entry "Negroes" in the first edition of the *Encyclopaedia Britannica*, which follows Chambers's original very closely, often word for word.[70] We see a similar growth in interest in the natural history of humanity and the human-animal divide in the *Encyclopaedia Britannica* as we saw between Chambers's *Cyclopaedia* to the *Supplement*. The new entry "Homo" is a Linnaean classification of the species into four principal races, with the addition of a fifth "monstrous" race but without the inclusion of the character descriptions of each of the races that would appear in later editions of Linnaeus's *Systema naturae*.[71] This entry also contains a description of the orangutan, demonstrating the importance of interest in the great apes and the human-animal divide in the eighteenth century.[72] The second edition of the *Encyclopaedia Britannica* expands the field of humanity's natural history by including the new entry "Colour of the Human Species, Difference of."[73] The entry reveals just how controversial the topic of human physical diversity had become by the latter half of the eighteenth century, particularly with the rise of the abolitionist movement and the increasingly heated debate between monogenism and polygenism: "Few questions in philosophy have engaged the attention of naturalists more than the diversities among the human species, among which that of colour is the most remarkable. The great differences in this respect have given occasion to several authors to assert, that the whole human race have not sprung from one original; but that as many different species of men were at first created, as there are now different colours to be found among them."[74] The author then goes on to firmly back the monogenist perspective, referring the reader to the lengthier discussion of the subject in the article "America" and citing John Hunter's 1775 University of Edinburgh dissertation on the subject.[75]

While each of these additional eighteenth-century encyclopedias naturally reflects the particular context from which it emerged, they also reinforce the general trends in thinking about human diversity and use of the concepts of equality and race that I have outlined in the preceding chapters. The natural history of humanity has become a distinct field of inquiry, with the temperature of the debate rising in the second half of the eighteenth century as a result of the political issues thrown up by abolitionism. Relatedly, the uses and abuses of European empire came to the fore in salient ways in the wake of the Seven Years' War and the American Revolution, and one finds both Enlightenment defenses and Enlightenment criticism of empire in these works. Lastly, these encyclopedias reflect the growing contestation of inequality in the second half of the eighteenth century and the expanding sentiment that inequality is immoral, sometimes unwittingly revealed, as we have seen, by individual encyclopedists who vehemently asserted the necessity and justice of inequality.

The Naturalization of the Human Species

Most significantly, bringing together universalizing concepts like race and equality in a study of Enlightenment encyclopedias has revealed that the same intellectual movement, even often the same minds within that movement, politicized equality *and* contributed to the discourse of inequality that was nascent racial science. This tension can best be explained by the philosophes' attempt to provide a naturalistic account of humanity, including both our physical and moral attributes. In terms of the physical, this meant including the human species in a history of nature, which explains how "race" was used in Enlightenment texts as described above. In terms of the moral, what I mean by a naturalistic account of human morality is that the philosophes sought the origins of human morality outside of Scripture, in social experience alone. In the introduction, "Preliminary Discourse," to the *Encyclopédie*, d'Alembert, relying predominantly on the theories of John Locke and Étienne Bonnot de Condillac, constructs a conjectural history of how language and knowledge might have developed in early human history through sensory experience.[76]

Even our ideas of right and wrong come from our interactions with others, in that we all have an equal right to life's necessities, but the strongest among us invariably take more than is their due, from which originates our notion of the unjust. It is this violation of basic equality that teaches us what is just: "The evil we experience through the vices of our own species produces in us the reflective knowledge of the virtues opposed to these vices, a precious knowledge of which we might perhaps have been deprived if a perfect union and equality had prevailed among men."[77] And later, d'Alembert writes of the close connection between feeling and moral judgment, stating that "one could call it [conscience] evidence of the heart, for, although it differs greatly from the evidence of the mind which concerns speculative truths, it subjugates us with the same force."[78] The *Journal des sçavans* singled out these and other passages from the "Preliminary Discourse" to criticize the secular underpinnings of d'Alembert's philosophical tract, expressing particular outrage at his separation of morality from religion and his neglect to trace how knowledge of God was "perfected" under Christianity.[79]

Rousseau's *Second Discourse* captures even more conspicuously how the naturalization of humanity in physical and moral terms in the Enlightenment could engender both racialization and a powerful concept of equality: "Let us therefore begin by setting aside all the facts, for they do not affect the question. . . . Religion commands us to believe that since God himself drew Men out of the state of Nature immediately after the creation, they are unequal because he wanted them to be so; but it does not forbid us to form conjectures based solely on the nature of man and of the Beings that surround him, about what Mankind might have become if it had remained abandoned to itself."[80] By stating that he is putting aside the "facts," Rousseau was able to lay Scripture to one side and focus completely on conjectural history. He makes the crucial distinction between natural or physical inequalities between human beings, which are inevitable, and moral or political inequalities, which depend upon consent and convention. Emancipated from the constraints of a literal interpretation of the Pentateuch, he imaginatively reconstructed how political and moral inequality might or must have taken root in early agrarian societies and thus provided a nonprovidential account of early human history and definitively transformed the way we think about humanity's deep past.[81]

Equality had long been recognized as part of the state of nature, but inequality was often viewed as the inevitable consequence of humanity's fallen state, a natural and just consequence of the divinely instituted Great Chain of Being. That perspective was still alive and well in the eighteenth century, as demonstrated by the other submissions to the Dijon Academy's 1754 competition to answer the question, What is the source of inequality among men and is it authorized by natural law? Many of them argued that inequality resulted from divine will and is indeed justified by natural law.[82] This view demonstrates the break of the philosophes with the wider society in which they lived and the way in which the naturalization of morality led to granting equality a normative authority it did not previously possess.[83]

While they do not often receive much attention, race and human physical diversity are in fact important subjects of inquiry in Rousseau's *Second Discourse*. He remarks that humankind must have gone through "successive developments" and that, in the deep recesses of our past, there have been "changes that must have occurred in man's internal and the external conformation, as he gradually put his limbs to new uses, and took up new foods."[84] While he argues that proof of such transformation is still lacking, he suggests that comparative anatomists and naturalists may one day establish these conjectures on a more solid foundation. And in one of the more famous notes of the text, Rousseau writes of the "incontrovertible proof" of human physical diversity and of how this results from "the powerful effects of differences in Climates, air, foods, ways of life, habits in general and, above all, of the astonishing force of uniform causes acting continuously on long successions of generations."[85]

Here, as elsewhere, we see Rousseau's appropriation of Buffon's ideas; both were viewed by some of their contemporaries as speculative philosophers working in a similar vein.[86] And crucially, although inequality informs much of Buffon's work, the basis of his philosophy that "only individuals really exist in nature" destroyed inequality as an ordering principle that was part of the Great Chain of Being.[87] Rousseau appropriates these elements of Buffon's history of nature to deny the naturalness of inequality. Unlike Buffon, Rousseau is even silent—perhaps expressly so—about early humanity's morphology, leaving open the possibility that Europeans were not the first human beings.[88] Robert Wokler convincingly argues that Rousseau was the only Enlightenment thinker to postulate that humanity may have descended from the higher primates, rather than the more commonly held notion that the higher primates are degenerated human beings.[89] Rousseau is an example of how natural history and natural law were reconfigured during the Enlightenment to give birth to both a racialized worldview and a more politically consequential notion of equality.

Rousseau was not the only thinker to reject the "top-down" theory of human morality, which locates human moral behavior in the observance of supposedly divine precepts. The naturalization of morality—which was not always in conflict with religion—could take a number of forms in the eighteenth century, including derivatives of natural law theory, postulation of an innate moral sense or property, theories of rational duty, and materialist perspectives that derived ethics from vital matter.[90] Chambers provided his readers with a naturalistic account of morality, in that he relied on Anthony Ashley-Cooper, Third Earl of Shaftesbury's concept of the "moral sense."[91] Shaftesbury argued that there is a faculty, or a sense, common to all people that enables them to discover what is good and virtuous, thus separating morality from revelation.[92] In his article "Morality," Jaucourt takes the separation of morality and religion even further than Chambers, arguing that a person can have sincere religious faith yet be wicked, while another can lack faith entirely but be morally upright, thus advancing Pierre Bayle's famous defense of the possibility of a society of virtuous atheists.[93] And elsewhere we see that Jaucourt argued that virtuous action stems from the emotions, as when he writes that "sensitivity is the mother of humanity and of generosity; it increases worth, helps the mind, and incites persuasion."[94]

While the Yverdon encyclopedists espoused the importance of Christianity in instilling correct morals, they ultimately grounded morality in sentiment as well, as we have seen in their discussions of society and the social virtues. They also reproduced Jaucourt's article "Moral Sense," which follows Francis Hutcheson's work closely in arguing for the importance of feeling in the functioning of this moral faculty.[95] The search for the basis of morality outside of religious dogma was one of the most divisive elements of Enlightenment thought, drawing sharp battle lines between philosophes and anti-philosophes, particularly from mid-century onward.[96] By locating morality in the sentiments, Enlightenment thinkers invested each individual with the capacity to behave morally and to be morally worthy because emotions are a human universal.[97] Thus, human beings are equal in two senses: theoretically, they have equal capacities to behave morally, and they are equally worthy of respect because of the universality of the human emotions. In this way, the naturalization of morality gave impetus to an ethics of egalitarianism.

Enlightenment Legacies

The value of studying Enlightenment encyclopedias is that we have ample evidence that the compartmentalization of the Enlightenment—into radical versus moderate, religious versus secular, or egalitarian versus inegalitarian— quickly breaks down upon closer examination, thus calling into question the simplistic defenses and wholesale rejections of the Enlightenment variously advanced from the right or left. The Enlightenment nonetheless remains good to think with because it was a world-historical turning point in that it made self-criticism a programmatic tenet, which explains why it has a beginning but no well-defined end.[98] The fact that we find powerful discourses of both equality and inequality in the Enlightenment has led some disillusioned intellectuals to argue that the movement's inegalitarian strand of thought disqualifies it from any serious philosophical or historical engagement. And indeed we cannot simply write off the fact that Enlightenment concepts like race and civilization would be put to reprehensible uses in the nineteenth and twentieth centuries. It is telling that Buffon would be cited both by early nineteenth-century abolitionists to defend the humanity of Black slaves and by nineteenth-century physical anthropologists who argued that there is an inherent and ineradicable inequality between the so-called "races of humanity."[99]

What is the upshot of the Enlightenment's legacy of race and equality for our present moment? Given the dark history of racism in the nineteenth and twentieth centuries, humanities scholars and social scientists seek the origins of race in the workings of power alone. The anthropologist Peter Wade argues that we must understand ideas of race not as building on biological givens (phenotypes and genotypes), but rather as discourses imbued with assumptions about how the natural world works.[100] His argument is flawed, however, since he argues that because knowledge about nature, including humanity's place in nature, is discursively constructed, there are no "facts of biology."[101] For example, he states that "the human organism is in a constant state of change; sexual reproduction involves the random recombination of parental genetic material, not its fixed transmission."[102] While this is indeed true, he deliberately obscures the fact that genes do ensure the transmission of certain characteristics that are not random and that scientists can trace a person's ancestry using their genes precisely because of predictable mechanisms of inheritance.

In one of the few articles to directly address the conflict between race-thinking and equality, the prominent evolutionary biologist Ernst Mayr states unequivocally that "recognizing races is only recognizing a biological fact."[103] He argues that there are average genetic differences between human populations or races but forcefully asserts that there is no biological basis for racism; there are no culturally or socially relevant ways in which races are unequal. Mayr's assertion of the biological reality of race runs counter to arguments proposed by many prominent scholars, including geneticists, who assert that the genome does not reveal clear and well-defined "races" of humankind.[104] Despite some dissenting voices,[105] there is a general consensus that race is a biologically incoherent concept—using skin color, or any other physical feature, does not result in any meaningful division of the human species.[106] Race comes into being in a complex social and political process that privileges some traits above others.[107] The history of how physical or other features came to be used as identity markers demonstrates that race, like all identities, is a social construct.[108] While "races" certainly do not carve nature at its joints, advances in genetics have allowed scientists to trace ancestry and human migration across the millennia.[109] And, as David Nirenberg has argued, one of the signal achievements of the social sciences of the second half of the twentieth century was the dismantling of racism's claim to provide a natural explanation for the existence of cultural and social differences.[110]

But I resist the strong constructionists like Peter Wade because they open the door to absurd metaphysical explanations for human diversity.[111] This position is not a call to revive the perspective of the biological reality of races, but is simply to reinforce support for the biological sciences and the importance of studying humanity's deep past.[112] Multifarious factors go into how we group human beings into categories, and all of the racial theories fail at the boundaries of a given racial group; there has never been a consensus about just how many "races" of humanity there are.[113] Ian Hacking strikes the best balance here in that he recognizes that there are differences between human populations which come from nature but demonstrates that so-called races do not meet the criteria to be considered natural kinds, in addition to rejecting those who hold that such differences affect the intellect.[114] But the Enlightenment philosophes analyzed in this study hit upon something crucial in their investigations into human diversity.[115] They sought an explanation in both environmental and hereditary causes and speculated that they may be linked, while stressing both humankind's unity and an innate malleability rooted in certain universal traits.[116] Many scholars argue that the social constructionist perspective on race no longer effectively serves progressive political ends and that we must pay more attention to the interplay of the materiality of the body and the cultural scripts written on the body.[117] In this regard, the Enlightenment presents us with a wellspring of ideas given that a materialist conception of humanity began to take root in educated circles at the same time as our common humanity was placed on a new footing. Enlightenment thinkers aimed at a naturalistic explanation for humanity's physical diversity in deep time and, in that sense, prepared the grounds for the development of paleoanthropology and other natural-scientific investigations of humanity.

The Enlightenment's most enduring legacy emphasizes the possibility and importance of human betterment in this world, a perspective founded on the recognition of individual rights, of freedom grounded in equality. Diderot believed that there is a connection between knowledge, virtue, and happiness. Analyzing the transformation of equality into a foundational concept in the Enlightenment supports his contention; increased knowledge of the extra-European world, particularly of the egalitarianism of many societies that Europeans encountered, taught those European thinkers willing to listen that inequality is neither just nor inevitable.[118] It is part of our heritage of the Enlightenment that the movement was involved in both setting up white/nonwhite binaries *and* in instilling in us an aversion to the inequalities that accompany such a worldview, in addition to bequeathing us the tools with which we can critique those very structures of inequality.

Rising inequality is one of the most pressing issues of our time, and one of the insights we might gain by studying the advent of equality in the Enlightenment is that countering the rising tide of inequality requires a strong affective commitment to equality as being central to how we imagine a just society to be. Enlightenment thinkers' reflections on equality and inequality do not offer us programmatic tenets that we can directly apply in our twenty-first-century societies. But their reflections reveal that perhaps one of the most revolutionary aspects of the advent of basic moral equality in the

Enlightenment is that the concept is a relational one, referring to the possibility of interacting with one another free of the stigma of inferiority or subordination, rather than referring directly to redistributive policies.[119]

Furthermore, Enlightenment debates demonstrate that there is a tension between cultural relativism and moral universalism that is perhaps unavoidable. Enlightenment thinkers defended toleration but realized that there are certain practices that one cannot tolerate, such as slavery. They set in motion an ever-ongoing struggle between the search for what should be tolerated because of the respect we owe to other cultures and ways of being, and what is deemed unacceptable, a striving toward a universal standard that conforms with, as Diderot stated, "the general welfare and individual utility."[120] The encyclopedists I have studied made an important innovation in placing humanity at the center of intellectual inquiry. This resulted not from a conflated sense of humanity's importance or from the conviction that humanity is the center of the universe in an ontological or religious sense, but rather from the realization that the omniscient perspective that their forebears so actively sought is unattainable. Human beings organize and make sense of the world, and so humankind must be at the center of any compendium of knowledge. If we cannot attain an omniscient perspective, can we at least make each other's lives more decent by recognizing the equal dignity not only of our fellow humans, but of all sentient beings? Such an ethical commitment would continue the expansion of the circle of morality that Enlightenment thinkers set in motion.

NOTES

Introduction

1. Barbara Taylor, "Enlightenment and the Uses of Woman," *History Workshop Journal* 74 (2012): 80.

2. William Max Nelson also emphasizes the importance of seeking the connections between discourses of equality and inequality within Enlightenment thought, rather than promoting a naïve and false choice between wholesale acceptance or rejection of the Enlightenment. See Nelson, "Making Men: Enlightenment Ideas of Racial Engineering," *American Historical Review* 115, no. 5 (2010): 1364–94. On rejecting the "blackmail of Enlightenment," see Michel Foucault, "What Is Enlightenment?" in Foucault, *Ethics: Subjectivity and Truth*, ed. Paul Rabinow, trans. Robert Hurley et al. (New York: New Press, 1997), 313.

3. Only volumes of text (not plates) have been included in these publication dates.

4. Richard Yeo, *Encyclopaedic Visions: Scientific Dictionaries and Enlightenment Culture* (Cambridge: Cambridge University Press, 2001). It should be noted, though, that alphabetical ordering and the use of cross-references long antedate the eighteenth century; for example, John Gerarde's *Herball or Generall Historie of Plantes* (London, 1633) was alphabetically ordered and used cross-references. See Anthony Grafton, *New Worlds, Ancient Texts: The Power of Tradition and the Shock of Discovery* (Cambridge, MA: Harvard University Press, 1992), 167. See, more generally, Judith Flanders, *A Place for Everything: The Curious History of Alphabetical Order* (London: Picador, 2020).

5. Arthur M. Wilson, *Diderot* (New York: Oxford University Press, 1972), 73.

6. Clorinda Donato, "Heresy in the *Encyclopédie d'Yverdon* (1770–1780)," in *Histories of Heresy in Early Modern Europe: For, Against, and Beyond Persecution and Toleration*, ed. John Christian Laursen (New York: Palgrave Macmillan, 2002), 241.

7. A good overview of the role and use of reference works, mostly in the sixteenth and seventeenth centuries, is provided by Ann M. Blair, *Too Much to Know: Managing Scholarly Information Before the Modern Age* (New Haven, CT: Yale University Press, 2010), chap. 5; see also Jeff Loveland, *The European Encyclopedia: From 1650 to the Twenty-First Century* (Cambridge: Cambridge University Press, 2019).

8. Prospectus to the *Encyclopédie, ou dictionnaire raisonné des sciences, des arts et des métiers*, etc., ed. Denis Diderot and Jean le Rond d'Alembert, University of Chicago: ARTFL Encyclopédie Project (autumn 2017 ed.), ed. Robert Morrissey and Glenn Roe, http://encyclopedie.uchicago.edu/, n.p., my translation. Unless otherwise noted, all translations are my own. Subsequent references to the *Encyclopédie* are to the ARTFL online edition.

9. Panckoucke in a 1776 letter to the *Société Typographique de Neuchâtel*, quoted in Robert Darnton, "The *Encyclopédie* Wars of Prerevolutionary France," *American Historical Review* 78, no. 5 (1973): 1352.

10. Paul Hazard, *The Crisis of the European Mind, 1680–1715*, trans. J. Lewis May (New York: New York Review of Books, 2013), 53–79; John Marshall, *John Locke, Toleration, and Early Enlightenment Culture: Religious Intolerance and Arguments for Religious Toleration in Early Modern and "Early Enlightenment" Europe* (Cambridge: Cambridge University Press, 2006).

11. J. B. Shank, *The Newton Wars and the Beginning of the French Enlightenment* (Chicago: University of Chicago Press, 2008), 481–506; Robert Darnton, "Philosophers Trim the Tree of Knowledge: The Epistemological Strategy of the *Encyclopédie*," in *The Great Cat Massacre and Other Episodes in French Cultural History* (New York: Basic Books, 1984), 191–214.

12. Yeo, *Encyclopaedic Visions*, 57; and see Carey McIntosh, "Eighteenth-Century English Dictionaries and the Enlightenment," *Yearbook of English Studies* 28 (1998): 3–18; Daniel Roche, "Encyclopedias and the Diffusion of Knowledge," in *The Cambridge History of Eighteenth-Century Political Thought*, ed. Mark Goldie and Robert Wokler (Cambridge: Cambridge University Press, 2006), 172–94.

13. Dena Goodman, *The Republic of Letters: A Cultural History of the French Enlightenment* (Ithaca, NY: Cornell University Press, 1994), chap. 1.

14. Daniel Brewer, "The *Encyclopédie*: Innovation and Legacy," in *New Essays on Diderot*, ed. James Fowler (Cambridge: Cambridge University Press, 2011), 48.

15. Michel Foucault, *The Order of Things: An Archaeology of the Human Sciences* (New York: Vintage, 1994), 131; also see Paul Rabinow, introduction to *The Foucault Reader* (New York: Pantheon Books, 1984).

16. Charles W. J. Withers, "Encyclopaedism, Modernism and the Classification of Geographical Knowledge," *Transactions of the Institute of British Geographers* 21, no. 1 (1996): 280.

17. Gunnar Broberg, "The Broken Circle," in *The Quantifying Spirit in the Eighteenth Century*, ed. Tore Frangsmyr, J. L. Heilbron, and Robin E. Rider (Berkeley: University of California Press, 1990), 46–47.

18. Sidney I. Landau, *Dictionaries: The Art and Craft of Lexicography*, 2nd ed. (Cambridge: Cambridge University Press, 2001), 420–24.

19. Aude Doody, *Pliny's Encyclopedia: The Reception of the "Natural History"* (Cambridge: Cambridge University Press, 2010), chap. 2.

20. Throughout this study, I use the anachronistic term "egalitarian," a nineteenth-century neologism, as a convenient shorthand to refer to early modern discourses of equality.

21. Louis de Jaucourt, "Egalité naturelle" (Droit naturel), *Encyclopédie*, ed. Diderot and d'Alembert (1755), 5:415; Jaucourt, "Traite des negres" (Commerce d'Afrique), *Encyclopédie*, ed. Diderot and d'Alembert (1765), 16:532–33. The entry on equality in the so-called *Dictionnaire de Trévoux* does mention that an honest judge maintains equality, not engaging in unjust preferential treatment; see *Dictionnaire universel français et latin* (Nancy, 1740), 3:63.

22. Jean-Baptiste-Pierre Le Romain, "Negres, considérés comme esclaves dans les colonies de l'Amérique" [unclassified], *Encyclopédie*, ed. Diderot and d'Alembert (1765), 11:80–83.

23. Quentin Skinner, "Meaning and Understanding in the History of Ideas," *History and Theory* 8, no. 1 (1969): 3–53; Anthony Pagden, "Introduction," in *The Language of Political Theory in Early Modern Europe*, ed. Anthony Pagden (Cambridge: Cambridge University Press, 1987), 1.

24. Quentin Skinner, *Visions of Politics*, vol. 1, *Regarding Method* (Cambridge: Cambridge University Press, 2002), 1–7 and chap. 5.

25. Quentin Skinner, "'Social Meaning' and the Explanation of Social Action," in *Meaning and Context: Quentin Skinner and His Critics*, ed. James Tully (Cambridge: Polity Press, 1988), 95.

26. Peter E. Gordon, "Contextualism and Criticism in the History of Ideas," in *Rethinking Modern European Intellectual History*, ed. Darrin M. McMahon and Samuel Moyn (Oxford: Oxford University Press, 2014), 32–55.

27. Judith Surkis, "Of Scandals and Supplements: Relating Intellectual and Cultural History," in ibid., 96.

28. J. G. A. Pocock, *Politics, Language and Time: Essays on Political Thought and History* (Chicago: University of Chicago Press, 1989), 35.

29. Siep Stuurman, "On Intellectual Innovation and the Methodology of the History of Ideas," *Rethinking History* 4, no. 3 (2000): 315.

30. Lynn Hunt, *Inventing Human Rights: A History* (New York: W. W. Norton, 2007), 27.

31. On the emotional, particularly empathic, elements necessary to egalitarian thought, see Christopher Lebron, "Equality from a Human Point of View," *Critical Philosophy of Race* 2, no. 2 (2014): 125–59; and G. A. Starr, "Egalitarian and Elitist Implications of Sensibility," in *L'Égalité*, ed. Léon Ingber (Brussels: Établissements E. Bruylant, 1984), 9:126–35.

32. One of the most important being David Hume, *An Enquiry Concerning the Principles of Morals* (London, 1751).

33. On how the conception of Europe changed in the Enlightenment, see Peter Hulme and Ludmilla Jordanova, eds., *The Enlightenment and Its Shadows* (London and New York: Routledge, 1990), 5–9; Larry Wolff, *Inventing Eastern Europe: The Map of Civilization on the Mind of the Enlightenment* (Stanford: Stanford University Press, 1994); Antoine Lilti and Céline Spector, eds., *Penser l'Europe au XVIIIe siècle: Commerce, civilisation, empire* (Oxford: Voltaire Foundation, 2014).

34. On the ethnographic sources of the Parisian *Encyclopédie*, see René Hubert, "Introduction bibliographique à l'étude des sources de la science ethnographique dans l'*Encyclopédie*," *Revue d'histoire de la philosophie* 1 (1933): 160–72; on the English republican tradition in Jaucourt's articles, see Céline Spector, "Voix du républicanisme dans l'*Encyclopédie*: Harrington, Montesquieu, Jaucourt," in *Le chevalier de Jaucourt: L'homme aux dix-sept mille articles*, ed. Gilles Barroux and François Pépin (Paris: Société Diderot, 2015), 119–42; Timothy Allen et al., "Plundering Philosophers: Identifying Sources of the *Encyclopédie*," *Journal of the Association for History and Computing* 13, no. 1 (2010), https://quod.lib.umich.edu/j/jahc/3310410.0013.107/ -plundering-philosophers-identifying-sources?rgn=main;view=fulltext.

35. Marie Leca-Tsiomis, "The Use and Abuse of the Digital Humanities in the History of Ideas: How to Study the *Encyclopédie*," *History of European Ideas* 39, no. 4 (2013): 472; see also Marie Leca-Tsiomis, *Écrire l'Encyclopédie—Diderot: De l'usage des dictionnaires à la grammaire philosophique* (Oxford: Voltaire Foundation, 1999).

36. Leca-Tsiomis, *Ecrire l'Encyclopédie—Diderot*, 185; John Lough, "The *Encyclopédie* and Chambers's *Cyclopaedia*," *Studies on Voltaire and the Eighteenth Century* 185 (1980): 221–24.

37. Frank A. Kafker and Serena L. Kafker, *The Encyclopedists as Individuals: A Biographical Dictionary of the Authors of the "Encyclopédie"* (Oxford: Voltaire Foundation, 1988); Frank A. Kafker, *The Encyclopedists as a Group: A Collective Biography of the Authors of the "Encyclopédie"* (Oxford: Voltaire Foundation, 1996).

38. I draw upon Ezra Tawil's approach in *The Making of Racial Sentiment: Slavery and the Birth of the Frontier Romance* (Cambridge: Cambridge University Press, 2006), 6. The way the *Encyclopédie* was used and read is addressed in Isabelle Regis, Maryse Guerlais, Jean-Yves Cochai, and Jean Biou, "Lire l'*Encyclopédie*," *Littérature* 42 (1981): 20–38; and Daniel Brewer and Julie Candler Hayes, eds., *Using the "Encyclopédie": Ways of Knowing, Ways of Reading* (Oxford: Voltaire Foundation, 2002).

39. Montesquieu, *The Spirit of the Laws*, trans. and ed. Anne M. Cohler, Basia C. Miller, and Harold S. Stone (Cambridge: Cambridge University Press, 1989), 93; Thomas Jefferson, *Political Writings*, ed. Joyce Appleby and Terrence Ball (Cambridge: Cambridge University Press, 1999), 475.

40. These tensions are analyzed in Fernando Vidal, "Onanism, Enlightenment Medicine, and the Immanent Justice of Nature," in *The Moral Authority of Nature*, ed. Lorraine Daston and Fernando Vidal (Chicago: University of Chicago Press, 2004), 254–81; and Jean Ehrard, *L'Idée de nature en France dans la première moitié du XVIIIe siècle* (Paris: Albin Michel, 1994).

41. Jonathan Israel, *Radical Enlightenment: Philosophy and the Making of Modernity* (Oxford: Oxford University Press, 2001), vi.

42. Darrin M. McMahon, "What Are Enlightenments?" *Modern Intellectual History* 4, no. 3 (2007): 614; for similar observations, see Siep Stuurman, "Pathways to the Enlightenment: From Paul Hazard to Jonathan Israel," *History Workshop Journal* 54 (2002): 233; Anthony J. La Vopa, "A New Intellectual History?" *Historical Journal* 52, no. 3 (2009): 724; Margaret Jacob, "Spinoza Got It," *London Review of Books* 34, no. 21 (November 8, 2012): 26–27.

43. Antoine Lilti, "Comment écrit-on l'histoire intellectuelle des Lumières? Spinozisme, radicalisme et philosophie," *Annales. Histoire, Sciences Sociales* 64, no. 1 (2009): 171–206.

44. Siep Stuurman, *The Invention of Humanity: Equality and Cultural Difference in World History* (Cambridge, MA: Harvard University Press, 2017), 259.

45. Eric Mark Kramer and Richiko Ikeda, "What Is a 'Japanese'? Culture, Diversity, and Social Harmony in Japan," in *Postmodernism and Race*, ed. Eric M. Kramer (Westport: Greenwood Press, 1997), 90.

46. Catherine Belsey, "Afterword: A Future for Materialist-Feminist Criticism", in *The Matter of Difference: Materialist-Feminist Criticism of Shakespeare*, ed. Valerie Wayne (Ithaca, NY: Cornell University Press, 1991), 262.

47. Nikita Dhawan, ed., introduction to *Decolonizing Enlightenment: Transnational Justice, Human Rights and Democracy in a Postcolonial World* (Opladen: Barbara Budrich, 2014), 9.

48. David Hollinger, "The Enlightenment and the Genealogy of Cultural Conflict in the United States," in *What's Left of Enlightenment? A Postmodern Question*, ed. Keith Michael Baker and Peter Hanns Reill (Stanford, CA: Stanford University Press, 2001), 7–18.

49. Antoine Lilti, *L'Héritage des Lumières: Ambivalences de la modernité* (Paris: Seuil, 2019), 30; Barbara Stollberg-Rilinger, *Die Aufklärung: Europa im 18. Jahrhundert* (Stuttgart: Reclam, 2011).

50. Hazard, *Crisis of the European Mind*, xiii.

51. Peter Gay, *The Enlightenment: An Interpretation*, vol. 2, *The Science of Freedom* (New York: W. W. Norton, 1969), 529–44; Robert Darnton, *George Washington's False Teeth* (New York: W. W. Norton, 2003), 129ff.; Roy Porter, *Enlightenment: Britain and the Creation of the Modern World* (London: Penguin, 2000); Annelien de Dijn, "The Politics of Enlightenment: From Peter Gay to Jonathan Israel," *Historical Journal* 55, no. 3 (2012): 785–805.

52. Alphonse Dupront, *Qu'est-ce que les Lumières?* (Paris: Gallimard, 1996 [1962]); Daniel Roche, *La France des Lumières* (Paris: Fayard, 1993), 259ff.

53. Edward Said, *Orientalism* (New York: Vintage Book, 1979); Michel Foucault, *Power/ Knowledge: Selected Interviews and Other Writings*, ed. Colin Gordon, trans. Colin Gordon, Leo Marshall, John Mepham, and Kate Soper (New York: Pantheon Books, 1980).

54. Michèle Duchet, *Anthropologie et histoire au siècle des Lumières* (Paris: François Maspero, 1971; repr., Paris: Albin Michel, 1995), I have used the 1995 reprint throughout; Harold E. Pagliaro, ed., *Racism in the Eighteenth Century* (Cleveland: Case Western Reserve University Press, 1973).

55. Duchet, *Anthropologie et histoire*, 18.

56. Ibid., 160.

57. Ibid., 125–36.

58. Ibid., 145ff.; and see Laurent Dubois's important remarks on Duchet's legacy in his article "An Enslaved Enlightenment: Rethinking the Intellectual History of the French Atlantic," *Social History* 31, no. 1 (February 2006): 1–14.

59. William B. Cohen, *The French Encounter with Africans: White Response to Blacks, 1530–1880* (Bloomington: Indiana University Press, 1980).

60. Ibid., 60–99.

61. Claude Blanckaert, postface to Duchet, *Anthropologie et histoire*, 594–95.

62. Sankar Muthu, *Enlightenment Against Empire* (Princeton, NJ: Princeton University Press, 2003), 7, though given my encyclopedists' lack of engagement with Kant, I do not include him in this study. For Kant on race, see Pauline Kleingeld, "Kant's Second Thoughts on Race," *Philosophical Quarterly* 57, no. 229 (2007): 573–92; and Katrin Flikschuh and Lea Ypi, eds., *Kant and Colonialism: Historical and Critical Perspectives* (Oxford: Oxford University Press, 2014).

63. Andrew S. Curran, *The Anatomy of Blackness: Science and Slavery in an Age of Enlightenment* (Baltimore: Johns Hopkins University Press, 2011).

64. Ibid., 14; emphasis in original.

65. For more on the social vocabulary of the ancien regime, see William H. Sewell, "Etat, Corps, and Ordre: Some Notes on the Social Vocabulary of the French Old Regime," in *Sozialgeschichte Heute: Festschrift für Hans Rosenberg zum 70. Geburtstag*, ed. Hans-Ulrich Wehler (Göttingen: Vandenhoeck and Ruprecht, 1974), 49–68.

66. W. B. Gallie, "Essentially Contested Concepts," *Proceedings of the Aristotelian Society* 56 (1955–56): 167–98.

67. Stuart White, *Equality* (Cambridge: Polity Press, 2007), 4–14. The literature on the subject is vast; particularly important are Elizabeth S. Anderson, "What Is the Point of Equality?" *Ethics* 109, no. 2 (1999): 287–337; Ronald Dworkin, *Sovereign Virtue: The Theory and Practice of Equality* (Cambridge, MA: Harvard University Press, 2000); Jeremy Waldron, *One Another's Equals: The Basis of Human Equality* (Cambridge, MA: Harvard University Press, 2017); T. M. Scanlon, *Why Does Inequality Matter?* (Oxford: Oxford University Press, 2018).

68. Siep Stuurman, *François Poulain de la Barre and the Invention of Modern Equality* (Cambridge, MA: Harvard University Press, 2004), 296.

69. Hunt, *Inventing Human Rights*, 28; Aldo Schiavone, *Une Histoire de l'égalité: Leçons pour le XXIᵉ siècle*, trans. Giulia Puma (Paris: Fayard, 2020), Part 3.

70. Stuurman, *François Poulain*, 283–89.

71. Ibid., 286; Louis de Jaucourt, "Femme" (Droit naturel), *Encyclopédie*, ed. Diderot and d'Alembert (1756), 6:471–72.

72. Sara Ellen Procious Malueg, "Women and the *Encyclopédie*," in *French Women and the Age of Enlightenment*, ed. Samia I. Spencer (Bloomington: Indiana University Press, 1984), 269; Siep Stuurman, "The Deconstruction of Gender: Seventeenth-Century Feminism and Modern Equality," in *Women, Gender and Enlightenment*, ed. Sarah Knott and Barbara Taylor (Basingstoke: Palgrave Macmillan, 2005), 371–88.

73. Keith Michael Baker, "Enlightenment and the Institution of Society: Notes for a Conceptual History," in *Main Trends in Cultural History*, ed. Willem Melching and Wyger Velema (Amsterdam: Rodopi, 1994), 95–120. Reinhart Koselleck also emphasizes the importance of the emergence of "society" in the seventeenth and eighteenth century, though from a very different perspective and with very different implications than Baker; see his *Critique and Crisis: Enlightenment and the Pathogenesis of Modern Society* (Cambridge, MA: MIT Press, 1988), esp. Part 2.

74. Keith Michael Baker, "Enlightenment Idioms, Old Regime Discourses, and Revolutionary Improvisation," in *From Deficit to Deluge: The Origins of the French Revolution*, ed. Dale K. Van Kley and Thomas E. Kaiser (Stanford, CA: Stanford University Press, 2011), 165–97; Brian C. J. Singer, *Society, Theory, and the French Revolution: Studies in the Revolutionary Imaginary* (New York: Palgrave Macmillan, 1986), wherein on the Enlightenment specifically, see 17–20; Brian C. J. Singer, "Montesquieu, Adam Smith, and the Discovery of the Social," *Journal of Classical Sociology* 4, no. 1 (2004): 31–57.

75. Charles Taylor, *Sources of the Self: The Making of the Modern Identity* (Cambridge, MA: Harvard University Press, 1989), 13.

76. Louis Dumont, *Essays on Individualism: Modern Ideology in Anthropological Perspective* (Chicago: University of Chicago Press, 1986), 76; Dumont, *From Mandeville to Marx: The Genesis and Triumph of Economic Ideology* (Chicago: University of Chicago Press, 1977); J. B. Schneewind, *The Invention of Autonomy: A History of Modern Moral Philosophy* (Cambridge: Cambridge University Press, 1998), 4–5. The advent of the individual has led some scholars to argue that Enlightenment thinkers promulgated an unrealistic and dangerous view of the self-realizing, atomistic individual, but such a perspective is largely misleading. See Dennis C. Rasmussen, *The Pragmatic Enlightenment: Recovering the Liberalism of Hume, Smith, Montesquieu, and Voltaire* (Cambridge: Cambridge University Press, 2014), chap. 5.

77. André Béteille, "Individualism and Equality," *Current Anthropology* 27, no. 2 (1986): 121–34.

78. Pierre Rosanvallon, *The Society of Equals*, trans. Arthur Goldhammer (Cambridge, MA: Harvard University Press, 2013), chap. 1; Schiavone, *Une Histoire de l'égalité*, 107–14.

79. Jaucourt, "Egalité naturelle," *Encyclopédie*, ed. Diderot and d'Alembert (1755), 5:415.

80. Harvey Chisick, "The Ambivalence of the Idea of Equality in the French Enlightenment," *History of European Ideas* 13, no. 3 (1991): 215–23.

81. Jean Marie Goulemot, "Egalité et inégalité," in *Dictionnaire européen des Lumières*, ed. Michel Delon (Paris: Presses Universitaires de France, 1997), 374.

82. Pierre Fala also emphasizes the Enlightenment as a foundational moment in the transformation of the concept of equality: see Fala, "Les Termes de l'égalité et de l'inégalité: Flux et reflux," in *In/Égalité/s: Usages lexicaux et variations discursives (18e—20e siècles)*, ed. Pierre Fala (Paris: L'Harmattan, 1999), 7–20.

83. Hunt, *Inventing Human Rights*, 19.

84. Devin J. Vartija, "Empathy, Equality, and the Radical Enlightenment," in *Reassessing the Radical Enlightenment*, ed. Steffen Ducheyne (London: Routledge, 2017), 274–91.

85. Thus, I disagree with Jonathan Israel's contention that equality followed logically from atheist, monist philosophy; see Israel, *Enlightenment Contested: Philosophy, Modernity, and the Emancipation of Man, 1670–1752* (Oxford: Oxford University Press, 2006), 545–71.

86. David A. Bell, *The Cult of the Nation in France: Inventing Nationalism, 1680–1800* (Cambridge, MA: Harvard University Press, 2001), 7–8, my emphasis; see also Robert Morrissey, "The *Encyclopédie*: Monument for a Nation," in *Using the "Encyclopédie": Ways of Knowing, Ways of Reading*, ed. Daniel Brewer and Julie Candler Hayes (Oxford: Voltaire Foundation, 2002), 143–61.

87. Jaucourt, "Traite des negres," *Encyclopédie*, ed. Diderot and d'Alembert (1765), 16:532, emphasis added. On this article, see David Brion Davis, "New Sidelights on Early Antislavery Radicalism," *William and Mary Quarterly* 28, no. 4 (1971): 585–94. Jaucourt translated large tracts from George Wallace, *A System of the Principles of the Law of Scotland*, vol. 1 (Edinburgh, 1760).

88. Hans-Jürgen Lüsebrink, "De l'*Encyclopédie* de Paris à l'*Encyclopédie d'Yverdon*: La diffusion des savoirs sur le monde colonial (l'exemple de l'Amérique Latine)," in *L'Encyclopédie d'Yverdon et sa résonance européenne*, ed. Jean-Daniel Candaux, Alain Cernuschi, Clorinda Donato, and Jens Häseler (Geneva: Slatkine, 2005), 257–76.

89. As such, I develop a theme explored by David Brion Davis. See Davis, *The Problem of Slavery in the Age of Revolution, 1770–1823* (Ithaca, NY: Cornell University Press, 1975); see also John S. Spink, "Diderot et la réhabilitation de la pitié," in *Diderot (1713–1784), Colloque International*, ed. Anne-Marie Chouillet (Paris: Aux Amateurs de Livres, 1985), 51–60; Stephen Ahern, ed., *Affect and Abolition in the Anglo-Atlantic, 1770–1830* (Farnham, UK: Ashgate, 2013). Claudine Hunting also emphasizes the importance of empathy in the philosophes' antislavery arguments in Hunting, "The *Philosophes* and Black Slavery: 1748–1765," in *Race, Gender, and Rank: Early Modern Ideas of Humanity*, ed. Maryanne Cline Horowitz (Rochester, NY: University of Rochester Press, 1992), 17–30.

90. Benjamin Isaac, *The Invention of Racism in Classical Antiquity* (Princeton, NJ: Princeton University Press, 2004).

91. Geraldine Heng, *The Invention of Race in the European Middle Ages* (Cambridge: Cambridge University Press, 2018).

92. Jean E. Feerick, *Strangers in Blood: Relocating Race in the Renaissance* (Toronto: University of Toronto Press, 2010); Margo Hendricks and Patricia Parker, eds., introduction to *Women, "Race," and Writing in the Early Modern Period* (London: Routledge, 1994); Ania Loomba and John Burton, eds., introduction to *Race in Early Modern England: A Documentary Companion* (New York: Palgrave Macmillan, 2007); Francisco Bethencourt, *Racisms: From the Crusades to the Twentieth Century* (Princeton, NJ: Princeton University Press, 2013); James H. Sweet, "The Iberian Roots of American Racist Thought," *William and Mary Quarterly* 54, no. 1 (1997): 143–66.

93. Kenan Malik, *The Meaning of Race: Race, History and Culture in Western Society* (New York: New York University Press, 1996); Hannah Augstein, ed., *Race: The Origins of an Idea, 1760–1850* (Bristol: Thoemmes Press, 1996), xxxii; Douglas A. Lorimer, *Colour, Class and the Victorians: English Attitudes to the Negro in the Mid-Nineteenth Century* (Leicester: Leicester University Press, 1978); Roxann Wheeler, *The Complexion of Race: Categories of Difference in Eighteenth-Century British Culture* (Philadelphia: University of Pennsylvania

Press, 2000); for a very effective critique from the perspective of intellectual history of the "origins debate" on race and racism, see Vanita Seth, "The Origins of Racism: A Critique of the History of Ideas," *History and Theory* 59, no. 3 (2020): 343–68.

94. Tzvetan Todorov, *On Human Diversity: Nationalism, Racism, and Exoticism in French Thought*, trans. Catherine Porter (Cambridge, MA: Harvard University Press, 1993), chap. 2; Claude-Olivier Doron, *L'Homme altéré: Races et dégénérescence (XVIIe–XIXe siècles)* (Ceyzérieu: Champ Vallon, 2016), 18–19.

95. Charles de Miramon, "Noble Dogs, Noble Blood: The Invention of the Concept of Race in the Late Middle Ages," in *The Origins of Racism in the West*, ed. Miriam Elav-Feldon, Benjamin Isaac, and Joseph Ziegler (Cambridge: Cambridge University Press, 2009), 200–216.

96. Bronwen Douglas, "Notes on 'Race' and the Biologisation of Human Difference," *Journal of Pacific History* 40, no. 3 (2005): 331–38; see also Jean-Frédéric Schaub and Silvia Sebastiani, "Between Genealogy and Physicality: A Historiographical Perspective on Race in the *Ancien Régime*," *Graduate Faculty Philosophy Journal* 35, nos. 1–2 (2014): 23–51.

97. George M. Fredrickson, *Racism: A Short History* (Princeton, NJ: Princeton University Press, 2002), 9.

98. Thierry Hoquet, "Biologization of Race and Racialization of the Human: Bernier, Buffon, Linnaeus," in *The Invention of Race: Scientific and Popular Representations*, ed. Nicolas Bancel, Thomas David, and Dominic Thomas (London: Routledge, 2014), 23.

99. Ernst Mayr, "The Biology of Race and the Concept of Equality," *Daedalus* 131, no. 1 (2002): 89–94; George L. Mosse, "The Jews: Myth and Counter-Myth," in *Theories of Race and Racism: A Reader*, ed. Les Back and John Solomos (London, 2000), 201. Throughout, I have avoided placing "race" in quotation marks because of how frequently I use the word; however, the reader should be aware of my critical distance from the values associated with the concept.

100. Sue Peabody, "'A Nation Born to Slavery': Missionaries and Racial Discourse in Seventeenth-Century French Antilles," *Journal of Social History* 38, no. 1 (2004): 113.

101. Eric Williams, *Capitalism and Slavery* (Chapel Hill: University of North Carolina Press, 1944), 7. For more recent contributions to this debate, see Rebecca Anne Goetz, "Rethinking the 'Unthinking Decision': Old Questions and New Problems in the History of Slavery and Race in the Colonial South," *Journal of Southern History* 75 (2009): 599–612.

102. Seymour Drescher, *Econocide: British Slavery in the Era of Abolition* (Pittsburgh: University of Pittsburgh Press, 1977).

103. Susan Dwyer Amussen, *Caribbean Exchanges: Slavery and the Transformation of English Society, 1640–1700* (Chapel Hill: University of North Carolina Press, 2007), 134.

104. Cristina Malcolmson, *Studies of Skin Color in the Early Royal Society* (Farnham, UK: Ashgate, 2013).

105. Sue Peabody, *"There Are No Slaves in France": The Political Culture of Race and Slavery in the Ancien Régime* (New York: Oxford University Press, 1996), 68ff.; John D. Garrigus, *Before Haiti: Race and Citizenship in French Saint-Domingue* (New York: Palgrave Macmillan, 2006); Yvan Debbasch, *Couleur et liberté: Le jeu du critère ethnique dans un ordre juridique esclavagiste* (Paris: Librairie Dalloz, 1967).

106. Theodore W. Allen, *The Invention of the White Race*, vol. 1, *Racial Oppression and Social Control* (London: Verso, 1994), introduction. This is a standard feature of Marxist historiography. See also Robin Blackburn, *American Crucible: Slavery, Emancipation, and Human Rights* (London: Verso, 2011).

107. Silvia Sebastiani, *The Scottish Enlightenment: Race, Gender and the Limits of Progress*, trans. Jeremy Carden (New York: Palgrave Macmillan, 2013), 12.

108. Richard H. Popkin, "The Philosophical Basis of Eighteenth-Century Racism," in *Racism in the Eighteenth Century*, ed. Harold E. Pagliaro (Cleveland: Case Western Reserve University Press, 1973), 245–62.

109. I have also developed this argument elsewhere: Devin Vartija, "Revisiting Enlightenment Racial Classification: Time and the Question of Human Diversity," *Intellectual History Review* (2020): DOI: 10.1080/17496977.2020.1794161.

110. Joan-Pau Rubiés, "Were Early Modern Europeans Racist?" in *Ideas of "Race" in the History of the Humanities*, ed. Amos Morris-Reich and Dirk Rupnow (Cham: Palgrave Macmillan, 2017), 66.

111. Malick W. Ghachem, "Montesquieu in the Caribbean: The Colonial Enlightenment between 'Code Noir' and 'Code Civil,'" *Historical Reflections / Réflexions Historiques* 25, no. 2 (1999): 183–210.

112. Davis, *Problem of Slavery*, 41–42. Winthrop D. Jordan and Lynn Hunt also find the decades around mid-century to be a turning point: Jordan, *White over Black: American Attitudes Toward the Negro, 1550–1812* (Chapel Hill: The University of North Carolina Press, 1968), Part 3; Hunt, *Inventing Human Rights*, chap. 2.

113. David Allen Harvey, *The French Enlightenment and Its Others: The Mandarin, the Savage and the Invention of the Human Sciences* (New York: Palgrave Macmillan, 2012), 7.

114. Saliha Belmessous, "Assimilation and Racialism in Seventeenth and Eighteenth-Century French Colonial Policy," *American Historical Review* 110, no. 2 (2005): 344.

115. Rubiés, "Were Early Modern Europeans Racist?" 51–53.

116. Justin E. H. Smith, *Nature, Human Nature, and Human Difference: Race in Early Modern Philosophy* (Princeton, NJ: Princeton University Press, 2015), 230.

117. Jacques Roger, *The Life Sciences in Eighteenth-Century French Thought*, trans. Robert Ellrich, ed. Keith R. Benson (Stanford, CA: Stanford University Press, 1997), 435ff.; Jacques Roger, *Buffon: A Life in Natural History*, trans. Sarah Lucille Bonnefoi (Ithaca, NY: Cornell University Press, 1997), 176.

118. This confirms Roxann Wheeler's central argument in her study *The Complexion of Race*.

119. Ephraim Chambers, "[Dedication] to the King," *Cyclopaedia* (London, 1728), 1:n.p. Emphasis in original. I have maintained original spelling throughout and have used the version digitized by the University of Wisconsin–Madison: https://uwdc.library.wisc.edu /collections/HistSciTech/Cyclopaedia/. On which version of Chambers's work Diderot, d'Alembert, and their collaborators used, see Irène Passeron, "Quelle(s) édition(s) de la *Cyclopædia* les encyclopédistes ont-ils utilisée(s)?," *Recherches sur Diderot et sur l'Encyclopédie* 40–41 (2006): 287–92.

120. Siep Stuurman, "How to Write a History of Equality," *Leidschrift* 19, no. 3 (2004): 37.

121. Georges Benrekassa, "De Robert Antelme à Diderot," in *L'Idée de "race" dans les sciences humaines et littérature (XVIIIe–XIXe siècles)*, ed. Sarga Moussa (Paris: L'Harmattan, 2003), 55–70.

122. John C. Greene, *The Death of Adam: Evolution and Its Impact on Western Thought* (1959; repr., Ames: Iowa State University Press, 1996); Herbert Dieckmann, "Natural History from Bacon to Diderot: A Few Guideposts," in *Essays on the Age of Enlightenment in Honor of Ira O. Wade*, ed. Jean Macary (Geneva: Librairie Droz, 1977), 93–112; Aram Vartanian,

Diderot and Descartes: A Study of Scientific Naturalism in the Enlightenment (Princeton, NJ: Princeton University Press, 1953), 97 and chap. 4; Kurt Ballstadt, *Diderot: Natural Philosopher* (Oxford: Voltaire Foundation, 2008), chap. 4.

123. Colin Kidd, *The Forging of Races: Race and Scripture in the Protestant Atlantic World, 1600–2000* (Cambridge: Cambridge University Press, 2006).

124. Sebastiani, *Scottish Enlightenment.*

125. Denis Diderot, *D'Alembert's Dream*, trans. Leonard Tancock (London: Penguin Books, 1966), 175–76; Denis Diderot, *Pensées sur l'interprétation de la nature*, ed. Colas Duflo (Paris: Flammarion, 2005), 114; Paolo Rossi, *The Dark Abyss of Time: The History of the Earth and the History of Nations from Hooke to Vico*, trans. Lydia G. Cochrane (Chicago: University of Chicago Press, 1984), 109; Ann Thomson, "Diderot, le matérialisme et la division de l'espèce humaine," *Recherches sur Diderot et sur l'Encyclopédie* 26 (1999): 197–211.

126. Dienke Hondius, *Blackness in Western Europe: Racial Patterns of Paternalism and Exclusion* (New Brunswick, NJ: Transaction Publishers, 2014); Harvey Chisick, *The Limits of Reform in the Enlightenment: Attitudes Toward the Education of the Lower Classes in Eighteenth-Century France* (Princeton, NJ: Princeton University Press, 1981).

127. Stuurman, *Invention of Humanity*, 338–45; Frederick G. Whelan, *Enlightenment Political Thought and Non-Western Societies: Sultans and Savages* (New York: Routledge, 2009), esp. chaps. 1 and 2.

128. Clifford Geertz, "The Impact of the Concept of Culture on the Concept of Man," in *The Interpretation of Cultures* (New York: Basic Books, 1973), 33–54; Alan Frost, "The Perception of Culture's Relativity in the Second Half of the Eighteenth Century," in *Studies in the Eighteenth Century, 5. Papers Presented at the Fifth David Nichol Smith Memorial Seminar*, ed. J. P. Hardy and J. C. Eade (Oxford: Voltaire Foundation, 1983), 129–42; Michael C. Carhart, *The Science of Culture in Enlightenment Germany* (Cambridge, MA: Harvard University Press, 2007); Larry Wolff and Marco Cipolloni, eds., *The Anthropology of the Enlightenment* (Stanford, CA: Stanford University Press, 2007); Muthu, *Enlightenment Against Empire.*

129. Ashley Montagu, *Man's Most Dangerous Myth: The Fallacy of Race* (New York: Columbia University Press, 1942).

130. I would like to thank Amade M'charek for this formulation.

131. Toni Morrison, "Home," in *The House That Race Built*, ed. Wahneema Lubiano (New York: Vintage Books, 1998), 5.

132. Fredrickson, *Racism*, 64.

Chapter 1

1. Stuurman, *Invention of Humanity*, 2.

2. Kent Flannery and Joyce Marcus, *The Creation of Inequality* (Cambridge, MA: Harvard University Press, 2012).

3. Aristotle, *Politics* 1.2.1253b20–3 and 1.2.1255a3–12.

4. Alfred Tuttle Williams, "The Concept of Equality in the Writings of Rousseau, Bentham, and Kant" (PhD diss., Columbia University, 1907), 5.

5. Kinch Hoekstra, "Hobbesian Equality," in *Hobbes Today: Insights for the 21st Century*, ed. S. A. Lloyd (Cambridge: Cambridge University Press, 2013), 93–98.

6. Tim Mc Inerney, "Ham's Curse and Genealogical Race in the Early Modern World," in *Catégoriser l'autre*, ed. Michel Prum (Paris: L'Harmattan, 2017), 91–107.

7. David M. Goldenberg, *The Curse of Ham: Race and Slavery in Early Judaism, Christianity, and Islam* (Princeton, NJ: Princeton University Press, 2003).

8. Robert E. Hood, *Begrimed and Black: Christian Traditions on Blacks and Blackness* (Minneapolis: Fortress Press, 1994); Fredrickson, *Racism*, 26.

9. Margaret T. Hodgen, *Early Anthropology in the Sixteenth and Seventeenth Centuries* (Philadelphia: University of Pennsylvania Press, 1964), 213.

10. Kidd, *Forging of Races*.

11. Quoted in Hodgen, *Early Anthropology*, 167.

12. Grafton, *New Worlds, Ancient Texts*.

13. Anthony Pagden, *The Fall of Natural Man: The American Indian and the Origins of Comparative Ethnology* (Cambridge: Cambridge University Press, 1982), 24.

14. Ibid., 94.

15. Ibid., 105.

16. Stuurman, *Invention of Humanity*, chap. 5.

17. Pagden, *Fall of Natural Man*, 137.

18. Daniel R. Brunstetter, *Tensions of Modernity: Las Casas and His Legacy in the French Enlightenment* (New York: Routledge, 2012).

19. José de Acosta, *The Natural and Moral History of the Indies*, trans. Edward Grimston (London, 1604; London 1880), 2:301; citations are to the reprinted 1880 edition.

20. Ibid., 390.

21. Ibid., 403.

22. Ibid., 455.

23. Hodgen, *Early Anthropology*, 255–58.

24. Quoted in Hodgen, *Early Anthropology*, 199.

25. Pagden, *Fall of Natural Man*, 200.

26. Stuurman, *François Poulain*, 189.

27. Erik Jorink, *Reading the Book of Nature in the Dutch Golden Age, 1575–1715*, trans. Peter Mason (Leiden: Brill, 2010), 73.

28. Goulven Laurent, "Classification" in *La science classique, XVIe-XVIIIe siècle: Dictionnaire critique*, ed. Michel Blay and Robert Halleux (Paris: Flammrion, 1998), 457–64.

29. Francis Bacon, *The New Organon*, ed. Lisa Jardine and Michael Silverthorne (Cambridge: Cambridge University Press, 2000), 222.

30. Ibid., 235.

31. Jean le Rond D'Alembert, "Discours préliminaire," *Encyclopédie*, ed. Diderot and d'Alembert (1751), 1:xxiv.

32. Hodgen, *Early Anthropology*, 422.

33. Rhodri Lewis, "William Petty's Anthropology: Religion, Colonialism, and the Problem of Human Diversity," *Huntington Library Quarterly* 74, no. 2 (2011): 261–88; on La Peyrère, see Richard H. Popkin, *Isaac La Peyrère, 1596–1676: His Life, Work, and Influence* (Leiden: Brill, 1987).

34. William B. Ashworth, "Emblematic Natural History of the Renaissance," in *Cultures of Natural History*, ed. N. Jardine, J. A. Secord, and E. C. Spary (Cambridge: Cambridge University Press, 1996), 17–37.

35. [François Bernier], "Nouvelle Division de la Terre, par les differentes Especes ou Races d'hommes . . . ," *Journal des Sçavans* (24 April 1684): 133–40.

36. Siep Stuurman, "François Bernier and the Invention of Racial Classification," *History Workshop Journal*, no. 50 (2000): 1–21; Pierre H. Boulle, "François Bernier and the Origins of the Modern Concept of Race," in *The Color of Liberty: Histories of Race in France*, ed. Sue Peabody and Tyler Stovall (Durham, NC: Duke University Press, 2003), 11–27.

37. Doron, *L'Homme altéré*, 430–33.

38. [Bernier], "Nouvelle Division," 134–35. Silvia Sebastiani also emphasizes the importance of Bernier's innovations in Sebastiani, "François Bernier," *Dictionnaire historique et critique du racisme*, ed. Pierre-André Taguieff (Paris: Presses universitaires de France, 2013) 206–7.

39. Lee E. Huddleston, *Origins of the American Indians: European Concepts, 1492–1729* (Austin: University of Texas Press, 1967).

40. Londa Schiebinger, "The Anatomy of Difference: Race and Sex in Eighteenth-Century Science," *Eighteenth Century Studies* 23, no. 4 (1990): 387–405.

41. Londa Schiebinger, *Nature's Body: Gender in the Making of Modern Science* (Boston: Beacon Press, 1993), 144–45.

42. Schiebinger, "Anatomy of Difference," 393.

43. William Harvey, *On the Generation of Animals*, in *The Works of William Harvey*, trans. R. Willis (London, 1847), 170; Clara Pinto-Correia, *The Ovary of Eve: Egg and Sperm and Preformation* (Chicago: University of Chicago Press, 1997); Justin E. H. Smith, ed., *The Problem of Animal Generation in Early Modern Philosophy* (Cambridge: Cambridge University Press, 2006).

44. Roger, *Life Sciences*, 259ff.

45. George Garden, "A Discourse Concerning the Modern Theory of Generation," *Philosophical Transactions* 16, nos. 179–91 (1691): 474–83; Elizabeth B. Gasking, *Investigations into Generation, 1651–1828* (Baltimore: Johns Hopkins University Press, 1967), 51–61.

46. Philip R. Sloan, "The Idea of Racial Degeneracy in Buffon's *Histoire Naturelle*," in *Racism in the Eighteenth Century*, ed. Harold E. Pagliaro (Cleveland: Case Western Reserve University, 1973), 295–97.

47. For a very clear overview of the philosophical and religious issues at stake in these debates, see Shirley Roe, *Matter, Life, and Generation: Eighteenth-Century Embryology and the Haller-Wolff Debate* (Cambridge: Cambridge University Press, 1981).

48. Nancy Shoemaker, "How Indians Got to Be Red," *American Historical Review* 102, no. 3 (1997): 629; Shoemaker, *A Strange Likeness: Becoming Red and White in Eighteenth-Century North America* (Oxford: Oxford University Press, 2004).

49. Amussen, *Caribbean Exchanges*.

50. Withers, "Encyclopaedism," 280.

51. Anthony Pagden, "Introduction," in *The Idea of Europe: From Antiquity to the European Union*, ed. Anthony Pagden (Cambridge: Cambridge University Press, 2002), 10.

52. Robert Wokler, "Anthropology and Conjectural History in the Enlightenment," in *Inventing Human Science: Eighteenth-Century Domains*, ed. Christopher Fox, Roy Porter, and Robert Wokler (Berkeley: University of California Press, 1995), 31–52; Smith, *Nature, Human Nature*, chap. 5.

53. Silvia Sebastiani, "A 'Monster with Human Visage': The Orangutan, Savagery, and the Borders of Humanity in the Global Enlightenment," *History of the Human Sciences* 32, no. 4 (2019): 82–83.

54. Raymond Corbey and Bert Theunissen, eds., *Ape, Man, Apeman: Changing Views Since 1600* (Leiden: Department of Prehistory, 1995), section 1.

55. Gunnar Broberg, "Homo sapiens: Linnaeus's Classification of Man," in *Linnaeus: The Man and His Work*, ed. Tore Frängsmyr (Berkeley: University of California Press, 1983), 156–94.

56. Shoemaker, "How Indians Got to Be Red," 626.

57. Knud Haakonssen, "Natural Law," in *Routledge Encyclopedia of Ethics*, ed. Lawrence C. Becker and Charlotte B. Becker, 2nd ed. (New York: Routledge, 2001), 2:1205–12.

58. Stuurman, *François Poulain*, 200.

59. Adam Smith, *An Inquiry into the Nature and Causes of the Wealth of Nations*, 3rd ed. (London, 1784), 3:76.

60. Duchet, *Anthropologie et histoire*, 11.

61. Hugo Grotius, *Commentary on the Law of Prize and Booty*, ed. Martine Julia van Ittersum, trans. Gwladys L. Williams (Indianapolis: Liberty Fund, 2006), 28.

62. Knud Haakonssen, *Natural Law and Moral Philosophy: From Grotius to the Scottish Enlightenment* (Cambridge: Cambridge University Press, 1996), 26–27.

63. Cited in ibid., 27.

64. Thomas Hobbes, *Leviathan*, ed. Richard Tuck (Cambridge: Cambridge University Press, 1991), 107, emphasis in original.

65. Kinch Hoekstra, "Hobbesian Equality," in *Hobbes Today: Insights for the 21st Century*, ed. S. A. Lloyd (Cambridge: Cambridge University Press, 2012), 77.

66. Don Herzog, *Happy Slaves: A Critique of Consent Theory* (Chicago: University of Chicago Press, 1989). The literature on this topic is vast, but see especially J. C. Davis "Equality in an Unequal Commonwealth: James Harrington's Republicanism and the Meaning of Equality," in *Soldiers, Writers and Statesmen of the English Revolution*, ed. Ian Gentles, John Morril, and Blair Worden (Cambridge: Cambridge University Press, 1998), 229–42.

67. However, Dan Edelstein argues that many treatments of the early modern revolution in natural law are misguided; see Edelstein, "Is There a 'Modern' Natural Law Theory?: Notes on the History of Human Rights," *Humanity: An International Journal of Human Rights, Humanitarianism, and Development* 7, no. 3 (2016): 345–64.

68. Lawrence Stone, *The Family, Sex and Marriage in England, 1500–1800* (London: Weidenfeld and Nicolson, 1977), 226–69; James H. Johnson, *Listening in Paris: A Cultural History* (Berkeley: University of California Press, 1995); Hunt, *Inventing Human Rights*, chaps. 1 and 2.

69. Haakonssen, *Natural Law*, 35.

70. Richard Tuck, *The Rights of War and Peace: Political Thought and the International Order from Grotius to Kant* (Oxford: Oxford University Press, 1999), 142.

71. Kari Saastamoinen, "Pufendorf on Natural Equality, Human Dignity, and Self-Esteem," *Journal of the History of Ideas* 71, no. 1 (2010): 42.

72. Samuel Pufendorf, *On the Duty of Man and Citizen According to Natural Law*, ed. James Tully, trans. Michael Silverthorne (Cambridge: Cambridge University Press, 1991), 61.

73. Anthony Pagden, *The Enlightenment: And Why It Still Matters* (Oxford: Oxford University Press, 2013), 57.

74. Saastamoinen, "Pufendorf on Natural Equality," 62.

75. Jeremy Waldron, *God, Locke, and Equality: Christian Foundations in Locke's Political Thought* (Cambridge: Cambridge University Press, 2002), 6.

76. John Locke, *Two Treatises of Government*, ed. Peter Laslett (Cambridge: Cambridge University Press, 1998), 269.

77. Holly Brewer, "Slavery, Sovereignty, and 'Inheritable Blood': Reconsidering John Locke and the Origins of American Slavery," *American Historical Review* 122, no. 4 (2017): 1038–78.

78. Knud Haakonssen, "The Moral Conservatism of Natural Rights," in *Natural Law and Civil Sovereignty: Moral Right and State Authority in Early Modern Political Thought*, ed. Ian Hunter and David Saunders (Basingstoke, UK: Palgrave Macmillan, 2002), 27–42; Helena Rosenblatt, *Rousseau and Geneva: From the "First Discourse" to the "Social Contract," 1749–1762* (Cambridge: Cambridge University Press, 1997), 101.

79. Dan Edelstein, "Enlightenment Rights Talk," *Journal of Modern History* 86, no. 3 (2014): 530–65.

80. Lynn Hunt also emphasizes the fundamental role that the equality-autonomy pairing played in the invention of human rights: Hunt, *Inventing Human Rights*, 28–29.

81. Frederick Neuhouser, *Rousseau's Critique of Inequality: Reconstructing the Second Discourse* (Cambridge: Cambridge University Press, 2014), 9.

82. Stuurman, *François Poulain*, 296–97.

83. François Poulain de la Barre, *A Physical and Moral Discourse on the Equality of the Sexes*, trans. Desmond M. Clarke (Oxford: Oxford University Press, 2013), 46. Throughout, I have used the anachronistic term "feminist" as convenient shorthand to describe people or arguments supportive of the equality of the sexes.

84. Poulain de la Barre, *Physical and Moral Discourse*, 44.

85. Stuurman, "Deconstruction of Gender," 371–88.

86. This was a commonplace among defenders of women's equality. See Desmond M. Clarke, *The Equality of the Sexes: Three Feminist Treatises of the Seventeenth Century* (Oxford: Oxford University Press, 2013), 157.

87. Stuurman, "Deconstruction of Gender," 371.

88. François Poulain de la Barre, *Physical and Moral Discourse*, 70.

89. Stuurman, *Invention of Humanity*, 9.

90. Herodotus, *The Histories*, trans. Robin Waterfield (Oxford: Oxford University Press, 1998), 185–86.

91. Stuurman, *François Poulain*, 41.

92. Michele de Montaigne, *Essays*, trans. J. M. Cohen (London: Penguin Books, 1993), 108.

93. Ibid., 277.

94. Muthu, *Enlightenment Against Empire*, chap. 2.

95. Wolff and Cipolloni, *Anthropology of the Enlightenment*, xii; Lynn Hunt, Margaret C. Jacob, and Wijnand Mijnhardt, *The Book That Changed Europe: Picart and Bernard's "Religious Ceremonies of the World"* (Cambridge, MA: Harvard University Press, 2010).

96. Malik, *Meaning of Race*.

97. Eric Voegelin, "The Growth of the Race Idea," *Review of Politics* 2, no. 3 (1940): 283–317.

98. Feerick, *Strangers in Blood*, 142.

99. Ibid., chap. 5.

100. Johann Friedrich Blumenbach, *The Anthropological Treatises of Johann Friedrich Blumenbach*, trans. and ed. Thomas Bendyshe (London, 1865), 298–99.

101. Smith, *Nature, Human Nature*, 10.

102. Sebastiani, *Scottish Enlightenment*, 9–10; Isaac La Peyrère, *Men Before Adam* (London, 1656).

103. Sebastiani, *Scottish Enlightenment*, 10.

104. On the importance of Hume's polygenism to his overall thought and the infamous footnote from his essay "Of National Characters," see Aaron Garrett and Silvia Sebastiani, "Hume on Race," in *The Oxford Handbook of Philosophy and Race*, ed. Naomi Zack (Oxford: Oxford University Press, 2017), 31–43.

105. David N. Livingstone, *Adam's Ancestors: Race, Religion, and the Politics of Human Origins* (Baltimore: Johns Hopkins University Press, 2008); Ann Thomson, "Issues at Stake in Eighteenth-Century Racial Classification," *Cromohs* 8 (2003): 1–20.

106. Livingstone, *Adam's Ancestors*, 65–66.

107. Richard S. Dunn, *Sugar and Slaves: The Rise of the Planter Class in the English West Indies, 1624–1713* (Chapel Hill: University of North Carolina Press, 1972); Gary Puckrein, *Little England: Plantation Society and Anglo-Barbadian Politics, 1627–1700* (New York: New York University Press, 1984); Brewer, "Slavery, Sovereignty.'"

108. Richard Ligon, *A True & Exact History of the Island of Barbados* (London, 1657), 44.

109. Hilary McD. Beckles, *White Servitude and Black Slavery in Barbados, 1627–1715* (Knoxville: University of Tennessee Press, 1989); Russell R. Menard, *Sweet Negotiations: Sugar, Slavery, and Plantation Agriculture in Early Barbados* (Charlottesville: University of Virginia Press, 2006); Simon P. Newman, *A New World of Labor: The Development of Plantation Slavery in the British Atlantic* (Philadelphia: University of Pennsylvania Press, 2013).

110. Cited in Newman, *New World of Labor*, 192.

111. Jordan, *White over Black*, 95–96; Shoemaker, "How Indians Got to Be Red," 631.

112. Rebecca Anne Goetz, *The Baptism of Early Virginia: How Christianity Created Race* (Baltimore: Johns Hopkins University Press, 2012).

113. Jordan, *White over Black*, 96.

114. Katharine Gerbner, *Christian Slavery: Conversion and Race in the Protestant Atlantic World* (Philadelphia: University of Pennsylvania Press, 2018).

115. *Le Code Noir ou recueil des reglements rendus jusqu'a present* (Paris, 1788); Louis Sala-Molins, *Le Code Noir ou le calvaire de Canaan* (Paris: Presses universitaires de France, 1987).

116. Debbasch, *Couleur et liberté*, 1:33; see also Garrigus, *Before Haiti*, 41.

117. Garrigus, *Before Haiti*, chaps. 4 and 5.

118. Peabody, *"There Are No Slaves."*

119. Ibid., chaps. 4 and 5.

120. Garrigus, *Before Haiti*, 44.

121. Jennifer L. Palmer, *Intimate Bonds: Family and Slavery in the French Atlantic* (Philadelphia: University of Pennsylvania Press, 2016), 16.

122. Ibid., 185; Hunt, *Inventing Human Rights*, chap. 5; Devin Vartija, "Racism and Modernity," *International Journal for History, Culture, and Modernity* 7 (2019): 1–15.

123. Brett Rushforth, *Bonds of Alliance: Indigenous and Atlantic Slaveries in New France* (Chapel Hill: University of North Carolina Press, 2012), 369–70.

124. George L. Mosse, *Toward the Final Solution: A History of European Racism* (New York: Howard Fertig, 1978), 1.

125. Malik, *Meaning of Race*, 7.

126. Harvey, *French Enlightenment*, chap. 5.

127. Hannah Arendt pursued a more nuanced approach to race-thinking and racism than does much recent scholarship, emphasizing the power of the humanist tradition in Enlightenment interest in the non-European world: Arendt, *The Origins of Totalitarianism* (New York: Harcourt Brace Jovanovich, 1973), chap. 6.

128. Seymour Drescher, *Abolition: A History of Slavery and Antislavery* (Cambridge: Cambridge University Press, 2009), 84. On the relationship between race and early modern imperialism more generally, see Anthony Pagden, "The Peopling of the New World: Ethnos, Race, and Empire in Early Modern Europe," in *The Origins of Racism in the West*, ed. Miriam Elav-Feldon, Benjamin Isaac, and Joseph Ziegler (Cambridge: Cambridge University Press, 2009), 292–312.

129. Seymour Drescher, *Capitalism and Antislavery: British Mobilization in Comparative Perspective* (Basingstoke, UK: Macmillan Press, 1986), 164.

130. Daniel Mornet, "Les enseignements des Bibliothèques privées (1750–1780)," *Revue d'histoire littéraire de la France* 3 (1910): 464.

131. Thierry Hoquet, *Buffon/Linné: Éternels rivaux de la biologie?* (Paris: Dunod, 2007), 88–101; Rosanvallon, *Society of Equals*, 19; Jacques Roger, *Les Sciences de la vie dans la pensée française du XVIIIe siècle*, 2nd ed. (Paris: Armand Colin, 1971), 528–41.

132. Louis Sala-Molins, *Dark Side of the Light: Slavery and the French Enlightenment*, trans. John Conteh-Morgan (Minneapolis: University of Minnesota Press, 2006), 103ff.; Duchet, *Anthropologie et histoire*, 194–226.

133. Stuurman, "How to Write a History," 37.

134. Phillip R. Sloan, "Natural History," in *The Cambridge History of Eighteenth-Century Philosophy*, ed. Knud Haakonssen (Cambridge: Cambridge University Press, 2006), 2:903–938.

135. Ibid., 916.

136. Duchet, *Anthropologie et histoire*, 274.

137. Buffon, *Histoire naturelle, générale et particulière* (Paris, 1749), 3:528.

138. *Le Dictionnaire de l'Académie françoise* (Paris, 1694), 2:364. On the origins of the concept of race, see Miramon, "Noble Dogs, Noble Blood"; Ivan Hannaford, *Race: The History of an Idea in the West* (Washington, DC: Woodrow Wilson Center Press, 1996), esp. chaps. 6 and 7.

139. Guillaume Aubert, "'The Blood of France': Race and Purity of Blood in the French Atlantic World," *William and Mary Quarterly* 61, no. 3 (2004): 439–78; Arlette Jouanna, *L'Idée de race en France au XVIème siècle et au début du XVIIème siècle, 1498–1614* (Paris: Champion, 1976).

140. Nicholas Hudson, "From 'Nation' to 'Race': The Origin of Racial Classification in Eighteenth-Century Thought," *Eighteenth-Century Studies* 29, no. 3 (1996): 253–54.

141. Buffon, *Histoire naturelle*, 3:384.

142. Ibid., 453; emphasis added.

143. Claude-Olivier Doron, "Race and Genealogy: Buffon and the Formation of the Concept of 'Race,'" *Humana Mente Journal of Philosophical Studies* 22 (2012): 75.

144. Doron, "Race and Genealogy," 87–88.

145. John Atkins, *A Voyage to Guinea, Brasil, and the West Indies* (London, 1735), 39; Henry Home, Lord Kames, *Sketches of the History of Man*, vol. 1 (Dublin, 1775), sketch I, "Diversity of Men and of Languages." On Kames, see Sebastiani, *Scottish Enlightenment*, 85–99.

146. Doron, *L'Homme altéré*, chap. 9; Douglas, "Notes on 'Race.'"

147. David M. Whitford, *The Curse of Ham in the Early Modern Era: The Bible and the Justifications for Slavery* (Farnham, UK: Ashgate, 2009).

148. Roger, *Buffon*, 176.

149. Buffon, *Premier discours*, in John Lyon and Phillip R. Sloan, ed. and trans., *From Natural History to the History of Nature: Readings from Buffon and His Critics* (Notre Dame, IN: University of Notre Dame Press, 1981), 102.

150. Buffon, *Histoire naturelle*, 3:529–30.

151. The best overview of how Enlightenment thinkers used travel literature for their anthropological reflections is provided by Duchet, *Anthropologie et histoire*, 65–136.

152. Sebastiani, *Scottish Enlightenment*, 115; Nelson, "Making Men," 1389; Schiebinger, *Nature's Body*, 172–73.

153. Camper cited in J. S. Slotkin, ed., *Readings in Early Anthropology* (New York: Viking Fund, 1965), 198.

154. Thomson, "Diderot, le matérialisme," 207; Miriam Claude Meijer, *Race and Aesthetics in the Anthropology of Petrus Camper (1722–1789)* (Leiden: Brill, 1999).

155. Blumenbach, quoted in Slotkin, *Readings in Early Anthropology*, 189.

156. Griffith Hughes, *The Natural History of Barbados* (London, 1750); Oliver Goldsmith, *History of Earth and Animated Nature*, 8 vols. (London, 1774); Kames, *Sketches of the History of Man*.

157. Stefano Fabri Bertoletti, "The Anthropological Theory of Johann Friedrich Blumenbach," in *Romanticism in Science: Science in Europe, 1790–1840*, ed. Stefano Poggi and Maurizio Bossi (Dordrecht: Springer Science, 1994), 103–25.

158. Hudson, "From 'Nation' to 'Race,'" 257.

159. Blumenbach, quoted in Slotkin, *Readings in Early Anthropology*, 191.

160. Schiebinger, *Nature's Body*, 140–41; Bruce Baum, *The Rise and Fall of the Caucasian Race: A Political History of Racial Identity* (New York: New York University Press, 2006), 75.

161. Schiebinger, *Nature's Body*, 119.

162. David Bindman, *Ape to Apollo: Aesthetics and the Idea of Race in the 18th Century* (Ithaca, NY: Cornell University Press, 2002).

163. Edward Long, *The History of Jamaica* (London, 1774), 2:353.

164. Seymour Drescher, "The Ending of the Slave Trade and the Evolution of European Scientific Racism," *Social Science History* 14, no. 3 (1990): 423.

165. Ibid., 425.

166. Ibid.

167. Ibid., 423; Bethencourt, *Racisms*, 215.

168. Cohen, *French Encounter with Africans*, 112.

169. Quoted in Drescher, "Ending of the Slave Trade," 423.

170. Voltaire, *Essai sur les moeurs et l'esprit des nations* (Paris: Garnier Frères, 1963), 2:335. I have maintained the French word *negre* (sometimes accented, sometimes not) throughout to preserve the set of assumptions and values that were intended by the term. See Curran, *Anatomy of Blackness*, x–xi.

171. Arthur Hertzberg, *The French Enlightenment and the Jews: The Origins of Modern Anti-Semitism* (New York: Columbia University Press, 1968); Pierre Pluchon, *Nègres et Juifs au XVIIIe siècle: Le racisme au siècle des Lumières* (Paris: Tallandier, 1984).

172. J. J. Clarke, *Oriental Enlightenment: The Encounter Between Asian and Western Thought* (Routledge: London, 1997), 46.

173. Lilti, *L'Héritage des Lumières*, 25–28; on the addition of the antislavery chapter, see Voltaire, *Candide*, ed. and trans. Daniel Gordon (Boston: Bedford/St. Martin's, 1999), 82–83.

174. Claude-Adrien Helvétius, *De l'esprit* (Paris, 1758), 458.

175. Jacques Necker, *Traité de l'administration des finances de la France* (np, 1784), 318.

176. Condorcet, *Political Writings*, trans. and ed. Steven Lukes and Nadia Urbinati (Cambridge: Cambridge University Press, 2012), 150.

177. Claude-Nicolas Le Cat, *Traité de la couleur de la peau humaine* (Amsterdam, 1765), 44ff.

178. Harvey, *French Enlightenment*, 213.

179. Pierre Boulle does not sufficiently distinguish the discriminatory laws of European states from Enlightenment thought; see Boulle, "In Defense of Slavery: Eighteenth-Century Opposition to Abolition and the Origins of a Racist Ideology in France," in *History from Below*, ed. Frederick Krantz (Oxford: Basil Blackwell, 1988), 219–46.

180. Jonathan Israel, Siep Stuurman, David Armitage, and Darrin McMahon all note this lacuna in scholarly research: Israel, *Enlightenment Contested*, 545; Stuurman, *Invention of Humanity*, 3–4; Armitage, foreword to R. R. Palmer, *The Age of Democratic Revolutions: A Political History of Europe and America, 1760–1800* (Princeton, NJ: Princeton University Press, 2014), xx; McMahon, "To Write the History of Equality," *History and Theory* 58, no. 1 (2019): 112–25.

181. Sanford Lakoff, *Equality in Political Philosophy* (Cambridge, MA: Harvard University Press, 1964), 7.

182. Chisick, "Ambivalence," 219.

183. André Delaporte, *L'Idée d'égalité en France au XVIIIe siècle* (Paris: Presses universitaires de France, 1987).

184. Ibid., 50; Margaret C. Jacob, *Living the Enlightenment: Freemasonry and Politics in Eighteenth-Century Europe* (New York: Oxford University Press, 1991), 14.

185. Stuurman, *Invention of Humanity*, 557.

186. Israel, *Enlightenment Contested*, 545–63.

187. Richard Rorty, "The Continuity Between the Enlightenment and 'Postmodernism,'" in *What's Left of Enlightenment? A Postmodern Question*, ed. Keith Michael Baker and Peter Hanns Reill (Stanford, CA: Stanford University Press, 2001), 19.

188. Ibid., 27.

189. Margaret C. Jacob, *The Radical Enlightenment: Pantheists, Freemasons, and Republicans*, 2nd ed. (Lafayette: Cornerstone, 2006), xi, 229.

190. Matthew Kadane, "Original Sin and the Path to the Enlightenment," *Past and Present* 235 (2017): 105–40; Roger Mercier, *La Réhabilitation de la nature humaine (1700–1750)* (Villemonble: Balance, 1960).

191. Charly Coleman, "Resacralizing the World: The Fate of Secularization in Enlightenment Historiography," *Journal of Modern History* 82, no. 2 (2010): 368–95; Bell, *Cult of the Nation*.

192. R. R. Palmer, "Equality," in *Dictionary of the History of Ideas*, ed. Philip Wiener (New York: Charles Scribner's Sons, 1973), 2:139.

193. Dumont, *Essays on Individualism*, 61.

194. Keith Michael Baker, "Enlightenment and the Institution of Society," 108–9.

195. Dumont, *Essays on Individualism*, 76; Schneewind, *Invention of Autonomy*, 4–5.

Chapter 2

1. Full title: *Cyclopaedia: Or, an Universal Dictionary of Arts and Sciences: Containing the Definitions of the Terms, and Accounts of the Things Signify'd Thereby, in the Several Arts, both Liberal and Mechanical, and the Several Sciences, Human and Divine: the Figures, Kinds, Properties, Productions, Preparations, and Uses, of Things Natural and Artificial; the Rise, Progress, and State of Things Ecclesiastical, Civil, Military, and Commercial: with the Several Systems, Sects, Opinions, etc; among Philosophers, Divines, Mathematicians, Physicians,*

Antiquaries, Criticks, etc.: The Whole Intended as a Course of Ancient and Modern Learning (London, 1728).

2. Robert Collison, *Encyclopaedias: Their History Throughout the Ages* (New York: Hafner Publishing Company, 1964), 103.

3. Lawrence E. Sullivan, "Circumscribing Knowledge: Encyclopedias in Historical Perspective," *Journal of Religion* 70, no. 3 (1990): 317.

4. For a significant revaluation of the "quarrel of the ancients and the moderns" and its relationship to the Enlightenment, see Larry F. Norman, *The Shock of the Ancient: Literature and History in Early Modern France* (Chicago: University of Chicago Press, 2011), 219–26.

5. Richard Yeo, *Encyclopaedic Visions: Scientific Dictionaries and Enlightenment Culture* (Cambridge: Cambridge University Press, 2001), 49; P. J. Wallis, "Book Subscription Lists," *Library*, 5th series, 29, no. 3 (1974): 256–57.

6. G. S. Rousseau, "Science Books and Their Readers in the Eighteenth Century," in *Books and Their Readers in Eighteenth-Century England*, ed. Isabel Rivers (Leicester: Leicester University Press, 1982), 197–237.

7. Yeo, *Encyclopaedic Visions*, 142.

8. Jacqueline Hamesse, "The Scholastic Model of Reading," in *A History of Reading in the West*, ed. Guglielmo Cavallo and Roger Chartier, trans. Lydia G. Cochrane (Cambridge: Polity Press, 1999), 103–19; Blair, *Too Much to Know*.

9. Joseph M. Levine, *The Battle of the Books: History and Literature in the Augustan Age* (Ithaca, NY: Cornell University Press, 1991). Dan Edelstein has argued that the Enlightenment arose as a new narrative of the specificity of European, especially French, society out of the quarrel of the ancients and the moderns; Edelstein, *The Enlightenment: A Genealogy* (Chicago: University of Chicago Press, 2010).

10. Yeo, *Encyclopaedic Visions*, 56.

11. Jacob, *Living the Enlightenment*, 151.

12. Judith Hawley, "The Anatomy of 'Tristram Shandy,'" in *Literature and Medicine During the Eighteenth Century*, ed. Marie Mulvey Roberts and Roy Porter (London: Routledge, 1993), 84–100.

13. Chambers, "Preface," *Cyclopaedia*, 1:xxix.

14. James Van Horn Melton, *The Rise of the Public in Enlightenment Europe* (Cambridge: Cambridge University Press, 2001), 88.

15. Yeo, *Encyclopaedic Visions*, 11.

16. Ibid., 50.

17. Richard Yeo, "Encyclopaedism and Enlightenment," in *The Enlightenment World*, ed. Martin Fitzpatrick, Peter Jones, Christa Knellwolf, and Iain McCalman (London: Routledge, 2004), 359–60.

18. Richard Yeo, "A Solution to the Multitude of Books: Ephraim Chambers's *Cyclopaedia* (1728) as 'the Best Book in the Universe,'" *Journal of the History of Ideas* 64, no. 1 (2003): 68; see also Richard Yeo, *Encyclopaedic Visions*, chaps. 2 and 3.

19. Keith Michael Baker, *Inventing the French Revolution* (Cambridge: Cambridge University Press, 1990), chap. 8.

20. Ephraim Chambers, "Preface," *The Literary Magazine: Or, the History of the Works of the Learned* (London, 1735).

21. Yeo, "Encyclopaedism and Enlightenment," 355; John Robertson, *The Case for the Enlightenment: Scotland and Naples, 1680–1760* (Cambridge: Cambridge University Press, 2005), 35.

22. Chambers, "[Dedication] to the King," *Cyclopaedia*, 1:n.p.

23. Thomas Sprat, *The History of the Royal Society of London, for the Improving of Natural Knowledge* (London, 1667), 388–89.

24. Wheeler, *Complexion of Race*, 7.

25. Ibid., chap. 1.

26. Chambers, "Savages," *Cyclopaedia*, 2:24.

27. Chambers, "Barbarian," *Cyclopaedia*, 1:82.

28. Teresa M. Bejan, *Mere Civility: Disagreement and the Limits of Toleration* (Cambridge, MA: Harvard University Press, 2017), 150; Keith Thomas, *In Pursuit of Civility: Manners and Civilization in Early Modern England* (New Haven, CT: Yale University Press, 2018), chap. 2.

29. Hodgen, *Early Anthropology*, 360; Ronald L. Meek, *Social Science and the Ignoble Savage* (Cambridge: Cambridge University Press, 1976).

30. "Proposals for the propagating of the Christian Religion and converting of Slaves, whether Negroes or Indians in the English Plantations," in Ruth Paley, Cristina Malcolmson, and Michael Hunter, "Parliament and Slavery, 1660–c. 1710," *Slavery & Abolition* 31, no. 2 (2010): 271.

31. On the transformation of toleration into a positive value, see Marshall, *John Locke* , chap. 20; on secular explanations, see Margaret C. Jacob, *The Secular Enlightenment* (Princeton, NJ: Princeton University Press, 2019).

32. Chambers, "Negro's," *Cyclopaedia*, 2:623.

33. Paley, Malcolmson, and Hunter, "Parliament and Slavery," 258; Susan Dwyer Amussen, *Caribbean Exchanges: Slavery and the Transformation of English Society, 1640–1700* (Chapel Hill: University of North Carolina Press, 2007), 134.

34. Chambers, "Negro's," *Cyclopaedia*, 2:623; emphasis in original.

35. David Brion Davis, *Inhuman Bondage: The Rise and Fall of Slavery in the New World* (Oxford: Oxford University Press, 2006), 126–27.

36. Chambers, "Negro's," *Cyclopaedia*, 2:623.

37. Jack P. Greene, *Evaluating Empire and Confronting Colonialism in Eighteenth-Century Britain* (Cambridge: Cambridge University Press, 2013), 157.

38. "Estimates," Voyages: The Trans-Atlantic Slave Trade Database, http://www.slavevoyages.org/assessment/estimates.

39. James Walvin, *Black and White: The Negro and English Society, 1555–1945* (London: Allen Lane, 1973), chap. 3.

40. Quoted in ibid., 39.

41. Craig Koslofsky, "Knowing Skin in Early Modern Europe, c. 1450–1750," *History Compass* 12, no. 10 (2014): 794–806.

42. Chambers, "Cutis," *Cyclopaedia*, 1:363.

43. John Harris, *Lexicon technicum* (London, 1708), vol. 1, entries "Cuticle" and "Cutis," n.p.

44. James J. Nordlund et al., eds., *The Pigmentary System: Physiology and Pathophysiology*, 2nd ed. (Malden, MA: Blackwell, 2006), 6–7.

45. Chambers, "Reticular," *Cyclopaedia*, 2:1008; emphasis added.

46. Koslofsky, "Knowing Skin," 800–801; David M. Whitford, *The Curse of Ham in the Early Modern Era: The Bible and the Justifications for Slavery* (Farnham, UK: Ashgate, 2009); Craig Koslofsky, "Superficial Blackness? Johann Nicolas Pechlin's *De Habitu et Colore Aethiopum Qui Vulgo Nigritae* (1677)," *Journal for Early Modern Cultural Studies* 18, no. 1, (2018): 140–58.

47. Koslofsky, "Knowing Skin," 800.

48. Kidd, *Forging of Races*; Stuurman, "François Bernier."

49. Chambers, "Trope," *Cyclopaedia*, 2:256; emphasis in original.

50. Jordan, *White over Black*, 15.

51. Srinivas Aravamudan, *Tropicopolitans: Colonialism and Agency, 1688–1804* (Durham, NC: Duke University Press, 1999), 1.

52. Ibid., 326–31.

53. Ibid., 4.

54. Philip Shorr, *Science and Superstition in the Eighteenth Century: A Study of the Treatment of Science in Two Encyclopedias of 1725–1750* (New York: AMS Press, 1967).

55. Wheeler, *Complexion of Race*, 28.

56. Koslofsky, "Knowing Skin," 798.

57. Chambers, "Complexion," *Cyclopaedia*, 1:289.

58. Chambers, "Humour," *Cyclopaedia*, 1:262. For further discussion of how Chambers's view of the humors differs from that of the ancients, see Bettina Hitzer, "Healing Emotions," in *Emotional Lexicons: Continuity and Change in the Vocabulary of Feeling, 1700–2000*, ed. Ute Frevert et al. (Oxford: Oxford University Press, 2014), 118–50.

59. Koslofsky, "Knowing Skin," 798.

60. Elizabeth D. Harvey, ed., *Sensible Flesh: On Touch in Early Modern Culture* (Philadelphia: University of Pennsylvania Press, 2003), 15.

61. Chambers, "Cutis," *Cyclopaedia*, 1:363.

62. Gasking, *Investigations into Generation*, 51–61.

63. Chambers, "Generation," *Cyclopaedia*, 1:133–36; Garden, "Discourse Concerning the Modern Theory."

64. Joyce Chaplin, "Race," in *The British Atlantic World, 1500–1800*, ed. David Armitage and Michael J. Braddick (Basingstoke, UK: Palgrave Macmillan, 2002), 164.

65. Martha C. Nussbaum, *Liberty of Conscience: In Defense of America's Tradition of Religious Equality* (New York: Basic Books, 2008), chap. 2.

66. Gordon S. Wood, *The Radicalism of the American Revolution* (New York: Alfred A. Knopf, 1993), chap. 13.

67. Nussbaum, *Liberty of Conscience*, 52.

68. Stuurman, *Invention of Humanity*, 89–96.

69. Benjamin J. Kaplan, *Divided by Faith: Religious Conflict and the Practice of Toleration in Early Modern Europe* (Cambridge, MA: Harvard University Press, 2007), 223ff.

70. Ibid., 355. Joris van Eijnatten has traced the development of arguments for religious toleration and their relationship with Enlightenment philosophy in the Dutch Republic; see van Eijnatten, *Liberty and Concord in the United Provinces: Religious Toleration and the Public in the Eighteenth-Century Netherlands* (Leiden: Brill, 2003); and van Eijnatten, "Gerard Noodt's Standing in the Eighteenth-Century Dutch Debates on Religious Freedom," *Dutch Review of Church History* 79, no. 1 (1999): 74–98.

71. Margaret C. Jacob, *Strangers Nowhere in the World: The Rise of Cosmopolitanism in Early Modern Europe* (Philadelphia: University of Pennsylvania Press, 2006), chap. 2.

72. Jacob, *Radical Enlightenment*, 95.

73. Larry Stewart, *The Rise of Public Science: Rhetoric, Technology, and Natural Philosophy in Newtonian Britain, 1660–1750* (Cambridge: Cambridge University Press, 1992), 173.

74. E. G. R. Taylor, *The Mathematical Practitioners of Hanoverian England, 1714–1840* (Cambridge: Cambridge University Press, 1966), 15.

75. Chambers, "Religion," *Cyclopaedia*, 2:990.

76. Porter, *Enlightenment*, chaps. 5 and 9.

77. Chambers, "Religion," *Cyclopaedia*, 2:991; for the original, see Guy Tachard, *A Relation of the Voyage to Siam* (London, 1688), Book 5, 224.

78. Hunt, Jacob, and Mijnhardt, *Book that Changed Europe*, 64–65.

79. Peter Harrison, *"Religion" and the Religions in the English Enlightenment* (Cambridge: Cambridge University Press, 1990).

80. Sullivan, "Circumscribing Knowledge," 323.

81. Louis Moréri, *Le Grand dictionnaire historique*, 20th ed. (Paris, 1759), 9:116.

82. Sullivan, "Circumscribing Knowledge," 322.

83. Mark Goldie, introduction to *A Letter Concerning Toleration and Other Writings*, by John Locke (Indianapolis: Liberty Fund, 2010), x.

84. Chambers, "Deists," *Cyclopaedia*, 1:179.

85. Chambers, "Liberty of Conscience," *Cyclopaedia*, 2:451.

86. Chambers, "Toleration," *Cyclopaedia*, 2:222.

87. Chambers, "Mahometanism," *Cyclopaedia*, 2:488; "Alcoran," 1:57–58; "Rabbi," 2:951; "Talmud," 2:172–73; and "Tabernacle" 2:167.

88. Chambers, "Enthusiasm," *Cyclopaedia*, 1:316; J. G. A. Pocock, "Enthusiasm: The Antiself of Enlightenment," *Huntington Library Quarterly* 60, nos. 1–2 (1997): 7–28.

89. John Locke, *A Letter Concerning Toleration and Other Writings*, ed. Mark Goldie (Indianapolis: Liberty Fund, 2010), 57; emphasis in original.

90. Ibid., 42; Lynn Hunt, *The Enlightenment and the Origins of Religious Toleration*, Burgerhart Lectures of the Dutch-Belgian Society for Eighteenth-Century Studies, No. 4 (Utrecht: Werkgroep 18e Eeuw, 2011), 12.

91. Waldron, *God, Locke, and Equality*.

92. Yeo, *Encyclopaedic Visions*, xiv.

93. Chambers, "Nature," *Cyclopaedia*, 2:617.

94. Chambers, "Primogeniture," *Cyclopaedia*, 2:872.

95. Randolph Trumbach, *The Rise of the Egalitarian Family: Aristocratic Kinship and Domestic Relations in Eighteenth-Century England* (New York: Academic Press, 1978); on the decline of primogeniture specifically, see p. 71. On the rise of new conceptions of the family, its more egalitarian dimensions, and its place in Enlightenment culture in the French case, see Meghan K. Roberts, *Sentimental Savants: Philosophical Families in Enlightenment France* (Chicago: University of Chicago Press, 2016).

96. Chambers, "Wife," *Cyclopaedia*, 2:366.

97. Chambers, "Woman," *Cyclopaedia*, 2:377.

98. Chambers, "Democracy," *Cyclopaedia*, 1:184.

99. Chambers, "Monarchy," *Cyclopaedia*, 2:568.

100. Caroline Robbins, *The Eighteenth-Century Commonwealthman: Studies in the Transmission, Development and Circumstance of English Liberal Thought from the Restoration of Charles II Until the War with the Thirteen Colonies* (Cambridge, MA: Harvard University Press, 1961), 13–16.

101. Chambers, "Charity," *Cyclopaedia*, 1:201; Mary Gwladys Jones, *The Charity School Movement: A Study of Eighteenth Century Puritanism in Action* (Cambridge: Cambridge University Press, 1938), 74.

102. Lael Ely Bradshaw, "Ephraim Chambers' *Cyclopaedia*," in *Notable Encyclopedias of the Seventeenth and Eighteenth Centuries: Nine Predecessors of the Encyclopédie*, ed. Frank A. Kafker (Oxford: Voltaire Foundation, 1981), 135.

103. Chambers, "Tories," *Cyclopaedia*, 2:225.

104. Chambers, "Faction," *Cyclopaedia*, 1:4.

105. Margaret C. Jacob, *The Newtonians and the English Revolution, 1689–1720* (Ithaca, NY: Cornell University Press, 1976), 190.

106. Jacob, *Radical Enlightenment*.

107. Chambers, "Preface," *Cyclopaedia*, 1:xiv.

108. Chambers, "Soul," *Cyclopaedia*, 2:99.

109. Chambers, "Epicureans," *Cyclopaedia*, 1:322.

110. Chambers, "Spinosism," *Cyclopaedia*, 2:111.

111. Chambers, "Spinozism," *Cyclopaedia*, 3rd ed. (Dublin, 1740), 2:n.p.

112. Collison, *Encyclopaedias*, 104.

113. "To the Reader," *A Supplement to Mr. Chambers's Cyclopaedia: Or, Universal Dictionary of Arts and Sciences* (London, 1753), vol. 1, University of Wisconsin Digital Collections, http://digital.library.wisc.edu/1711.dl/HistSciTech.CycloSupple01. All subsequent citations of this work will simply state *Supplement* and the volume number. The *Supplement* does not contain page numbers.

114. Yeo, *Encyclopaedic Visions*, 66; S. Padraig Walsh, *Anglo-American General Encyclopedias: A Historical Bibliography, 1703–1967* (New York: R. R. Bowker, 1968), 38.

115. "To the Reader," *Supplement*, vol. 1.

116. W. P. Jones, "The Vogue of Natural History in England, 1750–1770," *Annals of Science* 2, no. 3 (1937): 346. Jones's negative view of Hill is qualified with more evidence in G. S. Rousseau, "The Much-Maligned Doctor: 'Sir' John Hill (1707–1775)," *Journal of the American Medical Association* 212, no. 1 (1970): 103–8.

117. The growth of natural history in the post-1750 period is also emphasized by David Elliston Allen, *Naturalists and Society: The Culture of Natural History in Britain, 1700–1900* (Farnham, UK: Ashgate, 2001), 333–47.

118. Chambers, "Negro," *Supplement*, vol. 2, emphasis in original.

119. A prize was never awarded. The submissions are analyzed in Curran, *Anatomy of Blackness*, 81–87; James Delbourgo, "The Newtonian Slave Body: Racial Enlightenment in the Atlantic World," *Atlantic Studies* 9, no. 2 (2012): 191.

120. John Mitchell, "An Essay upon the Causes of the Different Colours of People in Different Climates," *Philosophical Transactions* 43 (1744–45): 102–50.

121. Delbourgo, "Newtonian Slave Body," 199.

122. John Ray, *The Wisdom of God Manifested in the Works of the Creation* (London, 1691); Léon Poliakov, *The Aryan Myth: A History of Racist and Nationalist Ideas in Europe*, trans. Edmund Howard (London: Sussex University Press, 1974), 157.

123. Broberg, "Homo sapiens," 158.

124. Chambers, "Animal," *Cyclopaedia*, 1:100.

125. Smith, *Nature, Human Nature*, 7–9.

126. Silvia Sebastiani, "Challenging Boundaries: Apes and Savages in Enlightenment," in *Simianization: Apes, Gender, Class, and Race*, ed. Wulf D. Hund, Charles W. Mills, and Silvia Sebastiani (Zurich: Lit Verlag, 2015), 105–38.

127. Chambers, *Supplement*, "Chimpanzee," vol. 1.

128. Jordan, *White over Black*, 28–32.

129. Quoted in Dror Wahrman, *The Making of the Modern Self: Identity and Culture in Eighteenth-Century England* (New Haven, CT: Yale University Press, 2004), 134.

130. Sebastiani, "'Monster with Human Visage,'" 88.

131. Richard Nash, *Wild Enlightenment: The Borders of Human Identity in the Eighteenth Century* (Charlottesville: University of Virginia Press, 2003).

132. Chambers, "Natural History," *Cyclopaedia*, 2:617.

133. Chambers, "Natural History," *Supplement*, vol. 2.

134. Robert Boyle, "General Heads for a Natural History of a Countrey, Great or Small, Imparted Likewise by Mr. Boyle," *Philosophical Transactions* 1, no. 11 (1665–66): 186–89.

135. Malcolmson, *Studies of Skin Color*, introduction and chaps. 1–3.

136. Robert Boyle, *Experiments and Considerations Touching Colours* (London, 1664).

137. Helen Tunnicliff Catterall, ed., *Judicial Cases Concerning American Slavery and the Negro* (Washington, DC: Carnegie Institution, 1926), 1:3.

138. *Pearne v. Lisle*, Ambler 75, October 1749, in ibid., 12.

139. "Weekly Essays," *Gentleman's Magazine* (January 1735), 5:21, emphasis in original.

140. Mercator Honestus, "A Letter to the Gentlemen Merchants in the Guinea Trade, particularly addressed to the Merchants in Bristol and Liverpool," *Gentleman's Magazine* (July, 1740), 10:341. Although a criticism of slavery based on natural rights arguments was not completely unprecedented at this time, it was rare. See Jack P. Greene, "'A plain and natural Right to Life and Liberty': An Early Natural Rights Attack on the Excesses of the Slave System in Colonial British America," *William and Mary Quarterly* 57, no. 4 (2000): 793–808.

141. "The African Slave Trade defended: And Corruption the worst of Slaveries," *London Magazine* (1740), 9:493–94.

142. Elizabeth Donnan, ed., *Documents Illustrative of the History of the Slave Trade to America* (Washington, DC: Carnegie Institute, 1931), 2:471.

143. T. O. Lloyd, *The British Empire, 1558–1995*, 2nd ed. (Oxford: Oxford University Press, 1996), 70–72.

144. Chambers, "Torture," *Cyclopaedia*, 2:227–28.

145. Yeo, *Encyclopaedic Visions*, 63.

146. Withers, "Encyclopaedism," 275–98.

Chapter 3

All references to Diderot and d'Alembert's *Encyclopédie* will be to *Encyclopédie, ou dictionnaire raisonné des sciences, des arts et des métiers*, etc., ed. Denis Diderot and Jean le Rond d'Alembert, University of Chicago: ARTFL Encyclopédie Project (autumn 2017 ed.), ed. Robert Morrissey and Glenn Roe, http://encyclopedie.uchicago.edu/. They will include the author (if known), article headword, classification (if stated), *EP* (*Encyclopédie de Paris*; to distinguish this encyclopedia from the *Encyclopédie d'Yverdon* [*EY*]), publication date, volume, and page number. The ARTFL version is a digitization of the first Paris edition of the *Encyclopédie*. For an explanation of the various editions, see Richard Schwab, *Inventory of Diderot's "Encyclopédie"* (Oxford: Voltaire Foundation, 1971).

1. Keith Michael Baker, "Épistémologie et politique: Pourquoi l'*Encyclopédie* est-elle un dictionnaire?," in *L'Encyclopédie: Du réseau au livre et du livre au réseau*, ed. Robert Morrissey and Philippe Roger (Paris: Honoré Champion, 2001), 51–58; Dale Van Kley, "The Jansenist

Constitutional Legacy in the French Revolution," in *The French Revolution and the Creation of Modern Political Culture*, vol. 1, *The Political Culture of the Old Regime*, ed. Keith Michael Baker (Oxford: Pergamon Press, 1987), 169–201.

2. Baker, *Inventing the French Revolution*, 9.

3. Daniel Roche stresses the importance of the emergence of an autonomous, human order in the Enlightenment in Roche, *La France des Lumières*, 259ff.; Baker, "Enlightenment and the Institution of Society," 95–120.

4. Yair Mintzker, "'A Word Newly Introduced into Language': The Appearance and Spread of 'Social' in French Enlightened Thought, 1745–1765," *History of European Ideas* 34 (2008): 500–513.

5. See the exchange between Henry C. Clark, Johnson Kent Wright, Andrew Jainchill, and Dan Edelstein at Clark, "How Radical Was the Political Thought of the *Encyclopédie*?," March 2018, Online Library of Liberty, https://oll.libertyfund.org/pages/lm-diderot. See also Henry C. Clark, introduction to *Encyclopedic Liberty: Political Articles in the Dictionary of Diderot and d'Alembert* (Indianapolis: Liberty Fund, 2016).

6. D. Brewer, "*Encyclopédie*: Innovation and Legacy," 55–56.

7. Frank A. Kafker, "Some Observations on Five Interpretations of the *Encyclopédie*," *Diderot Studies* 23 (1988): 85–100.

8. Dorinda Outram, *The Enlightenment*, 3rd ed. (Cambridge: Cambridge University Press, 2013), 3.

9. For helpful overviews of a vast literature, see John Robertson, *The Case for the Enlightenment: Scotland and Naples, 1680–1760* (Cambridge: Cambridge University Press, 2005), chap. 1; McMahon, "What Are Enlightenments?," 137–60.

10. Denis Diderot, "Encyclopédie" (Philosophie), *EP* (1755), 5:644, 642.

11. Diderot, in a letter to Sophie Volland quoted in John Lough, *The "Encyclopédie"* (London: Longman, 1971), 95.

12. Israel, *Enlightenment Contested*, 843.

13. Jean Ehrard, "Slavery Before the Moral Conscience of the French Enlightenment: Indifference, Unease and Revolt," in *The Abolitions of Slavery: From Léger Félicité Sonthonax to Victor Schoelcher, 1793, 1794, 1848*, ed. Marcel Dorigny (New York: Berghahn Books, 2003), 116. This perspective is echoed and strengthened by Harvey Chisick in Chisick, "On the Margins of the Enlightenment: Blacks and Jews," *The European Legacy* 21, no. 2 (2016): 127–44.

14. Siep Stuurman, "Diderot en Raynal: Verlichtingsvisies op de Europese koloniale expansie," *De Achttiende Eeuw* 47, no. 2 (2015): 106–126. See also Ursula Vogel, "The Sceptical Enlightenment: Philosopher Travellers Look Back at Europe," in *The Enlightenment and Modernity*, ed. Norman Geras and Robert Wokler (Basingstoke: Palgrave Macmillan, 2000), 3–24. Antoine Lilti also emphasizes the importance of a new perspective on Europe and its place in the wider world as a key feature of Enlightenment thought: Lilti, *L'Héritage des Lumières*, chap. 2.

15. Raynal, *Histoire philosophique et politique des établissements et du commerce des Européens dans les deux Indes* (Geneva, 1780), 1:1–2; Anthony Pagden, *Lords of All the World: Ideologies of Empire in Spain, Britain and France, c.1500–c.1800* (New Haven, CT: Yale University Press, 1998), 2.

16. Cited in Lilti, *L'Héritage*, 23.

17. Franck Tinland, *L'Homme sauvage: Homo ferus et homo sylvestris; De l'animal à l'homme* (Paris: Payot, 1968), 23.

18. Françoise Le Borgne, "Les savoirs des barbares et des sauvages dans l'*Encyclopédie*: Du rejet polémique à l'intégration dans une odyssée de l'esprit humain," in *Les Savoirs des barbares, des primitifs et des sauvages: Lectures de l'Autre aux XVIIIe et XIXe siècles*, ed. Françoise Le Borgne, Odile Parsis-Barubé, and Nathalie Vuillemin (Paris: Classiques Garnier, 2018), 79–95.

19. *Dictionnaire universel françois et latin* (Nancy, 1740), "Esclavage," 3:349, "Négre," 4:1498.

20. Adolf Reichwein, *China and Europe: Intellectual and Artistic Contacts in the Eighteenth Century* (London: Kegan Paul, 1925), 77.

21. Jaucourt, "Égalité naturelle" (Droit naturel), *EP* (1755), 5:415. Peter Schröder has shown that Jaucourt was relying principally, sometimes word-for-word, on Samuel Pufendorf in this article. See Schröder, "Natural Law and Enlightenment in France and Scotland: A Comparative Perspective," in *Early Modern Natural Law Theories: Contexts and Strategies in the Early Enlightenment*, ed. T. J. Hochstrasser and P. Schröder (Dordrecht: Kluwer Academic Publishers, 2003), 300. Jaucourt's use of Locke's ideas is also clear. On Jaucourt's debt to Locke, see Jean Haechler, *L'Encyclopédie de Diderot et de . . . Jaucourt: Essai biographique sur le chevalier Louis de Jaucourt* (Paris: Honoré Champion Éditeur, 1995), 465ff.

22. Rosanvallon, *Society of Equals*, chap. 1.

23. Jean Starobinski, introduction to *Discours sur l'origine et les fondements de l'inégalité parmi les hommes* (Paris: Gallimard, 1989), 15.

24. Jaucourt, "Égalité naturelle," *EP* (1755), 5:415.

25. Gilles Barroux and François Pépin argue that it is particularly Jaucourt's use of the concept of equality that demonstrates how radical his commitment sometimes was to Enlightenment thought: Barroux and Pépin, eds., *Le chevalier de Jaucourt: L'homme aux dix-sept mille articles* (Paris: Société Diderot, 2015), 15.

26. Montesquieu, *Spirit of the Laws*, book 8, chap. 3.

27. On the importance of the idea of equality in Montesquieu's thought, see Paul Foriers, "L'Égalité et sa dialectique démocratique chez Montesquieu," in *L'Égalité*, vol. 1, ed. Henri Buch, Paul Foriers, and Ch. Perelman (Brussels: Emile Bruylant, 1971), 247–57.

28. Brian C. J. Singer, *Montesquieu and the Discovery of the Social* (New York: Palgrave Macmillan, 2013), 36. On *The Spirit of the* Laws as a monarchist tract, see Annelien de Dijn, "Montesquieu's Controversial Context: *The Spirit of the Laws* as a Monarchist Tract," *History of Political Thought* 34, no. 1 (2013): 66–88. On how the encyclopedists used Montesquieu, see Georges Benrekassa, "*L'Esprit des lois* dans l'*Encyclopédie*: De la liberté civile à la contribution citoyenne, des droits subjectifs au 'pacte social,'" in *Le Temps de Montesquieu*, ed. Michel Porret and Catherine Volpilhac-Auger (Geneva: Librairie Droz, 2002), 253–74.

29. Chisick, "Ambivalence," 216.

30. Stuurman, *François Poulain*, 285–86.

31. Jaucourt, "Femme" (Droit naturel), *EP* (1756), 6:471.

32. Desmahis, "Femme" (Morale), *EP* (1756), 6:472–75.

33. Kafker and Kafker, *Encyclopedists as Individuals*, 102.

34. Lieselotte Steinbrügge, *The Moral Sex: Woman's Nature in the French Enlightenment*, trans. Pamela E. Selwyn (New York: Oxford University Press, 1995), chap. 2.

35. Antoine-Gaspard Boucher d'Argis, "Femme" (Jurisprudence), *EP* (1756), 6:475–76; Boucher d'Argis, "Mari" (Jurisprudence), *EP* (1765), 10:101–3.

36. Paul Joseph Barthez, "Femme" (Anthropologie), *EP* (1756), 6:468–71.

37. Louis de Jaucourt, "Pouvoir paternel" (Droit naturel et civil), *EP* (1765), 13:255–56.

38. Sara Ellen Procious Malueg, "Women and the *Encyclopédie*," in *French Women and the Age of Enlightenment*, ed. Samia I. Spencer (Bloomington: Indiana University Press, 1984), 260.

39. Françoise Gardey, "Notices biographiques des dessinateurs et des graveurs," in *L'Univers de l'Encyclopédie: 135 planches de l'Encyclopédie de Diderot et d'Alembert*, ed. Roland Barthes, Robert Mauzi, and Jean Pierre Seguin (Paris: Libraires Associés, 1964), 37–41.

40. Glenn Roe, "'A Sheep in Wolff's Clothing': Émilie du Châtelet and the *Encyclopédie*," *Eighteenth-Century Studies* 51, no. 2 (2018): 179–96.

41. Danielle Johnson-Cousin, "La 'Construction' du féminin dans l'*Encyclopédie* d'Yverdon et dans l'*Encyclopédie* de Paris," *Studies on Voltaire and the Eighteenth Century* 304 (1992): 752–58; Nicole Arnold and Annie Geffroy, "Les Femmes de l'*Encyclopédie* font-elles partie du genre humain?," *Recherches sur Diderot et sur l'Encyclopédie* 31–32 (2002): 71–90; Janie Vanpée, "*La Femme mode d'emploi*: How to Read the Article 'Femme' in the *Encyclopédie*," in *Using the "Encyclopédie*," ed. Daniel Brewer and Julie Candler Hayes (Oxford: Voltaire Foundation, 2002), 229–46.

42. Lieselotte Steinbrügge, "Le concept de 'nature féminine' dans le discours philosophique et littéraire du dix-huitième siècle," *Studies on Voltaire and the Eighteenth Century* 304 (1992): 743–45; Terry Smiley Dock, *Woman in the "Encyclopédie": A Compendium* (Potomac, MD: Studia Humanitatis, 1983).

43. Karen Offen, *The Woman Question in France, 1400–1870* (Cambridge: Cambridge University Press, 2017), 40.

44. Céline Spector, "Y a-t-il une politique des renvois dans *L'Encyclopédie*? Montesquieu lu par Jaucourt," in "L'ordre des renvois dans l'*Encyclopédie*," ed. F. Markovits and M.-F. Spallanzani, *Corpus* 51 (2007): 215–48.

45. Louis de Jaucourt, "Démocratie" (Droit politique), *EP* (1754), 4:816.

46. Spector, "Y a-t-il une politique des renvois," 227.

47. Stuurman, *François Poulain*, 285–86.

48. Louis de Jaucourt, "République" (Gouvernement politique), *EP* (1765), 14:151.

49. Jaucourt, "Démocratie," *EP* (1754), 4:818; Montesquieu, *Spirit of the Laws*, book 8, chap. 2.

50. Istvan Hont, *Politics in Commercial Society: Jean-Jacques Rousseau and Adam Smith*, ed. Béla Kapossy and Michael Sonenscher (Cambridge, MA: Harvard University Press, 2015), 77.

51. The classics remain Lough, "*Encyclopédie*," chap. 8; and Jacques Proust, *Diderot et l'Encyclopédie* (Paris: Albin Michel, 1995), chaps. 10–12.

52. Denis Diderot, "Autorité politique," *EP* (1751), 1:898–900.

53. John Lough, *Essays on the "Encyclopédie" of Diderot and d'Alembert* (London: Oxford University Press, 1968). See Proust, *Diderot et l'Encyclopédie*, 432, for possible interpretations of this article.

54. Diderot, "Autorité politique," 899.

55. "Souverains" (Droit naturel et politique), *EP* (1765), 15:423.

56. Ibid., 424.

57. Dan Edelstein, "Humanism, l'*Esprit Philosophique*, and the *Encyclopédie*," *Republics of Letters: A Journal for the Study of Knowledge, Politics, and the Arts* 1, no. 1 (2009): 1–17; Joshua T. Kirby, "Natural Law in the *Encyclopédie*" (PhD diss., University of Manchester, 2014).

58. Edelstein, "Enlightenment Rights Talk."

59. Denis Diderot, "Citoyen" (Droit public, histoire ancienne et moderne), *EP* (1753), 3:489.

60. Spector, "Y a-t-il une politique des renvois," 224–25.

61. Louis de Jaucourt, "Gouvernement" (Droit naturel et politique), *EP* (1757), 7:788.

62. Jaucourt returned to the concept of happiness again and again in his articles. See Haechler, *L'Encyclopédie*, 263.

63. Dan Edelstein, Robert Morrissey, and Glenn Roe, "To Quote or Not to Quote: Citation Strategies in the *Encyclopédie*," *Journal of the History of Ideas* 74, no. 2 (2013): 213–36.

64. S.-J. Savonius, "Locke in French: The *Du Gouvernement Civil* of 1691 and Its Readers," *Historical Journal* 47, no. 1 (2004): 47–79.

65. Jean-François de Saint-Lambert, "Législateur" (Politique), *EP* (1765), 9:357; for commentary on this article, see Lough, *"Encyclopédie,"* 304–9.

66. Denis Diderot, "Oppresseur, Opprimer" (Grammaire), *EP* (1765), 11:515.

67. Anthony Strugnell, *Diderot's Politics: A Study of the Evolution of Diderot's Political Thought After the "Encyclopédie"* (The Hague: Martinus Nijhoff, 1973); Ellen Marie Strenski, "Diderot: For and Against the Physiocrats," *Studies on Voltaire and the Eighteenth Century* 57 (1967): 1435–55; Gianluigi Goggi, *De l'Encyclopédie à l'éloquence républicaine: Étude sur Diderot et autour de Diderot* (Paris: Honoré Champion, 2013).

68. Proust, *Diderot et l'Encyclopédie*, 451; Annelien de Dijn, *French Political Thought from Montesquieu to Tocqueville: Liberty in a Levelled Society?* (Cambridge: Cambridge University Press, 2008), 30; Nicolas Antoine Boulanger, "Oeconomie Politique" (Histoire, Politique, Religion ancienne et moderne), *EP* (1765), 11:366–83.

69. Diderot, "Encyclopédie" (Philosophie), *EP* (1765), 5:642; on philosophical skepticism in the *Encyclopédie*, see Anton M. Matytsin, "Taming Thought with Practice: Philosophical Skepticism in the *Encyclopédie*," in *The Skeptical Enlightenment: Doubt and Certainty in the Age of Reason*, ed. Jeffrey D. Burson and Anton M. Matytsin (Liverpool: Liverpool University Press, 2019), 161–82.

70. The literature on these subjects is extensive, but see especially Jürgen Habermas, *The Structural Transformation of the Public Sphere: Inquiry into a Category of Bourgeois Society*, trans. Thomas Burger and Frederick Lawrence (London: Polity Press, 1989); Melton, *Rise of the Public*; Daniel Gordon, *Citizens Without Sovereignty: Equality and Sociability in French Thought, 1670–1789* (Princeton, NJ: Princeton University Press, 1994); Anthony J. La Vopa, "Conceiving a Public: Ideas and Society in Eighteenth-Century Europe," *Journal of Modern History* 64, no. 1 (1992), 79–116.

71. Roger Chartier, *The Cultural Origins of the French Revolution*, trans. Lydia G. Cochrane (Durham, NC: Duke University Press, 1991), 69.

72. On the connections between urbanization and the social and intellectual history of the Enlightenment, see Wijnand W. Mijnhardt, "Urbanization, Culture and the Dutch Origins of the European Enlightenment," *BMGN—Low Countries Historical Review* 125, nos. 2–3 (2010): 141–77.

73. Baker, *Inventing the French Revolution*, chap. 8.

74. William H. Sewell, Jr., "Connecting Capitalism to the French Revolution: The Parisian Promenade and the Origins of Civic Equality in Eighteenth-Century France," *Critical Historical Studies* 1, no. 1 (2014): 5–46.

75. Gordon, *Citizens Without Sovereignty*, 33.

76. Antoine Lilti, *The World of the Salons: Sociability and Worldliness in Eighteenth-Century Paris*, trans. Lydia G. Cochrane (Oxford: Oxford University Press, 2015).

77. Gordon, *Citizens Without Sovereignty*, 6.

78. Ibid., 56–60.

79. Ibid., 61.

80. Louis de Jaucourt, "Sociabilité" (Droit naturel et morale), *EP* (1765), 15:251.

81. Ibid.

82. Louis de Jaucourt "Saturnales" (Mythologie, Littérature, Médailles, Antiquité romaine), *EP* (1765), 14:694.

83. Ephraim Chambers, "Society," *Cyclopaedia*, 2:90–91.

84. "Société" (Morale), *EP* (1765), 15:252.

85. Ibid.

86. Ibid., 253.

87. Ibid.

88. Baker, "Enlightenment and the Institution of Society," 105.

89. [Denis Diderot?], "Privilege" (Grammaire), *EP* (1765), 13:389.

90. Jaucourt, "Oisiveté" (Droit naturel, moral, politique), *EP* (1765), 11:445–46.

91. Helvétius, *De l'esprit*, 251ff.

92. Denis Diderot, *Oeuvres philosophiques*, ed. Paul Vernière (Paris: Classiques Garnier, 2018), 581–87.

93. Pierre Bayle, *Pensées diverses, écrites à un docteur de Sorbonne, a l'occasion de la cométe qui parut au mois de décembre 1680* (Rotterdam, 1683), 2:429ff.

94. Denis Diderot, "Irreligieux" (Grammaire), *EP* (1765), 8:909.

95. "Philosophe" [unclassified], *EP* (1765), 12:510. On the original text, see Herbert Dieckmann, *Le Philosophe: Texts and Interpretation* (Saint Louis: Washington University Studies, 1948).

96. "Philosophe," *EP* (1765), 12:510; Terence's famous statement, "I am human, I think nothing human alien to me," was used as the caption to Jean-Michel Moreau le Jeune's engraving for the frontispiece to Bernardin de Saint-Pierre's *Voyage à l'Île de France* (Amsterdam, 1773); on the importance of the images in this text to its status as an antislavery tract, see Vladimir Kapor, "Reading the Image, Reviewing the Text: On the Reception of Bernardin de Saint-Pierre's *Voyage à l'Ile de France* (1773)," *Word & Image* 28, no. 3 (2012): 302–16.

97. Lough, *"Encyclopédie,"* 382–85.

98. Jean le Rond D'Alembert, "Fortune" (Morale), *EP* (1757), 7:205–6.

99. Denis Diderot, "Indigent" (Grammaire), *EP* (1765), 8:676; Denis Diderot, "Journalier" (Grammaire), *EP* (1765), 8:898; Louis de Jaucourt, "Peuple, le" (Gouvernement politique), *EP* (1765), 12:475–77.

100. Proust, *Diderot et l'Encyclopédie*, 474–84.

101. Harry C. Payne, *The Philosophes and the People* (New Haven, CT: Yale University Press, 1976), chap. 8.

102. For biographical information, see Kafker and Kafker, *Encyclopedists as Individuals*, 238–43.

103. Walter E. Rex, "'Arche de Noé' and Other Religious Articles by Abbé Mallet in the *Encyclopédie*," *Eighteenth-Century Studies* 9, no. 3 (1976): 333–52.

104. Douglas H. Gordon and Norman Lewis Torey, *The Censoring of Diderot's "Encyclopédie" and the Re-established Text* (New York: Columbia University Press, 1947).

105. "Religion" (Théologie), *EP* (1765), 14:78–79.

106. Abbé Mallet, "Déistes" (Théologie), *EP* (1754), 4:773–74.

107. Jacques Abbadie, *Traité de la vérité de la religion chrétienne*, 2 vols. (Rotterdam, 1684).

108. François Ilharat de La Chambre, *Traité de la véritable religion*, 2 vols. (Paris, 1737).

109. "Miracle" (Théologie), *EP* (1765), 10:560–62; "Pentateuque" (Théologie), *EP* (1765), 12:315–17.

110. Darnton, "Philosophers Trim the Tree," 201.

111. Jean-Edme Romilly, "Tolérance" (Ordre encyclopédique, Théologique Morale, Politique), *EP* (1765), 16:393.

112. Ibid., 394.

113. The passages can be found at Jean-Jacques Rousseau, *Du contrat social*, ed. Bruno Bernardi (Paris: Flammarion, 2001), book 4, chap. 8.

114. Louis de Jaucourt, "Superstition" (Métaphysique, Philosophie), *EP* (1765), 15:670. On Plutarch's criticism of superstition as worse than atheism, see Plutarch, *Moralia*, trans. Frank Cole Babbitt, Loeb Classical Library 242 (Cambridge, MA: Harvard University Press, 1928), 2:452–96.

115. Alexandre Deleyre, "Fanatisme" (Philosophie), *EP* (1756), 6:393–401. On how the concept of fanaticism was transformed in the early Enlightenment, see Frederick C. Beiser, *The Sovereignty of Reason: The Defense of Rationality in the Early English Enlightenment* (Princeton, NJ: Princeton University Press, 1996), chap. 5.

116. "Juif," *Le Dictionnaire de l'Académie française*, 4th ed. (1762).

117. Louis de Jaucourt, "Juif" (Histoire ancienne et moderne), *EP* (1765), 9:24–25; Ronald Schechter, *Obstinate Hebrews: Representations of Jews in France, 1715–1815* (Berkeley: University of California Press, 2003), 56–62.

118. Lough, *"Encyclopédie,"* chap. 6. On the counter-Enlightenment more generally, see Darrin M. McMahon, *Enemies of Enlightenment: The French Counter-Enlightenment and the Making of Modernity* (Oxford: Oxford University Press, 2001).

119. Locke, *Two Treatises of Government*, 301; emphasis in original.

120. P. J. Marshall and Glyndwr Williams, *The Great Map of Mankind: British Perceptions of the World in the Age of Enlightenment* (London: J. M. Dent & Sons, 1982); Adam Smith, *Lectures on Jurisprudence*, ed. R. L. Meek, D. D. Raphael, and P. G. Stein (Oxford: Clarendon Press, 1978). Turgot's key texts on conjectural history are available in English in Anne Robert Jacques Turgot, *Turgot on Progress, Sociology and Economics*, trans. and ed. Ronald L. Meek (Cambridge: Cambridge University Press, 2010).

121. Robert Launay, *Savages, Romans, and Despots: Thinking About Others from Montaigne to Herder* (Chicago: University of Chicago Press, 2018).

122. Hodgen, *Early Anthropology*, 360–61.

123. Philipp Blom, *Enlightening the World: "Encyclopédie," the Book That Changed the Course of History* (New York: Palgrave Macmillan, 2005), 150.

124. James Llana, "Natural History and the *Encyclopédie*," *Journal of the History of Biology* 33, no. 1 (2000): 1–25; Jacques Roger, "Diderot et Buffon en 1749," *Diderot Studies* 4 (1963): 221–36.

125. Béatrice Didier, "Le Métissage de l'*Encyclopédie* à la Révolution: De l'anthropologie à la politique," in *Métissages*, ed. Jean-Claude Carpanin Marimoutou and Jean-Michel Racault (Paris: L'Harmattan, 1992), 1:11–24.

126. Denis Diderot, "Humaine espece" (Histoire naturelle), *EP* (1765), 8:347–48.

127. Curran, *Anatomy of Blackness*, 87–95.

128. Diderot, "Humaine espece," *EP* (1765), 8:348.

129. For a discussion of the debates surrounding race and theories of inheritance, see Curran, *Anatomy of Blackness*, 144–45.

130. Arnold and Geffroy, "Les Femmes de l'*Encyclopédie*," emphasis added.

131. Joseph-François Lafitau, *Mœurs des sauvages américains comparées aux mœurs des premiers temps*, 2 vols. (Paris, 1724); Andreas Motsch, *Lafitau et l'émergence du discours ethnographique* (Sillery: Septentrion, 2001); Hunt, Jacob, and Mijnhardt, *Book That Changed Europe*, 10 and 213–15.

132. Denis Diderot, "Aricouri" (Géographie), *EP* (1751), 1:650.

133. Denis Diderot, "Brésil' (Géographie), *EP* (1752), 2:412, emphasis added.

134. Michel de Montaigne, *Essays*, trans. J. M. Cohen (London: Penguin, 1993), 105–19; Jerome Schwartz, *Diderot and Montaigne: The "Essais" and the Shaping of Diderot's Humanism* (Geneva: Droz, 1966).

135. Louis de Jaucourt, "Eskimaux" (Géographie), *EP* (1755), 5:949.

136. Le Borgne, "Les saviors des barbares," 87–88.

137. Louis de Jaucourt, "Hudson (Henry)," *EP* (1765), 8:331; Jaucourt, "Laponie, la ou Lapponie" (Géographie), *EP* (1765), 9:287–88.

138. Jaucourt, "Laponie," *EP* (1765), 9:288.

139. Louis de Jaucourt, "Etat de nature" (Droit naturel), *EP* (1756), 6:17–18.

140. René Hubert, *Les Sciences sociales dans l'Encyclopédie: La philosophie de l'histoire et le problème des origines sociales* (Paris: Librairie Félix Alcan, 1923).

141. Hubert, *Les Sciences sociales*, 84. See Ronald Meek's criticism in *Social Science*, 97–98.

142. Jaucourt, "Etat de nature," *EP* (1756), 6:618.

143. Hubert argues that the encyclopedists, on the whole, conceived of the state of nature as a depravity and thus that the encyclopedists did not adhere to a noble savage discourse: Hubert, *Les Sciences sociales*, 188.

144. Jaucourt, "Etat de nature," *EP* (1756), 6:618.

145. Jaucourt, "Gouvernement," *EP* (1757), 7:788.

146. Olive Patricia Dickason, *The Myth of the Savage and the Beginnings of French Colonialism in the Americas* (Edmonton: University of Alberta Press, 1984).

147. Louis de Jaucourt, "Industrie" (Droit politique et commerce), *EP* (1765), 8:694–95.

148. Louis de Jaucourt, "Mexico, ville de" (Géographie), *EP* (1765), 10:480.

149. Ibid.

150. Louis de Jaucourt, "Mexique, l'empire du" (Géographie), *EP* (1765), 10:481.

151. Muthu, *Enlightenment Against Empire*.

152. Saint-Lambert, "Législateur" (Politique), *EP* (1765), 9:359.

153. Yves Benot, *Les Lumières, l'esclavage, la colonisation* (Paris: Éditions La Découverte, 2005), 164–72.

154. Christy Pichichero, *The Military Enlightenment: War and Culture in the French Empire from Louis XIV to Napoleon* (Ithaca, NY: Cornell University Press, 2017).

155. Madeleine Dobie, "The Enlightenment at War," *PMLA* 124, no. 5, (2009): 1851–54.

156. François Véron de Forbonnais, "Colonie" (Histoire ancienne et moderne, Commerce), *EP* (1753), 3:650.

157. Etienne-Noël Damilaville, "Population" (Physique, Morale, Politique), *EP* (1765), 13:100–102.

158. Benot, *Les Lumières*, 172.

159. Louis de Jaucourt, "Espagne" (Géographie historique), *EP* (1755), 5:953.

160. Louis de Jaucourt, "Superstition," *EP* (1765), 15: 669.

161. Louis de Jaucourt, "Japon" (Géographie), *EP* (1765), 8:455.

162. Louis de Jaucourt, "Guerre" (Droit naturel et politique), *EP* (1757), 7:996.

163. Louis de Jaucourt, "Lucayes, les" (Géographie), *EP* (1765), 9:710.

164. Louis de Jaucourt, "Japon" (Géographie), *EP* (1765), 8:454.

165. Jean Pestré, "Canadiens (Philosophie des)," *EP* (1752), 2:581–82.

166. Louis-Armand de Lom d'Arce de Lahontan, *Nouveaux voyages de Mr. Le Baron de Lahontan dans l'Amérique Septontrionale* (The Hague, 1703), 2 vols. On this work and its influence across the eighteenth century, see Anthony Pagden, *European Encounters with the New World: From Renaissance to Romanticism* (New Haven, CT: Yale University Press, 1993), chap. 4; and Gordon M. Sayre, *"Les Sauvages Américains": Representations of Native Americans in French and English Colonial Literature* (Chapel Hill: University of North Carolina Press, 1997), 31ff.

167. Pestré, "Canadiens," *EP* (1752), 2:581.

168. Stuurman, *Invention of Humanity*, 9.

169. Pestré, "Canadiens," *EP* (1752), 2:582. For the original discussion of the reasonableness of Native Canadians, see Lahontan, *Nouveaux voyages*, 2:131.

170. Walter E. Rex, "The Philosophical Articles by Abbé Pestré in Diderot's *Encyclopédie*," *Studies in Eighteenth-Century Culture* 7 (1978): 251–62.

171. Louis de Jaucourt, "Iroquois" (Géographie), *EP* (1765), 8:906.

172. Louis de Jaucourt, "Hurons, les" (Géographie), *EP* (1765), 8:356. On the role of language in Enlightenment debates about the "stages of societal development," see Sean P. Harvey, *Native Tongues: Colonialism and Race from Encounter to the Reservation* (Cambridge, MA: Harvard University Press, 2015), chap. 1.

173. T. C. Newland, "D'Holbach, Religion, and the *Encyclopédie*," *Modern Language Review* 69, no. 3 (1974): 523–33; Lough, *Essays on the "Encyclopédie,"* chap. 3.

174. D'Holbach, "Michabou" (Histoire moderne, Cultes), *EP* (1765), 10:485.

175. Drescher, *Capitalism and Antislavery*, 164.

176. For an examination of these articles, see Andrew Curran, "Diderot and the *Encyclopédie*'s Construction of the Black African," in *Diderot and European Culture*, ed. Frédéric Ogée and Anthony Strugnell (Oxford: Voltaire Foundation, 2006), 35–53; Curran, *Anatomy of Blackness*, 149–56.

177. Pierre Barrère, *Dissertation sur la cause physique de la couleur des nègres, de la qualité de leurs cheveux, et de la dégénération de l'un et de l'autre* (Paris, 1741).

178. Éric Saugera, *Bordeaux, port négrier: Chronologie, économie, idéologie, XVIIe–XIXe siècles* (Paris: Karthala, 1995).

179. Numa Broc, *La Géographie des philosophes: Géographes et voyageurs français au XVIIIe siècle* (Paris: Editions Ophrys, 1975), 246.

180. Mitchell, "An Essay upon the Causes."

181. Pierre-Louis Moreau de Maupertuis, *Vénus physique* (n.p., 1745); Antoine François Prévost, *Histoire générale des voyages*, 19 vols. (Paris, 1746–1770); Buffon, *Histoire naturelle, générale et particulière*, vols. 1–3 (Paris, 1749).

182. Andrew Curran also emphasizes the importance of the 1740s in the development of anatomical interest in blackness in *Anatomy of Blackness*, chap. 2.

183. Johan Heinrich Samuel Formey, "Negre" (Histoire naturelle), *EP* (1765), 11:76–79. On Formey, see François Moureau, "*L'Encyclopédie* d'après les correspondants de Formey," *Recherches sur Diderot et sur l'Encyclopédie* 3 (1987): 125–45.

184. Formey, "Negre," *EP* (1765), 11:76. For the original passage, copied verbatim by Formey, see Maupertuis, *Vénus physique* (n.p., 1745), 120–21.

185. Formey, "Negre," *EP* (1765), 11:77.

186. Curran, *Anatomy of Blackness*, 90.

187. Maupertuis, *Vénus physique*.

188. Formey, "Negre," *EP* (1765), 11:77.

189. Kafker and Kafker, *Encyclopedists as Individuals*, 140–44.

190. Johan Heinrich Samuel Formey, *Traité d'éducation morale* (Liège, 1773), 23; Roe, "'Sheep in Wolff's Clothing,'" 183.

191. "Negres blancs" (Histoire naturelle), *EP* (1765), 11:79.

192. Le Romain, "Negres," *EP* (1765), 11:80–83. On Le Romain, see Kafker and Kafker, *Encyclopedists as Individuals*, 212.

193. Le Romain, "Negres," *EP* (1765), 11:81.

194. Duchet, *Anthropologie et histoire*, 260.

195. Curran, *Anatomy of Blackness*, 157.

196. "Negres" (Commerce), *EP* (1765), 11:80. The source for this entry is the entry "Negre" in Jacques Savary Des Bruslons, *Dictionnaire universel de commerce* (Paris, 1748), 3:552–64.

197. Antoine-Gaspard Boucher d'Argis, "Esclave" (Jurisprudence), *EP* (1755), 5:940–41.

198. Peabody, *"There Are No Slaves in France,"* 15–22; Palmer, *Intimate Bonds*, 50–56.

199. Diderot, "Humaine espece," *EP* (1765), 8:347.

200. Ibid.

201. Stuurman, "How to Write a History," 37.

202. Louis de Jaucourt, "Peau des negres" (Anatomie), *EP* (1765), 12:215–17.

203. Ibid., 216. For the original passage, see Buffon, *De l'homme*, ed. Michèle Duchet (Paris: L'Harmattan, 1971), 320.

204. Denis Diderot, "Benin" (Géographie), *EP* (1752), 2:204.

205. Denis Diderot, "Ethiopiens (Philosophie des)" (Histoire de la philosophie), *EP* (1756), 6:55–56. Jaucourt's article "Ethiopie" (Géographie), *EP* (1756), 6:54–55, does not alter the picture of this region of Africa in any way, as it is a terse account of the region.

206. "Hottentots les" (Géographie), *EP* (1765), 8:320.

207. Louis de Jaucourt, "Samoyèdes, les, ou Samoiedes" (Géographie moderne), *EP* (1765), 14:603.

208. Ibid.

209. Louis de Jaucourt, "Guinée, (la)" (Géographie), *EP* (1757), 7:1009.

210. D'Holbach, "Jagas, Giagas ou Giagues" (Histoire moderne, Géographie), *EP* (1765), 8:433.

211. D'Holbach, "Kraals" (Histoire moderne), *EP* (1765), 9:138.

212. D'Holbach, "Siratick" (Histoire moderne), *EP* (1765), 15:225.

213. Ehrard, "Slavery Before the Moral Conscience," 111–20.

214. Madeleine F. Morris, *Le Chevalier de Jaucourt: Un ami de la terre (1704–1780)* (Geneva: Librairie Droz, 1979), 120.

215. Louis de Jaucourt, "Esclavage" (Droit naturel, Morale, Religion), *EP* (1755), 5:934.

216. Montesquieu, *Spirit of the Laws*, book 15, chap. 7.

217. Ehrard, "Slavery Before the Moral Conscience"; Georges Benrekassa, "Montesquieu et le problème de l'esclavage: Ce que nous apprend l'étude du manuscrit du Livre XV de *L'Esprit des Lois*," *Bulletin de la Société Montesquieu* no. 3 (1991): 4–10; Edward Derbyshire Seeber, *Anti-Slavery Opinion in France During the Second Half of the Eighteenth Century* (Baltimore: Johns Hopkins University Press, 1937), 28–35; Céline Spector, "'Il est impossible que nous supposions que ces gens-là soient des hommes': La théorie de l'esclavage au livre XV de *L'Esprit des lois*," *Lumières* 3 (2004): 15–51. But see also Ghachem, "Montesquieu in the Caribbean," 183–210, for how colonists used Montesquieu to reform slave laws.

218. Montesquieu, *My Thoughts*, trans. Henry C. Clark (Indianapolis: Liberty Fund, 2012), 660.

219. Jean Ehrard, "*L'Encyclopédie* et l'esclavage: Deux lectures de Montesquieu," in *Enlightenment Essays in Memory of Robert Shackleton*, ed. Giles Barber and C. P. Courtney (Oxford: Voltaire Foundation, 1988), 121–29.

220. Jaucourt, "Esclavage," *EP* (1755), 5:937–38.

221. Hunt, *Inventing Human Rights*, 31.

222. Jaucourt, "Esclavage," *EP* (1755), 5:937.

223. Ibid., 938–39.

224. Dan Edelstein, *On the Spirit of Rights* (Chicago: University of Chicago Press, 2019), 135.

225. Jaucourt, "Esclavage," *EP* (1755), 5:938.

226. Jaucourt, "Traite des negres" (Commerce d'Afrique), *EP* (1765), 16:532.

227. Wallace, *System of the Principles*. See also D. Davis, "New Sidelights."

228. Wallace, *System of the Principles*, 90.

229. Jaucourt, "Traite des negres," *EP* (1765), 16:532.

230. Hunt, *Inventing Human Rights*. On how empathy and humanitarian sensibility influenced the portrayal of the enslaved in eighteenth-century art, see Elmer Kolfin, "Becoming Human: The Iconography of Black Slavery in French, British and Dutch Book Illustrations, c. 1600–c.1800," in *The Slave in European Art: From Renaissance Trophy to Abolitionist Emblem*, ed. Elizabeth McGrath and Jean Michel Massing (London: Warburg Institute, 2012), 253–96.

231. Jean Ehrard, *Lumières et esclavage: L'esclavage colonial et l'opinion publique en France au XVIIIe siècle* (Paris: André Versaille, 2008), 180.

232. Formey, "Negre," *EP* (1765), 11:77.

233. Phillip R. Sloan, "The Idea of Racial Degeneracy in Buffon's *Histoire Naturelle*," in *Racism in the Eighteenth Century*, ed. Harold E. Pagliaro (Cleveland, OH: Case Western Reserve University, 1973), 295–99. On Maupertuis's contributions to the life sciences, see Mary Terrall, *The Man Who Flattened the Earth: Maupertuis and the Sciences in the Enlightenment* (Chicago: University of Chicago Press, 2002), chaps. 7 and 10.

234. On the life sciences in the *Encyclopédie*, see Roger, *Les Sciences de la vie*, 614–53. On the role of the "medical vitalists" from Montpellier in the *Encyclopédie* and the Enlightenment, see Elizabeth A. Williams, *A Cultural History of Medical Vitalism in Enlightenment Montpellier* (Aldershot, UK: Ashgate, 2003), chap. 5.

235. Roger, *Buffon*, 137–38; Michael H. Hoffheimer, "Maupertuis and the Eighteenth-Century Critique of Preexistence," *Journal of the History of Biology* 15, no. 1 (1982): 119–44.

236. Mary Terrall, "Speculation and Experiment in Enlightenment Life Sciences," in *Heredity Produced: At the Crossroads of Biology, Politics, and Culture, 1500–1800*, ed. Staffan

Müller-Wille and Hans-Jörg Rheinberger (Cambridge, MA: MIT Press, 2007), 253–76; Charles T. Wolfe, "Epigenesis as Spinozism in Diderot's Biological Project," in *The Life Sciences in Early Modern Philosophy*, ed. Ohad Nachtomy and Justin E. H. Smith (Oxford: Oxford University Press, 2014), 181–201.

237. Denis Diderot and Louis-Jean-Marie Daubenton, "Animal" (Zoologie), *EP* (1751), 1:474. See also Roselyne Rey, "Diderot et les sciences de la vie dans l'*Encyclopédie*," *Recherches sur Diderot et sur l'Encyclopédie* 18–19 (1995): 47–53.

238. Thomson, "Issues at Stake"; Ann Thomson, "Diderot, le matérialisme et la division de l'espèce humaine," *Recherches sur Diderot et sur l'Encyclopédie* 26 (1999): 197–211.

239. Nathan G. Alexander, *Race in a Godless World: Atheism, Race, and Civilization, 1850–1914* (Manchester: Manchester University Press, 2019).

240. Daniel Lord Smail, *On Deep History and the Brain* (Berkeley: University of California Press, 2008), chap. 1.

241. Rossi, *Dark Abyss of Time*, 107–9; Stephen Toulmin and June Goodfield, *The Discovery of Time* (London: Penguin Books, 1967), 174–83; Jacques Roger, "Buffon et l'introduction de l'histoire dans l'*Histoire naturelle*," in *Buffon 88*, ed. Jean Gayon (Paris: Vrin, 1992), 193–205.

242. D'Holbach, "Fossile," (Histoire naturelle, Minéralogie), *EP* (1757), 7:210.

243. Rossi, *Dark Abyss of Time*, esp. Parts 1 and 2.

244. Phillip R. Sloan, "The Gaze of Natural History," in *Inventing Human Science: Eighteenth-Century Domains*, ed. Christopher Fox, Roy Porter, and Robert Wokler (Berkeley: University of California Press, 1995), 112–51.

245. Phillip R. Sloan, "The Buffon-Linnaeus Controversy," *Isis* 67, no. 3 (1976): 356–75.

246. Roger, *Buffon*, 181.

247. Denis Diderot, "Chine, la" (Gégographie), *EP* (1753), 3:339.

248. Siep Stuurman, "Common Humanity and Cultural Difference on the Sedentary-Nomadic Frontier: Herodotus, Sima Qian, and Ibn Khaldun," in *Global Intellectual History*, ed. Samuel Moyn and Andrew Sartori (New York: Columbia University Press, 2013), 33–58.

249. Diderot, "Humaine espece," *EP* (1765), 8:345.

250. Guillaume d'Abbes, "Figure" (Physiologie), *EP* (1756), 6:773.

251. Schiebinger, *Nature's Body*, 134–36; Schiebinger, "Anatomy of Difference," 393.

252. Stuurman, "François Bernier," 5.

253. d'Abbes, "Figure," *EP* (1756), 6:773.

254. J. A. G. Roberts, "L'Image de la Chine dans l'*Encyclopédie*," *Recherches sur Diderot et sur l'Encyclopédie* 22 (1997): 87–108; Basil Guy, *The French Image of China Before and After Voltaire* (Geneva: Publications de l'Institut et Musée Voltaire, 1963); Silvia Eichhorn-Jung, "Anthropologie et religion chinoises dans les encyclopédies françaises et allemandes du XVIIIe siècle," in *Les Lumières européennes dans leurs relations avec les autres grandes cultures et religions*, ed. Florence Lotterie and Darrin M. McMahon (Paris: Honoré Champion, 2002), 165–90.

255. Virgile Pinot, *La Chine et la formation de l'esprit philosophique en France (1640–1740)* (Paris: Paul Geuthner, 1932).

256. Pierre Bayle, *Continuation des pensées diverses* (Rotterdam, 1705), 2:785; Pinot, *La Chine*, 314–27; Joy Charnley, *Pierre Bayle: Reader of Travel Literature* (Bern: Peter Lang, 1998), chap. 4.

257. Denis Diderot, "Asiatiques: Philosophie des Asiatiques en général," *EP* (1751), 1:752–55; Pierre Rétat, *Le Dictionnaire de Bayle et la lutte philosophique au XVIIIe siècle* (Paris: Société d'Édition Les Belles Lettres, 1971), 391.

258. Jean François de Saint-Lambert, "Honnête" (Morale), *EP* (1765), 8:287.

259. Additional examples can be found in the following articles by d'Holbach: "Ju-Kiau," (Philosophie, Histoire moderne), *EP* (1765), 9:53; "King" (Histoire moderne, Philosophie), *EP* (1765), 9:129; "Siuto" (Histoire moderne religieuse, Philosophie), *EP* (1765), 15:233–34.

260. "Bibliothèque," *EP* (1752), 2:232.

261. "Noblesse Littéraire ou Spirituelle," *EP* (1765), 11:174. See similar remarks in another anonymously-authored article: "Mandarin" (Histoire moderne), *EP* (1765), 10:11–12.

262. Joachim Faiguet de Villeneuve, "Etudes" (Littérature), *EP* (1756), 6:87–94.

263. Michael Adas, *Machines as the Measure of Men: Science, Technology, and Ideologies of Western Dominance* (Ithaca, NY: Cornell University Press, 1989), chap. 2.

264. Jean le Rond D'Alembert and Johan Heinrich Samuel Formey, "Astronomie, Astronomia" (Astronomie), *EP* (1751), 1:789.

265. Roberts, "L'Image de la Chine," 87–108.

266. Louis de Jaucourt, "Peine" (Droit naturel, civil et politique), *EP* (1765), 12:248.

267. Louis de Jaucourt, "Fe, Fo, Foé" (Histoire d'Asie), *EP* (1756), 6:460–61.

268. Huguette Cohen, "Diderot and the Image of China in Eighteenth-Century France," *Studies on Voltaire and the Eighteenth Century* 242 (1986): 222.

269. Denis Diderot, "Chinois, philosophie des," *EP* (1753), 3:343.

270. Ibid., 346.

271. Ibid., 347.

272. Ibid., 348.

273. Said, *Orientalism*.

274. Clarke, *Oriental Enlightenment*, 9.

275. Harvey, *French Enlightenment*, 42.

276. Michael Keevak, *Becoming Yellow: A Short History of Racial Thinking* (Princeton, NJ: Princeton University Press, 2011), 24–28.

277. Diderot, "Humaine espece," *EP* (1765), 8:345.

278. Louis de Jaucourt, "Galles, (les)," (Géographie), *EP* (1757), 7:449.

279. Louis de Jaucourt, "Japon" (Géographie), *EP* (1765), 8:455. For the original, see Voltaire, *Essai sur les mœurs*, vol. 2, chap. 142.

280. On "regimes of temporality" in thinking about equality and common humanity in world history, see Stuurman, *Invention of Humanity*, 14–16 and chap. 6 on the Enlightenment; François Hartog, *Regimes of Historicity: Presentism and Experiences of Time*, trans. Saskia Brown (New York: Columbia University Press, 2015).

281. Keith Michael Baker, ed., *The French Revolution and the Creation of Modern Political Culture*, vol. 1, *The Political Culture of the Old Regime* (Oxford: Pergamon Press, 1987), xvi.

282. David Northrup, *Africa's Discovery of Europe, 1450–1850*, 2nd ed. (New York: Oxford University Press, 2009); John Thornton, *Africa and Africans in the Making of the Atlantic World, 1400–1800*, 2nd ed. (Cambridge: Cambridge University Press, 2013); Snait B. Gissis, "Visualizing 'Race' in the Eighteenth Century," *Historical Studies in the Natural Sciences* 41, no. 1 (2011): 41–103.

283. Duchet, *Anthropologie et histoire*, 260.

284. Hudson, "From 'Nation' to 'Race,'" 253.

285. Louis de Jaucourt, "Race" (Généalogie), *EP* (1765), 13:740.

286. Ibid.

287. Plutarch, *Moralia*, vol. 3, *Sayings of Kings and Commanders*, trans. Frank Cole Babbitt, Loeb Classical Library 245 (Cambridge, MA: Harvard University Press, 1931), 103.

288. Jean Ehrard, "Diderot, l'*Encyclopédie*, et l'*Histoire et théorie de la Terre*," in *Buffon 88*, 135–42; Llana, "Natural History."

289. Claudine Cohen, *Science, libertinage et clandestinité à l'aube des Lumières: Le transformisme de Telliamed* (Paris: Presses Universitaires de France, 2011), 361–63.

290. D'Holbach, "Terre, révolutions de la" (Histoire naturelle, Minéralogie), *EP* (1765), 16:171; d'Holbach, "Terre, couches de la" (Histoire naturelle, Minéralogie), *EP* (1765), 16:169–67; d'Holbach, "Tremblemens de terre" (Histoire naturelle, Minéralogie), *EP* (1765), 16:580–83. On d'Holbach and his place in eighteenth-century discussions of the history of the earth, see Rossi, *Dark Abyss of Time*, 88–91.

291. D'Holbach, "Fossile" (Histoire naturelle, Minéralogie), *EP* (1757), 7:209–211.

292. Martin J. S. Rudwick, *Bursting the Limits of Time: The Reconstruction of Geohistory in the Age of Revolution* (Chicago: University of Chicago Press, 2005), chap. 5.

293. Jean Starobinski, "Remarques sur l'*Encyclopédie*," *Revue de métaphysique et de morale* 75, no. 3 (1970): 288–90; William H. Sewell, Jr., *Work and Revolution in France: The Language of Labor from the Old Regime to 1848* (Cambridge: Cambridge University Press, 1980), chap. 4.

294. Goodman, *Republic of Letters*, 28.

295. Ibid., 33.

296. James Schmidt, "What Enlightenment Project?," *Political Theory* 28, no. 6 (2000): 734–57.

297. Muthu, *Enlightenment Against Empire*, 265; Margaret Jacob also highlights the basic principles which united a disparate and disputatious group of thinkers: Jacob, *Secular Enlightenment*, 134.

298. Diderot, "Encyclopédie," *EP*, 635.

Chapter 4

All citations to the *Encyclopédie d'Yverdon* are to this online version: *Encyclopédie, ou Dictionnaire universel raisonné des connoissances humaines*, ed. Fortunato Bartolomeo De Felice, 42 vols. (Yverdon, 1770–1775); Paris: Classiques Garnier, ed. Claude Blum, https://classiques-garnier.com/encyclopedie-d-yverdon.html; hereafter cited as *EY*.

1. Jonathan Israel, *Democratic Enlightenment: Philosophy, Revolution, and Human Rights* (Oxford: Oxford University Press, 2011).

2. Gabriel Mingard, "Philosophe," *EY* (1774), 33:344; emphasis in original.

3. Fortunato De Felice, "Preface," *EY* (1770), 1:viii.

4. Ibid., xiii.

5. Christian and Sylviane Albertan, "Foi et Lumières dans l'*Encyclopédie d'Yverdon*," in *L'Encyclopédie d'Yverdon et sa résonance européenne*, ed. Jean-Daniel Candaux, Alain Cernuschi, Clorinda Donato, and Jens Häseler (Geneva: Slatkine, 2005), 159.

6. Fortunato De Felice, "Sensibilité" (R) (Morale), *EY* (1774), 38:307; emphasis added.

7. Fortunato De Felice, "Société" (R) (Droit naturel et politique), *EY* (1774), 38:664.

8. "Inégalité" (R) (Morale), *EY* (1773), 24:500.

9. Fortunato De Felice, "Égalité politique" (N) (Droit politique), *EY* (1772), 15:383.

10. "Inégalité," *Dictionnaire universel François et Latin* (Nancy, 1740), 4:240.

11. Antoine Touron, *De la providence: Traité historique, dogmatique, et moral* (Paris, 1752), 269–70.

12. Louis-Mayeul Chaudon, *Dictionnaire anti-philosophique* (Avignon, 1767), 99.

13. Robert Darnton, *The Business of Enlightenment: A Publishing History of the "Encyclopédie," 1775–1800* (Cambridge, MA: Harvard University Press, 1979), 19–21, 36.

14. The biographical information is drawn from Eugène Macccabez, *F. B. De Félice et son Encyclopédie Yverdon* (Basel: Emile Birkhaeuser, 1903), chap. 1; and Jean-Pierre Perret, *Les Imprimeries d'Yverdon au XVIIe et au XVIIIe siècle* (Lausanne: F. Roth et Cie, 1945), 80–96. More recent scholarship includes Léonard Burnand, "Les coulisses de l'*Encyclopédie d'Yverdon*: L'éditeur Fortunato Bartolomeo De Felice et son réseau épistolaire," *Revue historique vaudoise* 120 (2012): 55–66; Burnand, "La correspondance de F.-B. De Felice: Une source pour l'étude des transferts culturels dans l'Europe des Lumières," *Recherches sur Diderot et sur l'Encyclopédie* 49 (2014): 107–121; Clorinda Donato, "A Commercial, Personal and Philosophical Foe: F. B. De Felice, Disseminator of Anti-Voltairian Sentiment from Florence to Berlin," in *Voltaire et ses combats*, ed. Ulla Kölving and Christiane Mervaud (Oxford: Voltaire Foundation, 1997) 2:997–1006; Donato, "Religion et Lumières en Italie, 1745–1775: Le choix protestant de Fortunato Bartolomeo De Felice," in *L'Encyclopédie d'Yverdon et sa résonance européenne*, ed. Jean-Daniel Candaux, Alain Cernuschi, Clorinda Donato, and Jens Häseler (Geneva: Slatkine, 2005), 89–120; Giulietta Pejrone, "Fortunato Bartolomeo De Felice: éducateur, publiciste, éditeur," *Annales Benjamin Constant* 14 (1993): 57–62.

15. Clorinda Donato, "Inventory of the *Encyclopédie d'Yverdon*: A Comparative Study with Diderot's *Encyclopédie*" (PhD diss., University of California, Los Angeles, 1987), 133.

16. On their friendship, see Donato, "Inventory," 134–36. On Genovesi and Sangro's activities in Enlightenment culture, see John Robertson, *The Case for the Enlightenment: Scotland and Naples, 1680–1760* (Cambridge: Cambridge University Press, 2007), 350ff.

17. Maccabez, *F. B. De Félice*, 6.

18. Ibid., 8.

19. Ibid., 10–11.

20. Jean-Jacques Burlamaqui, *Principes du droit de la nature et des gens avec la suite du Droit de la nature qui n'avait point encore paru: Le tout considérablement augmenté par Mr. le professeur De Felice*, 8 vols. (Yverdon, 1766–68). On this work, see Luigi Delia, "The Enlightenment, Encyclopedism and the Natural Rights of Man: The Case of the *Code of Humanity* (1778)," in *Thinking about the Enlightenment: Modernity and Its Ramifications*, ed. Martin L. Davies (London: Routledge, 2016), 69–85.

21. Fortunato De Felice, *Dictionnaire géographique, historique et politique de la Suisse*, 2 vols. (Neuchatel, 1775). The *Code de l'humanité* was officially titled *Dictionnaire universel raisonné de justice naturelle et civile*, 8 vols. (Yverdon, 1777–78). On the latter work, see Delia, "Enlightenment, Encyclopedism."

22. Darnton, *Business of Enlightenment*, 19–21, 36.

23. The information in this paragraph is taken from Kathleen Hardesty Doig and Clorinda Donato, "Notices sur les auteurs des quarante-huit volumes de 'discours' de l'*Encyclopédie d'Yverdon*," *Recherches sur Diderot et sur l'Encyclopédie* 11 (1991): 133–41.

24. Marc Weidmann, "Un pasteur-naturaliste du XVIIIe siècle: Elie Bertrand (1713–1797)," *Revue historique vaudoise* 94 (1986): 63–108; Rossella Baldi, "Questionner la figure du

médiateur: Mises à jour archivistiques autour d'Élie Bertrand," *Annales de la Société suisse pour l'étude du XVIIIe siècle* 5 (2014): 191–202.

25. Etienne Hofmann, "Le Pasteur Gabriel Mingard, collaborateur de l'*Encyclopédie d'Yverdon*: Matériaux pour l'étude de sa pensée," in *Le Gout de l'histoire, des idées et des hommes: Mélanges offerts au professeur Jean-Pierre Aguet*, ed. Alain Clavien and Bertrand Müller (Lausanne: L'Aire, 1996), 86.

26. Pietro Verri, *Pensées sur le bonheur*, trans. Gabriel Mingard (Yverdon, 1766).

27. Fortunato De Felice, *Encyclopédie, etc., Planches* (1780), 10:n.p.

28. Helena Rosenblatt, "The Christian Enlightenment," in *The Cambridge History of Christianity*, vol. 7, *Enlightenment, Revolution and Reawakening (1660–1815)*, ed. Timothy Tackett and Stewart J. Brown (Cambridge University Press, 2006), 292.

29. Rosenblatt, "Christian Enlightenment," 297.

30. Roger Francillon, "The Enlightenment in Switzerland," in *Reconceptualizing Nature, Science, and Aesthetics: Contribution à une nouvelle approche des Lumières helvétiques*, ed. Patrick Coleman, Anne Hofman, and Simone Zurbuchen (Geneva: Slatkine, 1998), 14.

31. Andreas Würgler, "Conspiracy and Denunciation: A Local Affair and Its European Publics (Bern, 1749)," in *Cultures of Communication from the Reformation to the Enlightenment*, ed. James Van Horn Melton (Aldershot, UK: Ashgate, 2002), 119–31.

32. Samuel S. B. Taylor, "The Enlightenment in Switzerland," in *The Enlightenment in National Context*, ed. Roy Porter and Mikuláš Teich (Cambridge: Cambridge University Press, 1981), 72–89.

33. On Marie Huber and her influence on Rousseau, see E. R. Briggs, "Marie Huber and the Campaign Against Eternal Hell Torments," in *Woman and Society in Eighteenth-Century France: Essays in Honour of John Stephenson Spink*, ed. Eva Jacobs, et al. (London: Athlone Press, 1979), 218–28.

34. David Sorkin, *The Religious Enlightenment: Protestants, Jews, and Catholics from London to Vienna* (Princeton, NJ: Princeton University Press, 2008), chap. 2.

35. Sorkin, *Religious Enlightenment*, 96.

36. Fortunato De Felice, "Egalité naturelle" (Droit naturel) (R), *EY* (1772), 15:377–80.

37. On Barbeyrac, see Tim Hochstrasser, "Conscience and Reason: The Natural Law Theory of Jean Barbeyrac," *Historical Journal* 36, no. 2 (1993): 289–308.

38. De Felice, "Egalité naturelle," *EY* (1772), 15:377. For the original, see Samuel Pufendorf, *Le Droit de la nature et des gens*, trans. Jean Barbeyrac (London, 1740), 2:26.

39. De Felice, "Egalité naturelle," *EY* (1772), 15:378; emphasis added.

40. As we have already seen, this is not the only way of reading Hobbesian equality: Hoekstra, "Hobbesian Equality," 76–112.

41. De Felice, "Egalité naturelle," *EY* (1772), 15:379.

42. Ibid., 379.

43. De Felice, "Egalité politique," *EY*, 380.

44. Ibid., 383. This is copied verbatim from Jean-Charles de Lavie, *Abrégé de la République de Bodin* (London, 1755), 2:175–76.

45. Charly Guyot, *Le Rayonnement de l'Encyclopédie en Suisse française* (Neuchatel: Paul Attinger, 1955), 118. For further information on the political outlook of De Felice and his circle, see Kathleen Hardesty Doig, "The Yverdon *Encyclopédie*," in *Notable Encyclopedias of the*

Late Eighteenth Century: Eleven Successors of the "Encyclopédie," ed. Frank A. Kafker (Oxford: Voltaire Foundation, 1994), 85–116.

46. Fortunato De Felice, "Démocratie" (Droit politique), *EY* (1772), 13:371.

47. Haakonssen, "Moral Conservatism," in *Natural Law and Civil Sovereignty: Moral Right and State Authority in Early Modern Political Thought*, ed. Ian Hunter and David Saunders (Basingstoke: Palgrave Macmillan, 2002), 27–42.

48. Rosenblatt, *Rousseau and Geneva*, 101.

49. Fortunato De Felice, "Gouvernement" (R) (Droit politique), *EY* (1773), 22:78.

50. Fortunato De Felice, "Souveraineté," *EY* (1775), 39:134.

51. Gabriel Mingard, "Autorité" (R) (Grammaire, Morale, Politique), *EY* (1771), 4:316.

52. Diderot, "Autorité politique," *EP* (1751), 1:898.

53. Fortunato De Felice, "Femme" (Droit naturel), *EY* (1772), 18:495.

54. Fortunato De Felice, "Pouvoir paternel" (R) (Droit naturel et civil), *EY* (1774), 34:830–39.

55. Fortunato De Felice, "Législation" (R) (Grammaire, Politique), *EY* (1773), 25:821–22.

56. Kathleen Hardesty Doig, "Rousseau and the Republican Model in the Yverdon *Encyclopédie*: The *Contrat Social*," in *Republikanische Tugend: Ausbildung eines Schweizer Nationalbewusstseins und Erziehung eines neuen Bürgers; Contribution à une nouvelle approche des Lumières helvétiques*, ed. Michael Böhler (Geneva: Slatkine, 2000), 471–86.

57. Jean-Jacques Rousseau, *The Social Contract and Other Later Political Writings*, trans. and ed. Victor Gourevitch (Cambridge: Cambridge University Press, 1997), 78.

58. De Felice, "Législation," *EY* (1773), 25:822; Rousseau, *Social Contract*, 79.

59. Patrick Riley, *The General Will Before Rousseau: The Transformation of the Divine into the Civic* (Princeton, NJ: Princeton University Press, 1986), 219–20.

60. "Intolérance" (Morale), *Encyclopédie, ou dictionnaire universel raisonné des connoissances humaines; Supplément* (Yverdon, 1776), 4:55; hereafter cited as *SY*.

61. François Jost, *Jean-Jacques Rousseau Suisse* (Fribourg Suisse: Éditions Universitaires, 1961); Rosenblatt, *Rousseau and Geneva*; Béla Kapossy, "The Sociable Patriot: Isaak Iselin's Protestant Reading of Rousseau," *History of European Ideas* 27, no. 2 (2001): 153–70; Simone Zurbuchen, "Reacting to Rousseau: Difficult Relations Between Erudition and Politics in the Swiss Republics," in *Scholars in Action: The Practice of Knowledge and the Figure of the Savant in the 18th Century*, ed. André Holenstein, Hubert Steinke, Martin Stuber, and Philippe Rogger (Leiden: Brill, 2013), 481–501.

62. Bela Kapossy, *Iselin Contra Rousseau: Sociable Patriotism and the History of Mankind* (Basel: Schwabe Verlag, 2006).

63. Fortunato De Felice, "Souveraineté" (R) (Droit politique), *EY* (1775), 39:143. For the original, see Jean-Jacques Burlamaqui, *Principes du droit politique* (Amsterdam, 1751), 2:39.

64. Fortunato De Felice, "Législateur" (R) (Politique), *EY* (1773), 25:809; original in Rousseau, *Social Contract*, 69.

65. Rousseau, *Social Contract*, 72.

66. Doig, "Rousseau and the Republican Model," 478.

67. Ibid., 486.

68. Fortunato De Felice, "Vertu" (R) (Morale), *EY* (1775), 42:203.

69. Guyot, *Le Rayonnement de l'Encyclopédie*, 115.

70. Ibid., 119–20.

71. Enid Stoye, *Vincent Bernard de Tscharner, 1728–1778: A Study of Swiss Culture in the Eighteenth Century* (Fribourg: St-Paul, 1954).

72. "Projet" (N) (Philosophie politique), *EY* (1774), 35:341–55; Georg Ludwig Schmid, *Traités sur divers sujets intéressans de politique et de morale* (n.p., 1760).

73. Gabriel Mingard, "Perfectibilité" (N) (Métaphysique, Antropologie [*sic*], Morale), *EY* (1774), 33:38–41.

74. Robert Wokler, *Rousseau, the Age of Enlightenment, and Their Legacies*, ed. Bryan Garsten (Princeton, NJ: Princeton University Press, 2012), 190. This "project" or "culture" of improvement was intimately connected to the practice of natural history; see E. C. Spary, *Utopia's Garden: French Natural History from Old Regime to Revolution* (Chicago: University of Chicago Press, 2000).

75. The best overview of the field is provided in Robert Wokler, "Natural Law and the Meaning of Rousseau's Political Thought: A Correction to Two Misrenderings of His Doctrine," in *Enlightenment Essays in Memory of Robert Shackleton*, ed. G. Barber, C. Courtney, and D. Gilson (Oxford: Voltaire Foundation, 1988), 319–35; and Wokler, "Rousseau's Pufendorf: Natural Law and the Foundations of Commercial Society," *History of Political Thought* 15, no. 3 (1994): 373–402. See also Rosenblatt, *Rousseau and Geneva*, chaps. 3 and 4; and Gabriella Silvestrini, "Rousseau, Pufendorf, and the Eighteenth-Century Natural Law Tradition," *History of European Ideas* 36, no. 3 (2010): 280–301.

76. Wokler, "Rousseau's Pufendorf," 384. Wokler qualified the important work of Robert Derathé, *Rousseau et la science politique de son temps* (Paris: Presses Universitaires de France, 1950).

77. Gabriel Mingard, "Droit naturel" (R) (Philosophie), *EY* (1772), 14:549.

78. Ibid., 552.

79. Fortunato De Felice, "Loi naturelle" (R) (Morale), *EY* (1773), 26:524–40.

80. Jean-Jacques Burlamaqui, *The Principles of Natural and Politic Law*, ed. Petter Korkman, trans. Thomas Nugent (1763; Indianapolis: Liberty Fund, 2006), 280–81.

81. Mona Ozouf coined the phrase "transfer of sacrality" to refer to the matrix of religious, cultural, and political change during the French Revolution; Ozouf, *Festivals and the French Revolution*, trans. Alan Sheridan (Cambridge, MA: Harvard University Press, 1988), chap. 10; on Enlightenment antecedents, see Charly Coleman, "Resacralizing the World: The Fate of Secularization in Enlightenment Historiography," *Journal of Modern History* 82 (2010): 368–95; Bell, *Cult of the Nation*.

82. The asterisk allows the search to track all of the variations of the French word "social": "social," "sociale," and "sociales." I also searched "sociaux" separately and added it to the totals reported here.

83. Mintzker, "'Word Newly Introduced.'"

84. De Felice, "Société," *EY* (1774), 38:663–94.

85. Ibid., 663.

86. Ibid., 664.

87. François-André-Adrien Pluquet, *De la sociabilité*, 2 vols. (Paris, 1767). On Pluquet, see Michael Sonenscher, "Property, Community, and Citizenship," in *The Cambridge History of Eighteenth-Century Political Thought*, ed. Mark Goldie and Robert Wokler (Cambridge: Cambridge University Press, 2006), 481.

88. Jean-Jacques Rousseau, *The Discourses and Other Early Political Writings*, trans. and ed. Victor Gourevitch (Cambridge: Cambridge University Press, 1997), 131.

89. Rousseau, *Discourses*, 158–59; Judith N. Shklar, *Men and Citizens: A Study of Rousseau's Social Theory* (Cambridge: Cambridge University Press, 1985), 44–45.

90. De Felice, "Société," *EY* (1774), 38:664.

91. Ibid., 664.

92. Robert Mauzi, *L'Idée du bonheur au XVIIIe siècle*, 4th ed. (Paris: Armand Colin, 1969), 599ff.

93. De Felice, "Société," *EY* (1774), 38:664.

94. Ibid., 683.

95. Baker, "Enlightenment and the Institution of Society," 107.

96. Élie Bertrand, "Religion" (R) (Théologie, Morale), *EY* (1774), 36:419.

97. Baker, "Enlightenment Idioms," 165–97.

98. De Felice, "Société," *EY* (1774), 38:681.

99. "Tolérance" (R) (Théologie, Morale, Droit naturel), *EY* (1775), 40:794.

100. "Tolérance" (R), *EY* (1775), 40:801.

101. Guyot, *Le Rayonnement de l'Encyclopédie*, 105–6.

102. [Alexandre Deleyre], "Fanatisme" (Philosophie), *EY* (1772), 18:317–33; [Louis de Jaucourt], "Superstition" (Métaphysique, Philosophie), *EY* (1775), 39:555.

103. "Juif" (Histoire ancienne et moderne), *EY* (1773) 25:198–229.

104. Fortunato De Felice, "Dévot" (N) (Fourberie), *EY* (1772), 13:646.

105. Gabriel Mingard, "Athée" (R) (Histoire de la philosophie), (1771), 4:81.

106. Clorinda Donato, "Réfutation ou réconciliation? Fortunato Bartolomeo De Felice critique des *Préjugés légitimes contre l'Encyclopédie* et le libre *De l'Esprit*," in *Les Ennemis de Diderot*, ed. Anne-Marie Chouillet (Paris: Klincksieck, 1993), 101–12.

107. Elie Bertrand, "Calvin, Jean" (N) (Histoire littéraire), (1771), 7:123.

108. Gabriel Mingard and Fortunato De Felice, "Évangile" (N) (Théologie), *EY* (1772), 17:536.

109. Gabriel Mingard, "Résurrection" (R) (Philosophie, Théologie), *EY* (1774), 36:643.

110. Gay, *Enlightenment: An Interpretation*; Robertson, *Case for the Enlightenment*, 8.

111. Franco Venturi, *Italy and the Enlightenment: Studies in a Cosmopolitan Century*, ed. Stuart Woolf, trans. Susan Corsi (New York: New York University Press, 1972), 166.

112. Mingard, "Droit naturel," *EY* (1772), 14:549.

113. Darrin M. McMahon, in his sweeping history of happiness in the West, also argues that the Enlightenment was a crucial turning point in the development of the idea in the *longue durée*. See McMahon, *Happiness: A History* (New York: Grove Press, 2006), 13, 197–252.

114. On Beccaria's reflections on happiness and equality, see Venturi, *Italy and the Enlightenment*, 157ff.

115. McMahon, *Happiness: A History*, 209.

116. Fortunato De Felice, "Peine" (R) (Droit naturel, civil, et politique), *EY* (1774) 32:621.

117. Cesare Beccaria, *Traité des délits et des peines* (Lausanne, 1766), 16.

118. Cesare Beccaria, *On Crimes and Punishments and Other Writings*, ed. Richard Bellamy, trans. Richard Davies (Cambridge: Cambridge University Press, 1995), 51.

119. Hans-Jürgen Lüsebrink and Anthony Strugnell, eds., *L'Histoire des deux Indes: Réécriture et polygraphie* (Oxford: Voltaire Foundation, 1995).

120. When citing the *Histoire des deux Indes*, I include the date of publication to indicate which edition De Felice and his collaborators used. The passages that Diderot authored are traced in Michèle Duchet, *Diderot et l'Histoire des deux Indes, ou l'écriture fragmentaire* (Paris: A.-G. Nizet, 1978); and, more recently, Gianluigi Goggi, "La collaboration de Diderot à l'*Histoire des deux Indes*: L'édition de ses contributions," *Diderot Studies* 33 (2013): 167–212.

121. Madeleine Dobie, "Going Global: Diderot, 1770–1784," *Diderot Studies* 31 (2009): 7–23; Dobie, "Enlightenment at War"; Bell, *Cult of the Nation*, chap. 3.

122. Darrin M. McMahon, "Religious Enlightenment: A Useful Category of Research?" *European Journal* 14, no. 1 (2013): 3.

123. "Amérique" (R) (Géographie), *EY* (1770), 2:357–62; Diderot had written that the geographic entries were of varying quality and that many would have to be revised and expanded in an updated encyclopedia. See Charles W. J. Withers, *Placing the Enlightenment: Thinking Geographically about the Age of Reason* (Chicago: University of Chicago Press, 2007), 173.

124. Ibid., 358.

125. Ibid., 358.

126. José de Acosta, *The Natural and Moral History of the Indies*, trans. Edward Grimston (1604; repr., London: Hakluyt Society, 1880), 1:70.

127. Paul-Joseph Vallet, "Canada" (R) (Géographie), *EY* (1771), 7:207.

128. Ibid., 208.

129. Belmessous, "Assimilation and Racialism."

130. Fortunato De Felice, "Caractère des sauvages" (N) (Morale), *EY* (1771), 7:471–73; original in Cornelius De Pauw, *Recherches philosophiques sur les Américains* (London, 1771), 1:102.

131. De Felice, "Caractère des sauvages," *EY* (1771), 7:472; original in De Pauw, *Recherches philosophiques*, 1:103.

132. De Felice, "Caractère des sauvages," *EY* (1771), 7:471–73; original in De Pauw, *Recherches philosophiques*, 1:105.

133. Curran, *Anatomy of Blackness*, 192.

134. Fortunato De Felice, "Chair" (R) (Histoire ancienne et moderne), *EY* (1771) 8:515; original at De Pauw, *Recherches philosophiques*, 1:185.

135. Michèle Duchet, *Le Partage des savoirs: Discours historique et discours ethnologique* (Paris: Éditions La Découverte, 1984), 83; emphasis in original.

136. Ibid., 93–94.

137. Buffon, *De l'homme*, 368ff.; Cornelius J. Jaenen, "'Les Sauvages Ameriquains': Persistence into the 18th Century of Traditional French Concepts and Constructs for Comprehending Amerindians," *Ethnohistory* 29, no. 1 (1982): 50.

138. John D. Browning, "Cornelius de Pauw and Exiled Jesuits: The Development of Nationalism in Spanish America," *Eighteenth-Century Studies* 11, no. 3 (1978): 294.

139. Browning, "Cornelius de Pauw," 307.

140. Buffon, *Histoire naturelle: Supplément* (Paris, 1777), 4:525ff.

141. "Métis et Mulâtres" (N) (Histoire naturelle), *EY* (1773), 28:550.

142. Ibid.

143. Ibid., 551; original in De Pauw, *Recherches philosophiques*, 1:244.

144. De Pauw's racial theories are discussed in Curran, *Anatomy of Blackness*, 126ff.

145. Fortunato De Felice, "Inceste" (Théologie), *EY* (1773), 24:422–24; "Patagons, les" (R) (Géographie moderne), *EY* (1774) 33:455–58; De Felice, "Californie" (R) (Géographie), *EY* (1771) 7:81–85.

146. The article is divided into two sections. The first, by Albrecht von Haller, follows the model of Diderot's "Homme" (Histoire naturelle), and the second section is unsigned and follows the model of Diderot's "Humaine espece" (Histoire naturelle).

147. "Sauvages" (Histoire moderne), *EY* (1774), 37:715–18. The original can be found at Guillaume Thomas François Raynal, *Histoire des deux Indes* (Amsterdam, 1772), 6:199ff.

148. "Sauvages," *EY* (1774), 37:718.

149. Ibid.

150. Ibid.

151. Stuurman, *Invention of Humanity*, 14–16, 288–95.

152. Ibid., 295.

153. The article analyzed in this paragraph is drawn verbatim from Raynal, *Histoire des deux Indes* (Amsterdam, 1772), 3:24–25.

154. Lilti, *L'Héritage des Lumières*, chap. 2.

155. "Mexique, l'empire du" (R) (Géographie), *EY* (1773), 28:587.

156. Ibid., 591.

157. Stuurman, "Diderot en Raynal."

158. "Mexique, l'empire du," *EY* (1773), 28:595.

159. Ibid.

160. Anthony Strugnell, "Diderot's Anti-Colonialism: A Problematic Notion," in *New Essays on Diderot*, ed. James Fowler (Cambridge: Cambridge University Press, 2011), 74–85; Kenta Ohji, "La fin de l'Ancien Régime en Europe selon l'*Histoire des deux Indes*," in *Penser l'Europe au XVIIIe siècle*, ed. Antoine Lilti and Céline Spector (Oxford: Voltaire Foundation, 2014), 117–36. Sunil M. Agnani also provides an insightful discussion of the ambiguities of Enlightenment anti-colonialism in *Hating Empire Properly: The Two Indies and the Limits of Enlightenment Anticolonialism* (New York: Fordham University Press, 2013); Dorothee Sturkenboom also presents a brilliant analysis of the gendered assumptions and nationalist sentiments that colored views of international commerce in the *Histoire des deux Indes*. See Sturkenboom, *De ballen van de koopman: Mannelijkheid en Nederlandse identiteit in de tijd van de Republiek* (Gorredijk: Sterck en De Vreese, 2019), 170–92.

161. Stuurman, "Diderot en Raynal," 120–21.

162. Fortunato De Felice, "Devoirs des nations" (N) (Droits des gens), *EY* (1772), 13:639. The original passage can be found at Emer de Vattel, *The Law of Nations*, ed. Béla Kapossy and Richard Whatmore (Indianapolis: Liberty Fund, 2008), 164.

163. Tuck, *Rights of War and Peace*, 195. Jennifer Pitts also highlights Vattel's disregard for the violence of European colonial expansion: Pitts, *Boundaries of the International: Law and Empire* (Cambridge, MA: Harvard University Press, 2018), chap. 3.

164. [Jean Pestré], "Canadiens (Philosophie des)" (Histoire moderne), *EY* (1771), 7:209–11.

165. "Amérique," *SY* (1775), 1:315.

166. [Zacharie de Pazzi de Bonneville], *De l'Amérique et des Américains: Ou observations curieuses du philosophe La Douceur* (Berlin, 1771), 55–56. It is discussed in Antonello Gerbi, *The Dispute of the New World: The History of a Polemic, 1750–1900*, trans. Jeremy Moyle (Pittsburgh: University of Pittsburgh Press, 1973), 102–7.

167. "Canada," (Géographie moderne), *SY* (1775), 2:443–59.

168. Pierre-François-Xavier Charlevoix, *Histoire et description générale de la Nouvelle France* (Paris, 1744), 3:310–11.

169. "Canada," *SY* (1775), 2:443.

170. Ibid., 444.

171. The original can be found at Raynal, *Histoire des deux Indes* (Amsterdam, 1773), 6:11ff.

172. Pierre Berthiaume, "Raynal: Rhétorique sauvage, l'Amérindien dans l'*Histoire des deux Indes*," in *L'Histoire des deux Indes: Réécriture et polygraphie*, ed. Hans-Jürgen Lüsebrink and Anthony Strugnell (Oxford: Voltaire Foundation, 1995), 231–50; Ursula Haskins

Gonthier, "The 'Supplément au *Journal* de Bougainville': Representations of Native Canadians in the *Histoire des deux Indes*," in *Raynal's "Histoire des deux Indes": Colonialism, Networks and Global Exchange*, ed. Cecil Courtney and Jenny Mander (Oxford: Voltaire Foundation, 2015), 187–97.

173. Duchet, *Anthropologie et histoire*, 18; Muthu, *Enlightenment Against Empire*.

174. J. G. A. Pocock, *Barbarism and Religion*, vol. 4, *Barbarians, Savages and Empires* (Cambridge: Cambridge University Press, 2005), 231.

175. Jean Tarrade, "Colonialisme," in *Dictionnaire européen des Lumières*, ed. Michel Delon (Paris: Presses Universitaires de France, 1997), 235–36.

176. Stuurman, "Diderot en Raynal." Antoine Lilti and Ann Thomson also highlight the ambiguities of the anti-colonialism of the *Histoire des deux Indes*: Lilti, *L'Héritage des Lumières*, 62–68; Thomson, "Colonialism, Race and Slavery in Raynal's *Histoire des deux Indes*," *Global Intellectual History* 2, no. 3 (2017): 251–67.

177. Fortunato De Felice, "Missionnaire" (R) (Théologie), *EY* (1774), 29:13.

178. Alan Frost, "The Pacific Ocean: The Eighteenth Century's 'New World,'" *Studies on Voltaire and the Eighteenth Century* 152 (1976): 779–822.

179. "Taiti" (N) (Géographie moderne), *EY* (1775), 40:101–2. The original is extracted verbatim from Louis Antoine de Bougainville, *Voyage autour du monde par la frégate du roi la Boudeuse* (Paris, 1771), 214.

180. Bronwen Douglas, "'Novus Orbis Australis': Oceania in the Science of Race, 1750–1850," in *Foreign Bodies: Oceania and the Science of Race, 1750–1940*, ed. Bronwen Douglas and Chris Ballard (Canberra: ANU Press, 2008), 107–8.

181. Bronwen Douglas makes this point in greater detail in Douglas, "Slippery Word, Ambiguous Praxis: 'Race' and Late Eighteenth-Century Voyagers in Oceania," *Journal of Pacific History* 41, no. 1 (2006): 10–13.

182. "Taiti," *EY* (1775), 40:101.

183. Ibid., 104; Bougainville, *Voyage autour du monde*, 221.

184. Denis Diderot, *Supplément au voyage de Bougainville*, ed. Michel Delon (Paris: Gallimard, 2002); Andy Martin, "The Enlightenment in Paradise: Bougainville, Tahiti, and the Duty of Desire," *Eighteenth-Century Studies* 41, no. 2 (2008): 203–16.

185. "Taiti," *EY* (1775), 40:106.

186. John Gascoigne, *Encountering the Pacific in the Age of the Enlightenment* (Cambridge: Cambridge University Press, 2014), 145–48.

187. "Esclavage" (Droit naturel, Religion, Morale), *EY* (1772), 17:41–43; Rousseau, *Social Contract*, 45.

188. Jean-Baptiste-Pierre Le Romain, "Sucrerie" (Habitation), *EP* (1765), 15:618–19; [Le Romain], "Sucrerie" (Manufacture), *EY* (1775), 39:486–88.

189. "Negre" (Histoire naturelle), *EY* (1774), 30: 202–14.

190. Ibid., 211.

191. Ibid.

192. Ibid.

193. Hunt, *Inventing Human Rights*, chap. 1.

194. All of these passages are copied from Raynal, *Histoire des deux Indes* (Amsterdam, 1770), 4:167ff. On this borrowing, see Lüsebrink, "De l'*Encyclopédie*," 257–76.

195. "Domingue, Saint" (R) (Géographie moderne), *EY* (1775), 3:331; original at Raynal, *Histoire des deux Indes* (1772) 5:127.

196. Daniel Gordon, "Uncivilised Civilisation: Raynal and the Global Public Sphere," in *Raynal's "Histoire des deux Indes": Colonialism, Networks and Global Exchange*, ed. Cecil Courtney and Jenny Mander (Oxford: Voltaire Foundation, 2015), 103–17; Jean Starobinski, "The Word 'Civilization,'" in *Blessings in Disguise; or, the Morality of Evil*, trans. Arthur Goldhammer (Cambridge, MA: Harvard University Press, 1993), 1–35.

197. Stuurman, *Invention of Humanity*, 262–63.

198. Albrecht von Haller, "Génération" (Physiologie), *EY* (1773), 21:315–46. On the rivalry between Haller and Buffon, see Roger, *Les Sciences de la vie*, 705ff.

199. "Chananéens" (R) (Histoire sacrée), *EY* (1771), 8:672.

200. Haller, "Génération," *EY* (1773), 21:344.

201. "Homme" (Histoire naturelle), *EY* (1773), 23:392. The original is at Buffon, *De l'homme*, 283–84.

202. "Afrique" (R) (Géographie ancienne et moderne), *EY* (1770), 1:544.

203. Ibid., 545.

204. Andrew Wells, "Race and Racism in the Global European World Before 1800," *History Compass* 13, no. 9 (2015): 435–44.

205. [Denis Diderot], "Benin" (Géographie), *EY* 1771, 5:253–54.

206. [Denis Diderot], "Ethiopiens (Philosophie des)" (Histoire de la philosophie), *EY* (1772), 17:387–89.

207. "Hottentots, les," (Géographie), *EY* 1773, 23:497–98; [d'Holbach], "Jagas, Giagas ou Giagues" (Histoire moderne, Géographie), *EY* (1773), 23:786.

208. "Giagas, ou Jagas, ou Jagues" (R) (Géographie et histoire moderne), *EY* (1773), 21:541–43. This is drawn directly from Jean-François de La Croix, *Dictionnaire historique des cultes religieux* (Liège, 1772), 3:89–93.

209. "Guinée, la" (Géographie), *EY* (1773), 22:539–42.

210. The original can be found at Auguste Bruzen de la Martinière, *Le Grand dictionnaire géographique, historique et critique* (Paris, 1768), 3:251. On Martinière, see Hans-Jürgen Lüsebrink, "(Re)Inventing Encyclopedism in the Early European Enlightenment: Connecting Antoine-Augustin Bruzen de La Martinière with the *Cérémonies et Coutumes Religieuses*," in *Bernard Picart and the First Global Vision of Religion*, ed. Lynn Hunt, Margaret C. Jacob, and Wijnand Mijnhardt (Los Angeles: Getty Research Institute), 313–30. On the role of encyclopedias in consolidating stereotypes, see Patrick Graille and Andrew Curran, "Un Apologiste abolitionniste: L'Abbé Bergier et les *Nègres* de 1767 à 1789," *Dix-huitième siècle* 48 (2016): 521.

211. "Madagascar" (R) (Géographie), *EY* (1773), 27:90.

212. Ibid., 93.

213. Harvey, *French Enlightenment*, 56–57.

214. Pierre Poivre, *Voyages d'un philosophe ou observations sur les mœurs et les arts des peuples de l'Afrique, de l'Asie, et de l'Amérique* (Yverdon, 1768). The section on Madagascar can be found at pp. 20–24; on Pierre Poivre and his importance in the development of modern environmentalism, see Richard H. Grove, *Green Imperialism: Colonial Expansion, Tropical Island Edens and the Origins of Environmentalism, 1600–1860* (Cambridge: Cambridge University Press, 1995), chap. 5.

215. On the physiocrats' views of empire, see Pernille Røge, "A Natural Order of Empire: The Physiocratic Vision of Colonial France after the Seven Years' War," in *The Political Economy of Empire in the Early Modern World*, ed. Sophus A. Reinert and Pernille Røge (Basingstoke, UK: Palgrave Macmillan, 2013), 32–52.

216. "Juda" (N) (Géographie), *EY* (1773), 25:168.

217. Gabriel Mingard, "Coutume" (R) (Physique, Psychologie, Philosophie Morale), *EY* (1772), 12:194.

218. Stuurman, *Invention of Humanity*, 9–14.

219. Abbé Mallet, "Anthropologie" (Théologie), *EP* (1751), 1:497; Pierre Tarin, "Anthropologie" (Économie animale), *EP* (1751), 1:497.

220. Gabriel Mingard, "Anthropologie" (N) (Philosophie, Histoire naturelle, Physiologie, Métaphysique, Psychologie), *EY* (1771), 3:22.

221. Ibid.

222. Fernando Vidal, *The Sciences of the Soul: The Early Modern Origins of Psychology*, trans. Saskia Brown (Chicago: University of Chicago Press, 2011), chaps. 7 and 8.

223. Jean-Henri Andrié, "Europe" (R) (Géographie), *EY* (1772) 17:716–21.

224. Paul-Joseph Vallet, "Bibliotheque" (R) *EY* (1771), 5:429–65; "Honnête" (Morale), *EY* (1773), 23:427–30; "Mandarin" (Histoire moderne), *EY* (1773), 27:330–31; "Noblesse littéraire ou spirituelle," *EY* (1774), 30:405–6.

225. [Guillaume d'Abbes], "Figure" (Physiologie), *EY* (1773), 19:198–201.

226. [Paul-Joseph Vallet], "Canal artificiel' (Histoire et architecture), *EY* (1771), 7:214.

227. Paul-Joseph Vallet, "Chamoiseur" (Arts mécaniques), *EY* (1771), 8:651; Vallet, "Gazette" (Histoire moderne), *EY* (1773), 21:250–51.

228. "Chine, la" (R) (Géographie), *EY* (1771), 9:443. For the original, see Poivre, *Voyages d'un philosophe*, 120ff.

229. "Chine, la," *EY* (1771), 9:443.

230. Ibid., 446.

231. Martinière, *Le Grand dictionnaire*, 2:391.

232. [Denis Diderot], "Chinois (Philosophie des)," *EY* (1771), 9:466. This passage is taken verbatim from Jean Étienne Montucla, *Histoire des mathématiques* (Paris, 1758), 1:383.

233. Paul-Joseph Vallet, "Chou-King" (N) (Histoire, Antiquités), *SY* (1775), 2:607.

234. Joseph-Jérôme Le François de Lalande, "Astronomie des Chinois" [unclassified], *EY* (1771), 4:32–45. Although this article is not marked with an "N," it was in fact a new addition to the *Encyclopédie*. See also the addition to "Astrologie," *EY* (1771), 4:16–19.

235. Fortunato De Felice, "Cheou-King" (N) (Histoire littéraire), *EY* (1771), 9:316–17.

236. Vallet, "Chou-King," *SY* (1775), 2:607.

237. Gabriel Mingard, "Dieu" (R) (Métaphysique, Théologie naturelle, Religion), *EY* (1772), 13:787.

238. De Felice, "Société," *EY* (1774), 38:693.

239. Fortunato De Felice, "Homme" (R) (Morale), *EY* (1773), 23:405.

240. "Deuil' (R) (Histoire ancienne et moderne), *EY* (1772), 13:612–16; "Honneurs rendus aux morts" (N) (Histoire moderne), *SY* (1775), 3:675–78.

241. On the modernity of racial classification, see Stuurman, *Invention of Humanity*, 259–60.

242. Fortunato De Felice, "Climat" (N) (Morale), *EY* (1772), 10:100. This article draws extensively from Jean-Charles de Lavie's amendments to Jean Bodin's work: Lavie, *Abrégé de la République*, 2:286ff.

243. Israel, *Enlightenment Contested*, 545–71.

244. Ann Thomson, "(Why) Does the Enlightenment Matter?," *Diciottesimo Secolo* 1 (2016): 157.

245. Anthony Strugnell, "Postmodernism Versus Enlightenment and the Problem of the Other in Raynal's *Histoire des deux Indes*," *Studies on Voltaire and the Eighteenth Century* 341 (1996): 169–82.

Conclusion

1. Mintzker, "'Word Newly Introduced,'" 511.

2. Jonathan Sheehan, "Enlightenment, Religion, and the Enigma of Secularization: A Review Essay," *American Historical Review* 108, no. 4 (2003): 1061–80; Sorkin, *Religious Enlightenment*; William J. Bullman and Robert G. Ingram, eds., *God in the Enlightenment* (Oxford: Oxford University Press, 2016).

3. See the insightful essays in David Allen Harvey, ed., "Religion(s) and the Enlightenment," *Historical Reflections* 40, no. 2 (2014): 1–116. More generally, on the importance of the development of a "this-worldly" perspective, see Jacob, *Secular Enlightenment*.

4. Ernst Cassirer, *The Philosophy of the Enlightenment*, trans. Fritz C. A. Koelln and James P. Pettegrove (Princeton, NJ: Princeton University Press, 1951), 159.

5. Lilti, *L'Héritage des Lumières*, 20–21.

6. J. G. A. Pocock, "Conservative Enlightenment and Democratic Revolutions: The American and French Cases in British Perspective," *Government and Opposition* 24, no. 1 (1989): 81–105; Bell, *Cult of the Nation*, 30.

7. On the connections between secularization and equality, see Marcel Gauchet, *The Disenchantment of the World: A Political History of Religion*, trans. Oscar Burge (Princeton, NJ: Princeton University Press, 1997), 159.

8. Alan Charles Kors, *D'Holbach's Coterie: An Enlightenment in Paris* (Princeton, NJ: Princeton University Press, 1976), part 2.

9. Voltaire, *Zaïre, Le Fanatisme ou Mahomet le prophète, Nanine ou l'Homme sans préjugé, Le Café ou l'Écossaise*, ed. Jean Goldzink (Paris: Flammarion, 2004), 157.

10. Voltaire, *Dictionnaire philosophique*, ed. Alain Pons (Paris: Gallimard, 1994), 241.

11. Corrado Rosso, *Mythe de l'égalité et rayonnement des Lumières* (Pisa: Goliardica, 1980), 3.

12. Diderot, "Privilege," *EY* (1765), 13:389. Diderot also made an illegitimate son the central character in his play *Le Fils naturel*, emphasizing that nobility resides in character, not birth. See Rita Goldberg, *Sex and Enlightenment: Women in Richardson and Diderot* (Cambridge: Cambridge University Press, 1984), 130.

13. Louis de Jaucourt, "Oisiveté," *EP* (1765), 11:445–46.

14. John Carson, *The Measure of Merit: Talents, Intelligence, and Inequality in the French and American Republics, 1750–1940* (Princeton, NJ: Princeton University Press, 2007), chap. 1; Sylvana Tomaselli, "Political Economy: The Desire and Needs of Present and Future Generations," in *Inventing Human Science: Eighteenth-Century Domains*, ed. Christopher Fox, Roy Porter, and Robert Wokler (Berkeley: University of California Press, 1995), 292–322.

15. Rosanvallon, *Society of Equals*, 16–33.

16. Hunt, *Inventing Human Rights*, 26ff.

17. We might also add the effect of the spread of capitalism. See Thomas L. Haskell, "Capitalism and the Origins of the Humanitarian Sensibility," *American Historical Review* 90, no. 2 (1985): 339–61; Thomas Laqueur, "Bodies, Details, and the Humanitarian Narrative," in *The New Cultural History*, ed. Lynn Hunt (Berkeley: University of California Press, 1989), 176–204.

18. This argument has been advanced in Hans Joas, *The Sacredness of the Person: A New Genealogy of Human Rights*, trans. Alex Skinner (Washington, DC: Georgetown University Press, 2013).

19. Guy G. Stroumsa, *A New Science: The Discovery of Religion in the Age of Reason* (Cambridge, MA: Harvard University Press, 2010).

20. Hunt, Jacob, and Mijnhardt, *Book That Changed Europe*.

21. Waldron, *One Another's Equals*, 188.

22. Clifford Geertz, "Centers, Kings, and Charisma: Reflections on the Symbolics of Power," in *Culture and Its Creators: Essays in Honor of Edward Shils*, ed. Joseph Ben-David and Terry Nichols Clark (Chicago: University of Chicago Press, 1977), 150–71.

23. Eric M. Kramer, ed., *Postmodernism and Race* (Westport, CT: Greenwood Press, 1997); Hoquet, "Biologization of Race," 23; Malik, *Meaning of Race*.

24. Drescher, "Ending of the Slave Trade," 415–50; Herbert Odom, "Generalizations on Race in Nineteenth-Century Physical Anthropology," *Isis* 58, no. 1 (1967): 4–18; Nancy Stepan, *The Idea of Race in Science: Great Britain, 1800–1960* (Hamden, CT: Archon Books, 1982); Stuurman, *Invention of Humanity*, chap. 7; Frank Dikötter, "The Racialization of the Globe: Historical Perspectives," in *Racism in the Modern World: Historical Perspectives on Cultural Transfer and Adaptation*, ed. Manfred Berg and Simon Wendt (New York: Berghahn, 2011), 20–40.

25. Sebastiani, *Scottish Enlightenment*, 164.

26. There were exceptions to this, however, such as John Mitchell, who argued that humanity's original pigmentation was olive-toned or brown (based on biblical genealogies) and that whiteness and blackness are equally far from the original: Mitchell, "Essay upon the Causes," 102–50.

27. Simone Beate Borgstede, *"All Is Race": Benjamin Disraeli on Race, Nation and Empire* (Zurich: Lit Verlag, 2011).

28. Lester G. Crocker, "Diderot and Eighteenth-Century French Transformism," in *Forerunners of Darwin: 1745–1859*, ed. Bentley Glass, Owsei Temkin, and William L. Straus, Jr. (Baltimore: Johns Hopkins Press, 1959), 114–43.

29. Buffon, *Histoire naturelle, générale et particulière*, 2:35ff.

30. Andrew S. Curran, *Diderot and the Art of Thinking Freely* (New York: Other Press, 2019), chap. 8.

31. Diderot, *Pensées sur l'interprétation*, 114.

32. Vartanian, *Diderot and Descartes*, 97 and chap. 4; Ballstadt, *Diderot: Natural Philosopher*, chap. 4.

33. Diderot, *Pensées sur l'interprétation*, 115.

34. Nancy Stepan, "Biological Degeneration: Races and Proper Places," in *Degeneration: The Dark Side of Progress*, ed. J. Edward Chamberlin and Sander L. Gilman (New York: Columbia University Press, 1985), 97–120; Bindman, *Ape to Apollo*.

35. Jean Dagen, *L'Histoire de l'esprit humain dans la pensée française* (Paris: Klincsieck, 1977), 18.

36. Joseph-François Lafitau, *Mœurs des sauvages américains*, 2 vols. (Paris, 1724).

37. Denis Diderot, "Chasse" (Economie rustique), *EP* (1753), 3:225.

38. Louis de Jaucourt, "Sauvages" (Géographie moderne), *EP* (1765), 14:729; Montesquieu, *Spirit of the Laws*, book 18, chap. 11.

39. Jaucourt, "Industrie," *EP* (1765), 8:694–95.

40. Anne Robert Jacques Turgot, "Reflections on the Formation and the Distribution of Wealth," in *Turgot on Progress, Sociology and Economics*, trans. and ed. Ronald L. Meek (Cambridge: Cambridge University Press, 1973), 148.

41. Smith, *Lectures on Jurisprudence*, 459.

42. H. F. Augstein, ed., introduction to *Race: The Origins of an Idea, 1760–1850* (Bristol: Thoemmes Press, 1996), xviii.

43. Henry Vyverberg, *Human Nature, Cultural Diversity, and the French Enlightenment* (New York: Oxford University Press, 1989), chap. 2.

44. Marvin Harris, *The Rise of Anthropological Theory*, rev. ed. (Lanham, MD: Rowman & Littlefield, 2001), 83.

45. John Locke, *An Essay Concerning Human Understanding* (Oxford: Oxford University Press, 2008), 54; Frank E. Manuel, "From Equality to Organicism," *Journal of the History of Ideas* 17, no. 1 (1956): 54–69.

46. Claude-Adrien Helvétius, *De l'homme* (London, 1773), 1:255.

47. De Felice, "Climat," *EY* (1772), 10:95–100.

48. Stuurman, *Invention of Humanity*, 342.

49. Christopher L. Hill, "Conceptual Universalization in the Transnational Nineteenth Century," in *Global Intellectual History*, ed. Samuel Moyn and Andrew Sartori (New York: Columbia University Press, 2013), 134–58.

50. James Turner, *Philology: The Forgotten Origins of the Modern Humanities* (Princeton, NJ: Princeton University Press, 2014), 96–97.

51. Denis Diderot, *Political Writings*, trans. and ed. John Hope Mason and Robert Wokler (Cambridge: Cambridge University Press, 1992), 61.

52. Hill, "Conceptual Universalization," 150.

53. For the publishing history of the *Supplément*, see Darnton, *Business of Enlightenment*, 18–23.

54. Ibid., 26.

55. Albrecht von Haller, "Droit" (Anatomie), *Supplément à l'Encyclopédie*, ed. Jean-Baptiste Robinet (Paris, 1776), 2:741–42.

56. Samuel Engel, "Amérique" (Histoire et géographie), *Supplément* (1776), 1:343–62.

57. Ibid., 352.

58. Ibid., 361.

59. Kathleen Hardesty Doig, *The "Supplément" to the "Encyclopédie"* (The Hague: Martinus Nijhoff, 1977).

60. Ibid., 57.

61. Ibid., 101.

62. Jean-Baptiste-René Robinet, "Afrique" (Géographie ancienne et moderne), *Supplément* (1776), 1:194.

63. https://encyclopedie.uchicago.edu/content/encyclop%C3%A9die-m%C3%A9thodique; I write "approximately" because various editions of the encyclopedia comprised differing numbers of volumes.

64. For analyses of the various dictionaries of the *Encyclopédie méthodique*, see Claude Blanckaert and Michel Porret, eds., *L'"Encyclopédie méthodique" (1782–1832): Des Lumières au positivisme* (Geneva: Droz, 2006). See also Kathleen Hardesty Doig, *From "Encyclopédie" to "Encyclopédie méthodique": Revision and Expansion* (Oxford: Voltaire Foundation, 2013).

65. "Égalité" (Droit naturel et civil), *Encyclopédie méthodique, Jurisprudence*, ed. Jacques Peuchet (Paris, 1784), 4:213; emphasis added.

66. Frank A. Kafker and Jeff Loveland, eds., *The Early Britannica: The Growth of an Outstanding Encyclopedia* (Oxford: Voltaire Foundation, 2009).

67. Frank A. Kafker, "William Smellie's Edition of the Encyclopaedia Britannica," in *Notable Encyclopaedias of the Late Eighteenth Century: Eleven Successors of the "Encyclopédie,"* ed. Frank A. Kafker (Oxford: Voltaire Foundation, 1994), 145–82; Stephen W. Brown, "William Smellie and the Culture of the Edinburgh Book Trade, 1752–1795," in *The Culture of the Book in the Scottish Enlightenment*, ed. Roger Emerson et al. (Toronto: University of Toronto, 2000), 61–86.

68. Silvia Sebastiani, "L'Amérique des Lumières et la hiérarchie des races: Disputes sur l'écriture de l'histoire dans l'*Encyclopaedia Britannica* (1768–1788)," *Annales. Histoire, Sciences Sociales* 67, no. 2 (2012): 327–61.

69. Ibid., 347.

70. "Negroes," *Encyclopaedia Britannica* (Edinburgh, 1771), 3:395–96.

71. "Homo," *Encyclopaedia Britannica* (Edinburgh, 1771), 2:789; Carl Linnaeus, *Systema naturae per regna tria naturae*, 10th ed. (Stockholm, 1758), 20–24.

72. Sebastiani, "'Monster with Human Visage,'" 80–99.

73. "Colour of the Human Species, Difference of," *Encyclopaedia Britannica*, 2nd ed. (Edinburgh, 1778), 3:2083.

74. Ibid.

75. On John Hunter, see Sebastiani, *Scottish Enlightenment*, 115–19.

76. Étienne Bonnot de Condillac, *Essai sur l'origine des connoissances humaines*, 2 vols. (Amsterdam, 1746).

77. Jean Le Rond d'Alembert, *Preliminary Discourse to the Encyclopedia of Diderot*, trans. Richard N. Schwab (Chicago: University of Chicago Press, 1995), 13.

78. Ibid., 44–45.

79. *Journal des Sçavans* (September, 1751), 626–27. The anti-philosophe Abraham-Joseph de Chaumeix was outraged by these exact same passages; see Chaumeix, *Préjugés légitimes contre l'Encyclopédie* (Brussels, 1758), 1:46–47.

80. Rousseau, *Discourses*, 132.

81. On this transformation and its continued resonance today, see Frank Palmeri, *State of Nature, Stages of Society: Enlightenment Conjectural History and Modern Social Discourse* (New York: Columbia University Press, 2016). Modern archaeologists and anthropologists continue to find inspiration in Rousseau's analysis; see especially Flannery and Marcus, *Creation of Inequality*, ix–x.

82. Roger Tisserand, *Les Concurrents de J.-J. Rousseau à l'Académie de Dijon pour le prix de 1754* (Paris: Vesoul, 1936).

83. On Rousseau as an Enlightenment philosophe, see Mark Hulliung, *The Autocritique of Enlightenment: Rousseau and the Philosophes* (Cambridge, MA: Harvard University Press, 1994).

84. Rousseau, *Discourses*, 134.

85. Ibid., 204–205.

86. Jean Starobinski, *Jean Jacques Rousseau: Transparency and Obstruction*, trans. Arthur Goldhammer (Chicago: University of Chicago Press, 1988), 323–32.

87. Buffon, *Histoire naturelle, générale et particulière*, 1:38.

88. Francis Moran III, "Between Primates and Primitives: Natural Man as the Missing Link in Rousseau's *Second Discourse*," *Journal of the History of Ideas* 54, no. 1 (1994): 37–58.

89. Wokler, *Rousseau, the Age of Enlightenment*, chap. 1.

90. Phillip R. Sloan, "From Natural Law to Evolutionary Ethics in Enlightenment French Natural History," in *Biology and the Foundation of Ethics*, ed. Jane Maienschein and Michael Ruse (Cambridge: Cambridge University Press, 1999), 52–83.

91. Ephraim Chambers, "Morality," *Cyclopaedia*, 2:581.

92. Ephraim Chambers, "Moral," *Cyclopaedia*, 2:581; Anthony Ashley-Cooper, Third Earl of Shaftesbury, "An Inquiry Concerning Virtue and Merit," in *Characteristicks of Men, Manners, Opinions, Times* (Indianapolis: Liberty Fund, 2001), 2:1–100. On Shaftesbury's role in the Enlightenment, see Dorothy B. Schlegel, *Shaftesbury and the French Deists* (Chapel Hill: University of North Carolina Press, 1956); Daniel Carey, *Locke, Shaftesbury, and Hutcheson: Contesting Diversity in the Enlightenment and Beyond* (Cambridge: Cambridge University Press, 2005), chap. 6.

93. Louis de Jaucourt, "Morale" (Science des moeurs), *EP* (1765), 10:702.

94. Louis de Jaucourt, "Sensibilité" (Morale), *EP* (1765), 15:52.

95. [Louis de Jaucourt], "Sens moral" (Morale), *EY* (1774), 38:283–83; Francis Hutcheson, *An Essay on the Nature and Conduct of the Passions and Affections* (London, 1728).

96. Jacques Domenech, *L'Ethique des Lumières: Les fondements de la morale dans la philosophie française du XVIIIe siècle* (Paris: Librairie Philosophique J. Vrin, 1989).

97. Williams, "Concept of Equality," 22.

98. Keith Michael Baker and Peter Hanns Reill, eds., *What's Left of Enlightenment? A Postmodern Question* (Stanford: Stanford University Press, 2001); Daniel Gordon, ed., *Postmodernism and the Enlightenment: New Perspectives in Eighteenth-Century French Intellectual History* (New York: Routledge, 2001); Stuurman, *Invention of Humanity*, 561.

99. On the egalitarian legacy of Buffon, see Nicholas Guyatt, *Bind Us Apart: How Enlightened Americans Invented Racial Segregation* (New York: Basic Books, 2016), 22–26. On the role of Buffon in nineteenth-century (racist) physical anthropology, see Claude Blanckaert, "Buffon and the Natural History of Man: Writing History and the 'Foundational Myth' of Anthropology," *History of the Human Sciences* 6, no. 1 (1993): 13–50.

100. Peter Wade, *Race, Nature and Culture: An Anthropological Perspective* (London: Pluto Press, 2002).

101. Ibid., 42.

102. Ibid., 6–7.

103. Mayr, "Biology of Race," 90.

104. Jonathan Michael Kaplan and Rasmus Grønfeldt Winther, "Prisoners of Abstraction? The Theory and Measure of Genetic Variation, and the Very Concept of 'Race,'" *Biological Theory* 7 (2013): 401–12.

105. Neven Sesardic, "Race: A Social Destruction of a Biological Concept," *Biology and Philosophy* 25, no. 2 (2010): 143–62; Ron Mallon, "Was Race Thinking Invented in the Modern West?," *Studies in History and Philosophy of Science* 44 (2013): 77–88.

106. See the debate in Joshua Glasgow, Sally Haslanger, Chike Jeffers, and Quayshawn Spencer, *What Is Race? Four Philosophical Views* (Oxford: Oxford University Press, 2019).

107. Amade M'Charek, "Beyond Fact or Fiction: On the Materiality of Race in Practice," *Cultural Anthropology* 28, no. 3 (2013): 420–42; David Ludwig, "Against the New Metaphysics of Race," *Philosophy of Science* 82, no. 2 (2015): 244–65.

108. Noel Ignatiev, *How the Irish Became White* (New York: Routledge, 1995); Karen Brodkin, *How the Jews Became White Folks* (New Brunswick, NJ: Rutgers University Press, 1998).

109. Shiya Song, Elzbieta Sliwerska, Sarah Emery, and Jeffrey M. Kidd, "Modeling Human Population Separation History Using Physically Phased Genomes," *Genetics* 205, no. 1 (2017): 385–95; Garrett Hellenthal et al., "A Genetic Atlas of Human Admixture History," *Science* 343, no. 6172 (2014): 747–51; David Reich, *Who We Are and How We Got Here* (Oxford: Oxford University Press, 2018).

110. David Nirenberg, "Was There Race Before Modernity? The Example of 'Jewish' Blood in Late Medieval Spain," in *The Origins of Racism in the West*, ed. Miriam Elav-Feldon, Benjamin Isaac, and Joseph Ziegler (Cambridge: Cambridge University Press, 2009), 233.

111. See W. J. T. Mitchell's refutation of the extremes to which some postmodernists have gone in rejecting everything associated with naturalist explanation: Mitchell, *Seeing Through Race* (Cambridge, MA: Harvard University Press, 2012), 34.

112. Smail, *On Deep History*, 10–11.

113. Ann Morning, *The Nature of Race: How Scientists Think and Teach About Human Difference* (Berkeley: University of California Press, 2011); Smith, *Nature, Human Nature*, chap. 1.

114. Ian Hacking, "Why Race Still Matters," *Daedalus* 134, no. 1 (2005): 102–16; Hacking, "Making Up People," in *The Science Studies Reader*, ed. Mario Biagioli (New York: Routledge, 1999), 161–71.

115. Scott Atran examines the development from folk-biological categories to more theoretically sophisticated ones and demonstrates that thinking in terms of distinct ancestral origins, while always inflected locally, also has certain universal characteristics. See Atran, *Cognitive Foundations of Natural History: Towards an Anthropology of Science* (Cambridge: Cambridge University Press, 1990).

116. Buffon, *De l'homme*, 320; Renato G. Mazzolini, "Skin Color and the Origin of Physical Anthropology (1640–1850)," in *Reproduction, Race, and Gender in Philosophy and the Early Life Sciences*, ed. Susanne Lettow (Albany: State University of New York Press, 2014), 131–61.

117. Alana Lentin, *Why Race Still Matters* (Cambridge: Polity Press, 2020), chap. 1; Kyla Schuller, *The Biopolitics of Feeling: Race, Sex, and Science in the Nineteenth Century* (Durham, NC: Duke University Press, 2018), 205–6.

118. From the sixteenth century onward, Native North Americans, Australians, and New Zealanders who visited London, for example, often commented upon the gross inequalities and concomitant injustices of the city. See Coll Thrush, *Indigenous London: Native Travelers at the Heart of Empire* (New Haven, CT: Yale University Press, 2016), 24–25.

119. Elizabeth Anderson, "A World Turned Upside Down: Social Hierarchies and a New History of Egalitarianism," *Juncture* 20, no. 4 (2014): 258–67.

120. Diderot, *Political Writings*, 61.

INDEX

ACKNOWLEDGMENTS

This book grew out of my doctoral dissertation and I would first like to thank Siep Stuurman for his inimitable level and style of support over the past few years. I am deeply grateful for the stimulating discussions, the *gezelligheid*, and the encouragement. Along with Siep, thank you to Selma Leydesdorff for warmly welcoming Jelte and me into your lives. We are grateful for your friendship and always cherish the time we spend together. Paul Ziche helped to sharpen my arguments and stimulated new ways of thinking about my project along the way, for which I am grateful. I would like to thank the Dutch Research Council and the Social Sciences and Humanities Research Council of Canada for the doctoral fellowships that made this research possible, and to Utrecht University for providing such a pleasant and stimulating atmosphere in which to research and teach. The École des hautes études en sciences sociales provided a wonderful environment in which to work on the final hurdles of this book. I am also grateful to Damon Linker and Bob Lockhart and their colleagues at the University of Pennsylvania Press for the superb support. I would also like to thank the press's reviewers—Sue Peabody and one anonymous reviewer—for the constructive feedback that vastly improved the quality of this book.

Research stays at UCLA and Princeton University came at just the right moments. Thank you to Margaret Jacob and David Bell for the warm welcome and constructive feedback. I am grateful to Darrin McMahon and Udi Greenberg and the other participants at the inaugural Dartmouth History Institute in European Intellectual History for the stimulating discussions, and to Sophia Rosenfeld for her incisive comments on my work. I would also like to thank friends and colleagues who have carefully read part or all of this book and believed in its potential: Lars Behrisch, Annelien de Dijn, Joris van Eijnatten, Ido de Haan, Dienke Hondius, Lisa Kattenberg, René Koekkoek, Matt McDonald, Jan Rotmans, and Melvin Wevers. Lynn Hunt, Margaret Jacob, and Wijnand Mijnhardt have been particularly supportive and encouraging, and for that I am deeply grateful. Audiences at numerous conferences over the years have deepened my thinking on this topic, particularly at ISECS in Rotterdam in 2015. I would like to thank Clorinda Donato and Alain Cernuschi for sharing their vast knowledge of the *Encyclopédie d'Yverdon* with me. My warmest thanks also to Silvia Sebastiani for her generous support and for sharing her brilliant intellect with me. The seminar around my introduction at the EHESS came just in time for publication and I would like to thank the participants for their constructive feedback. I am grateful to Pamela Swett for believing in my potential as a scholar at such a crucial moment and to Willemijn Ruberg for her mentorship and friendship. Frances Nijssen has enriched the trajectory I have followed over the past few years in immeasurable ways, and I am very grateful for that enrichment.

Danielle DeMarsh and Sarah Levitt played a special role in the unfolding of this research, and for that I am grateful. Thank you to Alanna Magder for help with particularly difficult French passages and for our friendship, which is very dear to me. I dedicate this book to my parents in recognition, however inadequate, of their boundless love and support. I am grateful for the example you set of dedication and perseverance and for the opportunities you have consistently given me. I would also like to thank my grandmother, Christine Woytiw, who, with only a third-grade education, is one of the most intelligent people I know and who stimulated my curiosity and inquisitiveness from childhood. I am grateful to Jelte Krist for so many things, perhaps most of all for your ability to somehow both support and challenge me in equal measure. Although I was sometimes reluctant, I am thankful that you consistently reminded me how sweet life in the world outside of books can be. Our relationship has made me a better person and, in sticking with a theme that is close to my heart and central to this book, I would like to thank you for teaching me that, in the end, equality is love.